MW01629013

Fishing on Deep River

Civil War Memoir of Pvt. Samuel Baldwin Dunlap, C.S.A.

Researched and Annotated by

Suzanne Staker Lehr

Platte Purchase Publishers
A Division of
The St. Joseph Museums Inc.
St. Joseph, Missouri

P.O. Box 8096
St. Joseph, Missouri 64508

Editor, Alberto C. Meloni
Executive Director
The St. Joseph Museums Inc.

Production Manager, Jacqueline Lewin
Assistant Director for External Affairs
The St. Joseph Museums Inc.

Library of Congress Number: 2006903037

Lehr, Suzanne Staker.
Fishing on Deep River: Civil War Memoir of Pvt. Samuel Baldwin Dunlap, C.S.A./by Suzanne Staker Lehr-1st Ed. (A Platte Purchase Publishers Civil War Series)
Summary: Contains the written memoir compiled from the diary kept by Pvt. Samuel Baldwin Dunlap, C.S.A., during the American Civil War years of 1861-1865 with explanatory annotations, an introduction, and an epilogue by researcher Suzanne Staker Lehr.

ISBN 0-9725353-9-X
[1. Platte Purchase Publisher (Mo.)-Adult History
2. St. Joseph Museums Inc. (Mo.)-History/Local
3. American Civil War-History/Memoir
4. Confederacy-History/Memoir
5. Missouri-History/Memoir]

Printed in USA by
BookMasters, Inc.
Mansfield, Ohio

In loving memory of my mother,
Dorothy Lucille Roberts Staker

Publications of Platte Purchase Publishers

Saint Joseph Series

On the Winds of Destiny by Jacqueline Lewin and Marilyn Taylor

Old Saint Jo by Sheridan Logan

Rare and Scarce Saint Joseph Books, Pamphlets, and Music
by J. Marshall White

Robidoux's Town by Robert Willoughby

Children's Discovery Series

The Elephant Way by Joyce Rochambeau

Civil War Series

A Darkness Ablaze by Joseph K. Houts, Jr.

As the Mockingbird Sang by Suzanne S. Lehr

Fishing on Deep River by Suzanne S. Lehr

Preface

With this newest effort, St. Joseph Museums Inc. Research Associate Suzanne Lehr brings to a close the Civil War experiences of the Dunlap brothers from DeKalb, Buchanan County, Missouri. As she accomplished in her first volume, with the wartime diary of Robert Caldwell Dunlap, C.S.A., so she repeats with that of Samuel Baldwin Dunlap, C.S.A. Both brothers assiduously wrote their thoughts, feelings, and observations throughout the War. The respective families of each preserved these priceless documents of remembrance and were generous enough to share them with Mrs. Lehr and, through her, the rest of us. Through their generosity and Mrs. Lehr's research and annotating efforts, we can all learn respect for and the value of family memoirs and letters.

The two Dunlap brothers served together throughout most of the War, but there the similarities end. As the reader turns each page of their respective observations and viewpoints, the unique individual character of each emerges. At the end of both diaries, there stands two separate views of the same war's events and incidents. There stand two brothers, each committed and dedicated to the same cause, but each his own person, not easily dissuaded from those views that render them individual. What a grand opportunity to see such a momentous conflict through the eyes of two combatants, both on the same side and both related by blood, yet each with a singular and unique viewpoint.

The two volumes, in addition to their own intrinsic historical merit, are an excellent example of why personal diaries must never be discounted as profound evidence of time, place, and events. Nor should the efforts of individuals who labor, as Mrs. Lehr has done, ever be received with anything but support and praise. Each of us has the potential of discovering such precious historical evidence. Each of us can have the wherewithal to research and annotate with discerning insights. Each of us can find the opportunity to make such historical treasures available to greater and appreciative audiences. It is only the desire, hard work, and opportunities which are often lacking, but which we must inspire, teach and provide. This is our obligation to the past, to such men as Caldwell and Samuel Dunlap. This is the purpose for such interested and dedicated public historians as Suzanne Lehr. This is the meaning and purpose of history museums such as The St. Joseph Museums Inc. To these ends, for these treasured reasons, and their valiant efforts, we are proud to present this newest volume of the Dunlap saga.

Alberto C. Meloni
St. Joseph, Missouri, 2006

Acknowledgements

The last pages of Sam's memoir speak to these thoughts.

Hope is the pillar that holds up the world.
Hope is the dream of a waking man.
—Pliny, the Elder

All human wisdom is summed up in two words—wait and hope.
—Alexandre Dumas

On December 22, 2003, I saw for the first time a copy of Robert Caldwell Dunlap's Civil War diary. With Austill and Barbara Landis' help, I was able to locate the original diary and get permission from the owner, Glenn Sampson, for publication. *As the Mockingbird Sang* was released in December 2005.

In the midst of working on Caldwell's diary, I learned that Caldwell's brother, Samuel Baldwin Dunlap, also kept a diary throughout the war. I obtained permission from Janette Dunlap to publish Sam's memoir (*Fishing on Deep River*), and I am extremely grateful to both the Sampson family and the Dunlap family for, first of all, preserving these irreplaceable treasures, and secondly, being willing to share them with the rest of us.

Finding the diaries all began with my research project at Mount Mora Cemetery. I have not seen a more beautiful, nor more interesting historic cemetery. Despite the weeds and crumbling tombstones and mausoleums, one hundred and fifty-five years after its opening, the burial place of three Missouri governors, two pony express riders, inventors, senators and representatives, musicians, architects, writers, stone masons, preachers, generals, Englishmen, border ruffians, veterans of many wars, an ambassador and assistant secretary of the treasury, entrepreneurs, adventurers, and John C. Landis, the commanding officer of the Dunlap brothers, remains a fascinating place to visit.

It was, John C. Landis, himself, who was the catalyst for the discovery of these two diaries, which have totally captivated my interest. I was researching the

Israel Landis family, as Israel was one of the three original owners of the cemetery. His son John, sent to West Point for a military education, was exposed to the rigors of military discipline and did not find the strict requirements to his liking. By 1858, John had been given the "opportunity" to return home to work for his father at the Landis Saddlery. Just prior to the beginning of the Pony Express, John was busy designing and supervising the construction of the mochila, but when the winds of war began buffeting Saint Joseph, he immediately rose to the call of the Confederacy. First he joined in the raid of the Liberty arsenal, shipping back to Saint Joseph arms and munitions that were hidden in the cellars of sympathizers until he could trundle them into the back of an old negroe's wagon to be driven to the county line and transferred to Sterling Price's troops. Soon he was enrolled in the Missouri State Guard and ultimately became an officer in the Confederate States Army.

While researching John, I learned his grandson lives nearby. And, since it is more usual today for Civil War descendants to be great-grandchildren or great-great-grandchildren, I was intrigued. Immediately I initiated a meeting. One visit led to another, and one day Austill Landis said, "There's an old diary around here somewhere. Not John's, but someone's in his unit."

Once I began work on Caldwell's diary, I was led to Sam's memoir. Now with the publication of Caldwell's diary and Sam's memoir, I fulfill my goal of bringing these two young Confederate brothers back together, at least on the bookshelf. One hundred forty plus years have separated their experiences. The publication of the diary and the memoir preserves their descriptions for all who have interest in Civil War history. All of my proceeds from these publications will go directly to the preservation of Mount Mora Cemetery, the burial place of the Dunlaps' commanding officer and the place where for me it all began.

I am indebted to the Landis, Sampson, and Dunlap families. Their generosity and support of this project has brought these publications to fruition. Three brothers left northwest Missouri together to fight for "southren rights" and two kept diaries. The words of brothers who served together in the same unit for much of the war gives the unique perspective of a shared experience through two pair of eyes.

I very much appreciate my husband Jim who has shared my interest in this project through giving me the time and space to research, read, and write. He has also willingly accompanied me to battle sites, to gather living histories, as well as to the places where the Dunlaps lived, fought, and are buried.

My thanks and appreciation to Alberto Meloni, Executive Director of The St. Joseph Museums Inc. and Editor of Platte Purchase Publishers and to Jacqueline Lewin, Assistant Director of St. Joseph Museums Inc. and Editor for Platte Purchase Publishers. Without both of them, this project could not have happened.

In addition, I am extremely grateful to the many individuals who provided support information for my annotations. Special thank-yous to Catherine and Thomas Alison, Cedar Grove Plantation, Faunsdale, Alabama; Faye Andrews, North Carolina Wildlife Resources Commission, Raleigh, North Carolina; Bill Dunlap, Jr., St. Joseph, Missouri; Janette Dunlap, St. Joseph, Missouri; James "Gene" and Bobbie Dunlap, Faucett, Missouri; Sarah Elder, Curator of Collections at The St. Joseph Museums Inc.; Bob Furmanski, St. Joseph, Missouri; Margaret Gilbert, Gower, Missouri; Bill Glass, Centre College, Danville, Kentucky; Ryan Heise, North Carolina Wildlife Resources Commission, Raleigh, North Carolina; Mary Hillix, St. Joseph, Missouri; Joseph Houts, Jr., St. Joseph, Missouri; Willie R. Johnson, Park Ranger/Historian, Kennesaw Mountain National Battlefield Park, Kennesaw, Georgia; Gloria Kelley, St. Joseph, Missouri; the Landis Artillery Battery re-enactors led by Col. Russ Hautzenrader, Saint Joseph, Missouri; Shane Libel, St. Joseph, Missouri; Joy Mackin, Demopolis, Alabama; Nancy and George McKee, Faunsdale, Alabama; Robert Mershon, Elk River, Minnesota; Kenneth Neth, Clay County Archives & Historical Library, Liberty, Missouri; Northwest Missouri Genealogical Society, St Joseph, Missouri; Saint Joseph Public Library staff, St. Joseph, Missouri; Jim Pyles, Plattsburg, Missouri; Glenn Sampson, DeKalb, Missouri; Charles Spencer, St Joseph, Missouri; Angela Stiffler, William Jewell College, Liberty, Missouri; Janice and Bill Strop, St. Joseph, Missouri; Barbara Turner, St. Joseph, Missouri; Becky Willis, Marengo County, Alabama; and Patricia Young, Oxford, Mississippi.

It has been my privilege and pleasure to research and annotate Samuel Baldwin Dunlap's memoir. For any errors contained in the results, I alone take full responsibility.

Suzanne Staker Lehr
St. Joseph, Missouri
May 29, 2006

Table of Contents

Introduction

James Carnachan Dunlap III and family arrived in northwest Missouri from Montgomery County, Kentucky, in 1843, to settle near Bloomington (later renamed DeKalb), where he and his wife Patsy Hainline began farming. They had been drawn to Missouri by J. C.'s Aunt Elizabeth, who had married James Ellison and settled here first, to be followed by another sister, Sarah "Sallie," and her husband, Matthew Wills. They were soon joined by J. C.'s grandfather, James Carnachan I, and J.C.'s father, William, a brother to Elizabeth and Sallie.

James I, born in County Antrim, Northern Ireland, on August 1, 1740, had come to the Colonies in 1758 and, as a young man, had fought for America's independence from Great Britain in the Revolutionary War. He had already passed his 100th birthday when his great-grandson Sam, who would one day fight for the Confederacy, was born. James I's will was written June 1, 1841. To his five sons, James, Andrew, Alexander, John, and Thomas James and his daughters Elizabeth Elison and Sally Wills, he left one dollar each. He left all the rest of his property to his son William. The will was witnessed by Henry West, Samuel G. Dunlap, and James C. Dunlap and recorded in Platte County on October 9, 1844 (Hodges and Woodruff).

James I's son William was born February 19, 1785, in Virginia, the first state to secede after President Lincoln called for troops to suppress the rebellion.

Samuel Baldwin, the youngest child of J. C. and Patsy Dunlap, was born in 1843 in Montgomery County, Kentucky, the same year his great-grandfather and grandfather arrived following the family's move to Missouri. J. C. and Patsy had married December 30, 1834. Patsy had six children during the next eight and one-half years, and when Sam was two, his mother and his brother Alvan Marion died. Patsy was twenty-eight years old; Alva was six. Sam's father would marry again in March 1846, only to lose his second wife when Sam was five. J. C. would be widowed by three more wives before his death in 1894. J. C.'s third wife, who would be the mother to nurture Sam and his siblings during their formative years, was Mahala (Morrison) Dunlap, whom he married on November 18, 1849.

The births of six children and the deaths of two wives could not have been easy for that young farmer. And, it would not have been easy for that young family to live in northwest Missouri, in the 1850s, as by this time the region was becoming a battleground between the free-state "jayhawkers" and the pro-slavery sympathizers, the "border ruffians." Missouri had entered the Union in 1821 as a slave state, but the controversy over slavery, which was to have been settled by the Missouri Compromise, had not gone away. Arkansas, on Missouri's southern edge, had entered the Union in 1836 as a slave state. Iowa, to Missouri's north, had been strongly pro-Union since achieving statehood in 1846. During the early years of Sam's life, Kansas was a hotly contested territory, finally coming into the Union as a free state in 1860, when Sam was seventeen years old.

Despite the tension between Missouri and the area that was to become the state of Kansas, Sam's earliest years in the rolling hills of southern Buchanan County were peaceful. However, Wallace, who was six years older, would have had greater exposure to the developing war, which began when Kansas was opened for settlement in 1854. Sam was only eleven years old at that time; Wallace was seventeen. Northwest Missouri was somewhat protected at first by the wide Missouri River. During those years, J. C.'s farm prospered. His children attended the nearby Bloomington Academy. Their teacher, Professor Charles S. Raffington, had been trained in ancient and modern languages and, as Sam described, the students were drilled on "five times six are thirty - Columbus discovered America, the earth is round like a ball; or I love, you love, they love." As Sam grew older, rumors of impending war escalated. It would be just seven years before the Civil War would officially begin.

The Dunlaps had moved to Missouri eighteen years earlier from Kentucky, a state which considered itself pro-Union, despite the many Southern sympathizers there who supported a movement to establish an alternative state government with the goal of secession. However, they failed to displace the legitimate government, and Kentucky remained in the Union. J. C., born in Montgomery County in 1810 and a slave-owner in Missouri, felt strongly about southern rights.

Although the 1850 Slave Schedule for Buchanan County does not indicate that J. C. owned any slaves at that time, slave bills still in the Dunlap family's possession document J. C.'s purchase of slaves in subsequent years: February 11, 1853 — a girl, Sarah, for six hundred dollars; December 4, 1855 — a girl, Jane, five or six years old, and another, Elizabeth, about four years of age, for six hundred and fifty dollars; February 15, 1856 — Daniel, an eight year old boy, for seven hundred dollars; November 18, 1859 — a fifty-year-old male, George, for eighty-eight dollars and fifty-eight cents; a mother, Milly, and her son, George (ages unknown), for eight hundred dollars. The 1860 Slave Schedule reported J. C. owned at that time five slaves: a fifty-year-old black male; a forty-four-year-old black female; a twenty-eight-year-old black male; a fifteen-year-old black male; and a two-year-old black male.

There was much support for slavery in Buchanan County, Missouri. In 1858, ten percent of the population was enslaved, whereas across the state in St. Louis County, the slave population was less than one percent. The family believes J. C. may have owned as many as eleven slaves at the time the war ended and that most of them remained with him after emancipation. There is a section in the private cemetery on the land J. C. originally farmed that is believed to hold several of the slaves' graves.

Family legend says that on the day of the firing upon Fort Sumter, April 12, 1861, J.C.'s reaction was to purchase a Remington-Beals Navy Model .36 caliber 6 cylinder percussion revolver with walnut grips, one of an estimated 14,500 made during 1861-1862. This model was smaller, although identical in appearance to the Remington-Beals Army Model (Flayderman 138). Although all types of revolvers were used in the Civil War, this model was considered an outstanding weapon at this time, probably costing close to $12.00, which would translate in today's market to approximately $1,470 (Libel).

On April 28, 1861, Sam and Caldwell, along with thirty-eight others, were sworn into the Missouri State Guard by Col. M. Jeff Thompson and "organized into a company to be designated as the DeKalb Guards" (Lehr, Suzanne 14).

On May 20, 1861, J. C.'s oldest son, Wallace, returned home from Danville, Kentucky, where he had been enrolled at Centre College. Sam described Wallace as being very ambitious and well versed in both the civil and political affairs of his country. This had led to controversy between Wallace and his fellow students and "caused him to lay aside his studies, return to the state where he was reared, and hoist the Confederate banner as his battle flag" (Sam's memoir, page 10). For the next three weeks, Wallace joined in the town discussions about impending war. On or about June 10, 1861, Wallace and J. C. came home from town with news that the Federals had taken St. Joseph and were threatening to capture those enrolled in the Missouri State Guard. Caldwell and Sam, who were plowing in the field, stopped at once, unharnessed their horses, saddled others, gathered their guns, and went into DeKalb with Wallace to await the arrival of the rest of their company. About sundown, the DeKalb Guards started on their journey to find Sterling Price at Lexington (Lehr, Suzanne 15-6).

A family legend says that J. C. gave the .36 caliber revolver described above to his oldest son when he left for the war. A portrait of Wallace made just after the war shows a pistol of this description tucked into his belt. By giving this gun to his son, J. C. was insuring greater safety for Wallace. A Guard or Confederate soldier carrying a six chamber pistol along with his single shot musket or rifle had a significant advantage over the Federal soldier who typically would have been issued a single shot rifle or musket (Libel).

There is no information as to what J. C. might or might not have given Caldwell or Sam. According to James "Gene" Dunlap (Sam's great-great-grandson), his father, Ralph Wallace Dunlap, saw twin ivory handled revolvers and was told by Ralph's brother Dean, who owned them, that they had belonged to Sam. There is no information as to whether they might have been carried by Sam and Caldwell or as to what has become of them.

Caldwell states in his diary that he and Sam "gathered our guns" and left for war (Lehr, Suzanne 16). Sam wrote in this memoir that "our old Squirrel 'peices' were tried, to see if they would stand 'roostered' & being satisfied they would still do to trust" they mounted their horses for the long journey (13). (In the nineteenth century, the word *cocked* would not have been used in polite company. Sam's reluctance throughout the diary to spell out any questionable words may explain Sam's choice of *roostered* as a substitute (Lehr, James).

Three brothers grew up in northwest Missouri, living in a village with many, who like themselves, had roots deep in southern history and traditions. Believing the Constitution of the United States had established a confederacy and that the Union was violating that Constitution by restricting the rights of each state to determine its own destiny, the young men did not see themselves as *rebels* when they left home to defend their impassioned beliefs.

By January 1862, Wallace, an officer of the Missouri State Guard, was gravely ill with pneumonia and a weakened heart. Forced to abandon his dream, following the battle at Pea Ridge, he was honorably discharged and allowed to travel to Kentucky to recuperate. Wallace gave the .36 caliber pistol to his brothers, and at the end of the war, it was in Sam's possession. The gun was passed down from Sam to his second oldest son, William Caldwell. William then gave it to his grandson, Bill Dunlap, Sr., who bequeathed it to Bill Dunlap, Jr., with whom it remains today.

Caldwell and Sam's journey to Dixie was thrilling at first, but soon soured as the young foot soldiers faced the realities of war at Lexington, Pea Ridge, Iuka, Corinth, Hatchie's Bridge, Port Gibson, Big Black River, Champion's Hill, Vicksburg, and Atlanta. The violent battle at Kennesaw Mountain ended Caldwell's service; Sam went on to see action at Franklin and Murfeesboro before making his last camp on the banks of Deep River in North Carolina, where, in disbelief, he learned of Lee's surrender.

What was Sam to do as he waited for the generals to save the South's "way worn ship," that had been "tossed upon the rugged waves of the sea of war"? With hope in his heart and as much patience as possible, he "frequently went fishing on Deep River."

Civil War Memoir

of

Pvt. Samuel Baldwin Dunlap, C.S.A.

Note to Reader

Samuel Baldwin Dunlap's memoir has been transcribed directly from the original, with no changes. The reader will notice Sam's spelling variations of the same word, misspellings, spaces where he declined to write out the word or words, words written twice, changes to verb tenses in his transcription, quotation marks at one end of a thought but not the other, missing commas or periods, and a profuse use of the "—" symbol. All has been transcribed, when possible, in the way it appears in Sam's book, except for the headings which were written in the memoir along the margin of Sam's ruled ledger paper. For readability, those headings were interjected in the transcription near the related text.

As Sam explained, he transcribed his memoir in 1890 from the individual diaries he kept throughout the war. Those individual diaries were burned during the cleaning of a deceased relative's attic, but fortunately, William Clouser Dunlap (now deceased) arrived on the scene just before the memoir was to be consigned to the fire. The family reports that he cried out, "I would like to have that!", and it was casually tossed his way. We all owe Bill a huge thank you for having the foresight at age ten or eleven to recognize the value of what Sam had put on paper those many years before and to protect the book, leaving it in the hands of his widow Janette Dunlap, who continues to preserve it for the future. Because the diaries were transcribed into a single book twenty-five years after Sam returned from the war, what exists might be more properly defined as a memoir.

The memoir has been annotated to facilitate better understanding of Sam's references to people, places, mid-nineteenth century expressions, and items that may not be known today other than to Civil War enthusiasts. To avoid confusion, the annotations are in a boldface type and a font different from that used for Sam's words. A scanned copy of the original memoir has been placed in the archives of The St. Joseph Museums Inc.

A
Personal Record
By
Sam B. Dunlap

Kept during the war between
the Confederate States and the United
States of America, from date of
enlistment in the Confederate Service
April 10th 1861, until His arrival at
home June 21st 1865. A period of
four years two months and eleven days.

Revised and Enlarged
from notes kept by the writer.
1890

Introduction

In order that any one wishing to read a short sketch of the writer, I have concluded to take the notes that I kept while a Confederate Soldier, revise & enlarge them, so they may be more fully understood; and the reader can gain more information, feeling better recompensed for the time consumed in the perusal of the Records. There are many very interesting incidents I wish to describe, that in the old work I only made a passing remark. I do not intend this for a biographical sketch of myself, only for so much as was consumed by the ~~Rebellion~~ War between the states.

Then let us commence when I was a School boy of Seventeen Summers, let us raise the curtain, look at this first act performed as a Soldier & keep pace with the writer through the long lists of hardships privations & blood shed caused by the great devastations of war; until the trap is sprung and the Screen falls to obscure from view (but not from memory) one of the most heartrending dramas that was ever enacted before a civilized people. Although I am now past the meridian of life, more than as old again as I was when the war closed; Yet I have only to refer to my Diary & commence reading, to live over again, in imagination the life a Soldier; and often now while wrapped in the arms of Morpheus, I fight the Battles & while struggling with the "Feds" — awake only to find myself on a peaceful bed at home with my Family.

1861

1861 Apr

As I stated in the beginning of my introductory remarks this is only intended as a record of events principally, which happened under my own observation; the "ups & downs" of my company & most personal friends. The dates of occurrences found in this short narrative, can be relied upon with the most implicit confidence; with the exception of a few pages in the beginning; the notes were taken on the battle field or in camp; while the events were transpiring or soon afterwards.

Now kind reader I will ask you to go back with me to April 1861, and picture in your imagination the appearance of a school boy in antebellum days. Seventeen years of age with pouch of books hung over his shoulder, dinner basket in hand, dressed in a suit of home spun (generally brown jeans), cheeks flushed with health, bashful as a girl, yet displaying in countenance a determination of character Sufficient to undertake whatever duty devolved upon him; and you will have some idea of the appearance of myself & many other Boys as we trod along our pleasant road to school at DeKalb. Our Teacher was Charles Raffington, who died but a short time ago. (1887).

DeKalb, Missouri, the oldest town in Buchanan County, was platted in the late 1830s by James G. Finch. Although it was laid out with a town square to allow for a courthouse, it never became the county seat as expected. Originally called Bloomington, the town's name was changed around 1851 to avoid confusion with another town of the same name in Missouri (*Daily News'* 69-70; Union 370).

Sam's teacher Professor Charles Raffington founded the Bloomington Academy on a site near where the Sleepy Hollow School later stood. Mrs. Henriella Prather Crossno described the academy as a typical log building with hand-hewn split log benches and desks (Crossno).

The country was full of tumult, the sectional lines were being drawn with greater distinction, men had began to array themselves on one side or the other, at the school at noon us boys instead of taking the ball and bat, to engage in a game for the championship of the day; would talk about war, go through with what ever performance like a soldier we could, at the same time paint the most glowing picture of the scenes of battle, that were possible for our youthful imaginations.

This state of affairs would however soon be changed, my school days would soon be ended, the imaginative Soldier would soon become a real one; the tender face would become taned by the sun & smoke on the tented field; the good warm feather bed with its covers tucked in as none other than a mother can do, would have to be substituted by a blanket on a bunk at the beginning as my bed, a tent to protect me from wind & rain, But toward the close of the war if I could only find a few moments to rest without any of the above comforts, the opportunity was eagerly grasped And with a rock or chunk of wood for my pillow, the earth for my bed, the Heavens for my covering, I could rest my wearied limbs & sleep as soundly, as I once did, when I had the pleasure of enjoying the happiness and comforts of my own dear Father's home.

Enlisted under Jeff Thompson of St. Joseph Mo

Early in april, Several of the Boys of the School, my next to oldest Bro. Caldwell and myself were enrolled as Soldiers, to fight the battles of the south, by Capt. Jeff Thompson of St. Joseph, who was enlisting recruits for Camp Jackson (This camp was named in honor of Claiborn Jackson thhen Governor of the state) which was then established east of what was called the Patee House, a large Hotel, & east of the City limits at that time, Now laid out in town lots on which have been erected beautiful residences & business houses, & instead of the open plain where the voice of the lark was heard, now you hear the hum of a busy city.

Pvt. Robert Caldwell Dunlap's diary, titled *As the Mockingbird Sang*, has also been published in its entirety, with annotations, by Platte Purchase Publishers (Lehr).

Meriwether Jeff Thompson was born at Harper's Ferry, Virginia, on January 22, 1826. Following his first visit to St. Joseph in 1846, he returned in 1847 and soon began working in Middleton & Riley's mercantile store. (In 1851, Reuben Middleton joined Simeon Kemper and Israel Landis in founding Mount Mora Cemetery.) Thompson's career included work as a surveyor on the Hannibal & St. Joseph Railroad, grocer, city engineer for St. Joseph, officer of several small railroads, and mayor of St. Joseph. Following President Lincoln's request of Missouri for military support to help quell the rebellion, Governor Claiborne Jackson called for the formation of a state militia. Thompson helped form two companies in St. Joseph, becoming a colonel in the Missouri State Guard.

Thompson's service in the marshy regions of southeastern Missouri earned him the nickname "Confederate Swamp Fox," a play on the "Swamp Fox" moniker earned by General Francis Marion during the Revolutionary War. Following the war, Thompson took a position as chief engineer of the Board of Public Works for the state of Louisiana and never returned to St. Joseph to live. In 1876, Thompson was granted a leave of absence due to ill health and traveled north to Washington, D.C., New York, and other places before visiting in St. Joseph, where his health rapidly declined. Thompson died within six weeks and was buried beside his father's unmarked grave at Mount Mora Cemetery; he had buried his two young sons in that cemetery many years before ("Death"; Logan 373, 416-428; Proctor).

Construction of Patee House by John Patee began in 1856. Completed in 1858 at a cost of $130,000 and furnished for $20,000, it was losing money by the end of the first year. Patee's financial problems, accrued during the war partially because of his southern sympathies, were solved when he raffled off the hotel in a lottery on April 26, 1865, and drew the winning ticket himself (Union 626).

This was a beautiful, broad prairie valley covered with a nice green sod, facing the south, & when the beaming rays of an april sun were seen in the eastern horizon as they first began to shed their sparkling light on the Splendors of nature surrounding, as if extending an invitation to us to enjoy its beauties. This was a nice place affording us a good opportunity to practice drilling, become familiar horsemen & ~~become~~ also efficient in the use of arms. After enlisting, the next thing was to prepare ourselves for camp (Which I have already described) proceeded to the organization of a company, adopting a uniform Etc. We elected John Hart of DeKalb Captain. Also a full line of Subordinate Officers, and established for a company uniform, Black pants with yellow stripe down the out side seam of leg, (to indicate the cavelry service) gray caps, hunting shirts of the same color. After a Short interval I donned my uniform, mounted my horse, repaired to DeKalb having been ordered by the Captain to assemble at that place & march as a company to our camp at St. Joseph. 'Oh,' how grand I felt when dressed in my first uniform. I thought to become a soldier, I was a man, and the life in camp was play compared to the monotony of the schoolroom, to hear the commands, forward; march, right-shoulder shift arms, halt, ground arms; parade rest. Would be so much more animating, than five times six are thirty - Columbus discovered America, the earth is round like a ball; or I love, you love, they love.

You cannot picture in your imagination a more dazzling object than I painted in my mind, as I rode up to DeKalb about three miles from my Father's farm.

The Dunlap farm consisted of 120 acres on Section 17 outside of DeKalb. It is bounded today on the northwest corner by SW 66 Road and HH Highway.

I had read the many brilliant achievements of our forefathers, when fighting for the independence of our country, I had seen the smoke of battle, men fall dead & bleeding, horses running and dropping lifeless in all directions, artillery dismounted Etc. Etc. Yes — all this I had read & seen — "on paper". But now that the grim visage of war itself was to be seen, and I had a chance to play a part in the great drama. My heart was content at present.

After all of the company had arrived, we formed in two's & Started north in the direction of Sant Joseph, about fourteen miles distant. Our fire arms were such as could be gathered up at home, generally squirrel rifles, with barrels about four or five feet long, or single barrel shot guns (now and then you would find a farmer able to own a double barreled one) Some few had colts revolvers besides. After a ride of three hours, arrived at camp & was shown our place, which was soon filled with tents pitched in regular military order. I felt myself duly installed as a Soldier now.

Camp Jackson St. Joseph Mo

I had some blankets for bedding that I had taken from home, these thrown over some straw in the tents answered for my resting place at night. We did not have much cooking to do, as we drew from our Commissary Bakers bread, crackers dried beef Etc. ~~Our~~ The principal use for camp fires was to prepare our coffee. Our camp life at this place was somewhat monotonous, although ~~was~~ very exciting to me at that time, & highly enjoyed, but the comforts could not be so highly appreciated then as they would have been about three years afterwards. We had our daily rations which were good — and our daily drill – and such a "drill" it was. true we had drill masters who understood their business; but the principal part of the company were very ignorant about & unskilled in the use of firearms. We would be threatened with an attack of "Buck ager" before enough courage could be mustered to shoot a beef.

Dr. Jack Ward Thomas of the Boone and Crockett Club, founded by Theodore Roosevelt, describes buck agar as the pounding heart, shallow breathing, shaking limbs experience of a young hunter as he sights his first prey in the crosshairs of the gun (Thomas; "What does").

Our horses were untrained, they would become unmanageable, our guns & bridle reins would get "mixed up" with each other, and we bouncing up & down on our saddles like "rubber" men, get clear out of ranks. We would "pick" ourselves up, and after a few words of abuse to our horses, return into line in as good shape as possible while those who happened to be fortunate enough to keep in place better, would be laughing, & the Officers give us a Slight repremand for our awkwardness. But we went to this camp for this purpose, and while we remained, which was about six weeks, we improved greatly in drill & made a very good appearance from a military standpoint.

1861 May
Temporary Disbanded

About the 10th of May thinking it useless to remain in camp as a body any longer, disbanded, returning to our respective homes, with orders to assemble ourselves together at Company Headquarters at DeKalb, at a moments warning, fully equipped for the field.

My Bro. & I returned home, but not to be satisfied, the school book had losts its charms, the plow & hoe looked too much like work; the stillness of the house where my Father & Step-mother were the only occupants, was very oppressive to us; this cessation in our camp life only added fuel to the war flames that were already burning within us. The first gun of the war had been fired at Fort Sumpter, South Carolina; military companies were being formed all over the Northern and Southern states, preparations for war seemed to have begun in earnest; in fact all you could read or hear talked of, on the street corners or cross roads was war – war.

Return to Saint Joseph to repel the Kans. "JayHawkers"

We didn't remain but a few days at home, ~~we~~ were called together again at DeKalb, & ordered to ~~p~~ report to St. Joseph to repel what was thought to be real invasion of the "Kansas Jayhawkers", but turned out only an imaginary foe that time.

Kansas Jayhawkers were Union guerillas who engaged in guerilla warfare with the pro-slavery sympathizers known as Border Ruffians.

However, we reported, and was ordered to take up our quarters this time in the Oak hills south east of the City; to put out pickets, (this kindness made a lump come up in our throats) & not permit any one to enter camp, without the countersign & a satisfactory explanation annexed, – of his business. While at this camp one dark night rather an amusing incident, (but a very exciting one at that time) occurred.

False Alarm

As I said before, we were expecting the "Kansas Jayhawkers" our pickets were out with strict orders to fire on any one approaching the lines who failed to observe the orders given the guards. One of our Pickets who was stationed in some bushes in the outskirts of the camp, saw what he took to be the advance guard of the enemy mounted & coming in the direction of where he stood, gave the command to halt! with all the courage that a newly enlisted Soldier could, & after a repetition of the same word three times, and his summons not being obeyed, raised his double barreled shot gun to his Shoulder & with a feeling which is easier experienced than described; fired & fell back to camp in as good shape as possible. The report of the gun although not unexpected, was very exciting & the appearance of the picket so soon afterward almost produced a panic. But a short speech by way of encouragement from the Officers, quelled the excitement to a certain extent, & we proceeded to examine our old squirrel "pieces", to satisfy ourselves, they were all right. Saddled our horses put on our spurs & in obedience to orders reposed in line on our guns the remainder of the night.

Camp in Oak hills

When it was almost time for the gray streaks of early dawn to appear in the eastern horizon; Some of those who had seen a few more of the vacissitudes of life than the man who fired the shot, concluded to make a reconoiter, & they came to the conclusion after making quite an extended examination, that the imaginative enemy was none other than an old gray horse which had strayed away from camp & was feeding around through the bushes. Our great suspense was ended, the camp which we thought but a few hours previous, would be one of blood, carnage & weeping over our fallen comrades; was filled with mirth & laughter. Occurrences of a similar nature were frequent, at the beginning of the Rebellion, & it seems to me now, of prime importance; we should have had something of this nature to prepare us for the coming conflict. The stern qualities of our natures must be brought out, the timidity of Youth must be laid aside, & the mantle of modesty obscured from the middle aged. We had to meet the imaginary to prepare us for the real.

Second Disbanding

The enemy not making his appearance, and considering our services no longer necessary at this point, returned to our respective homes again, also a continuation of this order given to expect to be called, out for drill, or camp service as the necessity of the times seemed to demand. About this time (20th May) my oldest Bro Wallace (23 years of age) who had been attending College at Danville Ky. (Where he would have graduated with the highest honors in a short time) returned home. The age he was and being of a very ambitious disposition, well posted ~~in~~ in the affairs of his country, both civil & political, led to arguments & controvercies between him & his fellow students, caused him to lay aside his studies, return to the state where he was reared, and hoist the Confederate banner as his battle flag.

The 1890 General Catalogue of The Centre College of Danville, Kentucky, lists James W. Dunlap as a non-graduate in 1860. Centre College's 1861 catalogue lists Dunlap as a junior in the Scientific Department (Centre College 9).

At Home

Although many years have intervened, & many things happened to blight my memory; yet I remember well as if but yesterday, a few days after his arrival at home, he was chosen as orator of the day. The time of meeting at DeKalb was Set apart, guests were invited, a company from Iotan, & one from Taos neighboring villages were also requested to meet us & have a consolidated drill.

Iatan, Missouri, remains a small northwest Missouri village; the 2000 census lists the population at 54 people ("Iatan, Missouri").

Halleck, Missouri, once known as Birming and before that as Fansher's Cross Roads, received the Halleck name during the Civil War in honor of Union General Henry Wager Halleck. The Taos nickname was a compliment to Mexican war soldier John McGuire who, comparing the whisky sold there in an 1848-49 saloon to Taos [Mexico at the time] whiskey, rode through the village shouting, "Hurrah for Taos!" (Union 375-6).

According to arrangements previously decided upon, when the day set apart for the meeting arrived, our fondest anticipations were more than gratified. The cavalry companies from the Sister towns arrived; the Rebel flag (Red white & red) was unfurled to the breeze in the middle of the Square, on a pole about fifty feet high, which had been prepared for that special occasion. We ~~had our~~ had our drill in a beautiful bluegrass pasture, owned by Edwin Hart, lying immediately west of the town, after which we returned to the square, which was completely packed with people (as was the streets also) of all parties, discussing the leading topics of the day, (War & it consequences) excitement ran very high, everything seemed to be at fever heat. Brothers were arrayed against brothers & Father against Son. There was a Company of home guards who had been drilling on the opposite side of town from where we were in the morning, but as the evening approached they mostly disappeared, after they had viewed our crowd, came to the conclusion they were much in the manority.

Home guards
Oration at DeKalb by J.W. Dunlap

About 1 P.M. the Taos, Iotan & DeKalb companies were formed in line on foot in front of the brick store then owned by "Nick" Oliver, my Bro Wallace mounted the awning over the door (to deliver his Speech) & was greeted with long, loud & welcome cheers from the sea of upturned faces which met his gaze as he looked down upon them, who had assembled themselves to hear the topics of the times discussed, which was done in a very able & impressive manner.

I cannot refrain from calling to memory, the beautiful picture presented when he mounted the rostrum with his firm tred. Countenance glowing with the reflection of a noble heart within, Straight as an arrow, a smile playing upon his lips; his dark eyes sparkling with the inteligence of a broad & comprehensive brain, every jesture was words unspoken, & every word uttered, took deep hold in the minds of his hearers. He was every inch a man.

I felt proud that I could call him Brother. I rejoiced to think he had come back home, while the country was clouded with such uncertainty, that he might give me advice concerning an approaching danger, or give me council in the hours of trouble; how often it is that good advice is not appreciated by the person upon whom it is bestowed, at the time it is given, but in this case my actions met with his most hearty approval. He said that war was inevitable, & if he had to take sides, would fight with the defenders of the soil that gave him birth. He was stopped several times during his speech by his enemies, asking questions which were not pertinent, for the purpose of confusing, & leading his mind astray from his subject; but it seemed to have the opposite effect, new points would be brought to bear, & as his cheeks colored blood red, the flow of eloquence would break forth anew, & as his adversary turned to walk away badly worsted, the victory gained was saluted by a long round of applause from his enthusiastic friends.

DeKalb hero

The oration lasted about three hours, closing as it commenced, amid deafening & prolonged cheers. But man: poor frail man is bound to die.

Alas! there is never a star so bright, that there isn't a cloud appears to obscure it, and this bright star in the intellectual world was destined to fill a premature grave.

James Wallace Dunlap died January 22, 1866.

Well, in short we had a full grown day of it; & after a short consultation was held by the officers in regard to our future plans for actions, returned to our respective homes, much wiser & more encouraged than when we met, & with the impression more deeply imbedded in our minds that the time for action had arrived.

Only those who were old enough to take sides, or conceive into their minds, some idea of the perils of war, can imagine any thing near the correct state of affairs at that time. If the people had been thrown into one tremendous reservoir, & an earthquake shock, sufficient to prostrate them, & numb their sensitiveness for a moment, produced; the tumult caused could not have been greater; the gray haired Sires were preparing for the field as well as the youth in this teens. Those who sympathized with the south were branded as cesessionists or southern Sympathizers; while those of the opposite side were called Abolitionists or Unionists, later on the appelation was shortened on both sides to "Reb" & "Yank".

1861 June
Taking Sides

About the first of June receiving orders to rally at Headquarters (DeKalb) our old Squirrel "peices" were tried, to see if they would stand "roostered" & being satisfied they would still do to trust, mounted our horses & were soon answering to roll call at the company rendezvous, and as a long journey was contemplated, the Officers endeavored to be very strict in their inspection, and everything proving satisfactory was soon marching in an eastern~~er~~ direction, after a few miles ride formed a junction with some other companies & started south with the intention of joining Prices army, which was then in Southern Mo., our journey was a pleasant one, seemed to be just what we had been longing for, it was a complete panacia for our troubled feelings. "Everthing went lovely & the Goose hung high".

From 1840-1844, Sterling Price served in the Missouri House of Representatives. He was then elected to the Twenty-

ninth Congress where he served from March 4, 1845, to August 12, 1846, when he resigned to raise a regiment for service in the Mexican War. Following his honorable discharge, he returned to Missouri to become a major tobacco planter. Price was governor of Missouri from 1853 to 1857, and, although he was a slave-owner, he presided over the Missouri State Convention in 1861 which opposed secession. Angered by Francis P. Blair and Nathaniel Lyon's inflammatory actions at St. Louis, he accepted command of Governor Jackson's newly formed Missouri State Guard in May 1861 and later served as a major general in the Confederate States Army. Price was highly respected by his men, but his military success was limited. He led a failed Confederate exile colony in Carlota, Veracruz, and died "a broken and impoverished man" (Boatner III 669; "Sterling Price").

The maxim "the goose hung high" comes from the old practice of curing meat by hanging the fowl. A goose hung high signaled good luck or good fortune ("The goose").

Sam drew the maxim from at least one of two popular song sheets of the time. The American Memory from The Library of Congress website describes song sheets as 6 x 8-inch single sheets of lyrics that could be matched to popular melodies of the time such as "Yankee Doodle Dandy."

One verse of the lyrics published by Doyle:

Now good folks I will sing you a song,
The tenor of my rhymes
Shall be a hit on the notions,
And a joke upon the times.
When things go well in these hard times.
The people loudly cry,
Everything is lovely and the goose hang's high.

One verse of the lyrics published by Johnson:

Sensation politicians, when they mount the boards,
They tickle up the voters, calling them creation's lords;
Crying out, "Dear fellow-citizens, for you I'm here to die,"
For they see a good fat office, *and the goose hangs high*.

From DeKalb to Liberty Clay Co Mo

Our march was by way of New Market & Platte City. About sundow,

Second day, stopped for the night at a large barn in the suburbs of Liberty Clay County. Although there were ~~were~~ quite a command of us banded together, their seemed be a very noticable absence of military tactics, we had not decided on any particular one as a leader. On our march we had not discovered the slightest sign of an early appearance of the enemy; all was peace & tranquality, every one seemed to be our friends, So with that assurance, not using the caution of putting out guards; ate supper, fed our horse, Spread our blankets, upon the ground and retired for the night. Our rest was unbroken, except a slight interruption caused by the Squealing of a horse while being kicked by his neighbor, or the buzz of the june bug as it would come to an abrupt halt in his wayward flight by meeting with an obstruction in the shape of a sleepers nose.

Liberty Mo

Our Officers before retiring, made arrangements for all hands to get breakfast the next morning at the Hotel ______ in Liberty, as we were not very well prepared to do our own cooking in Camp.

Yes we slept; but our enemy didn't, they were a little better up to "snuff" than we. If this had happened but one year later, and Officers made such an unpardonable blunder as this one made here, matters not if they had been doubly assured by the good people that there was not the slightest danger, (as they were at this place) they would have been tried by a courtmarshal, the stars or bars as an insignia of their rank torn from their collars, reduced to ranks with the lowest private and all their past glories buried in the darkest corner of military disgrace. There is never a stream so calm, but by close scrutiny a tiny ripple can be observed, a surface so smooth that a slight mark doesn't appear, a form so perfect that something else couldnot be added to make its beauties more attractive. Likewise there never was and never will be a community so nearly all of the same belief, that there is not one of the number who cannot be persuaded to turn traitor. Our Savior was deceived in this manner. He was betrayed by one of his own guests, one who had eaten from the same table, yea the same dish, and it is not surprising that one should be betrayed as we were, being ~~as we were~~ young in the arts of a Soldier.

A Traitor in Town

The man who was interested in the Hotel, was accused of being cognisant of the plot against us. A courier was mounted on a swift horse that night & sent to Fort leavenworth Kansas to inform the United states troops stationed there of our where abouts, and no doubt of the blunder we made in not putting out Pickets. As soon as the courier had delivered his message, a force of men armed and equipped for war were placed under command of Brigadier General Prentice, boarded a steamer which was tied at the wharf, and while the darkness of night obscurred them from view, & the gnats & mosquitos were singing their sweet lulabies over our tranquil forms as we snored away, Soon disembarked at liberty landing, (about four miles distant from our camp) and proceeded to deploy their forces so as to approach the town in all the principal thoroughfares.

Surrounded by the Enemy

Well now, to return to our camp, A beautiful June morning dawned, to find us in fine spirits, feeling very much refreshed after our undisturbed slumber, the warm sun was peeping through the heavy dew drops which hung in masses on the beautiful and luxuriant foliage, as if weeping tears of sorrow over our unconscious ignorance. The hour had come for us to pertake of the meal which had been ordered on the previous evening, & after which take up our line of march. We filed into the Hotel by Squads. ("By turns like going to mill") Our breakfast was gotten up in superb stile.

Breakfast at Liberty

I was eating at the last table, & just buttered my last half buiscuit, spreading molasses very profusely on it for a "fare well" bite, when the alarm was given that the "Bluecoats" were coming. You cannot imagine a more complete surprise than this was. just think of it; hemed up in a long narrow dining room, an enemy coming, & but few of us armed to defend ourselves; I ran with others to the front door, a hasty consultation was held by the few present. Some had their guns at the hotel, but most of us left them at camp with the horses. The Boys who had eaten at one of the first tables scattered all over town. Some were dressed in uniform, others in Citizens suits. My oldest Brother was dressed as a Citizen. He had attended the William Jewell College here, the year previous as a Student; went to his old boarding house, & avoided arrest, But the uniform of our company betrayed Caldwell and Myself; Suffice to say the excitement ran high.

Wallace Dunlap is listed in the William Jewell College catalogue for the year ending June 23, 1859. According to Angela Stiffler, William Jewell College Partee Center for Baptist Historical Studies, Dunlap is not listed for the 1858

class, but he is listed with the senior class in the Academic Department for 1859. There is no explanation in the catalog, but "around that time...there was a high school equivalency program" that was separate from the Collegiate Department (Stiffler).

The Capt. of our company and several of the Boys myself included, made a break for our horses & arms, Which were about two hundred yards distant. Did not run far before we saw the enemy intercede, turned our course only to run a short distance to find our way was again obstructed by the Bluecoats with glittering bayonetts, a third attempt was made & likewise foiled. Seeing all the ways of exit cut off the Capt Sugjested we go back to the place from where we started & Surrender "like men" seeing no other alternative we very willingly assented. When we returned found "Federals" in force and several of the Boys already corralled.

Captured by Gen Prentis U S.A

Only those who had been once guarded by a row of bayonetts, can imagine the deep chagrin we felt, as we sat on the curbstones, meditating about our destiny in the near future; we revolved in our minds some of the most direful scenes & consequences; the murderers gallows, the deserters stake, or the dingy, dreary & lonely walls of the prison, a long absence from Father Mother & Friends Etc. Etc. But we were more than agreeably disappointed. Lucky for us if we had to be slipped up on in this way, that the act was done by the Soldiers & General who effected our capture. These troops were Old United states regulars under command of a very gentlemanly Officer. His only desire, he said was to try to make us loyal to the Union cause. After capturing all those who could be easily overtaken, formed us in a line, took our guns, discharged their contents in the air, poured out our supply of ammunition on the ground in the streets, Administered an oath. (But not the "iron clad" Oath of 1865) this one was simply to support the constitution of the United states and the state of Missouri without any mental reservation; which we "swallowed" without any hesitation. The countenances which but a few moments before, were shrouded with gloomy forebodings, and disappointments; were now brightened up by a — great — big — broad — Smile.

Our arms and horses were returned to us, with the admonition from the Officer in command, to return to our homes and be good "Boys". Good advice wasn't it?

General Prentice having completed all that he started out to do, returned inhaste to the point from whence he came, no doubt thinking there might be some of our comrads, who would come to our relief.

In 1861, General Benjamin Mayberry Prentiss, in command of the area surrounding the Hannibal & St. Joseph Railroad, was ordered to keep communications open in northern Missouri. He fought multiple skirmishes with Southern sympathizers in an effort to remove secessionists from his area (Heidler and Heidler 1559-60).

Liberty

We were captured without a shot being fired or the shedding of blood in battle. The surprise was so complete & we not having out any guards to warn us of an approaching danger, their force being much greater & better equipped than ours, an effort to repel them would have been futile, & very distructive to property & Noncombattants.

John. Wallingford Wounded

We had a very sad mishap here about the time the "Feds" first came up. One of our company Boys John. Wallingford, lost the use of his left arm & came near loosing his life. He was standing in the Hotel office — his left hand on the muzzle of a double barreled shot gun & under his left armpit; foot upon the bottom of a chair, when by some means both barrels were discharged, the contents going through his hand & lacerating his shoulder in a fearful manner. This put an end to his career as a soldier, but by careful nursing got well & became a useful & honored citizen. This one circumstance learned me one lesson about fire arms, that has remained indelibly stamped on my memory ever since. As I previously Stated the Boys who had eaten at one of the first tables and started around "to take in the town" some of whom were fortunate enough to be in a position so as to discover the approach of the Enemy, avoided capture, Some of them took to the woods & kept going until they reached Price's army, others secreted themselves in some persons house who was friendly to the southern cause, and made their appearance after the disappearance of the "Feds". My oldest Brother mounted his horse "Bolivar" (as he was called at home) & after bidding us a friendly good bye — Started for Prices army. Those of us who were unfortunate enough to have to take the Oath — turned our backs upon Liberty, and started home by the same route, we came the day previous on our "going down to Dixie.

Returning Home

We didn't feel quite so cheerful though, we could not reconcile ourselves as to the manner in which we would answer the many interrogatories & prove satisfactory in every respect awaiting us by the numerous friends that we left at home, from whom we seperated but a few days previous with feelings that anticipate an affectionate farewell when a long absence is expected.

We did not think we were guilty of commiting any great crime, for which we deserved severe criticisms of our old associates; we had not lost any of the zeal for the great cause we had espoused, this little disappointment only caused us to think more serious in regard to the magnitude of the undertaking in which we had enlisted.

The Oath that was administered to us, we could not think it criminally violating to continue on our course south, for we were contending for our states rights under the constitution of the United states; but thought best under the present circumstances to return, reorganize, strengthen our force, & equip ourselves in a manner so as to insure success when we attempted another march South.

1861 July
At Home Reorganization Commenced

After a few days rest the reorganization of our somewhat scattered forces was commenced, but the purpose of our meetings were not made so public as they had been in the past, ~~our~~ the experience of a few weeks was a good schooling for us, we had learned caution. During the time I remained at home (about six weeks or two months) I had a gay time. Strange "ain't" it, how quick a boy gets to be a "man" or at least an imaginary one. Before this little experience as a soldier, I had not commenced going out "amongsts em". The "Gals" I mean; this seemed to have cleared away my bashfulness to a certain extent, & I took great pleasure in escorting them to church, parties, picnics Etc, & by the way I made such an impression on one of the Belle's of the neighborhood that She presented me with a beautiful plain gold ring as a memento of her affections for me.

I received the beautiful gift with as many thanks & bowing myself out of her presence & with a cheerful heart was soon away on the tented field again. I esteemed the gift very highly, but it soon became too small to wear on my finger, and I carefully wrapped it in paper, placed it in my pocket book, where it remained during the four years of untold hardships undergone by the writer, which had then just began. I had only to catch a glimpse of this little token of friendship, when on the swing south & many miles intervened between myself & the donor, to revive afresh in my memory the thought of home & the pleasant associations of the past.

At Home
Caldwell Started south

About the 15th of July my Bro. Caldwell became restless & thinking the signs of the times not indicating an early march south, in company with a young man "Newt." Baughman, started horse back on the perilous mission of joining Price's army, which they succeeded in doing in time to participate in the hand fought battle of Oakhills, near Springfield Mo.

Oak Hills was the Confederate name for the Battle of Wilson's Creek. The August 10, 1861, Confederate victory was the first major Civil War battle fought west of the Mississippi River.

1861 August

About the first of August, my Bro. Wallace returned home from Price's Army, to act in the capacity of a recruiting Officer, to make preperations for a final departure & return with the companies then almost ready to start south again. By this time we had our company in tolerably good trim, we had become much better skilled in the drill of small arms, our appearance in the saddle denoted one of ease & comfort. We were not in regular camp, but would meet according to orders on certain days & return to our places of residence with a definite understanding when & where to meet again.

August 26th Ordered to report for active duty

I received orders from company Head quarters at DeKalb, to report for active duty. A ride of three miles brought me to Town, & from the appearance of things in general, I thought there was something more than had been in the meaning of report for duty heretofore; But having been anticipating a move of some kind, took in the situation at a glance. I could tell from the actions of the crowd collected that they were really in earnest, that they meant business.

Preparing for Service

The old as well as the young seemed to be deeply interested in the matter, at one place you could see a squad of young men Selecting Saddles, bridles, halters, Spurs &c &c, & at another buying blankets overshirts, caps, in fact everything needed for an active camp life, the old gray haired Sires & Matrons assisting in the purchases, and occasionally you could catch the glympse of a youthful feminine hand as its owner passed something to her "Best young man" as a kind of remembrancer of an existing affection & a cheerful wish for health happiness & a speedy return, annexed. Oh! I tell you this made us feel as if we could grind the North into powder in a few days. There are nothing like words of encouragement, & more especially when spoken by a woman, who is always uppermost in a true mans affections; A woman can lead a man to the highest pinacle of true manhood, or sink him to the lowest pit of degradation. Well after completing our preperations as much as possible, & a good many of the Boys filling up on "Bug juice" enough to make them merry, left DeKalb 1 P.M. for Camp Gibson about 20 miles distant.

"Bug juice" was a Civil War slang term for whiskey ("Bug juice").

We were entertained on our way by the Boys who were given to vocalism by the favorite melodies of Dixie & the "Gal I left behind me".

One verse of "The Gal I Left Behind Me":

The dames of France are fond and free, and Flemish lips are willing,
And soft the maids of Italy, While Spanish eyes are thrilling.
Still tho' I bask beneath their smiles, Their arms all fail to bind me,
And my heart goes back to Erin's Isle, To the girl I left behind me ("The Gal").

We had a very pleasant trip. Marched in an eastern direction, passed through Taos (Now Halleck) a small village about Six miles from DeKalb. Also Agency situated on Platte river, a small but very old town.

In 1838 or 1839, Robert Gilmore of east Tennessee established a ferry on the Platte River, at a settlement known as Agency Ford. In 1865, William B. Smith founded Agency on that same site (*Daily News'* 73; Union 130-1).

Camp Gibson

Arrived at Camp Gibson 4 miles distant 9 P.M. where we found a small force, consisting of two companies of Infantry commanded by Capts Mintern & Gibson

Aug. 27th

Our camp here was beautifully situated in a nice grove of timber, and a never failing Spring as clean as crystal near at hand, from which we ~~can~~ quenched our thirst, we ~~are~~ were in the midst of a wealthy agricultural district, the fins ~~are~~ were full of last years crops, & the ground almost groaning under the productions of the present one; and what ~~is~~ was better still this bounteous supply ~~is~~ was in possession of a generous & chivalrous hearted people, who threw open their doors & Store rooms & as we appeared upon the threshold greeted us with that word which has an almost endless meaning — Welcome. This ~~is~~ was truely flattering indeed, well calculated to drive from our thoughts the realistic part of camp life, & cause us to think it nothing to be a Soldier. We didnot wait to eat when we got hungry, to drink when we got dry, or rest when tired; for we were situated so as not to be compelled to do either. Our camp was frequently visited by the ladies, & they didnot come on a mission of curiosity, they brought baskets well filled with meats of all kinds, pies, cakes &c &c, which were very delicious and highly appreciated by us. Heretofore or at least since my capture at Liberty, I had not enlisted for any definite time, or attached myself to any particular arm of Service. We were now called upon to make our choice.

Sworn into the Service for Six months as Cavalry

I enlisted as cavalry in Capt. John Harts company for Six months, also all persons who had not previously taken the oath, and desired to do so, were Sworn into service for the same length of time, & allowed to choose either Cavalry or Infantry.

Camp Gibson

We remained at this place about one week, & I assure you, I could not leave without a Sigh of regret, we had been supplied so bountifully with food for ourselves & horses, & our camp visited by the citizens of the Surrounding country, who encouraged us in our undertaking in a manner that the memory of which only brightens as time passes

Sept 4th

Broke up camp - Our company Capt Harts were ordered to Rushville, about 26 miles west of our present situation, the Citizens of that section of country becoming very much alarmed, a report having been circulated, that the Kansas Jayhawkers (our old foe) were crossing the Mo. River at Winthrop, and committing depredations in the adjacint country. We made haste to the scene of trouble as fast as our horses could carry us, arriving at Rushville late in the afternoon. We had been nerving ourselves all the way on our march for the coming conflict — but found the report false, laid aside our "fighting harness" again, tied our horses to the fence & hung ourselves "up" on the ground for the night, but before doing so stationed a strong picket guard at Winthrop a small village on the Mo River about 4 miles distant, & ~~at~~ other points at regular crossings. We were determined not to be caught napping here as we were at Liberty. Rushville is a small town Situated about Six miles west of DeKalb — In the Early history of Buchanan County it was called Columbus.

Rushville, known as Columbus until 1851, was laid out in 1847 by Perman Hudson and James Leachman on a quarter section claimed in 1839 by John Flannery. Winthrop, a once prosperous village, was settled by George Million in 1839. Million operated the first ferry across the Missouri River from Winthrop to what later became Atchison, Kansas. The Winthrop town company formed in 1857; the name was chosen in honor of Governor Winthrop of Massachusetts colony. In 1884, a portion of Winthrop washed into the Missouri River and necessitated the abandonment of the "Paw-Paw" railroad station between Winthrop and Rushville (*Daily News'* 70-1; Union 372-3).

5th

The Enemy not appearing, & not seeing any Signs to denote his near approach, concluded to retire to more comfortable quarters. In the forenoon we moved back about four miles, and camped in Christopher Hart's pasture, which was called Camp Hart. We pitched our tents in military order, on the beautiful blue grass sod, Shaded by the hanging boughs of the forest trees, and again we were the recipients of the bounteous supplies afforded by a rich & well tilled soil.

Camp Hart

We kept out a strong picket force to warn us of any approaching danger. My Oldest Brother (Wallace) was our commissary, who kept our tents crowded with all substantials as well as delicacies the surrounding country afforded.

To say we lived high doesn't express half enjoyment, unbounded. The Ladies often attended our camp and pardon me if I call them good looking — for one of the number was the same person spoken of in the beginning of my story, as presenting me with a beautiful memento, nor did they come and return as silent visitors, they were continually presenting some one with a remembrancer, or something that would increase their comfort and well being in future; this was not all; they didnot come to whisper words of sorrow or discouragement in our ears; but while their eyes were sparking from the light reflected from a kind and generous disposition within, their language was full of encouragement, especially as it was, when spoken, embellished with smiles. I have already given a discription of the firearms with which we were supplied, but a great many didnot think them sufficient, thought something was needed for close quarters, & in the absence of better material, concluded to have a substitute hammered out. All the Blacksmith shops in the country were ransacked for worn out files & rasps, which were soon converted into huge knives or Sabers, a rough scabbard was stiched up, a pistol (the larger the better) & the two were suspended from a belt around the body. Some of the knives bore a striking resemblance to the corn knives of the present day. These rude specimens however were soon abandoned as a useless appendage & as harmless in war.

Camp Hart

Any person who followed us for the next six or eight months, found them scattered along the roadside almost eaten up with rust. We remained at camp Hart about ten days, and it is unnessary to say, that the order to move was very reluctantly received.

September 14th

Having become satisfied that our services were no longer needed as a safe guard to this community, & Gen. Price having moved his forces upon Lexington which was garrisoned by a few thousand troops under command of Brigadier Gen Mulegan U.S.A. we resolved to make another effort to join our beloved chieftain. The company left camp early in the morning & went to DeKalb. I went by home to change horses & was soon again with them ~~company~~ & marching in a southeasterly direction, but our progress was some what retarded for a great many of the "Boys" like myself, had to go home and make a little more preperations than common, for we were inspired with more confidence this time than ever before, and on account of our friends being near by in force, caused us to redouble our energies.

Traveled 15 miles & camped for the night. This was a day long to be remembered by the writer. You may ask, Why? Well, I was 18 years old for one thing. Quite a difference between then & now. It seemed to me almost like an age from one birth day to another; thought I never would get to be 21 — but I almost imagined myself a man in stature any how for I had got to be a Soldier.

Leaving Home For four years

And another reason was leaving home & realizing if our march proved successful, might perhaps be the last time; grasping my kind old Father and Stepmother's hands, leaving the dear old hearthstone, around which I played in childhoods happy hours, parting with friends, old associates, neighbors, &c &c. I had a good home; I had one of the best Fathers that ever lived. Why not regret leaving all these? My Mother died when I was a child of two summers, this always left an aching void in my heart, for I never knew, or realized the fond carresses that only a loving mother can give, but as I said before I had a good home, and the dreadful experiences of the next four years through which I passed, made me look back with a shudder, when I took into consideration, how little I had appreciated home & its surroundings, when situated so as to enjoy them. Home! this word has a meaning that will last eternally, the fond recollections that cluster around our earthly home are indelibly stamped upon the minds of all, & those who have appreciated the benefits & luxuries of such, & acted accordingly, will be entitled to a home eternal in the Heavens.

Sam's mother (and the mother of Sam's siblings)was Patsy Hainline. She was born December 29, 1817, and died September 16, 1845. Sam's father James C. Dunlap then married Mary "Polly" Horn on March 4, 1846. She died December 10, 1848. James' third wife was Mahala Morrison. They married November 18, 1849. Mahala was born December 2, 1815, and died August 27, 1872. She was the stepmother whom Sam mentions in his diary. Following her death, James C. married Sallie Yates on November 3, 1873. She died September 8, 1884. James' last marriage was to Sarah "Sallie" Burgess on August 9, 1886. According to family legend, James C. planned to marry a 6th time, following Sallie's death, but his sons intervened and changed his plans (Sampson).

'Tis human to err, natural that we should not merit with due reverence, the true value of a favor, at the time the benefit is received. I was a Boy at this time, was clothed, fed & sheltered, and I did not stop to think from whence it came; but I looked back upon my forgetfulness with weeping eyes, while far away in the Sunny South, during the long years that intervened between my departure & return. At the time we left this camp (Hart) on that memorable day, these reflections did not appear. I left home with buoyant spirits believing the cause in which I was engaged, was a just one.

15th March from DeKalb to Lexington

Left camp at daylight, marched in a southern direction, formed a junction with Col. Patton's command of Andrew County at Union Mills, situated on Platte river. A grist mill, Store & Blacksmith shop constituted the burg. After resting a few hours resumed our march, camped at Smithville Clay Co 8 P M. The Boys all in good spirits, & the nearer we got to Price, the more anxiety ~~is~~ was displayed to form a junction with his forces.

16th

Moved out 4 A M. Although feeling somewhat sore, from my previous days ride, I crawled into my saddle & pushed on — the excitement of the times and merriment of the Boys, soon wore away the wearied feelings. Our line of march this time although we were nearing the same town, (Liberty) was on another road & under quite different & more encouraging circumstances, than those to which we were compelled to submit, at the time of our betrayal & capture at this place a few months ~~ago~~ previous. We had a larger & better equipped command, & had learned to keep our "eyes open".

Liberty Second Time

Passed through Liberty in the afternoon. This is the County Town of Clay Co. A beautifully situated inland town, inhabited by a highly enlightened & whole souled people, a very large majority of whom ~~are~~ were friendly to the Southern cause, & the demonstrations made by them as we passed through the streets, were very strong convincing evidences, that they most assuredly acquiessed in our movements. I almost imagined that I could hear a piano in every dwelling, for the air was full of music, both vocal & instrumental, the favorite airs at that time, Dixie & Bonnie blue flag, were sung & played in the most delicious manner, by the charming young Ladies (and I assure you they were plenty) who appeared on the varandas or in open windows.

Harry McCarthy's "The Bonnie Blue Flag" summarizes the secession of the first eleven states from South Carolina to Tennessee. A rousing chorus between verses proclaims:

Hurrah! Hurrah!
For Southern rights, hurrah!
Hurrah for the Bonnie Blue Flag that
bears a single star.

The old of both sexes, as well as the young, appeared on the scene & engaged in the highlarity of the occasion; they were all loud in their expressions of faith in the cause which we were defending. The Boys would greet these noble demonstrations with loud huzzas, & frequent shouts for "Jeff." Davis, And as we moved on, the waving of handkerchiefs, could yet be seen as we were disappearing, signaling us onward, which inspired us with renewed courage to defend the soil of our beloved state, & especially those noble men & women of Liberty.

Blue Mills Landing

We arrived at Blue mills landing a few miles south of Liberty late in the afternoon, where we crossed the Missouri river about sundown on an old rickety flat boat, & camped for the night. The United states troops having dicovered our movements, concentrated their forces in the rear of our men who were not yet across, & tried to prohibit them from doing so.

17th

Early in the morning the noise of the oars on the old flat boat could be heard, while the ferry man was transporting his loads of human freight, & the lashing of the mad waves against the sides of his frail craft, was sufficient evidence that his task was not an easy one. The Federals under command of Gen. Crayner, said to be chiefly composed of raw recruits, now made their appearance, and from what information could be gained, from Scouts who were seen hurrying in all directions on both sides of the river, a battle was iminent, There was great excitement on both sides. About 3 P.M, all of our men were across but Col Patton's command, and Crayner thinking our forces much weaker than they were, thought he would take advantage, of the situation. Opened the fracus by firing three rounds from his artillery in quick succession. This being the first engagement for our men, they seemed anxious, to turn upon their pursuers, & raising a deafening shout charged upon them with such a determination of spirit & unerving aim, that Crayners men fled in great confusion, leaving their artillery & many other articles of value on the field, as well as their dead & wounded. Our loss was trifling. Col Pattons men did themselves great honor, & if their last efforts can be crowned with the same success as the first, they will be hard competitors. Crayner gathered up the fragments of his forces, & returned to Liberty, leaving Col. Patton's men to cross the river at leisure. Our company marched back to cross the river to assist Patton's men, twice as infantry & once as cavalry, but were ordered ~~back~~ by our officers to remain where we were, Said when our services were considered necessary, we would be sent for. This engagement was called "Battle of Blue Mills landing," & the success with which we met was truely gratifying. Now that we were across the "Big muddy" considered ourselves safe, or atleast the main barrier between us & our Leader (Price) had been overcome, & served as a rear guard to keep our pursuing enemy at bey. Our rest for the night was unbroken.

According to the *History of Clay and Platte Counties, Missouri*, the Battle of Blue Mills was an "insignificant collision of hostile forces." Gen. Price had sent messages ordering the Missouri State Guards "and other Secession forces in Northeast and Northwest Missouri to meet him at Lexington." About 3,500 men from Gentry, Andrew, Nodaway,

Holt, Buchanan, and DeKalb counties responded but found it challenging to reach Gen. Price, as the Federals were guarding all the main fords and crossings of the Missouri River. About September 15, these men under Col. J. P. Saunders, Col. Wilfley, Col. Jeff. Patton, Col. Childs, and Capt. E. V. Kelly were able to assemble near St. Joseph, and immediately left for Lexington.

Gen. Pope learned of the troop movement in his area and set out to intercept the Confederates about three miles south of Liberty on the road to Blue Mills, or Owens' Landing. A skirmish ensued, halting the Federals, followed by a fall-back of the Missouri State Guards. The Federals determined to advance, but were met by a calculated ambush. About four miles south, Col. Jeff. Patton's regiment lined the road, supported by other battalions and companies.

> As the Federals were marching gaily along, 'eager for a fight,' as they said, suddenly a galling fire was opened upon them from both sides of the road. A fierce little fight was begun and kept up for nearly an hour. But the advantage was with the Missourians from the start until the close, and the federals were at least driven from the field, and retreated into Liberty in something like disorder and more of haste.

The Union troops returned to the field under cover of night and retrieved their wounded. At once, both sides began exaggerating the numbers of their opposition, as well as their losses. The following day, the wounded were brought to the William Jewell College building, which had been converted into a hospital, and their dead were buried on the college grounds. A small cemetery remains today in the midst of William Jewell's now expanded campus. Eventually, estimates placed Federal casualties at 56 and Missouri State Guard casualties at 70 (History 208-12; "Missouri: June-October 1861").

Before this battle, Southern sympathizers (among them John C. Landis of St. Joseph) seized the Liberty, Missouri, arsenal on April 20, 1861. Federal troops immediately arrived to fortify a hill across town from the hill on the William Jewell College campus. Sensing the danger nearby, the trustees of the college vacated all professorships and the presidency.

Almost five months later, following the September 17, 1861, Battle of Blue Mills Landing, Federal troops occupied the then 10-year-old Jewell Hall for use as an emergency hospital. The following summer and fall, the troops remained on campus, digging entrenchments around the Hall in anticipation of possible further hostilities, although those hostilities never came to pass. In 1891, the U.S. Congress passed a bill granting payment of $2,200 to William Jewell College for the use of the buildings and grounds during the war years. The last of the rifle pits were visible until campus expansion occurred in 1957 (Clark 33-4; King).

18th

Reveille was sounded, & at rollcall almost to a man reported for active duty. Left camp and moved down the river, Our march was a very leisurly one, & uneventful in character. Stopped again when night overtook us at Wellington, a small town on the south side of the river 7 miles from Lexington.

19th

An order, or rather a request, was sent to our camp by Gen Price, for all who wished to take a part in the battle of Lexington, to come forward & report for duty as infantry immediately. There were several new recruits in our company who were unarmed, those we left in charge of the horses & camp equipments, the rest of us reported according to orders & were assigned quarters in the courthouse yard.

Lexington Mo

A very nice, & by the way a very conspicuous position. Some skirmishing & cannonading around the lines. Our post of duty ~~is~~ was some distance from the "Feds" yet ~~can~~ could be reached by their artillery. They ~~are~~ were strongly fortified, in the suburbs of the City around the college which had been converted by them into an arsenal & store room. Our men had been beseiging them for several days, & as their means of supply of all kinds except water, had been cut off Price ~~is~~ was projecting plans for a final attack, with a view of compelling them to surrender.

Lexington

This began to look like 'business". As I said in the beginning of my diary, my Bro. Caldwell met Prices army at Springfield, coming north with him left the company to which he was attached & came to ours. He was almost destitute of clothing, having left home with only a change. But having anticipated meeting him here in that condition, made provisions to meet his wants before leaving home. Meeting him was a great satisfaction to me, for this was the longest period over which our seperation had extended up to this time.

20th

Remained in our position, momentarily expecting orders to move out & take position in line of battle. Every now and then we were reminded that our locality had been discovered, & the occasional bursting or buzzing of a shell, denoted an enemy near by. That night in anticipation of orders for active duty, our company received orders to load their guns & lay down in line with them in hand, side by side.

Camp in Court House yard

There were several horses tied to the fence around the courthouse yard; during the night one of them becoming frightened by the bursting of a shell near by, pulled off a plank, & while it was yet tied to his halter, ran with full speed the whole length of our company, while most of us were sound asleep. This created a wild excitement, we were all on our feet in less time, if possible, than it takes to think, the shock was so sudden & unexpected, we were completely bewildered; the first thought was, that the enemy had made a very precipitous dash upon us, & as a matter of course having our guns in hand, a few shots were fired, before the real cause of alarm was discovered & quiet restored; fortunately no harm was done by the firearms, but after we had all come to our senses, & an examination commenced, several of the Boys were found to be hurt by the horse's feet; some so badly as to render them unfit for duty for several days. Lexington is the County town of Lafayette Co. Mo. Inhabited by two or three thousand thrifty people, this ~~is~~ was the principal market for hemp the chief production of the rich soil, which surrounds it. At the beginning of the war a great many of the farmers of Lafayette were very wealthy, & owned a large number of slaves & when Lincoln's immancipation act went into effect, the immense loss rendered many of them penniless.

As I remarked before, there were immense fields devoted entirely, to the production of hemp, & these Negroes seemed peculiarly adapted to the raising & preparing for market, this great staple; especially cutting when ripe; which was done in the month of August, when the rays of "Old Sol" were very warm & oppressive to the white man.

Lexington

At the time of the Capture of Lexington by Price, there were several large ware-houses filled with hemp put up in bales of four or five hundred pounds each, ready to be shipped to the manufactory, to be made into bagging rope, twine &c &c; But Price thought instead of sending this crop off as had been the custom of the past, to utilize ~~them~~ it as breastworks to save the lives of his men would be the best in the case of necessity.

Hemp bales used for breast works

So He prepared to use the hemp as did Gen. Jackson the cotton bales at the memorable battle of Neworleans. All the drays and wagons that could be "pressed" into immediate service, were soon moving the hemp to a point near the river, at which the least protection was afforded to our men, and under fire of the enemy these movable breastworks were constructed.

21

Early in the morning the attack on the entrenched Enemy, was renewed with more than the usual determination.

Battle of Lexington

About 9 O.C. AM Gen Price thinking the time for capture ripe, having his plans fully matured, concluded to go in & gather the fruit; & before any possible attempt at liberation of the besieged enemy could be made, began preparations for a final & simultaneous attack from all sides. The roaring of Artillery intermingled with musketry had now become general. Our company were ordered to take position in line of battle behind the breastworks constructed of hempbales, and as fast as circumstances would permit, rolled them forward until our old "squirrel peices" would do effective service. Our advance was very slow, & often retarded by the firing of the Enemy; but "Old Paps" (Gen Price's Nic name given him in honor of his parentel care at all times over his men) movable fortifications proved too great a barier to be overcome by the already weakened garrison.

Capture of Lexington

Accordingly about 4 P.M stipulations for surrender were gladly received. Hurrah! Lexington ~~is~~ was ours! Once more She's free!! Hurrah, for Jeff Davis & the Southern Confederacy! Such were a few of the wild huzzahs that rent the air, as signals of the unbounded joy that filled the hearts of the captors on that occasion. This was the first victory for many of the men on our side, in fact the war was only in the earliest infancy, but small as it was compared with subsequent events, our feelings & heart swellings were almost uncontrollable. This was the first time your humble Servant ever heard a bullet whistle when a human being was used as a traget, & I assure you the "music" didn't put me to sleep. After a few moments delay our men were marched around the breastworks of the "Feds" as a guard, & I must acknowlage my bosom swelled with inexpressable joy, as I stood watching them stack their arms, & march out as prisinors of war. When the column was passing our position, you cannot imagine the feelings that crept over me, when in the moving column I recognized the familiar faces of three Cousins & one Uncle from the same section of country from which I came. At that time my sympathy for them did not reach out very far; I thought they "Should not have been Yanks". The color of their clothes (blue) did not suit me; And I never have, Since, opposing that color in line of battle so much, admired it when worn by a man. After the preliminary arrangements subsequent to a surrender were made, in obedience to orders received, we went into camp one mile south of town, which was very pleasantly situated, & our fare was very sumptuous while the provisions lasted that we captured from "Old Abe's" Commissary.

General Price lost 25 and had 75 wounded at the Battle of Lexington; the Federals lost 39 and had 120 wounded. Price gained five artillery pieces, 3,000 rifles, and 750 horses, all badly needed by his army. Respect for Price, as the South's great hero, spread when it was learned he returned to the bank the $900,000 (looted by the Federals), which belonged to the loyal Lexington supporters of the Confederacy ("The Battle of Lexington").

Camp near Lexington

We remained here several days, during which time a great many new recruits were added to our ranks; but there were many who returned home; this caused quite a damper on our cause in the hours of success all over the South, & the addition did not swell the number or cause the enthusiasm that it should. Those who didnot care to face the perils of war longer, & wanted an excuse to return to their "families" or "Sweethearts", almost imagined the war was over & the honors gained by the victory at Lexington, was sufficient glory for them as a Soldier.

Had we at this time been reinforced with a few thousand well equipped & well drilled troops from the Virginia army, & those of our army who had volunteered to fight the battle of Lexington remained in service, I always will think, would have put quite a different face on the affairs of the South. Instead of turning our backs to the North as we did, could have about faced & moved forward into the northern territory from all sides, & having the sympathy of Foreigner nations to encourage us as we did at that time, & the confidence of the Federal government at Washington being trembling on the verge of extreme uncertainty, we would have had a very promising show, to have our rights under the constitution acknowledged & liberal terms granted the Confederate Government.

Sept. 30

Broke up camp, leaving Lexington to be occupied by the enemy again as it was but a short time Since. Price not having troops sufficient to sustain his position during a fall & winter campaign, thought proper to move south in the direction of his friends. And under the circumstances it seemed to be the propper & only move for him to make, as the "Feds" were beginning to mass their forces in north Missouri ready for an assault & their numbers being so much greater, a defeat would have been almost certain & very hazzardous.

Leaving Lexington

We marched in the direction we started 12 miles & camped for the night. We thought an addition to the supply of rations on hand would not be amiss, & a chance to get something that was never issued to us; concluded to jaayhawk a few sweet potatoes for supper from a patch near by. This word "Jayhawk" don't sound very musical to my ears, on account of being harrassed by the Kansas Jayhawkers in my initial days as a Soldier. But when property is removed without the knowledge or consent of the owner, and not really necessary for food or rayment, it takes an ugly word like this to signify its meaning. I might add to the above that our experience as Soldiers, either in battle or camp was not very extended, our introduction had been short yet our experience had been quite varied in its nature. The majority of us had not been long from home, consequently we could not be scarce of clothing, (unless it might be those who left home against their Parents will) but we hadn't learned to be our own washerwomen; our experience as cooks did not amount to anything; as for myself, I could not make a "pankake" when I left home. I had been learned to wash dishes, milk & churn, Sweep make fires & carry water from the spring about two hundred yards, (I could write a long chapter here ~~about~~ about the "ups & downs" of life with out a mother, but might be considered by the reader as too great a deviation from the description of my career as a Soldier, But I will "beg leave" here to not be considered Irksome If I refer to this frequently in my "Tales of the war".) This completed my duties as a domestic; & I donot suppose my culinary education would have extended this far — had not our family, at home, for some time previous to the beginning of the war; ~~was~~ been composed of Boys; & as I imagined then being under the jurisdiction of a Stepmother.

First Camp life

We had not yet learned to take into consideration the laws of health, imagined the rougher we lived the better, as to cleanliness in preparing our meals, or with respect to our person; our bread after making a thick dough, was fried in bacon grease (when we had any) & eaten hot, for if we waited for it to get cold, a "dog could hardly chew it," our meats were prepared with the same nonchalance. No wonder that our stomachs had become clogged by the constant use of this indigestible food & our appetites longed for a change; No wonder, that while the cold Autumn wind was whistling around our scanty messfires on the prairie, that the propriety of appropriating a few of the Sweet potatoes from a patch near; to our own use; without consulting the owner; was accepted as an unavoidable necessity & as rapidly as they could be grabbled from their hiding places in the ground & a little of the dirt brushed off, were hidden again, this time in hot ashes instead of the ground & when scarcely done, were taken from their hot beds, & with as little attention to ashes ~~v~~ as had been given to the dirt before cooking, not allowing them time to cool, were eaten with a relish that could only be characterized by a child: we had to "live & learn" as our future life will show, & the lessons taken at this time, were not passed by unheeded.

Oct. 1st

Early in the morning the Army received orders to continue their march south, when the command struck camp, & in company with nine other men was sent back as a detachment to Lexington for, the purpose of bringing up a piece of artillery, which had been abandoned on account of the scarcty of horses in the command to which it belonged. Before leaving camp however, we examined our old trusty rifles, mounted our horses & commenced ~~our~~ the retrograde movement in haste; because the reports that came from the direction in which we had started were anything but agreeable or favorable to us. After two hours ride, arrived at Lexington & found the property for which we had been sent; but found it "badly" disconnected, & none of us being drilled in artillery tactics our situation was rather embarrassing, the front wheels or (limber) of the gun could not be found; our conclusions had to be made rapidly. So in the absence of the thing proper, the next best substitute must be adopted; the corresponding wheels of a farm wagon were brought into service. The trail of the gun was secured to the front axle by ropes. This mounted the gun ready for transportation, the next thing was to procure something to move it with; two span of mules & harness belonging to an old Plantir were "Pressed" into service. (this was the mild army expression for Stealing) hitched to the gun, when our little band headed southward, applying the lash to the mules, that our progress might be as rapid as possible & the main army be overtaken at the earliest time practicable. As I said before this enterprise, was a new one for us, ~~A~~ our introduction was very abrupt & we were not desirous of extending our acquaintance.

Moving South from Lexington

Our progress at times was very much impeded, the mules becoming wearied from climbing the slippery hills; we were all willing to drop the subject, consequently the trip was not refered to afterwards as one of pleasantry. Well we overtook the Army in camp, thirty miles south of Lexington 9 O.C P.M, & to say that I was glad of it, would only faintly describe my joy, I had been traveling in the rain all day, without any extra wrappings, & my haversack furnished rather a scanty supply of food & cold at that; boo-ho-ho-oo-oo.— I almost shiver yet, when I think of it! After warming up by the fire & eating a hearty supper which had been prepared by my messmates, rolled up in my blankets by the side of a comrad (John. D. McCormack) to snatch a few hours sleep.

A mess was not considered an official unit, but was an informal small group of men who organized themselves "to share equipment, duties, and talents." Chores of cooking, obtaining food, sewing, and laundry were divided among the men, thus giving "a measure of stability to a soldier's day-to-day existence" (Flagel 123).

On the next morning, as on several subsequent days our march was continued; on the 3rd Oct. passed through Rosehill a small village in Johnson Co. & After marching through Henry Co. crossed the Osage River on the night of the 9th 9 O.C. P.M, camped in St. Clair Co. about 2 miles south of river. Here we remained three days waiting for the balance of the army to cross, the progress of which was greatly impeded, the only means of crossing was an old dilapidated flat boat which had been considered dangerous for some time, but like many other things, put off from time, to time & "patched up" with the excuse "that will do for the present." This country is very poor, the habits of the people very antique & manner of cultivating the soil on the same level judging from the appearance of a large proportion of the inhabitants they have not been very extensively blest in the accumulation of this worlds goods. Our rations at the place were of poor quality & very scarce in quantity — I tell you it made a new recruit think of the jonny cake & spare ribs, & wish himself at home again, any-way, long enough to "shove" his knees under the table & enjoy a good cup of coffee or a glass of milk: -- but we only thought such things, for if we dared express them in words; our timidity, & "homesickness" was ridiculed & laughed at in the most derisive manner by those who were in for "during the war"– In this way one after another firm resolution was scared to stand up to the rack "hay or no hay", ration or no ration.

Johnny cake is made of maize or corn meal and, in the South, is toasted before a fire. In other regions the batter is more often baked in a pan. One recipe calls for 1 cup white or yellow cornmeal, 1 tsp. salt, 1 cup boiling water, and ½ cup milk. Early day cornbreads of many names such as sad bread, water cake, flat cake, hoecake, corn dodgers, and johnny cakes were nourishing, but not particularly palatable. The characteristic dry, hard texture served to make the johnny cake (or journey cake) travel well, but improvement in taste came in the 1800s with the addition of eggs, milk, and/or baking powder, when available ("Johnny cake"; "Pioneer Cooking"; Southern Heritage 11).

My Father always said, when we had plenty of corn there was no reason to think of starving. We had corn, but not very abundant & not very hard; however it would do to eat, and as subsequent events will show, would have proven quite a desert to the bill of fare, that adorned our messplates. We soon converted some tin vessels into graters, by punching holes with nails, & by this means managed to grate enough meal to keep us from starving. You can imagine, the kind of bread we had, coarse meal not Sived not seasoned with shortning, or anything else but Salt, if we had not, mixed it with boiling water our efforts to have made it into "pones" would have resulted in a most complete failure. The scarcty of rations would have been sufficient inconvenience to withstand, but coupled with this, the weather was very unfavorable for camp life, rainy & cold. In order that the reader in these days of prosperity & fruitfulness; innumerable facilities of production & transportation, may not conclude that the state of affairs at that time was due to the criminal carlessness of those in command, I will add a few words by way of explanation & if possible reconcile the mind of the reader by a reasonable excuse for the scarcty so early in the campaign.

Camp Near Osage river St. Clair Co

There was not a railroad or telegraph line in that country when occupied by Gen. Price's Army, we had to depend on wagons drawn by horses or mules (Sometimes oxen) for transportation, & couriers mounted on horseback for news.

Our march was again resumed on the 12th & continued in a southerly direction for two or three days, passed through Clintonville & Centreville, Cedar Co. two small country villages; the streets were not numbered by the twenties, neither were the inhabitants. After you had read the following superscriptions over that many doors, you had exhausted the stock of business houses in town. Blacksmith shop. Post Office & Drygoods. As a general thing the towns and crossroads would be crowded with the citizens ~~for~~ from several miles around to see the army pass; thought it quite a treat to see a soldier. Homespun jeans of all colors was the costume of the men & Boys; ~~calico~~ The female portion of the inhabitants dressed in calico principally. Split bonnets, hoopskirt made of grapevines, we were frequently greeted with flying handkerchiefs, & a few songs; some familiar southern airs sung by some of the rosy cheeked maidens, whose delight it was to cheer us on our weary march. Our march was continued, as I said before in a southern or Southwestern direction, the country was mostly prairie on uplands, the small ravines were fringed with timber. The uplands were very sparsely settled. The soil along the ravines was better suited to cultivate & the log cabins were numerous & generally well filled with children "white headed" at that. It looked as if they raised "two crops" of children to one of corn.

March South Continued

I guess this state of affairs have long since changed for the better; I sincerely hope not for the worse. I failed to keep the number of miles traveled while on this march, but I remember very distinctly that we made good speed.

15th

Passed through Greenfield, Dade Co, and camped near by 12 O C M. Our rations were again getting short; & after a short consultation among the commanding officers it was decided to send a detail of cavalry to assist in procuring same, a detachment of men 150 strong (I in the bunch) were sent out in a southeastern direction several miles from the army — to a small grist mill on Sack River for the purpose of threshing wheat in the adjoining country, & having it converted into flour at the mill, for the use of the army.

In 1840, "Hulston Grist Mill was established at the confluence of the Sac River and Turnback Creek in Dade County, Missouri....The Hulston family owned and operated the mill until 1897, when John Christopher Hulston was murdered." The mill last operated June 25, 1967. The mill has been moved to a proposed heritage park site which will feature the reconstructed Hulston Mill, circa 1850 ("Greenfield").

On detail Threshing & grinding wheat

This change was greeted with applause, everyone was in the saddle on time; we were each of us glad to be one of the detail. The major part of us were country Boys & used to threshing what at home. You may rest assured that we lived fat while our camp was near the Old Mill; we had plenty of flour issued us by the commissary of the Squad, & by the addition of the "stray" "mudlark" (Army phrase for hog) that happened in our camp occasionally; supplied us with a dish to which we had not been accustomed for some time past. The wheat crops were not very extensive or numerous in this section, nevertheless, we succeeded in "hulling" out several bus. with a small horse power thresher & having it converted into flour at the mill.

Camp near the Old mill on Sack river

We had become well satisfied with our job & extremely well pleased with our situation, If we could have done our share of the fighting at this place & in this manner, we would have Shouted in concert. "be it So." But the duties & life of a Soldier are very changable & at this Juncture, the change in store for us was a very sudden one.

Forced March

A courier galloped into our camp & informed us that the main portion of our army was again moving south, & the enemy coming in the direction of our position in force, So to use the army phrase, had to pick up in a hurry & "Skedaddle", the place at which we were located, was some distance from the road traveled by the main army, & as a matter of necessity were compelled to make a force march of several days & nights duration; we became very much fatigued, if we slept at all it was while in the saddle, this was very irksome, but the actions of some of the "Boys" while asleep, weaving from side to side, backward then forward, afforded a great deal of merriment at intervals to those who happened to have their "eyes open."

Skedaddle, a Civil War slang term, meant "to retreat" ("Skedaddled").

When we came to the outskirts of the main army in camp, one of the Boys got seperated from the company, by going to sleep and his horse stopping with another one, picketed by the roadside, when he woke up, was so bewildered, & the night was dark, that he failed to overtake the company until sometime next day. Many others would have done likewise, had they not been noticed and aroused by a nudge in the ribs from a companion. While on this march we passed through Sarcoxie, Jasper Co. Grandby, Newton Co. & arrived at Neosho, Same Co Oct 21st Sometime after night.

Army Overtaken
Camp Near Neosho Mo

here we fo~~uned~~und the army in camp. Remained at this place several days, during which time Missouri passed the Ordinance of Secession, which was looked upon as a very ~~of~~ important, & propper step to take, & greeted with loud applause. Salutes were fired throughout the army; our company fired 13 rounds; this was one round for every Southern or Slave state in the Union, which afterwards (for a short time only) constituted the Confederate states of America (C.S.A)

> **Following the secession of eleven states, Missouri Governor Claiborne Fox Jackson called a legislative session that approved the Ordinance of Secession on October 31, 1861, as the 12th state in the Confederacy. However, this ordinance was not recognized by the Unionist state convention, and a provisional government was established to replace the secessionist state government. Hamilton Gamble was named governor, and Willard Prebble Hall was named lieutenant governor. Hall succeeded Gamble upon Gambel's death and served from 1864 to 1865. Hall is buried at Mount Mora Cemetery, Saint Joseph, Missouri (Heidler and Heidler 1055).**

The army remained in quarters here for several days, our commissary department was better supplied with rations here, than it was on the Osage; yet our craving appetites could have relished a greater variety.

29th March resumed

"Pulled up stakes" & left Neosho, & as our line of march was in the direction of "Dixie"; thought probable some of the "Sunny" states would be our winter quarters, arrived at Cassville Barry Co 31st Inst. Here we formed a junction with Gen. McCullough's army from Texas. This proved to be a great Stimulant to us, imagined ourselves ready for any emergency, we thought then a Texan could whip a dozen more men than, a trooper from any other state. Gen. McCullough had become quite famous, by the many brilliant achievements won by him & his brave band of Rangers, in the border Indian war in Northern & Western Texas. The time consumed in resting & recruiting the army was about a week. Several changes in military affairs were made, among other things our company was dismounted, you may rest assured, that this order was not very pleasantly received, we would have remonstrated in earnest, could we have seen a probability of retaining our horses by so doing.

Gen. Benjamin McCulloch, former Texas Ranger and an extremely popular leader in Texas, had commanded the Confederate forces at Wilson's Creek (Boatner III 530).

Entered Infantry Service

Most of the horses were our own individual property & had been brought from home; & as a matter of course, could not, very readily entertain the idea of parting with them, & the thought of becoming Infantry was really demoralizing in its nature; in short we were greatly stirred up over the matter – but when we found there was no other alternative, "knocked under", as quietly as possible. The excuse for the change was ascribed to the scarcity of forage. After a moments reflection this seemed very plausable, for there ~~aw~~ were many places ~~here~~ there, that the earth ~~as~~ was so void of nutriment, that it would be a matter of impossibility, to find enough animal production, to "Sprout a blackeyed pea". The greater portion of the Boys sold their horses. I got a forage master by name, McClannahan to keep mine, (a large fine bay mare, well gaited & when in the saddle on her felt, "at home") She remained with the army in the possession of the person to whom I entrusted her, until after the battle of Pea Ridge Ark. & the Missouri state troops received their discharges at Vanburen Ark. Previous to this she was attacked with the dread disease Grease-heel, but could yet travel tolerably well, and W. A. Bowen a member of the company to which I belonged, after receiving his discharge, from the state guards, declared his intention of returning to his home in North Missouri, & by my request undertook the task of riding her through. (I was very desirous of having her returned to my Father) I afterwards learned that she becoming too lame to travel, was left "in the possession of a farmer in Jackson Co. Mo.

Grease-heel, sometimes known as "grease" or "scratches," is an inflammation of the back of the pastern (area of the foot between the fetlock and hoof) that can lead to chronic dermatitis. Continual wetness, manure, mud, and long coarse hair covering the area all contribute to the cause ("Grease-heel").

Oct.

Well there was one thought that proved to be a great "Soothing Syrup" to our minds & balm to our bodies; we had no horse to curry or procure forage for & feed.

Here we ~~are~~ were! And had been during the last days of an other month, also a few of the Ides of its Successor had passed away, & ~~are~~ were watching & waiting. The Enemy ~~are~~ were still making demonstrations on the north of our situation, & it ~~is~~ was "whispered' that our army ~~is~~ was on the eve of another move South. Rumored that Gen. Fremont ~~is~~ was advancing in force. Orders to move. They all said let's follow "Old Pap." (Gen Price) & we ~~will~~ would come out alright at last.

Lincoln appointed John Charles Frémont major general upon the advice of Postmaster General Montgomery Blair and gave him command of the Western Department. Not up to the task of organizing, arming, and commanding his largely untrained and poorly equipped army in the midst of a hotbed of Confederate sympathizers, Frémont's position deteriorated and was ultimately lost when he established martial law in Missouri on August 30, 1861, and freed the slaves of all those opposing the Federal government. Lincoln rescinded Frémont's emancipation proclamation and eventually relieved him of his command. Frémont was then given command of the Mountain Department in Virginia, and after the battle of Cross Keys, General Pope was given command of Frémont's corps. Fremont refused to serve under him and ultimately resigned (Boatner III 314-5; Heidler and Heidler 786-7).

Nov 7th March resumed

Yesterday when the order to march was received, rations were cooked. This morning, left Cassville & moved in a southwestern direction, This country ~~is~~ was similar to some other we had passed through on this march; very poor, a great many of the hills resemble mountains, especially when viewed at a distance, Plenty of rock. The roads in most places ~~are~~ were furnished with a natural Macadam. Our march as usual, was attended with success & the distance traveled was sufficient. Camped near Pineville McDonald Co. on the following day Nov. 8th.

Camp Near Pineville McDonald Co. Mo

This is the southwestern corner of the state. Our situation ~~is~~ was very near the corner of Mo. Ark. Kas. – & the Indian Territory. Well it seems to me, the purpose for which Gen. Price had decided to use this country, ~~is~~ was undoubtedly the best that had been applied up to that ~~present~~ time, of the events come to pass that at present writing seem inevitable. Gen. Fremont ~~is~~ was advancing rapibly with a force of men outnumbering ours by great odds, & we had come to the conclusion that he did not propose to halt until compeled to do so.

Nov.

Our position here ~~is~~ was in a deep narrow ravine ~~it is~~ was about three fourths of a mile from one summit to the other, the hills ~~are~~ were about half mile high, extending in long ranges from N. E. to S. W.

Pineville

This ravine ~~is~~ was coursed by a small clear stream of water, a narrow strip of table land on either side. These high hills, or mountains are almost hidden by rocks of every description, the timber ~~is~~ was very thick of which Scrub Oak, hickory & Cedar ~~are~~ were the principal growth, & the great secret of our position being so formidable, ~~is~~ was we ~~cannot~~ could not be approached by an enemy from any other direction, than the one by which we came, or from the South west, & then only in broken columns. Gen. Price's intention was to form his men on both sides of the ravine, draw Fremont in by an attack & sham retreat; and once into the ambush, we could have whipped a half score to one; In the event of our ammunition becoming exhausted, could have "Stoned them to death," as did the unbelievers — St. Stephen of old.

Remained in camp here about one week. Our company was quartered where corn had been raised, any way the stalks were yet standing. I guess there had been some soil in sight when the corn was planted; (some of the Boys sugjested that it might have been planted with a shotgun) at the time we were there, the marks of the plow could be seen, but all signs of earth had vanished, which left small ridges around the stalks, of fine "Jack" rock & gravel. I tell you this looked like hard times & "worse coming". The little log cabins were dotted here & there, in close proximity, and the number of persons (especially little ones) occupying each cabin, impressed one with the belief, that this country originated the phrase "A poor man for children":

A jack rock, also known as a caltrop or star nail, is a weapon made of four sharp nails or spines arranged so that one spine always protrudes up. Used militarily, these weapons slow the progression of horses or troops. Applying this definition to the rock around the campsite allows the reader to appreciate the ruggedness of the landscape ("Caltrop").

We received the first army supplies from the Confederate States while at this point, but the amount sent, fell far short of meeting our present wants. We had been changing from place to place so much; & this manner of living being entirely new & strange to us; the supplies brought from home had become almost exhausted; yet, we felt very buoyant; over the prospects ahead! Air castle, after air castle, was built! having heard that Fremont had fallen back from his position at the mouth of the canyon in which we were stationed, making the prospects of a speedy move north certain; we almost imagined ourselves in North Missouri; once there would receive an abundant supply of food & rayment, from extended arms & open hearts, that were always ready to give, & give bountifully to those in whose hands & strong arms they had entrusted their destiny.

16th
Northward bound

The report of Fremont falling back having been confirmed, our command in obedience to orders received, left Pineville, & as had been predicted, longed & almost prayed for by the Mo's, commenced our northward march. This was a delightful time & by way of explaining to what extent the minds & actions of Soldiers can be aroused, by the appearance of prospects that may lead to gaining the prise desired, I ask a little indulgence. The greatest excitement imaginable was visible. A hurried examination was made for odd relics that had been hidden away for safe keeping, thinking they might soon be face to face, with the one who presented them; wild huzzahs were heard! Three cheers for North Missouri were given time & again! Shout after shout rent the air! was echoed & echoed from hill to hill, again & again; till wafted away down the valley on the cool november breeze & died away in the distance. It seemed as though the rocks & trees had joined in the chorus. I wouldn't be surprised that wild game was scarce in that country for sometime after our departure.

March continued

At the call of the bugle every cavalry man was in his saddle, as the rattle of the drum brought every "foot pad" (Infantry man) to his place in ranks, no "stragglers," while the fifes were blowing, drums beating, & bands playing the most favorite southern airs; we stepped off with an elastic pace, facing the cool, north breeze, and as the days passed by & distance shortened, between us & the "promised land", would pull our half worn, buttonless coat around our otherwise thinly clad bodies & march on. When the progress of the army was sufficiently checked, extricate a pebble that would occasionally intrude on our (sockless in many cases) toes, through the holes in our more than half worn shoes; when night overtook us, after a hasty meal, commonly called supper, (frequently two meals in one) our blankets were spread upon the ground, often a rock or chunk of wood for a pillow; the blue canopy of heaven for our shelter, (if not raining) & while in this position, pass off to dreamland, feasting our minds (in fiction) on things of long-ago. The route traveled on our north bound trip, was the same, as previously used going south.

24th

On the 24th after crossing the Sack River our tents were pitched ~~our tents~~ near Osceola St. Clair Co. It soon occurred to our minds from the movements of the Commanding Officers, that the signs of the times denoted a ~~stop~~ for several days, & perhaps, the final overthrow of our northern adventure, we however concluded to wait coming events, & as obedience was one of the first laws taught us in childhood, thought it wise to observe the same rule in the beginning of our soldier life.

Camp On Sack river Near Osceola Mo

Our army remained in this camp, or near this place about four weeks, recruiting at the same time watching the movements of the Enemy. Fremont was a hard Gen. to locate, & the manner in which He maneuvered his men was something of a mystery to his adversaries, he had obtained quite an extended foreknowledge in the science of war, while engaged in the Kansas troubles, under "Old jim Lane".

Maj. Gen. James Henry Lane, militia leader of the Free State movement in Kansas during the "bleeding Kansas" period

from 1854 through 1859, became known as the "Liberator of Kansas" (Boatner III 471).

But "Old Pap," had been ready for any emergency, so far, & ~~can be~~ could have been at any time, if only furnished with something near an eaqual number of men. While in camp at this place the measles broke out amongst the troops; the weather being cold, the majority of the men poorly clad & badly sheltered, many of the cases proved fatal, or left its victim a physical reck. I was making myself perfectly content, by recconciling my thoughts in that direction, in the belief that I had — had them while at home with the "rest of the children". I was enjoying the pleasures of camp life, with my companions as well as circumstance would permit. One evening in company with a few of my friends, procured an old skift from ~~an old~~ farmer, crossed a Bayou, on the river & after filling ourselves with ripe percimons, returned to camp late in the afternoon, as full as you ever saw a "possum". I guess you are aware of the fact, that it requires several heavy frosts to make a percimon palitable, otherwise it is bitter & will "pucker" your mouth ready to "whistle" all the time. There are a great many "whistlers" in that country, I expect "Arkinsaw" Traveler originated near there. The percimons we got, were not lacking for frost for a great many of them were ice cold when eaten. I retired to my humble couch of leaves that night as happy as a Soldier could be, under such circumstances, & I tell you the happiest days that a Soldier ever saw, was when he had plenty to eat. But a person don't always feel as well when arising, as they do on retiring, this happened to be my feelings on this particular occasion.

Col. Sanford C. Faulkner, a wealthy planter from Chicot County, Arkansas, is given credit for writing the melody for "The Arkansaw Traveler." Sources vary on the origin of the words; some give credit to Faulkner and others to David Stevens. The song is believed to have been inspired by Faulkner's travels in 1840 to Pope County, Arkansas, where he met an old fiddler. At the time of Sam's memoir entry, the troops were in St. Clair County, Missouri, and not particularly close to Chicot County, Arkansas, the most southeastern county of that state ("Arkansas Traveler"; Boni 58; "Chicot County"; "Osceola"; "The Arkansas State").

Measles in Camp

When I awoke from my slumbers on the following morning, I was sick. My face swollen, & as red as a beet; raising myself up – on my elbow, &

peeping out through the door of the tent, discovered that the ground was covered with snow; concluded to settle back & await as patiently as possible the termination of events. I had already learned several lessons on the line of patience, while "roughing it" through, that had not come up for study before leaving home.

I had not remained in this position long before some one came around that knew what anything was when he looked at it, & as he pulled down the cover remarked, "Old fellow" You've got the measles. Well, I imagined myself fortified against anything almost; but I tell you, the measle scare was one shock for which I found myself wholly unprepared, for this contradicted my "Father's word", I was a great boy for Father while at home, & after leaving, many sentences were verified, by the assertion "Father said so." The overdose of percimons, taken the evening before, acted as a cathartic (which was very necessary) & my messmates kept me well stimulated with hot tea made from spice wood, (which was a spontaneous growth in that country) kept as close as possible to my tent — was over the worst & doing well, but the weather got colder, & according to orders received, the army had to move — on this march, which I will hereafter describe; a great many poor fellows, were wrapped in their blankets & laid away in their final resting places, to await the judgement day. This was caused in most instances by having to expose themselves, before out of danger of measles; but thanks be to God, & the kindness & good attention of my army companions for my restoration to health. At this camp quite a number of Missourians were sworn into the Confederate Service for twelve months — as my time had not yet expired for which I had sworn to serve the state, & as I had commenced with the determination of serving through the war — considered it useless to multiply oaths.

Diseases during the Civil War claimed two lives for every one soldier who died from wounds caused by grape, cannister, and minie balls ("Civil War Medicine"; Marszalek and Williams).

Spice-wood, also called spice-bush, benjamin bush, or wild allspice, grows along the swampy edges of woodlands and beside stream banks. Some believe it indicates the water table is near the earth's surface. "The twigs and bark have been used in rural sections for making an infusion which is used in the treatment of intermittent fevers" ("Spice-wood"; Grimm 145-6).

Dec. 19-61

As I remarked before, the order to march was again received, & with unmistakeable emotions of joy of all those enjoying good health, having been confined to our quarters so close by the stormy weather, felt as though a little exercise would be beneficial & more especially, when the indications favored a move in the direction to us most desirable.

From Sack R. to Springfield

We moved out early on the morning of the 19th, in a northern direction as had been predicted, & it would be useless to render another description of a similar character to the one when breaking camp at Pineville, yet could not be considered erroneous or out of place by those who participated in both occasions — this was an occasion of great mirth, & highly enjoyable, by all who were not suffering from any disease or its effects, but my health was greatly improved by sickness, the measles propper had disappeared, but the inroads made upon my system by that loathsome disease, left me as an easy prey for some other enemy to health, to "step in" & claim its prize after a well directed siege upon the weakest parts. This weighed heavily upon my mind as I trudged along through the snow & over the frozen ground. Sometimes when the road was not too hilly, I was favored with a short ride in the company "Messkit" wagon, which was a great relief. On this march there were many weary limbs & sore feet, but the same nerve & determination displayed on similar occassions, made itself manifest, again, especially when marching in the desired direction. Frequent shouts for "North Mo" could be heard. But alas! It seems to me, especially in a Soldiers life, for every joy, there is always two sads; or atleast it appeared to ~~me~~ one that such was the case on this trip, for it looked as though, when the climax of our most earnest desires, had almost appeared, & the sunshine of contentment & success, was almost ready to rise up over us in brilliancy, would always go down, leaving us in gloom & dispair. The great change that came over us at this particular time was caused by turning our course from north to east, & after continuing in this direction for a day or two, it soon became very apparent, that the close of the winter would find us much worse off, so far as clothing was concerned & no nearer the source from whence the first supply came.

Camp at Springfield

Arrived at Springfield Green Co on the 23rd Dec where we went into winter quarters for a short time, This sudden termination of our campaign completely smothered, the last hope we had of seeing that portion of Missouri which lies north of the river, as an army again, soon, & those of us who had placed our mementoes near at hand, that we might show our sweethearts, how well we had preserved them, & by that means, express the degree in which they were esteemed in our affections; returned them, with a sad heart, to their old hiding places, for safe keeping, & by way of consolation, commenced singing — "Sweet Evilena" & the "Gal" I left behind me.

"Dear Evelina, Sweet Evelina" was published in New York in 1863, but was sung earlier by minstrel bands; Sam and his fellow soldiers were singing this song in 1861. A popular song among the Confederate troops, a series of verses describe unrequited love for a beautiful maiden. Each verse is followed by the chorus ("Dear Evelina").

Dear Evelina, sweet Evelina,
My love for thee shall never, never die.
Dear Evelina, sweet Evelina,
My love for thee shall, never, never die.

We soon became reconciled to our fate & settled down to the hum drum life of a regular camp. Christmas day passed, with but little demonstation of any kind. I remembered well the joy that swelled my bosom to overflowing in days passed, how anxiously & impatiently, I counted the long days as they dragged along & time drew near, & at the earliest dawn of that great boon of happiness; would rise from my downy bed & enjoy the immense store of "fun let loose" that was waiting for me. I could only call back to memory these cherished relics of the past, & console myself with the thought, that if spared, by a kind Providence, so as to enjoy such pleasures in future, the true worth of them would be appreciated. Our mess however made some little endeavor toward a feast. We had a goose, (but I disremember now just how we got it) but not such a powerful fat one though, & we not having had any experience in the art of dressing one ready for the "pot," & not caring to be very particular either, there was quite a destruction of the undeveloped crop of feathers, when spread before us on the board used as a table. "Anything for a change though" was the motto. I have used the word mess in several places since I commenced this book, & will have occasion to use it many more times. by way of explanation, will say it consists of a number of men who cook & eat around the same camp fire. There ~~is~~ was no certain number, I think we had Six or eight in ours. The old year had passed away & the new one; had been ushered in with the same heedlessness that marked the keeping sacred to memory, the birth day of our Savior.

1862

January

The funeral cortege had already been sent out with the remains of 1861. She had passed the records over to the historian, & that never ending Something, denominated time, had rolled up its boundless pages to view & on the first & most prominent corner, the figures 1862 ~~can~~ could be seen & read in letters of blood, & judging from the signs of the times, the rumors of coming battles from different sections occupied by the two Beligerant armies, the wild conversations indulged in around the camp-fires; there remained to be enacted, innumerable scenes of blood shed in the coming year, & many poor fellows would be forced to drink the bitter cup of sorrow to the dregs.

Cabins built

Some of the messes, that felt ~~so~~ disposed to perform a "little" extra work for a "great - deal" of extra comfort, built cabins out of the oak & hickory saplings that grew in abundance, near our camp, erected chimneys, as of old, mud & sticks, dirt floor.

Chosen as a Cook

My mess built a cabin, & after moving into it, thought best to have certain persons detailed, for certain duties: Some to procure the wood, others carry water, & two chosen for cooks, I was one of the cooks. J. D. McCormack the other. We had plenty to cook; three of the principal articles being cornmeal, beef & pork, the cornbread was cooked in "dodgers" & "you bet" I made them rich. My outside clothing soon became as "slick" & greasy as a butchers overalls. Our dishrags were scarce, & very frequently when in a hurry & a "little" careless, would use our Jacket sleeve, or knee of our pants instead.

A dodger is a hard-baked cake made of corn ("Dodger").

This gross diet & close confinement soon had its effects on me, coming to the surface in the shape of a very large boil on my right wrist, & after the large one had somewhat decreased in size, there were more than a dozen smaller ones, covered the wrist, this was very painful, rendering rest impossible night or day, Several of the scars are to be seen at the present time. There was a great deal of sickness among the troops while in quarters here, & several deaths, one a young man by the name of George. Copp, late of Ohio a member of our company & had once lived at my Father's house, for a short time. My Oldest Bro. Wallace, was taken very sick with Pneumonia, & in order that he could receive better attention, was moved to a private residence in the City. My Bro. Caldwell & I went to nurse him & by the skill of the Physicians, the kindness offered by the good people of the house, the untiring attention & devotion given by us; was considered sufficiently convalescent to be hauled in a wagon, when the retreat from Springfield commenced, but as subsequent events will show never regained his former health & vigor.

Jan & Feb

Our duties in camp were very monotonous, the amount of coarse diet eaten without exercise in the open air, was one cause of so much sickness; had not commenced regular drill. Our position was somewhat remote, the nearest Railroad station then was Rolla one hundred miles north, & not having the advantage of telegraph to warn us of danger, were frequently placed in rather an ugly dilema, by a danger following in too close proximity to the warning. This coupled with inexperience in military tactics in the field, was frequently the occasion of great confusion & excitement in our camp.

Feb. 12 Evacuation of Springfield

The retreat from Springfield began. While in Camp, Our plan for future action had been marked out to a certain extent, but a premature retreat had not been considered, much less received a passing thought. But the

"Feds" had all the advantage, in fact, everything at their command that adds to strength & durability. They were backed by millions of men & Billions of money; had the use of the telegraph & controll of the Railroads north of us to consolidate their forces in a few hours sufficient to over power & wipe out the handfull of troops under Price's Command. After consolidating their forces at Rolla they swept down upon our camp by force march in overwhelming numbers, & a hurried retreat was the only alternative, left ~~us~~, & to do this with as much system & as little loss entailed as possible, was left to & accomplished by our noble Old benefactor Gen. Price; who afterward rendered himself famous for his cunning & daring exploits in this direction.

When a body of troops remain in camp for some length of time, they pertake of habits similar in character to a permanent resident: A Soldier will have his gun in one place, knapsack in another, his canteen, haversack & blankets scattered promiscuously about the cabin or tent, & no wonder a sudden surprise creates consternation & confusion under such circumstances. Any way we "picked" ourselves up in as good shape as possible & left Springfield to the mercies of the "Feds" (If they had any). Camped first night, on the same ground on which the memorable Battle of Wilson Creek, or Oak hills was fought. Saw the spot of ground said to have been dyed by the life blood of Gen. Lyon, one of the most daring commanders of the Union Army.

In early 1861, Capt. Nathaniel Lyon and Francis P. Blair captured the southern rebels they believed were attempting to raid the St. Louis, Missouri, arsenal. Through Blair's influence, Lyon was appointed brigadier general on May 12, 1861. Lyon became the North's first military hero upon his death at the battle of Wilson's Creek (Boatner 497-8).

13th

Marched through a portion of Christian Co. Our progress was not attended with the success that might have followed, had we been given time to prepare & permitted to travel at will. We were continually dogged by the Enemy, & every step contested with the greed of an infuriated beast of prey. Our rearguard was compelled to halt several times during the days march in the most secure places of defense, to hold the advance guard of the enemy in check sufficient time to allow our main column to get out of danger.

Crane Creek
Feb 14

On the night of the 14th camped on Crane Creek Stone Co. The surface of the country here ~~is~~ was similar to other sections of this portion of the State already described, hilly covered with a dense growth of small timber of various kinds, in many places matted together with the wild grape & muscadine vines. Small field & garden spots ~~are~~ were seen along the creek bottoms dotted here & there with houses, principally log.

Soon after camping, one of the Boys started out with a gun; when he had been absent but a few moments & made a short reconnoiter, a shot was heard; a few minutes elapsed, returned dragging after him a very lean specimen of the hog (mud lark) kind. I tell you she was a regular "razor blade," "hazel splinter". Someone lost their old "Sandy" brood sow. Oh but she was thin, for after we had skinned her, could almost count the stars through the middlings — we didn't take into consideration her condition in regard to flesh —but the meat was prepared for the frying pan, in less time than it takes to describe the manner in which it was done, & eaten with an appetite sharpened by the hardships of an eventful days march. This seemed to satisfy the inner man pretty well, the next thing was to prepare as comfortably as possible for a nights rest. My Bedfellow (John D. McCormack) & I soon succeeded in collecting quite a pile of dry leaves in our tent, on which to spread our blankets, this looked like comfort, & I know would have been enjoyed as a rare treat.

A Sudden Surprise

But — about the time, we were spreading the first blanket, some body said in subdued tones — hold on — hush! What's that!! boom, boom the ~~distinct~~ sound of cannon ~~is~~ was heard in the distance. The command to arms! ~~is~~ was given, twenty rounds of ammunition to the man; tents struck, & with mess kit hurriedly thrown into the transportation wagons & ordered to the rear on double quick time; there goes another shot tearing through the timber from their light cavalry howitzers. Hurry up, was the order. The companies were formed & marched back a short distance where a line of battle was formed. We remained in this position for an hour or two, all demonstrations of attack in front being dispelled, our retreat was again resumed & continued for several consecutive nights & days.

Feb 15
Line of Battle formed

On the evening of the 15th our rearguard was again attacked near Cassville, but after the exchange of a few shots, were permitted to move on. Our march was one of continual hardships & unrest, having to about-face & form in line of battle as often as three times in one day; Yet, we were not engaged in battle with all our troops at any time. It is only a Soldier who has participated in the hardships of a similar campaign to this, that can weigh with candor, & give sanction to the truthfulness of the details, as they are written by his companion; But I will ask you kind reader, to draw on your imaginations for truthfulness & rest assured the half has not been told, the real feelings of one so situated cannot be expressed, in words, the true & only test is to participate in the act itself. But While we were deprived of many other of the comforts & luxuries of life, we had an abundance of clear pure water. The boiling springs were numerous & very large, the water from which coursed the country in many beautiful pebbly streams, & when consolidated formed, what was called Spring River, which was quite a stream & when not aggravated by rain the bottom could be seen in water four or five ft deep.

Fed Retreat continued

Frequently on the trip, & more especially after night, when the progress of the army was checked for a moment, by some blockade in front, the wearied infantry-man would drop to the ground, completely overcome, in the middle of the road or by the roadside, & in a moment would be sound asleep, to be roused by an Officer or companion when the command was ordered to move on; or his nap was frequently interrupted, while asleep on foot & moving, by his nose coming in contact with the gun strapped upon the back of a comrad in front when some unexpected circumstance would cause a sudden halt. It required the very closest attention possible, of the Officers & men who were blest with superior nerve power to their comrads, to avoid straggling & capture to a great extent, but our losses from these causes were comparitively small. Great credit is due Gen. Price (more than was ever awarded him) for the manner in which this retreat was conducted, The courage displayed, the kindness shown his men, while sharing the hardships as one of them, was remarkable. Although passed from earth long ago to an eternal home, his acts remain as burning lights upon the memory of those who sympathized, or participated in the privations of those dark days.

Gen. Sterling Price died September 29, 1867. Sam was writing this memoir twenty-three years later in 1890.

Such noble men, & such noble deeds as those committed by him & persons of like character should be treasured up by the historian as the most costly jewels & placed upon the brightest pages of the escutcheon of time; for ~~never~~ fear not, they will never become dim.

16th

On the morning of the 16th our army crossed the state line between Missouri & Arkansas near the western border, soon after which we met the Ark. troops under command of Gen. McCullough. (One matter that I neglected to state in the order that it should have been was, when we broke camp at Pineville, & started north (Price's Army). Gen. McCullough returned to his native state with his troops, thinking perhaps our destination was north missouri, It would have been ~~be~~ very indiscreet in him to have left ~~leave~~ his own home unprotected, At that time the majority of his men were under ~~the~~ orders of the Governor of Ark. so were the Mo's controlled by Mo's Gov.) When we met the Ark. troops they received orders to countermarch by the Gen by whom they were commanded, after which both armies moved on south together. After coming to, & crossing cross hollows, it was considered a very strong possition, & the commanding Gens. soon determined to make a stand.

Sam does not appear to be aware that shortly after Brig. Gen. Benjamin McCulloch's success at the battle of Wilson's Creek with the aid of Gen. Sterling Price's Missouri State Guard, McCulloch split from Price and wrote:

> **We have little to hope or expect from the people of this state. This force now in the field is undisciplined and led by men who are mere politicians; not a soldier among them to control and organize this mass of humanity. The Missouri forces are in no condition to meet an organized army, nor will they ever be whilst under the present leaders. I dare not join them in my present condition, for fear of having my men completely demoralized (Gillespie 3).**

Cross Hollows Ark

Accordingly the troops were soon formed in line of battle, to check this enemy who were advancing rapidly. This a natural barricade, for which this mountainous country is noted & it proved to be an invaluable shield to an army acting on the defense as ours was at that time. I thought then if we could hold out some inducements by which to draw them into this trap, or great agent of destruction at our controll, could heap upon them sufficient punishment to more than compensate us for the inconvenience caused by their harrassments on the late retreat. But it seems that the position was recognized by our adversaries as a formidable one, & not caring to test the superior advantage held by us, by direct attack, commenced to flank our left wing. Their numbers being so much greater than ours, & equipments so far superior, the only alternative left us was to fall back, to protect our supplies in the rear.

19th Retreat from Cross hollows

Accordingly on the 19th the Enemy had all disappeared in our front & the retrograde movement was again commenced. We had been retreating, retreating! so much & so long, that it became a second nature to us, when we arose from our scantily furnished couches, to don the still more scanty & greasy wardrobe by our side or from our heads, as we frequently used them as a pillow when we had time to undress; pack the messkit turn our faces south & move out. Our task was a hard one, rations scarce, & the country over which we had to march, very rough & rocky. But we were nerved to endurance, by confiding in the belief that our cause was a just one & decided to defend it at all hazzards.

20th Fayetteevill Ark

Passed through Fayetteville Ark. This is a very nice little town & was considered at that time the Metropolis of North Arkansas, one thing in particular, that impressed the beauties of the village more forcably on my mind, was the appearance on the porticos & porches in front of several houses, some nicely dressed good looking young ladies. Doubtless the same impression was made upon the minds of all admirers of the gentler sex, such sights had a great influence over me, my spirits were very much enlivened for a time, the duties of a Soldier seemed light; but these pleasant thoughts would soon pass away, & the sad recollection of the more pleasant moments spent in company with the "Gal I left behind Me" would step in & say wait; wait! your time has not come yet, the future is dark & full of mystery. At this place, a large amount of bacon, flour, sugar & molasses had been stored. The troops in an unguarded, unthoughted moment, when their reasoning power was over thrown, by the inward gnawing & cravings of an unsatisfied & ungovernable appetite; when their haversacks had been filled (when filled at all) by a very scanty ration & poor quality of cornbread & "Blue beef", gave way to their animal natures & took possession of everything for awhile, in their greed to get the best, wasted as much as was put to proper use.

Wastefulness of Soldiers

They would tear open a sack or knock in the head of a barrel of flour, fill their haversacks or anything they had that would hold flour, knock in the head of a barrel of molasses to fill their canteens, or turn a faucett to fill them & in their hurry leave the contents running on the cellar floor, fill sacks with sugar or scatter it promiscuously over the house, throw bacon sides across their backs, & I saw several men carrying a half side each on their bayonets as they marched out to camp about one mile from town. Surround a person, with plenty in times of peace & let them read this account, would be ready to render a verdict, that we were a set of villians, unfit for recognition in civil life as men of honor & virtue. But as I have said before, in similar comparisons, this is not a fair test of mens honesty & manliness — in order to make one qualified to pronounce sentence in a case like this, should partake of some of the discomfeitures incident to such a life. Rest assured we lived fat as long as these delicacies (as we termed them) lasted. That evening when we went into camp every man looked like a miller & his haversack resembled one of his "bags".

21st

When reveille was sounded early in the morning, the order to march was again given & during our days journey passed over the Boston Mountains & camped on Cove Creek, a beautiful stream, which wends its way at a rapid rate between two ranges of the aforesaid mountains. The narrow bottom on either side of this stream — & the mountain side were covered with a heavy growth of large fine timber, which afterwards proved to be very valuable, when the people became more enlightened & the facilities for turning the timber into money became greater.

The Boston Mountains, at more than 2,000 feet, make up the highest part of the Ozark plateau which

stretches from southwest Missouri across northwest Arkansas into eastern Oklahoma.

Camp on Cove Creek

At this time the people that lived in that country were almost void of energy & as a general rule very ignorant. It is an old saying, yet a very true one, where you find a poor rough country, you fine it inhabited by people of the same discription. The habits & manners of citizens generally conform to the country in which they live. I invariably found this the case, while traveling with the army. This assertion is not made, or written as a slur upon the inhabitants of one section of country more than another; there were people living in many other sections of country as ignorant as these, in the isolated & mountainous districts. We actually found persons of mature years in this part of the state & a little farther south, living within Six or eight miles of a small village, who said they didnot know how far it was & had never been there. One of the most universal & seemed to be hereditary habits of the women here, was to go barefoot. I heard one young fellow say: by the way— too, he was a closer observer of such "things" than myself, ~~say~~ that he had seen some with their feet run down, he said they ~~done~~ did this by climbing around the mountain sides. This sounded a little queer, but at the same time there was some foundation from which to reason, their feet not being braced by anything & especially while young & growing could have become a little creeled. They were undoubtedly very hard especially on the bottom, from coming in contact with the rocks appearing on every side. But remember this was in 1862 — times have changed some.

Cove Creek Ark

We had a very nice time while in camp on Cove Creek & a rest of about ten days which was greatly needed & highly appreciated. But we had again began to feel restless, as a week or ten days, was our usual period for remaining at one place, except Springfield; And it seems that our restful feelings were not unfounded, for when Gen McIntosh's command from Texas arrived as reinforcements, the rumor of a northward move was soon circulated throughout the camp, which created considerable excitement, the prospects of a battle seemed good, the Enemy having concentrated several thousand men at Elk horn Tavern. This Elk Horn Tavern was situated on Pea Ridge. The Battle which occurred at this place was recorded in history as the Battle of Pea Ridge. Gen. McIntosh's command was composed chiefly of Indians, (Cherokees) had some Texas Rangers. The Indian troops were a great curiosity to us, as a great many had never seen one. some had been fortunate enough to see the red man on exhibition in a side show. They came to us with the reputation of being great fighters, they claimed if they could not win a contest by true courage, the wild Indian yell would be resorted to, which would create confusion & result in a defeat of the enemy. This stimulated us very much & caused us to deceive ourselves, at the Battle of Pea Ridge as subsequent events will show.

March 3rd

The same old bustle & hum, familiar to the old soldier could be seen & heard in camp when the order to cook three days rations, was received. Our rations consisted of cornbread & "blue" beef. We called it blue, because there was scarcely any tallow or morrow about the meat, when prepared for the kettle it looked slick & flabby. The majority of which didnot have enough fatty substance to season soup. There were some good beeves in the heard, but the worst were always butchered first — we used to think they were killed on account of not having sufficient strength to travel farther. Well, we cooked our cornbread & beef, & three days rations, made quite a bulk & considerable load on the first days march, but before supper time of the third day, our haversacks were entirely empty. These corn "dodgers" were reasonably good when we had the opportunity as well as the pleasure of eating them warm, but when cold you could knock a "calf" down with one of them. The greatest obstacle that we had to contend with in making bread, being compelled to put the "shortning" in the "long" way.

Elk Horn Campaign

On the morning of the 4th according to orders our army was again on the move. The plan as matured by the Officers in command, was for a portion of our army to gain the rear — or north of the Enemy, while the other would advance from the south & attack simultaneously. Price's troops were selected to gain their rear, while McCullough & McIntosh were to be the attacking parties in front. Price headed his column in a north westerly direction & commenced a force march. At Bentonville our progress was checked for a few hours. Gen. Seigle occupied the town with a small body of Cavalry, & made some resistance, we formed a line of battle & after exchanging a few shots the village was ours. But Seigle didnot give it up without leaving his mark with the fire brand in several residences &

business houses; this mode of warfare became very common & destructive, when used as it was by some of the Federal Genl's before the war closed. The punishment of noncombattants by burning their houses from over their heads, kindled anew the courage within us & we resolved to pursue them as a lion does his prey.

March 4th

Our progress was checked in many places, by trees which the enemy had fallen to obstruct the road, in order to detain us sufficient time, to make their escape sure. This had to be removed, to clear the way for our artillery, & as a natural consequence our game was always a little out of range. Our march was almost continuous, not desiring to risk much time in resting, for fear our prize would be lost. The bleak march winds were coming from the northwest, & I almost imagine now that I can feel a cold chill, when any memory is refreshed with the thought of how we tramped along those dreary valleys & climbed the mountain like hills, half clad & insuficient food to stimulate our wearied frames. Yet, regardless of all our mishaps & hardships, the long sought for position was reached on the night of the 6th. By a circuitous route & a forced march of three days & the most of two nights, Price gained exactly the position that was in contemplation when the campaign commenced. McCullough & McIntosh had also fulfilled their mission, But the time to perform the last act of the bloody drama was yet quivering in the balance, night had drawn her sable curtain, over the two beligerent armies; the only sound to break the stillness of the night, was the sentrys tread, or the sharp crack of the rifle in the hands of some lonely picket, as he attempted to "pluck" off his opponent on similar duty — But Alas! what a change, when the darkness rolled back, before the sun had began to peep up in the eastern horizon, the sound of the horses feet could be heard as the Courier galloped by carrying messages to different parts of the army, the moving of artillery, the rattle of the drum, or the shrill notes of the bugle as they mingled their discordant tones together & passed down the rocky valleys, were singing unaware the last sad requiem in the ears of many poor mortals; but who would be the unfortunate ones was as it should have been hidden by an Alwise God.

March 7th Battle of Pearidge or Elkhorn

The early hours of the morning of March 7th were taken up, in selecting positions, forming lines, & getting the artillery up the ridge & planted in a commanding position, which was quite a task. All things ready, the Battle of Pea Ridge was opened 10 O C A. M by Capt. Churchill Clark's (of St. Louis Mo) battery firing the first shot. This acted like magic, something similar to throwing a bombshell into a magazine of powder; this was a signal & spread like wild fire, was immediately taken up by the different batteries all around the line. McCullough & McIntosh were at the posts assigned them. The sullen roar of artillery was almost incessant, broken only by the sharp crack of the sharpshooters rifle; this was answered back in an instant by all the weapons of destruction in the hands of the enemy (& theirs were far superior to ours). The panting steeds went whirling by carrying Couriers with dispatches from one Officer to another; the stray minnies would zip, zip — by our heads & bury themselves in the trunk of some friendly tree that was shielding the body of some poor fellow who had been fortunate enough to get behind one. The sickening screach of the shell could be heard as it plowed its way through our ranks, or went tearing through the boughs of the timber over us & scattering them in every direction. But what's that? listen! the order to charge is given: The Infantry are formed in solid phalanx, & column after column, moved on in rapid succession. We were now into it; raising the yell, which was taken up on all sides, charge after charge was made & our struggles on the north were crowned with most flattering successes. We the Missourians on the night of the 7th had possession of the enemies camping ground. But, how was it on the south? While success had crowned ~~ef~~ our efforts in every instance & the most flattering prospects appeared, to brighten our hopes of final success; the darkest gloom had been cast over the poor unfortunates on the south, Gen's. McCullough & McIntosh were both killed early in the action, & when their men became aware of the fact, that their leaders were gone, after a short interval, they retired from the field; this left the south side unprotected except by a small body of cavalry, through whose heroic exertions our baggage wagons were saved from destruction, as we had left in the rear on Cove Creek. About three or four O C in the evening, when our company was changing position from one part of the line to another under a very heavy fire of Artillery & Musketry from the enemy, several of our company were wounded & Lovel. Bowen killed, his brains were splattered on his comrad's clothing.

Lovel Bowen's death

Among the wounded was my Bro. Caldwell, who was struck in the head & ankle with small fragments of a shell & bleeding very profusely, — the Capt. ordered me to take him off the field, also to assist in taking care of the other wounded of the company. After considerable trouble &

exposure, to the bullets of the enemy, succeeded in getting them to a place of safety under the hill, where they had a hospital to meet the ~~present~~ immediate needs of the wounded. I also assisted Alphonso. Bowen to carry his dead Bro. Lovel from the field. Oh! can you imagine the keen darts of anguish that pierce the heart, of one when forced to become one of the pall bearers of his dead Brother? No. to bear his almost lifeless form from the bloody field, while gasping for breath; his eyes turning backward in their sockets; the cold clamy sweat of death has come, the last sad farewell is spoken, not by him, but by a fond & loving Brother as he bent over the dead form, straightened the stilled limbs on the blanket saturated in his own life blood, which flowed from a warm heart while grasping a musket in defense of the noble cause he so zealously espoused. His comrads new him only through honor & respect. He was kind, affectionate, true & brave; although young, he lived life in earnest & died without a murmer. Another hero is gone. He has passed away to never again answer to roll call, until the last general muster. Everything favored a victory on our (the north) side. Our days work was a complete success. A short time after dark the bloody struggle ceased & the men dozed as best they could in line of battle without anything to eat.

8th

On the morning of the 8th instead of being roused as usual by the sound of the bugle or rattle of the drum, a sharp reveille of musketry & artillery brought every man to his place in the ranks & the battle was again resumed in earnest, but after about two hours fighting, Gen Price was compelled to, & very reluctantly gave the order to retreat, which was very disastrous & unfortunate. The Texas & Arkansas troops having retired from action to the south, the Federals concentrated their entire force on Pric's command, & that was more than our decimated corps could successfully oppose. The wounded were loaded in wagons & ambulances in charge of a surgeon & started in an eastern direction (Caldwell with them) & our only alternative was to follow them. The Enemy having succeeded in cutting off communications to our baggage wagons, left us without baggage, cooking utensils, anything to cook or eat & compelled to retreat across the Boston Mountains in order to escape capture.

Retreat From Elkhorn

There was considerable demoralization & straggling, which was, under the circumstances unavoidable & impossible to controll; for we were extremely hungry, the last crumb had been eaten from our haversacks more than forty eight hours since, the "blue beef" was all gone too; but luckily for us, the first night on the retreat as we were preparing to stop for the night, several hogs made their appearance near our bivouac, & I expect people in that neighborhood, thought Price's army had found another enemy, for the crack of the rifles, sounded similar to the advance skirmish line of an attacking army. But this time we were making war on our friends. Hogs were shot in every direction, ~~drug~~ dragged up to the mess fires, (log heaps) the skin cut in small strips, snatched off with the rapidity & dexterity only characteristic of a half starved Soldier of the late war.

Pork without bread or salt

I remember well as if but yesterday; cutting a chunk of meat from the bleeding hog almost before its pulse had ceased to beat, while yet quivering, stuck a stick through it & inserting into the fire, & as fast as the outside would become scorched a little, trim ~~of~~ off & eat without bread or salt; this was kept up until my inveterate appetite was partially satiated. I imagined it ~~this~~ the sweetest meal I ever ate. I most assuredly felt that way at that particular time. This retreat was attended with many hardships, some of which will be pronounced almost incredible by the reader of this narative, but as I obligated myself in the beginning to stick to the truth, I will not deviate. After crossing the mountains our line of march was continued for several days in a Southeastern direction, down a deep canyon which was traversed by a stream of water which in an ordinary way could be easily forded, but when aggravated by continued rains, footmen had to wade or resort to footlogs to cross. Well this state of affairs existed on this memorable escapade, the rain commenced falling on the second day of our march & continued a week.

Retreat continued

The valley was so narrow & the stream so crooked, that in the course of a days march, we were compelled to cross it 25 or 30 times. Sometimes we would fall small trees across to walk over on, but more frequently wade through; it mattered but little any way. Our clothing was already wet by incessant rain. Some of the Boys on this trip, (I could name some but I will avoid personating) becoming greatly discouraged, let their lips fall & displayed unmistakable signs of "home sickness" & more than once every day, I have seen a mischievous comrad, catch some one of these fellows in an unguarded moment & shake him from the trembling footlog into the middle of the stream. This would create great merriment, to see them crawl out "as wet as a rat;" shaking themselves while heaping unmentionable epithets of abuse upon the person or persons who caused so much fun at their expense & discomfeiture. We found this part of the country very sparsely settled. Now & then would pass a small house where the valley widened sufficient to give room for a small field & garden spot. It looked as though they belonged to a recluse class of people, for they undoubtedly lived that kind of life to a great extent. The cabins were built of logs, chinked, & daubed with mud, stick chimneys plastered with the same material, the hand used as a trowel. The cabins were set close up to the hills on either side, which were so steep, a person on the summit of one could almost look down the chimney & see the children playing around the fire. I imagine it was seldom they ever saw a stranger traveling in that valley previous to the war. I think some where in this part of the state, the man resided who originated the first part of the tune called "Arkensaw" traveler & kept the man over night as a guest for learning him the other "side".

Retreat of Elkhorn continued

On the second day of the retreat Forage masters were sent out in every direction to procure something for the men to eat, their labors were slightly rewarded, by obtaining a very scanty supply of coarse corn meal, we had no salt or meat — & the meal was too scarce to seive & no cooking utensils, so it was every fellow for himself. The meal was issued to every man seperate & he was his own cook. We ~~would~~ mixed the meal with water in a tin plate, that was generally carried in our haversacks: spread upon a thin flat rock, (which were numerous in that country) & set up before the fire, similar to the manner in which our mothers used to bake "Jonny cakes", when done were eaten with a relish that only a hungry, or rather half starved man can appreciate. It frequently happened though, that a fellow lost all his bread, by being two hasty, thinking the process of cooking a side at a time too slow, place the rock upon the fire, the heat would cause it to burst, scattering the bread in every direction, & "you bet" a person need not to have been extremely near by, to have heard the adjectives qualified by a few well regulated oaths; at the same time picking up what scraps he was lucky enough to find. The loss of the bread was enough to throw a fellow "off the handle" for awhile, but that wasn't all, his actions & ugly expressions generally wound up in a "free for all" laugh. After a few days we managed to get some salt, & our supply of rations was somewhat increased, though during the whole time, which extended over ten days, we didnot have enough rations issued to us per day for one good meal. There were a great many of the men barefooted, staining the ground over which they passed with blood. My shoes had disappeared except part of the vamps & soles. The enemy did not make any attempt to follow us, having been too badly crippled by "Old Pap" at the recent engagement at Elkhorn, to desire a more extended acquaintence at present.

Retreat Continued

They made several unsuccessful attempts to capture our transportation wagons on the other road. After pursuing the direction in which we started for several days, & having learned that our transportation wagons were camped near Vanburen Ark. changed our line of march to a southwestern direction, & I need not tell you that it filled our hearts with gratitude overflowing, when we found our wagons at the place designated on the 19th day of March. To say that I was tired; this word in not "big" enough to express half. I was ragged (but not lousey) dirty, hungry, sleepy — in short I had kind of an alloverishness" good for nothing — woe begone feeling, that I cannot just exactly describe, I will let the reader try to imagine how I felt.

Camp Near Vanburen Ark

The men with the wagons had heard of our near approach, & had very correctly conjectured that we could almost eat up the Boston Mountains if roasted, were busily engaged in cooking edibles which were bountiful at that time. At sight of the tents pitched (which we had not seen for some time) & the bright mess fires burning, our hearts leaped for joy, which found expressions in loud & prolonged cheers; the scent of the cooking viands only tended to increase the desire, to appease our ungovernable & unbridled appetites. The Boys often made the remark, that they could eat a "sow & nine pigs" or a horse if "skinned". The use of these expressions were freely indulged in at this time. But, to make a long story short, I was not long in locating the mess fire, at which I had a right, & cramming the "grub" down my neck as fast as possible. I dinot have any table to stick my legs under; I used the Soldiers substitute, my knees, while seated upon the ground, & it was astonishing how quickly & without ceremony I emptied the huge tin plate filled with cornbread beans, bacon & washed them down with "old fashioned" coffee. Which was such a rarity. (You will excuse me for making mention) we sometimes made a substitute of burned cornmeal — when not too scarce.

Camp at Vanburen

After getting a good nights sleep in a tent I felt like Sam. again, but didnot feel sufficientlly invigorated to rehearse the lessons of the past fifteen days, unless they could be reversed. Here I again found my Oldest Bro. Wallace, whose health had improved ~~some~~ but little since I last saw him, before the Battle of Elkhorn. He had been traveling with the baggage wagons most of the time since we left springfield Mo, & being advised by his friends as to the condition of his health at that time, concluded that his strength was insufficient to undergo the duties & privations of a soldier. His heart was in the cause, & he gave his strength as long as it lasted in defense thereof. After receiving an honorable discharge from Price's Army, went to Montgomery County Ky. Where he remained until sometime in the year 1863 teaching school, then returned to Buchanan Co, Mo. his old home, & resided there until the close of the war, taught school in Platte Co, a short time, where he died in the winter of 1866 in his 31st year. At this place (Vanburen) all the Missouri state troops whose time had expired were discharged. (One matter that I wish to explain here, that should have been attended to in proper order. nevertheless, better now than not at all.) When we were in camp on cove creek Ark, some of the Mo state troops whose time expired, having enlisted for Six months; Gen. Price in view of the pending battle, issued an order, or rather an urgent request, appealing to all Soldiers under his command to remain in ranks until after the immediate crisis had passed. There were quite a number though; regardless of his entreaties called for, & received their discharges, & (some few of our company) returned home; Some went farther south & remained as a citizen through the war, now & then one joined other commands, this number however, compared with the others was insignificant, from the fact, it was immaterial, with those who expected to remain in service, whether they received their discharges at the exact date or not. Price's plea, & ~~a~~ it seems to me a just one too, ~~was~~ to issue discharges to men at that time, would produce a demoralizing effect. This was human nature; To see a man with whom you had been intimately associated in camp life; stack arms & say that he is done fighting — this is a harder life than I expected, when I went in I thought the war would have been over before this time, I'm going home anyhow; would we line his comrad to do, or say likewise; If he's done, so am I —

Camp Churchill Clark

Our camp at Vanburen, was called Camp Churchill Clark, In honor of the

Artillery Captain who fired the first shot at the Battle of Pearidge & lost his life in the same engagement, while fighting at his post. He was a brave young Officer, by whose death the Confedercy lost a true & tried friend.

On the 21st I received my discharge from the state Service, which called for Six months & twenty three days. There were a great many others discharged at the same time & were sworn into the Confederate Service for twelve months. Several of my old neighborhood Boys concluded, they had faced the perils & uncertainties of war long enough; after giving me a parting farewell & asking what to tell the home folks, started, homeward, bound. Alphonzo. Bowen was one of the number, & as I have stated sometime previous in my memoirs, commenced his long journey on a mare that I rode from home. It seemed as though, after the death of his Bro. Lovel at Elk Horn, his hopes & asperations, in the life of a soldier, all vanished, seemed to be completely overwhelmed by the shock & his energies greatly impared by grief.

Camp at Vanburen

While these fellows were buoying themselves preparing to return home, Caldwell & I were meditating about what arm of service we would attach ourselves, that we might not become dissatisfied with our choice, the remainder of the war, if spared that long. As our first introduction was in the cavalry service, then Infantry — concluded to risk our chances in the field artillery, In which choice we were well pleased. We found it to be the cleanest service, more privilege extended, & less cramped in camp.

Entered Confederate States Army

On the 22nd day of March 1862, we were sworn into the Confederate service for twelve months. After this time we were intimately associated with each other, bunked together, eat around the same mess fire, sharing alike pleasures & hardships until seperated, by him receiving a wound at the Battle of Kennessaw Mountain Ga, June 23rd 1864 from the effects of which he lost his left arm.

We attached ourselves to a company commanded by Capt. John C. Landis of St. Joseph, Mo., who had made up a company & drawn a full battery ~~(4) of guns~~ four pieces, two twelve pound smoothe bore Napoleon guns & two twenty four pound howitzers, all brass. This company was attached to an Artillery Brigade quartered at Camp Sand Prairie, near Vanburen, under the supervision of Brig. Gen. Frost of St. Louis Mo. It has always been a query in my mind, since the war closed, & I found out what a Sandburr was, whether the name given to this camp, was on account of the Sandburr or the narrow strip of Prairie which was covered with sand. This camp was situated near the Arkansas river & the prairie looked as if it might have been the old river bed at an early day. The surface of the ground was sand; when dry & the wind blowing, it became very disagreeable.

John Christopher Landis, son of Israel and Sarah Landis, attended the United States Military Academy at West Point, but withdrew in 1860, and returned home to work in his father's saddlery, where he designed and supervised the construction of the mochila and saddle for the first run of the Pony Express on April 3, 1860. When the war between the states began, he organized a company of Confederate militia, commanding a battery of artillery at the battle of Lexington. Following the battle of Pea Ridge, Landis was commissioned lieutenant colonel, C.S.A. and assumed command of the Missouri Division of Artillery just prior to the siege of Vicksburg. He was breveted colonel of artillery after the surrender at Vicksburg and placed in charge of the Gulf Division of the Confederate artillery until Lee's surrender. Despite the higher ranks afforded him, Landis always preferred to be called Captain Landis. He died April 2, 1913, and is buried in Mount Mora Cemetery, Saint Joseph, Missouri ("Capt. Landis").

Gen. Daniel Marsh Frost commanded the militia that was captured by Nathaniel Lyon during the attempted seige of the St. Louis arsenal in 1861. Following his capture and exchange, he led his Missouri brigade at the battle of Pea Ridge and was commissioned brigadier general, C.S.A. He was no longer in service to the Confederate army after December 9, 1863. According to Boatner III, the Confederate Military History reports, "he was on 'detached duty' in 1864" (Boatner 318).

Camp Sand Prairie

The principal production was a thick growth of slender bladed grass, the stems of which were covered with small burrs & the burrs with numerous little jaggers as sharp as needles. Our blankets & clothing all got full of them before we became aware of the mischief there was in the little "strangers."

At this camp clothing was issued to us, (which we needed badly) consisting of hats, pants, Jackets & shoes, out of which I got a "pretty" good fit except pants. I was rather small of stature, consequently forced to carry a considerable surplus of goods. The pant legs were almost long enough for grain sacks & made of material that kept stretching, so every day or two I was compelled to add another roll, to the bottom of the legs in order to keep them from under my heels.

Early in the morning of the 26th, having received orders for the entire command to report to Memphis Tenn. commenced our march in the direction of Little Rock Ark. I felt very much recuperated, after the rest of the last several days, & everything being new & fresh, our progress was good for the first few days. Passed through Clarksville on the 30th this was a very nice little village, & perhaps would have been passed by with mere nominal notice, had it not been for the beautiful Covey of Young Ladies, who appeared on the balcony of a seminary. This took the eyes of all the Soldiers & their sweet songs, in which the girl of the South took such great delight, had a great tendency to lighten the burdens of camplife. These were nice young ladies, I tell you; but on this march we found others that were not near so nice. We saw & talked with all sorts of people. A great many of the men had enlisted as Soldiers at the beginning of the war.

March from Vanburen to Desark

Those at home were tall, slender of sallow complextion & in the country generally ignorant where the country was poor. The majority of them wore blue jeans, their pants looked as if they had been "pulled too soon", or the wearer ~~was~~ mad when he put them on & ran his feet through too far. "The cannon" the peoples name in this country for Artillery, ~~was~~ were a great curiosity. When we camped before night there was always several visitors to see the "cannon". And by the way we had some young men in the company, who went a great deal on their "shape", & the first one of these fellows who happened to notice the appearance of visitors, would be on hand to show them the "mysteries" of the Artillery. One evening shortly after parking the guns & "old sol" had just about gone to sleep in his western home; three young women made their appearance on the outskirts of the camp, wearing homespun dresses & bonnets of the same material; ~~when~~ & one of these "upper tens" of the company spied them & was soon making himself very interesting;

Webster's New International Dictionary of the English Language **defines upper ten or upper ten thousand as "the ten thousand, more or less, who are highest in position or wealth; the aristocracy."**

Showing the girls the ammunition, the manner in which the guns were loaded, the different duties of the cannoniers, how destructive the shells were when thrown into the enemies ranks &c &c. He made himself very interesting & in turn had become very much interested in his new companions, when in an unthoughted moment, forgetting that he was in the company of "ladies" & possibly thinking the time long between chews; took from his pocket some plug tobacco & bit off a chew. One of his companions, said, give me a "Chaw" of your "flat terbacker", & to his great amazement & perplexity, all three "indulged". Suffice to say his tobacco was a great deal smaller when returned to his pocket. All these proceedings were watched with scrutinizing eyes by the Boys around the mess fires, & the joke on the "young man" with "flat terbacker" was not forgotten soon. This march was one of varied experiences, intermingled with, suffering, ease & pleasure.

Under the wheel of a caisson

I had an accident happen me on this trip, that I would not desire to have repeated. One evening awhile before our days travel ended, becoming wearied from walking, & not feeling very well, mounted the middle chest of one of the caissons to ride, when our guns filed out of the road into the woods to camp for the night. As had been our custom for the cannoniers to procure as much good dry wood as possible, I attempted to make a jump & join in the race. On the foot board of every caisson was tied a pick & shovel, to be handy in case of an emergency. I had on those large pants drawn at Vanburen, of which you have already had a description, & just above the roll in one of the legs, I had worn a hole by flopping them together in walking. As I said before I made an attempt to spring off as quickly as possible to get my share of the dry wood, when my accelleration was brought to a very sudden stop, by the hole in my pant leg catching on the point of the pick, this threw me under one of the wheels so sudden that it was impossible to extricate myself before it started over my waist. I "yelled woe" with all the power within me, & had it not ~~then~~ been for the prompt action on the part of the wheel driver, in stopping his horses, my body would have been halved in an instant longer. As it was, the "pressing" made me so sore for several days, that I could scarcely stand to ride. This taught me a lesson, that has never been forgotten. The old adage, "look before you leap" was deeply impressed upon my memory. The rear of the caisson was very heavy, both chests being full of ammunition at the time.

Sam mentions the prompt action on the part of the wheel driver, but does not identify him. Sam's brother Caldwell clearly remembers the incident and reports in his March 28, 1862, diary entry:

> **Just as were going into park Sam came near loosing his life; as the caisson came near running over him. He aimed to jump off the ammunition chest when the leg of his pants caught on a pick & threw him under the wheel. I happened to be driving the wheel horses in place of one of the drivers & by a loud yell at the drivers ahead & a mighty surge on the bridle I succeeded in hindering the wheel from running over him & thus saved his life (Lehr 40-1).**

March to Memphis continued

Well — I had often heard & read of the Bogs of Ark, but on this march, the chance was afforded me to realize by feeling & seeing just what they were. The progress of the first few days was good, the weather was fine & roads in tolerable order, although in some places hilly. About the time we struck the swamps or bogs, rain commenced falling & continued several days. The entire command traveled the same road, which created a great deal of mud & slush. Our march was very slow & tiresome, the artillery wheels sinking to the axle many times through the day & we (the cannoniers) would have to wade in, put our shoulders to them & render assistance to the wearied horses.

Whenever it was possible, we cut roads through the woods to dodge miry places in the main one. But in case we could not do this, a corduroy was constructed, by halving saplings, or throwing in rails (when handy) or brush, any thing to hold the wheels out of the mud. Being so hastily & temporarily made, was very dangerous, a horse frequently caught his foot between the cross timbers, falling headlong, rider & all. The poor animal becoming worn out by plunging through the mud so long, too weak to rise, was left lying to dig his own grave in the mire in his desperate struggles for life.

Our loss in horses on this trip was immense, many of which could have been saved, if we could have stopped a few days to nurse them. Sometimes a man or boy would happen around & the Officers give them the horses.

1862 April

April 9th & 10 remained in camp to give the baggage wagons time to catch up, several of which got stuck in the mud. On the morning of the 10th about 10 O.C. A.M. the company was formed in line, & dispatch read which stated, that our forces had gained a complete victory over the "Yanks" at Shilo Miss, a few days ~~since~~ previous. This caused a great jubilee in camp for a while. One of our signals of great joy, was to wave our hats around the head, or throw them high in the air, both were indulged in freely on this occasion. A salute was ordered to be fired immediately. Our guns fired six rounds. This was our first introduction; a little awkward, but done the work "just the same".

> **The two-day battle of Shiloh (April 6-7, 1862) began with the Confederate army effecting a "complete strategic surprise" that made a Confederate victory seem likely. However, General Albert Sidney Johnston, considered by Jefferson Davis to be the top Confederate general, failed to develop his attack as planned and was fatally wounded in the afternoon of the first day. General Pierre Gustave Toutant Beauregard took command and held the entire battlefield, except for the landing. Beauregard made a decision not to attack the Union troops at the landing, which opened the way for Grant's strike the following morning at dawn. Ultimately, battle casualties reached nearly 24,000, making the battle of Shiloh the bloodiest up to that time. The Federal victory put control of the Memphis & Charleston Railroad in Union hands, which helped split the Confederacy, and ultimately led to its defeat (Boatner III 440; Heidler and Heidler 1775-80).**

March to Memphis continued

When we left Vanburen, it was surmised that our destination was Little Rock, but we never crossed the Ark. River; yet our march extended the principal part of the time near the north bank, this I suppose was partly the cause of our bad roads.

The "Stragglers" of all description having reported, the order was given Apr 11th to move on in the direction of Desark. This changed our direction a little to the northeast. Made good progress allthings considered. The country through which we passed for some distance previous to entering the town, was good. The country was well fenced, the dwellings were very comodious & tastefully constructed, an indication that occupants were well to do, & the country in a prosperous condition. This was about the first mark, so characteristic of the open hearted Southerners found on this march. The chief products of this country before the war, were cotton & tobacco, though Sugar cane was grown to some extent on the low lands.

Desark Ark

Arrived at Desark Apr 13th. This completed another weary march which consumed eighteen days. This Town is very nicely situated on White river, a deep & beautiful stream. At the time of our march, a great deal of the country through which we passed was very isolated, no sign of the woodman's ax, — as the mark of the plowshare could not be detected. You may, kind reader, think that I have overdrawn the mark, in the description given of the people — Not a bit — when the remoteness of the country at that time is taken into consideration; No railroads, no telegraph; Churches & School houses were almost unknown, Yet these people seemed happy & contented with their lot. They "basked" in the sunshine of the old addage, "Ignorance is bliss, tis folly to be wise". Yes, I could give a great deal more coloring to the picture describing our hardships on this trip, & then not tell all. Can you imagine just how one feels, when half fed & forced to sleep in a tent every night on the cold damp ground, & wet blankets too? Can you study up just how you would feel, when your shoes were filled with small gravel every night? Your socks wet & muddy & be compelled to return your feet into this cold mud on next morning? Or if dried were as stiff as boards. Did you ever stop to think of the blistered feet, by being hemed in these muddy prisons, while marching every day? did you ever notice the steam rise from a hogs bed, when first vacated on a cold morning? If so; you can imagine something similar to the fogg that rose from our tent doors, when we crawled out of them & fell into line, to answer to roll call, when the bugler sounded reveille. I did undergo all this, & found out afterwards, these were only initiation ceremonies compared to what, I was brought face to face, as the war neared the close. Soon after camping, we received orders to cook five days rations, preparatory to making the remainder of our journey to Memphis, by water.

Apr 13

Late in the afternoon of the same day on which we arrived, loaded our guns & horses on the steamer Clara Dolsen.

The *Clara Dolsen* was built in Cincinnati, Ohio, in 1861. She was a 1,200 ton "magnificent river steamer" with an estimated value of $60,000. She was captured on the White River by the Federals and absorbed into their operation as the USS *Clara Dolsen* (Ainsworth and Kirkley Vol. II 833; Ainsworth and Kirkley Vol. V 478; "Clara").

Desark to Memphis

This was the first time since my duties as a Soldier began, that I had an opportunity in sight of traveling by water; We had become accustomed to wading, & often glad when we could get to where we started by so doing; we had had long since learned to take things as they hapened. The river is said to be deep at this point, as an indication the warter moves sluggishly along toward its junction with the Miss. River. The water is sufficient to admit steamers of large capacity.

Early on the morning of the 14th we were again on the move, but this time we didn't have to roll on the wheels, build corduroy roads; or pull our feet out of the mud — ca-chuck; We just sat down & chatted, or stood where ever suited us, & "took in the beautiful scenery as it presented itsself on the banks.

Logs, rails, or other available materials can be laid horizontally across a roadbed to "corduroy" or make the surface stable for travel.

Spring time, with all its southern lovliness had come in this country, the trees had put forth their little leaflets, & the wild flowers had unbosomed their tiny folds to the soft balmy breeze; distributing their sweet & mellow perfumes, alike to all. This was a grand treat to a "high private." I tell you, almost "good enough for an Officer". Slowly but smoothly we glided along, down the crooked Stream, occasionally catching a word or two of some old time Negro melody while hoing in "de cotton & de corn", or passing a group of people assembled on the bank to see the "Soldiers" pass. This served to lighten our burdens & brighten our prospects, for the time being any way, although not furnished the accommodations of first class passengers, nevertheless our enjoyment was immense. We had an abundance of time & a good opportunity to rehearse a portion of our past biography & speak a few words about the "Gals" we left behind us. When roused from slumber in the morning of the 15th , found myself on the broad bosom of the Miss River. The name applied to this, "the Father of waters", seems to me, to be a contribution justly awarded for when all others get "dry", She will have an abundance left to quench their thirst.

Desark to Memphis continued

There were a great many things that happened me after leaving home that had never before, & one, here, for the first time in my recollection, I was on this immense body of water, watching with eager & delighted eyes, the beautiful scenery on either side, or gazing at the~~y~~ tiny blossoms ~~as~~ when they bended low to catch the waves as they bounded from shore to shore, or slashed against the sides of the boat, sparkling in the lovely spring morning sun, as the current was parted on our slow ascent; & when night came, weary of watching & trying to see everything, laid down to sleep; but not while listening to some sweet lullaby, such as our mothers used to sing, while trotting us on ~~our~~ their knees; but the clanking & banging of the iron doors, of a red hot furnace, while the fireman was plying the wood, the coarse voice of the mate giving orders to the deck hands, the roar of the immense drive wheels as they ploughed their way through the deep blue water & slashed it high in the air; the rattle of the bell by the pilot, indicating to the engineer how to govern the power. All these & more, mingled together made one grand chorus of clanking — clattering commotion & buzz.

Early on the morning of the 16th our boat hove insight of Memphis Tenn. All eyes were anxious to catch a glimpse of the beautiful City. Our hearts leaped within us for gladness, & when the flying handkerchiefs as a signal of welcome were seen, loud shouts pealed forth from every lip, in answer to the noble generosity extended us.

1862 April 16th
Memphis Tenn.

About 8 OC A M we landed at the wharf of the long talked of City. We were warmly received by the Citizens. They came with outstretched arms & open hearts, bid us enter & share their hospitality.

Old fort Pickering

The guns were soon unloaded & horses hitched to them, when we moved out, a little to the south & east of the city, to a point which had been selected for us called Old fort Pickering, situated on the bank of the Miss R. about fifty feet above the water's edge. We pitched our tents in regular military order, on the beautiful bluegrass sod. This was a nice clean camp, & we felt very much elated at our first introduction into the Trans Mississippi department.

Fort Pickering was constructed in 1796 to defend the United States against a Spanish invasion from Florida. During the War of 1812, the fort was blown up and burned. Rebuilding was never necessary, as seven years later Spain ceded Florida to the United States. The old Georgian fort settled under layers of dirt and was forgotten until archaeological exploration began in 2004, and the significance of this early site was revealed ("Archeologists").

While situated here Gen. Frost was removed from command of the artillery, & Louis. Clark of Mo. placed in his stead. This change was very satisfactory to all the Artillery men. Frost having proven himself undeserving the honor. He was disposed to be selfish, bigoted & somewhat inclined to tyranize over his subordinates. This inclination in an officer of the Southern Army was spurned with great contempt. We lost a great many of our company horses, killed by buffalo gnats; (an insect about the size of a house fly, differing some in shape) which were very destructive to horses in that country in ~~in~~ the spring of the year.

Buffalo gnats, also called black flies, are any of a variety of small, dark biting flies. The larvae of the family *Simuliidae* attach themselves to rocks in flowing streams ("Black flies").

Our horses being greatly fatigued by the march through the Ark. Swamps, were an easy prey to their small yet very destructive enemies. One of the victims was a large Bay horse, (Bolivar by name) that my Oldest Bro. Wallace, rode when leaving home the last time on his way south in Aug. 61. He was a noble animal, looked upon at home as a family pet; respected for his kind disposition in carrying with safety, what ever burdens that were placed upon him, & he was no less doted upon by his adopted master (Lieut. Harris of our Co) in whose charge he was at the time of his death. Our camp was very nice, but we were not permitted to enjoy its conveniences & pleasures long. On the 22nd general orders were issued to cook five days rations. Also, all those who were not able to undergo the fatigues consequent to a long march, ordered sent to the hospital.

Memphis
Irving Hospital

I was taken sick a short time after our arrival at Memphis, & not being able to travel, very reluctantly accepted the only alternative. I was placed in an ambulance & taken to the Irving House, which had up to a short time previous been occupied as a Hotel, but at that time converted into a hospital for the army. I remained there all night & most of the next day. This was my first introduction into a hospital as a patient, & previous to this had thought the intention of such a place was to try to better one's condition; to render them such help as required, in the manner of medicine, nursing; or in preparing nutritious food, to suit the delicate appetite of the invalid & seeing that they had rest & quiet. But all these very necessary commodities seemed to be entire strangers to this place. The noise, buzz & roar kept up day & night sounded more like that at a union freight depot distributing freight on several railroad lines, when a moments delay, would entail a loss of thousands of dollars. This was not the cause of the noise. But it was human beings handled as roughly. The sick were brought in on a stretcher & stowed away in some dark & dirty corner on the floor, a bed made of their blankets, (if lucky enough to have any); while the nurses of the hospital, were engaged with eaqual vigilance, carrying the dead to the undertakers room, in one end of the building, where for sake of convenience the coffins were rudely constructed of rough pine boards. The Scrash, Scrash Scrash of the saw as it tore its way through the soft lumber, resembles the screach of the long shells on the goary battle field as they tore through the timber or plowed their deadly swathe through the rank & file. The rap, rap, rap! of the hammer in the hands of workmen forcing nails into these hurried incasements, were driving fangs into my heart, deeper & deeper at every strike. Oh! I imagined, that I could see death, stealing in upon me, that night as I tossed my aching head, from side to side on the hard pillow made of my clothing, in that dark & lonely room; no friend to comfort me, no sound to be heard but the feeble cries of the sick for help, or the moans of the lonely dying Soldier as his soul passed out into eternity. When death claimed a victim, (& that was frequently) his blanket was used as a shroud, his body placed in one of those rude boxes (above described) hurried away to the potters field, where the remains were placed under the cold clods, in a shallow trench, prepared by negroes detailed to do the work.

A great many of these deaths were attributed, & justly too, to the criminal negligence of the Surgeons & nurses in charge. As a general rule the nurses employed in these army hospitals, were men who were too cowardly to go into the ranks & fight; & a man that is a coward is generally indolent & void of sympathy. This was a very trying period in my life. I was only a boy in my eighteenth year, far away from home, & when seperated from the company, was deprived of the association of all reliable friends, at whose hands I could expect a favor; no one to speak a word of consolation; or do an act of kindness, my lips were parched from inward fever, but there was no kind hand to bring the cool water to quench my thirst. My mind wandered back to the old homestead, where hearts & hands were always ready to meet my wants when overcome by sickness. But we will live on through these dark hours, by & by we will turn over & behold a brighter page. On the morning of the 23rd about 10 O.C. AM, one of the cooks brought me "something" to eat; the sight of which would make a sick man sicker, & a well one could not have relished it unless absent from his meals about three days previous. The meat was rare beef steak, tough at that, Stale bakers bread, & the "stuff" they called coffee was the worst I ever drank. I managed to swallow sufficient to gain a little strength, & nerved by the thought, that this was bad, but from indications, there was worse coming — resolved to make a change, if possible. Fortunately for me the company did not move immediately as ordered, & while I was yet revolving the surroundings in my mind, which under the circumstances could not be otherwise than dark & foreboding; when to my great surprise & joy my Bro. Caldwell & another one of the company Boys ("Bob" Welch) came into see me. This was a panacea more powerful in its effects, than any medicine that could have been pattented by human ingenuity. I told them I would sooner risk my chances in camp than remain at that place, & if compelled to do either would choose the ~~latter~~ camp, then I would have the consolation of being surrounded by friends, if nothing else. After watching the maneuvers a few moments, they concluded that my choice was well considered. They said it would not do for me to entertain the idea of returning to camp, but would assist me in procuring a place at a private house. The next thing was to devise some means by which to get me out, as the orders in regard to giving a patient a permit to leave the Hospital until able for duty, was very strict. "Kill" or cure" was the motto at this place, & the former doctrine seemed to be in the lead by a large majority. They went to the Surgeon in charge & after a short parley, procured a pass for me to go out in town with them for a while. Thanks to the Almighty I yet had sufficient strength to walk a short distance; so leaving my baggage at the hospital started out with buoyant spirits.

Memphis Private house

I did not care to trouble the most stylish people with my presence, I did not have any desire to enter one of those stately mansions on the busy thoroughfares; lest there would be more attention paid to style than me; as a general thing that class of citizens are not very enthusiastic in doing charity, they would prefer paying their way through on that line.

After a short ramble my attention was attracted by a neat story & a half frame residence, with a nice little portico in front filled with blooming flowers, set back from the street a few feet, giving room for the snug little front yard which was beautifully & tastefully decorated with shrubs & evergreens.

This was the first place that presented itself that pleased my fancy & as we came near the gate, I said to the Boys, let me try here! A rap on the door soon brought one of the occupants to it, who bade us enter & be seated. After a short hesitation, I made my errand known to the Lady of the house, who very kindly assured me that my request should be granted, my wants cared for as well as in her power to do, & still better, I could remain until entirely well. This generous expression of kindness, almost overwhelmed me with joy & gratitude, I realized the immense value of such a "free will" offering, & felt that I should say something in return to express my thankfullness — But I was so modest that I couldn't. I frequently abuse my self now for being so modest & awkward when young. The next thing was to get my knapsack & blankets from the hospital, without being detected by the scrutinizing eyes of the Surgeon or his assistants. The Boys had already been absent from home sufficiently long to take several lessons in cunning; So they went back after them & while the attention of the persons in charge of affairs, was occupied in another direction, slipped out unobserved & brought them to me; after which my Brother & companion returned to camp, leaving me quietly ensconsed in my new & comfortable home. I tell you, I slept about three nights in one, & repeated the dose until I had made up for lost time & rested in the same proportion through the day. My improvement was very noticable.

Memphis at Mrs. Haines

The members of the family at home then — consisted of Father, brother & Daughter, their surname was Haines. The Old folks were a little on the shady side of life, while their Daughter was a blushing maiden of 17 summers, & it is useless to say the longer I remained, the more beautiful she became in my sight. This was very natural, wasn't it? Oh! How often I wished for my "Store Clothes", that I could accompany her to church or theater, after gaining sufficient strength to walk some. She didnot object to my worn & faded uniforms, but my "bashfulness" again interceded. I became more & more attached to my adopted home day by day. I spent the day in reading or lounging around, & when night came, instead of the hard floor of a dark, noisy & dirty room to sleep in, & no one to offer a word of sympathy, or do an act of kindness; was tucked quietly away in a nice clean soft bed, & the last request spoken before the final goodnight, was if you need anything, call & your summons will be quickly & kindly answered. This assured me that I was among friends. The Old folks didnot believe in the use of strong medicine. Consequently I was treated with home remidies. In fact I did not need medicine as badly as rest & good nourishing food. I will always remember the Old Lady in kindness, for the pleasure she took in preparing & changing things to suit my dainty appetite. After I had been there a few days, these newly made acquaintences & friends, became very much interested in my behalf perhaps, on account of my youthful appearance & being so far from home. Every day I was called on to repeat a little more history of my parentage & young days. They asked me a great many questions, & I in truthfulness answered, while in turn was listened to with a confidential ear. I delight to refer to this period in my soldier life, in word & thought as one of the happiest. I take great pleasure in calling back to memory the many pleasant evenings that I passed with the small but happy family circle; Yes I can yet ponder in in thought how delightful it was to accompany the Old Lady & Daughter to market; the many kind admonitions of the Old Gentleman while sitting by my bedside, or taking a buggy ride with him, I assure you kind reader, it is not considered a task, to refresh in mind, the many pleasant hours passed in the company of that kind whole souled girl, while basking in the light of her beautiful countenance, reflected by the pleasant smiles as they played hide & seek, upon her cheeks radient with the true bloom of maidenhood & Youth; Is this a dream? no, 'tis reality. She spoke in unconcious flattering tones, that sank deep into the heart of her young & lonely companion; Yes they have all been treasured up, & with pleasure I place them on the brightest pages of my memoirs, that I may turn to at anytime, & bring vividly to mind, a picture, that requires not the skill of an Artist to portray its beauties. But should these lines become dim, or entirely obliterated by the ravages of time, an account of which has long since been indelibly registered on my memory in letters more costly than gold & more glittering than diamonds. I have often wondered why she became so deeply interested in my welfare, but upon reconsideration, I am reminded that it was only that promonent characteristic, which so often displayed itself in the lives of so many Southern Girls.

May

I remained with these generous hearted people about three weeks & all their kind deeds were gratuitously administered. I have often thought how foolish it looked in me, to leave this comfortable home & return to camp before able for duty. In the mean time, my company had moved with the main army to Corinth Miss. This left Memphis badly exposed, liable to be raided upon by the Federal cavalry at any time & having such a great detest for being captured, resolved to again risk my chances with the company. I informed the folks of my determination & the Old Lady soon had my haversack, crammed full of everything possible to be carried, that she had found, during our short acquaintence suited to my appetite. She was a noble Old woman, & I will always remember with the most profound feelings of gratitude, the thoughts that filled my mind & the tears that stole their way unconciously down my cheeks, as I offered my hand to give them the parting good bye & while yet shaking, the showers of supplications & well wishes for my health, happiness, preservation & protection that fell from the lips of that true & devoted Trio. My heart was chuck full; my tongue paralyzed with joy, as in silence I shouldered my knapsack & bent forward to meet the train for Corinth Miss. Long live & God protect such people, was the prayer that I uttered to myself. "A friend in need, is a friend indeed" Yet there are few who realize the true value of one until too late to offer a recompense. As I have previously remarked, it looked like an act of criminal indiscretion on my part, to leave such comfortable quarters & return to camp in the condition I was at that time, & the unavoidable exposure attending such a life. I did not leave my own dear home in Missouri on a pleasure trip, was not hunting easy places, did not expect to fare sumptuously every day, & being stimulated by the great responsibility resting upon all, & the desire burning within me to do my whole duty in helping to defend the noble cause which I had so early & unhesitatingly espoused, was anious to be with my old comrads again; at the same time trying to console myself with the belief that such a change would do no harm. Arrived in time & was soon moving in an eastern direction toward my destination, laid over first night at Grand junction, arrived at Corinth Miss May 20th & after making inquiry, ascertained the direction to take & a walk of a mile or two brought me to camp where I found the tents standing; together with the baggage wagons.

Corinth Miss

Some of the men on the sick list were guarding the camp. In anticipation of an engagement, our company had been ordered to take position at the breastworks in line of battle. Skirmishing on the left this evening. Corinth is situated in a low swampy country, only a few miles distant from Shiloh or Pittsburg Landing, where that ever memorable Battle was fought a few weeks since, in which that brave & gallant Confederate Gen. Sidney. Johnston fell mortally wounded while leading his men to victory.

There was a great deal of sickness here among the troops, water was very poor & scarce.

The poor camp sanitation allowed disease to greatly outdistance injuries and wounds as a cause of death. Diarrhea and dysentery were extremely common; Union physicians reported almost 500,000 cases a year. Overcrowded conditions and latrines built beside camp water sources resulted in contaminated water being used for bathing, cooking, and drinking. Physicians with little knowledge of cause and appropriate treatment were ill prepared in the early days of the war to make good decisions. As the war progressed, necessity forced implementation of more hygienic and sanitary measures (Rutkow 14, 126).

On the 23rd our company was all in again & remained for several days, very anxiously awaiting coming events, which seemed to drag very slowly along. I was very glad to again meet my old camp associates, & it is needless to remark that I was kept busy answering questions about the family at Memphis, & receive with as much dignity as possible the jokes that were thrown at me about the Young Lady. It was thought by many at the time that everything seemed to be on a balance & would require but little to turn the scales either way.

Corinth

The movements of both armies at that time was somewhat myterious. Large bodies of men were collecting as reinforcements for Northern & Southern armies alike. The two belligerent forces stood face to face with each other, & with eagle eyes watching every move, ready to spring upon the weakest point in their adversaries lives. Every body was very restless. You frequently heard the remark, if we are going to fight here! the sooner the better, & let us know our doom. Oh! what a nervous disagreeable feeling, one experiences, when so situated. If we could have marched up & commenced the wholesale slaughter of human beings immediately, & fought to a finish; our dread would not have been near so great, but, to remain in the dreary tented field, & in addition to all this be compelled to listen to the heavenly "Artillery" in the dark & lowring clouds (as on that occasion for a day or two) as they poured forth their torrents upon our frail coverings, drenching our blankets & provisions, or watch the vivid lightning flash, when depositing its destructive fluid near by, or throwing its blinding light in our eyes, when reflected by our smoothly polished guns parked in front of our tents. All was impatience, there was but little chance for rest, Sleep was almost a stranger. The stillness of the night was frequently broken & dreams of the soldier disturbed, by the sullen roar of the artillery, or the pop! pop! of the rifle in the hands of the lone picket, on duty perhaps for the last time. This firing was often continued all night, with but little damage, they could not see each other, only guessing at the position occupied by the flash of each others guns. On the morning of the 28th everything seemed to be on the move. The clouds had cleared away, & just as "Old Sol" had peeped up from his home in the eastern sky, throwing his brilliant rays through the sparkling dew, as it hung in immense drops upon the beautiful foliage, & moss that swung down from the limbs in ringlets, vividly painting before the excited imagination, all nature weeping, a very striking imitation of the many tears that would be shed by human eyes, as the greif of some distracted soul would gush forth in tears, to wash away the sad feelings, when hearing of the loss of some loved one. It was a grand sight to behold the glistening bayonets, as the men passed line after line, keeping step with the tap of the drum, flags waving high in the air, while the bands were pealing forth the most inspiring notes to cheer the men onward to battle; at the same time shout after shout was uttered, & the cry was on to victory or death! Both armies were entrenched & didnot seem inclined to make a direct attack. We labored under great disadvantage here, as on many other subsequent occasions. The Federals outnumbered our force sufficient to hold their front, & at the same time turn our flank & after holding our position as long as deemed advisable, to avoid the unnecessary sacrifice of life commenced falling back in a southern direction. Two days before our army commenced falling back a general engagement seemed imminent, but the principal part of the fighting was done by Artillery.

Our Battery was praised very highly by Gen's Vandorn & Price, for the manner in which they handled their guns. We had one man slightly wounded. During the two days (28 & 29th) engagement, all valuables were sent to the rear for safe keeping. Caldwell was taken sick & sent to the hospital on the 27th, & I after returning to camp, soon found my old & dreaded enemy (Dysentery) making inroads on my system again, the water that I was compelled to drink, & the food was very unwholesome rendering me unfit for field duty — so the morning of the 29th I was about eight miles south of Corinth with the baggage wagons & still moving, the weather was very warm, & not being accustomed to the climate, the heat almost overcame me. On the evening of the 29th, the baggage train halted near Baldwin Miss. & the company overtook us June 1st, Boys all in good health & spirits but hungry & tired.

Withdrawal from Corinth

The movements of our army at that time seemed to be completely enveloped in mystery, & the general tendency to the stagnation of military affairs, both in the eastern & western department, was a query that all acknowledged themselves incapable of solving although freely debated upon. In fact everything was rumor & restlessness. The report took the rounds of the messfires that our commander (Gen. Vandorn) intended to make a stand here, but it was similar to a great many other reports that gained considerable circulation, was only the private opinion of some "Smart Aleck" publicly expressed.

June

June 3rd in camp & still under the weather. Since leaving Memphis, I have often wished myself back, or that I could have brought some of the comforts with me, that I so lavishly enjoyed while at my pleasant home there; how nice it would have been to have breakfasted on buckwheat cakes, nice syrup, & good oldfashioned coffee; at the same time my life being made radient with the smiles of that bright eyed & pleasant faced girl, who was the queen of the household. Orders again received to cook three days rations & be ready to move at a moments warning. This set the camp all agog again, & in addition to the wild speculations concerning the movements of the troops in this department, news came that Lee had whipped the "Feds" in Virginia, also that England & France had acknowledged the independence of the South. This buoyed up our drooping Spirits, & as there had been a great deal Said & written in reference to foreign intervention the rumor gained considerable credence, we very earnestly hoped that the source from whence it came would prove to be reliable, for at that time we didnot care from whom we received assistance or sympathy, if by so doing the point for which we were contending could be gained.

Moving South

On the morning of the 4th when we again took up our march south, the boys were all in fine spirits & wishing the enemy would follow, believing it to be the intention of our commanding Officers to draw them a sufficient distance from their supplies, harrass their rear by cavalry raids, attacking in front at the same time with our main force, defeat them on open field, compelling a disastrous retreat, if not a wholesale capture. Not withstanding all our wild conjectures & building of air castles, we cooked our rations of cornbread & "blue" beef & moved on in the direction designated at the appointed time. Our march was a very quiet one, except an occasional & trivial attack in the rear by federal cavalry. Made very good headway notwithstanding some of the country over which we passed was rough.

Tupelo

Camped near Tupelo Miss. a small station on the railroad leading from Corinth to Meridian. The country around here is generally poor, sandy soil, covered with a thick growth of scrubby oak, hickory & some tall pine. Our army remained here for several days; our Captain was quite a military man & had us to devote considerable of our time to drilling while at this place. On the 9th the camp was wild with inthusiasm again, news having reached us, that "Stonewall." Jackson had gained a great victory over the enemy in Virginia. Hurrah! for Stonewall; was the cry that took the rounds of the different camps, making the woods ring with unbridled meriment & joy. These dispatches were frequently received at company headquarters & read by the Captain to the boys who would flock around him & listen with breathless silence to catch every word of good news, which was received with a shout, after which they would return to their tents to enter into a spirited discussion, in regard to our future prospects, but it is needless to say it generally terminated by our side coming out victorious.

Camp Near Tupelo

About the 15th the weather became very hot & dry, making the roads extremely dusty being continually traveled by wagons hauling supplies to the men & horses. Water also became scarce, so much so that the best (& that was hardly fit to drink) was kept under strict guard for hospital purposes. Our horses as well as men, suffered greatly for water. The horses had to drink from small mud puddles, covered with a green scrum, where the branch had stopped running, while the men drank from small seepy springs, into which the water collected so slow & being almost constantly stirred up by dipping, looked more like soapsuds than anything else, & very unpalatable unless you had time to allow it to settle & then the warm air would soon destroy its nutrative powers. The boys frequently in a joking way would tell one of their messmates, when going after a "fresh" drink to "cut" them out a piece & bring it back in their pockets. I have frequently sat by the spring for an hour at a time trying to get a clear cool drink. Had we been forced to fight at that time & place, many men would have perished on the field for want of water, for as you are aware kind reader excitement & heat are the forerunners of thirst. There is nothing more exhilarating to a person than a cool draught of water, & to see the wounded, bleeding soldier as he holds the canteen with a death like grip to his parched lips, & drink with all the power within him, or as was often the case calling piteously to his comrads to spare just one swallow of water, is really too impressive to behold.

July 4th
Tupelo continued

Well, let me see. I don't know just what to say about today, for my surroundings are so much different to what they were in years gone by. I have been accustomed to hearing the declaration of Independence read & commented upon, & the orator of the day speaking in flaming & eloquent tones, emphasized by the most spasmodic & impressive jestures imaginable the old story reiterated of how our forefathers fought bled & & even died upon their countries cross, struggling desperately for our independence, & to establish the best government under the Sun; & see the uncovered heads, glaring eyes, & mouths stretched to the utmost capacity, drinking in the noble patriotism & enthusiasm of the speaker, & when he retired from his elevated stand, was greeted with round after round of deafening shouts & exclamations of long live, these patriotic exponants of the government that our glorious Ancestors established. Yea! I have seen men fill themselves "brimin" full of the "overjoyful" & wallow in luxury, in their own imagination, all for "patriotism". And after the day of feasting & revelry was over the young folks would assemble at some public hall or private house, & to the sweet & facinating music of the violin, engage in a social dance until the "wee" hours next morning drove them home, & I tell you there was nothing that afforded me more plasure or from which I received greater joy than to be one of the number. But hold on! What's all this about? Why that's the way things used to be; let's look at them as they are now, or at least as they are with us "Rebels". What has become of all that glorious freedom of which those silvery tongued orators proclaimed from the house tops? Where has that great American eagle gone? Those stars & stripes that float over the "free & the brave"? All! All! Gone! Gone!! That which was intended by our Forefathers to be enjoyed by all, is monopolized by the few. That great "bird" has taken fright & flown from his exhalted position, to soar aloft, not caring to associte its fair name with disolution, or desiring to see one section tyrannized over by the other as we think the people of the South are by their northern brethren.

Camp at Tupelo

The "Star spangled" banner still waves; but how? Worshiped & applauded to the skies by one party, disowned & ignored as a false emblem by the other. That glorious freedom is vanished, all! vanished. Yes, & if one of those martyrs of, old, who poured out their life's blood, contending against the Anarchy of Great Brittain, on the same battle grounds where Lee & Jackson are so nobly contending for their rights; could rise up for a moment, would blush to Shame those who advocate the doctrine of Coercion. I could put a great deal more color in this & fix it up in gilt ede style, then not portray half the illwill we had toward our armed enemy, & what little respect we had for the Old nation's birthday — our thoughts were very bitter, felt as though we had been ostracized & that without a cause. One consolation, we had plenty of good news from Virginia to crow over, if nothing else, another report just received which tells of the wholesale defeat of McClellands Army. I'm afraid too good to be true. Yes, I wished that I could be so situated as to live over again some of those pleasures of long ago & feast awhile on the fat of the land as of yore! but I knew such things were impossible & tried to be as well contented as possible with my chosen lot. Satisfied to live on "Bull" beef &, cornbread, & coffee made of burned cornmeal, if we could only succeed in gaining our rights under the constitution.

Union Gen. George Brinton McClellan, known as the "Young Napoleon," caused great controversy. After successfully defending the peninsula at Malvern Hill on July 1, 1862, he withdrew his army to Harrison's Landing where they were protected by gunboats. This effectively ended the Peninsula Campaign. He put together the powerful Army of the Potomac, but commanded it weakly. After the war, Ulysses S. Grant said it best. "McClellan is to me one of the mysteries of the war" (Boatner III 504-7; Heidler and Heidler 1273-77; "Malvern Hill"; Moran).

Tupelo

I did not keep a daily record while at this camp, for the reason, the occurrences were so monotonous, the reading would become tiresome. The Officers were endeavoring to recruit the army in every way as much as possible & establish a move through system in all departments. On the 22nd & 23rd our army (the army of the west) had a general review, & I tell you it was a grand sight, to behold the long lines of glittering bayonets, as the Infantry marched in plattoons, keeping step with the drum, their knees bending as one man, at the same time stimulated by the sweet strains of music from all the brass bands playing some air worded to suit the sunny south, & as it appeared the almost endless chain of glistening artillery that passed slowly along, every driver & cannoneer sitting erect in their respective places. When the army was called upon to perform this duty, the department commander & Staff always situated themselves at a point from which they could obtain a good view, & as the different regiments & companies passed in review, recognize them with a bow & salute, & which in turn was honored with cheers & waving of hats. It inspired new life in a soldier to receive the courtesy of an Officer.

The Army of West Tennessee was a Confederate force created by the merger of Gen. Sterling Price's Army of the West with Gen. Earl Van Dorn's troops from Mississippi and eastern Louisiana. The same name was used by the Union army under the command of Maj. Gen. Ulysses S. Grant that organized in early 1862, and fought at Shiloh in April 1862 (Heidler and Heidler 107).

Gen. Earl Van Dorn was killed May 8, 1863, "at Spring Hill by a resident of the neighborhood, Dr. Peters, who stated in justification of his act that Van Dorn had 'violated the sanctity of his home.' Van Dorn's friends, on the other hand, indignantly deny there was any such reason. They say Van Dorn was shot in the back, in cold blood, and for political reasons" (Boatner III 867; Horn 453).

On an occasion like this every many of ambition, tried to look his best, he prepared himself as neatly as the scanty supply of his wardrobe & circumstances would permit. We were sometimes honored by the gentler sex turning out, to witness these grand procession, there were a few made their appearance here; but in my hurried glances at them as I passed, was not very favorably impressed, they were not tastefully dressed; not very goodlooking, & worse than all, I saw some of them dipping snuff. I found out afterwards, this was almost a universal practice among the women in north Miss. (I will give you an extended lesson on snuff dipping, farther on).

Saltilo Miss

As our supplies at this place & especially forage for horses, were running shorter & shorter every day, another move was commenced, & we arrived near Saltilo on the 30th a small village & station, on the same rail road Similar in size to the one we left, only our camp was much more pleasantly situated. Soon after arriving, we policed the company grounds. This was done by cutting all the underbrush as near the surface of the ground as possible, sweeping with brush brooms all the dead leaves & grass to one side, making the ground as clean as our mothers formerly kept their front yards, & this was repeated as often as filth accumulated. Our tents when in a regular camp, were pitched in a double row facing each other, & the space between was kept as clean of filth as the ground where the guns were parked. Sometimes when one of the men committed a trifling misdemeanor, was made to sweep the company ground as a punishment. We remained in camp at this place for some time, as the dates in my journal will show. Had a great many pleasant happenings, interspersed with some very sad ones.

Murder of Himen by Bradley

One of the most sad, & an occurrence which threw the veil of mourning over our entire company, was the killing of our company Bugler, (Himen) by Wm Bradley, & I suppose one of the reasons why the act is so easily refreshed in my memory, I was on guard at the time; & Bradley was arrested & put in my charge; another is, this was the first & last murderer I ever guarded. The loss of one of our company under any circumstance was sad enough. When we engaged in battle we were not so surprised or shocked, when leaving the field our number was diminished, or at the next reveille roll call — there was no response to the Seargents summons, where there ~~is~~ was once a merry voice, at the same time a radiant smile lit up a countenance where there was now a vacancy, aye! his lips were hushed, death had claimed him until the final reveille. But, kind reader, you must draw on your imagination, in order to judge how great the surprise would be, when in camp out of reach of the enemies bullets, where all should be friends, bound together in a bundle of love & affection united against one common foe, to fight & kill each other, it is a very sad, sad! thing.

Saltilo

Bradley was a stout heavy set young man, while Himen was small, slender & middle age. They had quarreled on several previous occasions, about their mess duties; each in turn accusing the other of being lazy, not doing enough work, etc etc, & early in the morning of the 31st July, while making a fire to prepare breakfast, the dispute was again renewed & finally ended by Bradley striking his opponent with the sharp corner of a spade just behind the ear, cutting a deep gash from which brains oozed out, causing death in a few moments. The deed being done in Miss; by order of the Gen. in command, Bradley was turned over to the state malitia taken to Jackson the Capitol, for trial & I donot know what became of him afterwards.

In camp is one of the best places in the world to study human nature, it affords one of the largest fields for the querist, & brings out the good as well as the bad points of the human character. Find a man that is a man, in camp; one who ~~is~~ is always ready to bear his part of the burdens, whether on the battle field, or around the messfires; as the old adage very truely says you have a friend that will do to "tie to."

A bug in my ear
1862 August

One day while I was laying stretched out in my tent asleep, taking things as easy as possible, on a rudely constructed bunk of small blackjack poles on forks, I was suddenly awakened & almost brought to my feet the first jump, by a bug crawling into my ear, & if you don't believe that I was excited just ask my Bro. Caldwell, W'y I tore around there worse than a horse with bots.

> **Bots are the insect larvae of horse bot flies. The flies lay eggs on the legs or around the muzzle of the horse. After hatching, they get into the mouth and burrow into the base of the tongue and below the gum line. They eventually move to the stomach, where they become full grown and create ulcers or intestinal problems. Results can be fatal ("Bots").**

It afforded some amusement for the boys for awhile. Well, reader did you ever have a real "bug" in your ear? If you you never, 'tis hardly worth while trying to tell you just how one feels under the circumstance, nevertheless if you will not think it tiresome I'll tell you what I did & had done. I gouged in my ear with a pin, pounded myself in the head with the palm of the hand, had the boys to look in my ear, for it was making such a noise & felt so large I thought they certainly could see it, had them blowing their breath in my ear, pouring in cold water etc etc, and everything that I or they could think of was done, but, yet the bug kept up his circuit, thump; thump! buzz! buzz! on the drum of my ear. Seemed as if it was as large as a walnut, & making a noise like thunder or siege artillery. Finally after all the remedies that we could call to mind had been exhausted, & myself worn out by rolling around, & I had about come to the conclusion that "mr bug" had gone in to take up permanent quarters; one of the Boys went after Dr. Wm Gough (who was ~~or~~ our Company Physician & Surgeon. He was soon on hands to render what assistance was possible & after a vain endeavor to extricate the intruder, said the only way by which the "racket" could be stopped was to kill it & let it rot out. The killing was done by pouring laudanum in my ear. This served the purpose for which it was intended, but the coming out of the bug was very slow & annoying. I experienced more or less pain for about three months, thought I would loose my hearing entirely on that side. I will say more in regard to it farther on.

Saltilo Miss

Excuse me kind reader for a moment until I speak a few words in respect to the noble qualities of this good (Dr. Wm Gough) man & fearless Physician & Surgeon; for otherwise I would consider my memoirs imperfect, or rather a very important link left out. His whole soul was with the south. His most earnest desire was to assist his fellow man, & he didnot hesitate when necissary to face the cannons mouth, to bandage the wound of a bleeding Soldier. His keen eyes were set well back under a high projecting forehead fringed with a heavy coat of eyebrows: his looks spoke language indisputable of untiring determination & perseverance. Was tall, & rugged looking, yet as gentle & sympathetic as a Mother, was slow in forming acquaintances, but when he made a friend, was for a longer period than a day. He enlisted in the Southern army about the same time & place that I did was associated with the same company to which I belonged almost the entire war, & soon after surrendering with Joseph A. Johnston in North Carolina, returned to Buchanan Co. Mo the place from which he started & renewed his practice, which proved to be very successful. At this writing is a resident of Los angeles Cal.

While at this place we had a change in Military affairs, which was very satisfactory to us. Our company was attached to the 3rd Mo Infantry Brigade, commanded by Brig. Gen. Martin. E. Green of Mo. He was a kind & noble old man; brave; true as steel & whose heart went out in sympathy for his men. He lived as they lived, fought as they fought, & shared alike victory or defeat. His command was composed of the very best material; men who had enlisted early in the action & left their homes & families far behind them, exposed to the depredations of an invading foe. It was a glorious satisfaction to know when we went into battle, that we had a support upon whom we could depend to stand by us as long as there was any hope, & in this confidence we could rest assured, as their reputation as fighters, "to a finish" had long since been established.

Gen. Martin Green led the 3rd Brigade of Sterling Price's army at Iuka, Corinth, Hatchie Bridge, and Port Gibson. He was killed at Vicksburg (Boatner III 355).

About this time we had a little extra to eat, & this was so seldom it might be well enough to tell something about it. Blackberries grew in abundance in this country, & for some time after moving to this camp, you could walk out a mile or so from our quarters & see the hillsides dotted all over with men gathering berries. Some of us became very well skilled in the art of making & making cobblers & as I was always a great boy for pie, thought them quite a delicacy. I remember when a little "shaver" I used to carry dry oak bark & chips for my Step Mother to bake pies, in order to get a piece. We had plenty of neworleans Sugar issued to us here & occasionally drew a ration of flour, from which we made the crust. The vessels in which we done our baking were old fashioned skillets. After the crust was carefully placed on the bottom & sides the skillet was filled full of berries & sugar, the top covered with another crust, this was put on the coals to bake & when done, it was eaten with a relish, & in a great deal less time than I have consumed in informing you.

Welch's Sickness

One of my messmates — an intimate friend & old acquaintance, whose name was Robert D. Welch, was taken sick with billious fever; & in order that he could be better attended to was taken to a private house near our camp, & I went along with him as a nurse. I was real sorry that my old friend had to suffer, while struggling against the ravages of that filthy disease, but if such a thing had to be, was glad that it happened just where & when it did, & with the surroundings; well, I guess you are wondering what were the surroundings? We had a good comfortable, old fashioned hewed log house to stay in, we had plenty of milk & butter, something that was rarely ever our good fortune to ~~to~~ enjoy; we were received with southern hospitality & treated very kindly. The family was what you would call common livers, but they bade us in & share with them what they had. Yes, we had all these substantials, & as rare delicacies, had three voluptuous girls, the youngest just blooming into womanhood, the oldest yet in her teens to drive away the blues, for they were a lively trio. They kept us besieged with interrogatories & in order to answer them correctly at the same time satisfactory, kept our wits busy.

Bilious fever was a term casually encompassing the symptoms associated with diseases of the liver such as typhoid, malaria, or hepatitis ("Old Time").

Saltilo

Welch was too sick to talk much, consequently the bulk of the responsibility fell upon me. But it was not long until my patient had sufficiently recovered, & being naturally of a lively disposition he amused the girls very much telling stories. Not casting any reflection in the least on the southern ladies, or speaking in flattering language of Missourians; yet it seemed that there was a peculiar attraction about them, that pleased the fancy, or mastered the affections of the girl of the south; perhaps it was on account of their ruddy, robust appearance, or a natural sympathy extended them on account of, being so far from home. I for one can speak from experience, their affections were reciprocated with interest, the girls had been accustomed to being indoors most of the time before the war began, & the warm climate gave them a tender appearance & genial disposition, well calculated to attract the eye & win the admiration of the rugged Soldier. Goats were raised to some extent in this country, at this house they seemed to have an abundant crop, about forty, & privileged to go where they pleased. They would get into a romp in the yard, run on the porch jump the banisters, & occasionally with a mah!—ah—ah! run through the house. Oh! I tell you, we had plenty of lively company, & a "bushel" of fun. Another flock I wish to make mention of; is they had a good sized herd of dogs, I think four, among them was a small one, which was a particular pet of the family. As I said before the troops were camped nearby. These dogs would run around the mess fires to pick up scraps, occasionally getting the "lips" into something that had not been cooked. This was not very agreeable as we didnot draw any more rations than we could easily consume. The boys drove them away several times, only to see them return again late some evening. The boys becoming tired of this, concluded to have a little fun at the dog's expense, so one evening shortly after night fall, when we were all quietly chatting in the old log house; Welch, by this time had become convalescent & very much interested in his new companions; when all of a sudden silence reigned supreme, for a moment; then broken by one of the girls exclaiming excitedly! listen! What's that? It was a dog running in full speed & yelping at every jump, clearing the yard fence ran through the yard, & fairly slid through the house, it happened to be the family pet. I suppose because he was easier to make up with strangers. The dog made a circuit around the house, & in he came again, under & on the bed, scooting & running around in all directions, at the same time whining. This was fun for Welch & I — but we could only bite our lips, pull our faces down as long & look as sactimonious as possible & profess ignorance. With the family; matters were more serious, many anxious looks were cast; they were completely dumbfounded as to the real cause of the trouble, thought the dog was really crazy or going mad. By this time the girls had become well enough acquainted with me to address me by given name, & they would come to me & say Sammy, (I looked so boyish) What in the world is the matter with our little dog? (They called him by name but I have forgotton it) Do you reckon them boys in camp have done something to him? Oh! I do wish they'd let him alone etc etc. I tried to console them as best I could, by professing ignorance as to the cause, & saying, in order to pacify them if I could find out for certain the one who did it, would break his neck. When morning came the dog was alright, except a little stiff; but I think that was his last visit to camp during our short stay afterwards. On the 23rd of August, Welch, having recovered sufficiently to take care of himself. I returned to camp, He returning also for duty in a few days. I fattened as fast as "Bob" improved. It was a long time after that before I heard the last of the Girls, Sammy & dog.

Saltilo

On the 31st we had a review of our division commanded by Maj. Gen. Little. All things passed off quietly & very orderly, as he was a strict disciplinarian & a good military man.

> **Gen. Henry Little served under Gen. Sterling Price in Missouri, then joined Beauregard at Corinth, where he assumed command of Price's 1st Div. in the Army of the West. He was killed September 29, 1862, at Iuka, Mississippi (Boatner III 485).**

Every man in line, seemed proud of the privilege & seemed anxious to try to do his whole duty. I was detailed as regular driver, to which I remonstrated some at first, but I had long since learned, to obey was one of the most imperitive commands as well as duties of a soldier, concluded to make the best of it while it lasted, having the promise of the Captain to release me as soon as possible. I took charge of the two lead horses of the gun. I might add here by way of explanation, that a man who was a driver did not have any guard duty to perform, only on extreme occasions. His duty was to feed, water & curry two horses in camp, & ride one & drive the other on a march, also feed etc etc. There were six horses for each gun & three drivers & the same for caisons. Men in battle the driver duty was, after the trail of the gun had been dropped by the cannoniers, to turn around in rear of the gun, about fifteen yards, & with horses facing the enemy, sit on the lead horse or stand by his side & watch both of which required a great deal of patience & nerve. A cannonier's mind was engaged in the labor of loading & discharging the gun; While the driver could only stand & look on in silence, listening to the whizz & zip of the minnie as it passed, or the scream of the murderous shell as it flew by on its mission of destruction, or burst near, scattering its deadly missels in all directions around him. When we had a full force, or number to constitute a detachment, for one gun, there were seven cannoniers, Six drivers, our Sergeant & one Corporal. It was the duty of the Cannoniers to stand guard over the guns day & night, when in camp or on picket duty.

Preparing for a N ward move

There was a detail made by the Orderly Sergant at roll call every evening, of three privates one Corporal & one Sargeant. One of these noncommissioned officers, took charge of the guard in the fore part of the night, the other in after, relieving the guards at proper time. A man was on post two hours & off four, his beat was in front of the guns & his duty was to keep up a slow pace, back & forth in front of them ~~guns~~, at the same time keeping a sharp look out in all directions. The guns were always parked in a straight row & from twelve to fifteen yards apart. The caisson belonging to each gun, directly in rear. The horses when possible to do so was tied to a large rope stretched for that purpose a short distance in front of the guns, this was done in order that one guard could watch all. Our division & the second received orders to move in the direction of Corinth on the following day. This was no surprise, for we had about eaten up everything around us, besides the "Feds" had began to make considerable demonstrations north of our position. Accordingly on the 1st day of September we moved out, but didnot travel in the direction designated (Northwest) only five miles, when we filed out of the road & camped in an old field near Guntown a small inland village. The sun was very oppressive, there not being even one little leaflet to get between us & the burning rays of "Old Sol." Quite different from the camp we had just vacated, & it was a great puzzle to us why we should leave such comfortable quarters, moving such a short distance & stop in such a ___ forsaken spot as this.

Guntown, a small rural town in northern Mississippi, is believed not to have been named for guns, but for James Gunn, an 1800s settler (Miller).

Campaign of Corinth

But our thoughts didnot change matters, we had to be mum, consoling ourselves in the belief that all thing would work out for our good.

On the night of the 2nd about 10 O.C. ~~PM.~~ there was great excitement in camp caused by the appearance of a very small bright light in the east, resembling a star, it was believed to be a federal balloon or signal light of some kind. The light was several miles from our position, the air was also filled with smoke from the camp fires of both armies, accounting for its diminished appearance. Both armies had been lying quietly in camp for some time, with out a great many miles intervening & as our army had commenced a move in a northwestern direction, was supposed that it had been noted by our adversaries out post or signal corps, & this light was to notify the commanders in chief. We remained at this camp several days & it would be impossible for you to imagine or me to describe, the anxiety that we felt in regard to the immediate future. The Boys would gather around in small groups frequently extending their conversations until late in the night, vainly endeavoring to solve the mysterious movements of both armies. The 9th day many souls were made happy, & our thoughts diverted from the all absorbing question, for a short time, by the company being paid off. We were without money so long, felt as proud as a child with his first nickle, had to count it over & look at it several times a day. Our Paymaster not having very much money on hands, only paid us up to the 1st of May last. Caldwell & I received $15.00 each. This was Confederate money, which at that time was at par in our own lives.

The use of ballooning for observation and intelligence gathering began during the French Revolution. As evidence of approaching hostilities mounted in the early 1860s, Thaddeus Sobieski Constantine Lowe, a man who on April 20, 1861, set a distance record of more than 900 miles in nine hours, joined others to suggest the use of ballooning to the U.S. War Department. Both the Union and Confederate armies ultimately formed balloon corps that used balloons for battlefield observations (Heidler and Heidler 163-4).

To Corinth Continued

Reveille was sounded early on the morning of the 11th, & at daylight we broke camp & with little confusion every brigade, regiment & company filed into their respective places in line, making very slow progress; for our march was continued over the roughest country I ever saw, the roads were very narrow & crooked; Finally, after the day ~~was~~ was well spent & the sun was passing out of sight in his western abode, we halted to camp for the night 12 miles from where we started at Marietta Miss. There were a small number of "Feds." here a few days since, but hearing of our northward move, "vamoused the ranch". Country poor & rough & as observations of the past have proven to be a good maxim, by which to judge the inhabitants of a country, persons can well justify themselves by applying the same comparison to this. They did not care for education, was seemingly content to live in ignorance of the "outside' world. Raised some grain, a very few stock, there was a loom & spinning wheel in almost every house in the country, on which the women made most of the wearing apparel for both sexes; the principal vocation of the men was fishing & hunting. Early on the morning of the 12th the same old song was sung, get your breakfast as soon as possible, harness up & move out. We did as ordered, but our progress was very slow & tiresome, having to march up & down hill continually. We frequently had a delay caused by some of the artillery horses refusing to pull after being stopped for some time on one of those steep hills. Some of the horses were giving out all the time & having to fill their places with raw ones & often with those that never had a collar on before. Camped near Bay spring a small village about dark, after traveling 12 miles. From reports of a short time past the prospect for a "fracus" at an early date was good. There was a skirmish here a few days since, between one hundred & fifty of our men & three hundred "Feds". Our side victorious, loss small, on both sides. The enemy were also reported in force at Iuka Miss. a small town on the Memphis & Charleston railroad.

March Continues

The thought struck us that the purpose for which that country was intended, was near at hand, it looked as if, it was too poor & hilly to be profitably applied to any other purpose, than the camping or battle ground of two hostile armies. After a short nights' rest & but little sleep the morning of the 13th dawned upon a wearied set of men, yet, regardless of this we had to move on early in the morning. Our horses half fed, & we had only a small ration in our haversacks of B____beef & cornbread. Also a few sweet potatoes which are "jayhawked" out of a patch as we passed. I tell you, hunger will cause a man to look around with an eye of inquisitiveness, & if he can pick up anything "loose" to eat, or can get it by scratching, he will most assuredly scratch. This gave us a very small ration for the day, without extending the time so much between meals, but we had to continue our tiresome trip all night without sleep or rations for horse or man. Traveled 25 miles. Some time during the nights' march, the report got circulated that our Officers were looking for a place to camp, (I suppose this was intended as a burlesque) or would stop if a suitable spot could be found, so we gave it the name of "Camp not yet found." I was almost worn out having been in the saddle all night, & the boys said my eyes looked as red as if I had been on a "whizz" for a week; if they looked as badly as they felt, they might have extended the time a little longer.

14th
Sept. Near Iuka

The morning of the 14th was one that I didnot have to wake up to see; however I was looking dreamily through a pair of highly inflamed orbs, only waiting for a moments halt to go off to "shut eye town". I would have murmered, but I saw Gen. Price passing, & I knew by the pleasant smile upon his weather beaten countenance, that what he was doing, he was sanguine in his expectations of success, & was aimed for our good. I was almost worn out, as lank as if prepared for the races, & five miles from Iuka, where the "Feds" ~~are~~ were said to be five thousand strong. As the troops came up "Old Pap" formed them in line of battle. At 8 O.C. AM. moved on, after going to within a short distance of town, stopped & prepared for action, our battery was planted directly across the road, but did not fire a shot.

The "Feds" thinking themselves too weak to stand the "pressure", "Skedaddled" leaving behind them an immense quantity of commissary and quartermaster stores. Gen. Armstrong's brigade of Forests Cavalry, pursued them with all haste possible. We "gobbled" up the stores that they forsook in their flight & did not think the task a hard one, for we were badly in need of both. We went yelling triumphantly into town, & in passing through, got a barrell of flour for every detachment (one for every gun) in our company, our mess also got a box of dried compressed vegetables, which we found very valuable in making soup for some time after the capture. The army also captured a large amount of bacon, Sugar & Coffee. Some of the Boys found some of the "how—come—you—so—hie"! We all partook of it to some extent, but we had a few men in the company, who indulged too freely when ever an opportunity offered itself — would soon have all the "Yanks" whipped out, & independence of the south acknowledged. One thing that I can truthfully add — In battle there were no better Soldiers.

Iuka Miss.

We passed through town & camped nearby on the same ground from whence we had driven the enemy. We thought we had peacable possession, for there was not an enemy in sight with a gun on his back, but were very much mistaken, we were soon aware that all our opponents did not carry guns, for the camp was yet numerously occupied by — "Gray backs" or body lice; & I'll tell you they were the largest I ever saw, Some of the boys, who were naturally adapted to close scrutinizing, said now & then they could find some with U.S. on their backs. We didnot pay much attention to the "insects" that night, for we were so dreadful hungry & the "grub" was so much better than common & our time so much taken up in gratifying the inner man, that we failed to take conizance of the little "busy bodies", nestling themselves away under our clothing, or playing hide & seek around the waistband of our pants or jacket collar. They did not stay with us long — our clothing didnot have enough wool to suit — the "Blue coats" & woolen shirts ~~was~~ were what they wanted".

Samuel Baldwin Dunlap was born September 14, 1843.

This was my nineteenth birthday. I felt proud that I was where I was, & helped to do what had been done; only hoping that while I remained in the army I could roll up a similar record, on every such day thereafter, or ere the next one come round that victory would crown our efforts & sweet, happy peace would nestle among us once more. Iuka was a very nice little town, having some note as a watering place. There were a great many nice & commodious residences. Our camp was near the Springs, which were somewhat out of repair, nevertheless I got several drinks of the water, of which there were several kinds. The 15th we remained in camp until late in the afternoon, when a dispatch came to report immediately one & a half miles from town. Boots & Saddles were sounded by the bugler, we harnessed & hitched up with all haste possible, & was soon at the point designated; only to find the alarm a false one. Remained at the place all night, returning to town early on the morning of the 16th unhitched, unharnessed & fed the horses, also cooked & eat breakfast. Early in the afternoon of the same day, roaring of cannon was heard, one & a half miles north of town, & the orders of previous day were again received & with the same promptness our Battery was at the position designated & ready for action. The "Feds" fired a few shots & disappeared, the cause of alarm likewise diminished; notwithstanding night soon came on & was very dark so that the movements of the enemy could not be discerned, & the consequence was we were compelled to remain on post all night, with horses hitched to the guns. This was very tiresome on a man & especially a driver, for his duty to watch his horses was very imperitive, & in addition to the arduous duties of being picketed on out post; the anxious expectations, mingled with the dread & danger of a sudden night attack, was constantly being revolved in our minds — & another thing which made our condition & duty a very unpleasant one, about midnight rain commenced falling, attended with a cool breeze. We did not have a shelter of any kind, & the attitude in which we were placed, debared the use of fire, lest our adversary discover our position & pick us off from ambush — so the only alternative & the wisest notion was to make the best of our lot possible. As a general thing on an occasion like this, the Boys "killed time" as they termed it, by talking over, their past adventures, or joking each other about some occurrance of a few days standing & occasionally quarrel a little, as a situation of this kind — Sleepy, hungry, tired, & wet besides — fitted a man for almost any thing — except having his countenance wreathed ~~wreathed~~ with a pleasant smile — or being polite & courteous in presence of ladies. Such surroundings became very familiar to us, befor the war closed.

Iuka Miss.

Daylight on the morning of the 17th was received with open arms, but considerable exertion was required on the part of the wearied trooper, to hold his eyes open long enough to recognize its appearance, however it gave us one great advantage, as well as comfort, & being in the woods, fires were soon burning brightly & soldiers warming their wet & chilly backs around them. This relieved our sufferings some little, but the rain continued to fall, we were also on half rations, without blankets & the only sleeping done was in "catnap" fashion. In a case of this kind, some men became very desperate & seemed to obtain more consolation in abusing the Commanding Officers for being in such a predicament, than anything else, while others weighed matters from a more conservative standpoint, endeavoring to believe that in time all things would turn around right. Yet they all consolidated on the one earnest hope that such a state of affairs would not continue long. While on this post we had a very dangerous & almost inexcusable circumstance to happen, which resulted in dangerously wounding two or three men. The person who did it was the son of a very promonent, brave & Successful Gen. & held the rank of first Lieutenant in Infantry.

"Fool Tom" Green

The experiment gave him the unsavory, insignia of 'Fool Tom", he justly deserved the "nickname" for I think his actions made it very applicable. The circumstances which lead to the second christening of this man, with this unenviable cognomen, which he bore through the war, was this.

On the evening we moved to this position, the "Feds" fired a few shots, at us from their artillery, & some of their shells failed to explode. This Lieutenant found one of them & brought it up to a fire where several men were grouped around, & contrary to the advice of all his comrads, entered into an examination of the fuze — wanted to see why it did not burn, or whether the shell had any pounds in it or not — in short he knew there was something wrong, & conceived the idea that he was doing a smart trick to make an examination. "Experience teaches a dear school" & it seems on this particular point, was unwilling to take a lesson in any other manner. He didnot get to see the powder, but after Scratching around the fuze enough to cause an explosion, & coming to his senses after being stunned by the deafning roar of the shell could see its effects. Strange to say, he escaped without injury, the one that should have received a punishment. Some of the peices fell near our position. A thing of this kind, was ridiculed very much by an artillery man. We know of what a shell was composed, & if one of these missionaries of death happened to fall near us without exploding, curiosity didnot lead us to investigate the cause; we were only too glad to let it remain unbroken & wishing the fuze would fail to burn in all of them.

Iuka continued

18th Same old song half rations, half sleep, tired & felt almost too bad to know just who I was or where situated. We remained on post until 2 OC PM, the enemy not making any demonstrations of an aggressive character, returned to our former camp — not the one though that was already "inhabited" we moved a short distace. One consolation we got a good "Square" warm supper, & all prospects led us to believe that our chances for a good nights sleep in a tent was a good one, had just laid down to rest on our scanty & hastily prepared beds, when the sharp clatter of a horses feet was heard, & the foaming charger was brought to a halt in front of the Captains quarters, a courier pulled from his pocket, a paper, which contained an order to move to the front immediately. We crawled out & harnessed with as much dispatch as possible.

The night was dark & we so tired & badly disappointed about our rest; left camp with our feelings somewhat ruffled, however we got out in some shape & after a march of two miles north, a position was selected, where we stopped, fed our horses in harness & laid down to finish our rest, as best we could. This move raised considerable excitement & a great many anxious looks were cast at each other, when on the morning of the 19th our battery was ordered to take position on a hill, a little in advance of our present one & prepare for action. We were soon at the place, pieces unlimbered & every man to his post. Our Capt (Landis) was very punctual in obeying & quick in executing orders, & his men prided themselves in being one of the banner artillery companies of the army of the west. Some firing on our left in the morning & as the day passed the firing became more general in that direction. About 3 OC PM the chances for a general engagement seemed imminent. The enemy having concentrated their forces on that portion of our lives, our company was ordered to that place to take part in the "fracus".

Brig. Gen. Nathaniel Lyon created The Army of the West when he took command of the Union forces in Springfield, Missouri, on July 13, 1861. Less than a month later, following Lyon's death, Gen. John C. Frémont disbanded it. Two other armies later became known as the Army of West Tennessee. The Confederate force mentioned above was in existence near the end of 1862 for about two months. It formed in September 1862 with the merger of Gen. Sterling Price and Gen. Earl Van Dorn's troops. The name also was used by the Union army commanded by Maj. Gen. Ulysses S. Grant (Heidler and Heidler 105-7).

Battle of Iuka Miss

We were on hands as soon as possible, but didnot have the opportunity of firing a shot, nevertheless we were not too late to be annoyed by the unpleasant buzz of the shell & "zip" of the minnie, but fortunately for us, was of short duration, the enemy soon gave way in confusion. One Brigade of Gen. Maurey's division, was attacked by double the number of "Feds", but Maurey's veterans repulsed them with heavy loss. The 3rd Texas regiment charged & captured three pieces of artillery. Maj. Gen Little of Mo was killed. This was a sad affair & a loss which was keenly felt by the South & especially the command with which he was immediately associated. He died the death of a hero, while bravely leading a charge. Before the engagement closed, the day was far spent & the woods were full of smoke from battle, when a great confusion & excitement was caused for a short time, by Gate's regiment firing into a body of our own troops. They had become bewildered, in the dark & smoke, having made a flank movement to cut off a portion of the enemy, thought when they met their friends, they had bagged their game & commenced firing. Fortunately, this regretful circumstance was only momentary, the mistake was discovered before much damage was done. This completed another days record of blood & carnage, after which we bivouaced on the battle ground to spend the remainder of the night.

Retreat from Iuka commenced

We felt very much like sticking another feather in our hats. After making the Feds "Skedaddle' again from Iuka, but concluded to wait awhile to see how things would "turn up". Well we did; for, when reveille was sounded & roll called on the morning of the 20th, the order of retreat was given. The smoke of battle was wafted back by the cool autumn breeze & settling away in the far distant hills & valleys. The pale faced moon which had traversed the heavens on his nightly visit, while looking down upon the two belligerent foes as they slept upon their arms, or giving light to the lonely guard while risking his life to warn others of their danger, looked as an immense ball of fire, disappearing in the far distant, western skies, & "Old Sol" was rolling up from his eastern home, blood red! & struggling to thrust his smoke bedimed rays through the branches of the majestic pine, among which the autumn winds were singing a mournful dirge, to the foot steps of a disappointed army, as they bowed their heads in grief & turned their backs upon an invading foe. We bid a dieu to Iuka early in the morning, burning everything that could be of importance to the enemy, that was impossible for us to move. We got all the baggage out safe. We very reluctantly consented to giving up the town, but didnot have any scruples in trying to outrun as many as possible of those "pests" which became so affectionate on short acquaintance. Made good progress. Heavy firing in the rear all day, but every attack resulted in a repulse of the enemy. We had the utmost confidence in "Old Pap" in everything & especially conducting a retreat, & the expression was often made if beaten that time would be the first. The enemies forces were estimated all the way from 25000 to 75000 troops.

Retreat continued

This move was very discouraging to us, as but a few days previous had been so successful in capturing such an immense supply of army stores & having lived so fat off them for some time, would have been pleased better, as our rations were dropping back into their old channel, to have been ordered forward to capture another depository.

On the morning of the 21st all was quiet in the rear, & the early morning hours passed before we left camp, on account of the baggage & supply train blockading the roads in the direction we wished to travel. Which was all ways one great drawback to an army on a retreat; but as a matter of course, it was a policy as well as a duty to do this; otherwise ~~loose~~ lose all & an army without supplies would soon become a demoralized mob, scattered & disorganized — ~~when~~ then defeat & destruction would surely be their lot. However we got started after a while, but made very slow progress as the roads, we were compelled to travel was very rough. We were very hungry as we had been deprived of the chance to cook anything to eat for two or three days, except a few sweet potatoes, we "hooked" from patches along the road, these were roasted in the fire when stopped in one place sufficient length of time. Passed through Bay springs a small town on the Tombigby river, where we crossed on a bridge, going up, a short time since, the bridge was considered unsafe, & we had to go down the river about seven miles before a suitable ford could be found, which caused a considerable delay, extra travel & the night was half consumed before our camp was reached. This brought us back near one of our old camping grounds, where we left a few weeks since in a great deal better spirits.

Near Baldwin Miss

Sept. 22nd Camp near Baldwin Miss. The Feds stopped thundering away at our rear, & after a very tiresome march extending over several miles of country, attended with enthusiasm, disappointed & danger bound ourselves near the old stamping ground, on 20 mile creek & 55 miles from Iuka, dirty, hungry, sleepy, tired, & a kind of a "woe begoneness" which makes a "feller" feel like he was good for nothing or if "sent for" couldn't go. There we were all in a pile, kicking around in an old field, cuckle burrs waist high, trying to cook something to eat, out of the scanty supplies on hand. Mad at everything, blankets, tents, knapsacks & cooking utensils, scattered promiscuously over the ground. I often think what a conglomeration of things it took to make up an outfit for a Soldiers life in active service, & how natural it was to get things badly mixed while undergoing a campaign similar to the one from which we had stopped to recruit. But if things were "mixed" our mess yet had a little of the compressed vegetables which we found in the rubish, left from our captures at Iuka & the night we camped here, although it was late, made a large camp kettle full of soup, which revived us very much

23rd Found me feeling very much revived. This was general wash day & I tell you it was needed. You could hear the battling sticks, or "clubs" going in all directions, reminding me of the way the women used to wash when I was a "shaver". Instead of using a bench smooth logs were substituted. Every man that was lucky enough to have an extra shirt, put it on & washed the dirty one; those who were not, stripped off any way, & while their shirt was drying sat in the shade of a tree. I did that frequently, when without a change, or seperated from our baggage wagons. This wasn't very pleasant, yet it beat going dirty.

Baldwin Miss

I made myself one or two shirts during the war, from flour sacks that I saved up. "You bet" they were "daisies". Well this washing & battling just about rid us of the "unpleasant company" we fell in with at Iuka. A great many Boys when they entered the army, imagined they had taken out license to do anything that was filthy & rough, such as swear, drink, smoke, chew, blackguard & gamble. I knew some boys who were members of our company, & who told me, they were scared strangers to all the foregoing habits & were looked upon by their parents or guardians as proof against all such. These very same boys seemed to be adept to all the above vices, I knew some of them to sit up all night, by the dim light of a torch or candle & play poker for money, at the same time puffing away at an old strong pipe. Some of them reconstructed themselves after the war & lived as reared in youth. As for myself I never swore an intentional oath, so far in my life, never used tobacco in any way, & a year or so previous to leaving home, made a promise to my Father, that I would never play cards for money, & the screen of war, being far away from home, & prospects of never reaching there again, did not cause me to break my pledge. I have played cards across a blanket or log, many a half day at a time with the Boys for passtime. Our camp was once more made jubilant over the news reaching us that our forces had again whipped the "feds" in virginia, & I earnestly joined the boys in the hope that our time would soon come to gain a victory.

On the 25th orders were given to cook two days rations. Orders of this kind were equivalent to a move, or at least that was what generally followed; but at this time was a great quarry in our minds to tell where was our destiny, but were anxious to go north & hoped with a sufficient force to drive the vandal hords of Abolition scoundrels from our soil & stop the starving & fighting business. "My health was very much improved, since returning from Iuka springs" or at least I felt like Sam, again, we had all been in camp a sufficient length of time to appear like ourselves again, But we came to the conclusion very suddenly that we could enjoy more rest, when on the morning of the 26th our slumbers were broken by the shrill notes of the bugle & we got our eyes open sufficient to see the Orderly Sergeant poke his head into the tent & yelling! roll out! roll out! at 3 OC AM. Well we did tumble out into line, in all kinds of shapes to answer to our names. Breakfast was eaten, horses fed, harnessed & all ready to move at sunrise, but didnot move until 10 O.C. AM & as desired commenced marching north. Our progress was slow, which was generally the case, first day after remaining in camp for a while. On the 27th our line of march was taken up in the direction marked out by the previous one. Crossed the Chestnut mountains of wilson hills, which were very steep & hard to climb with artillery. The distance across was said to be six miles & I think it was all of that if not more. Camped near the base. Crossing these mountains consumed most of the time we were on the move, & the task was made more arduous & disagreeable by drizzling rain. This was an awful poor, rough country, yet we found some cabins stuck around & as in Arkansas, filled with a good "crop" of white headed children. The 28th was consumed in trudging along through the mud & rain, over the rough narrow roads, in the direction aforesaid. One great consolation to us & an order that was received with much thankfulness, was the one which gave us the privilege of filing out side the woods to camp at 3 O.C. PM, after traveling 11 miles. Fared sumptuously on beef & soup.

Corinth Campaign

We were all right while our "Soup" lasted. On the 29th Reveille was blown early as usual, but we remained in camp, six miles, from Ripley Miss. until 2 O.C. PM. About 1 O.C. we received orders to cook three days rations, this was a great annoyance for we alredy had our mess kit & provisions loaded in the wagons, but we unloaded & commenced opperations, but had to remove the "grub" from the fire, before done reload, & move camp near Ripley. After our arrival cooking was again resumed. This was the cause of a great deal of trouble, as well as loss of rations. This looked like a very foolish & uncalled for move, mixed with a little too much desire, "just to show authority" We were accustomed to changes in the programme, often before the scene was half played, we wasted some of our rations but managed to save sufficient to live over. Here we formed a junction with Gen Vandorn's command, this was a great encouragement to us, gathering strength as we moved north toward the foe. Ripley is the county seat of Tippen county. It was said that this was the first time since arriving in miss, that we had been outside the limits of Tishamingo Co. Pretty large county, eh? & what I saw was very rough & poor, no wonder its appearance was not flattering to a new comer, for it had been foraged for the last Seven months by both armies. On the 30th all things ready.

Campaign of Corinth

Moved out early & passed through Ripley. As we moved along through the streets saw several young ladies, some of whom I thought were blest with more than the average amount of beauty, to which my attention was greatly attracted; being the first goodlooking ones I had seen, since leaving the "Old hewed log house" at Saltilo. But just as I was about to pronounce the final encomium & turning half round in my saddle taking a farewell look, noticed some of these participating in the abominable & filty practice of snuff dipping, & my "feathers" fell immediately, but they didn't know any better, "had been raised that way". Before leaving camp the Gallant Vandorn passed us. He was a brave, stern looking Gen. & prided himself very much on his fine military appearance. After spending most of another day on the weary march & traveling 12 miles camped on Hatchie river.

Oct. 1st

Horses harnessed & everything in shape for moving at day light, but didnot leave camp until 10 OC AM. Having to wait for Vandorn's command to get ahead of us. When our Captain gave the order our company filed out in the order designated & took up the same old routine of business. Passed through Jonesborough, a small village Situated four miles south of the Tenn. state line. Some of the country over which we passed was rough, & our march became very tiresome as it was 10 O.C. PM before we camped on the Hatchie river, to spend the remainder of the night. Traveled 16 miles. We were very much elated over the thought that we were once more out of Miss & we all earnestly hoped to God, that our shadows would never again darken her soil, while the war lasted. Yet we were only in Tenn. by a "squeeze & a grin". for it was said our guns were parked & we slept in Hardin Co. Tenn., while our cooking & eating was done in McNair Co. miss. The expression, made that our bodies might not again cast a shadow on miss. soil, may sound a little queer & harsh to the inteligence of the present day; but when you take into consideration, the "ups & downs" of the army for a few months previous & follow the meanderings of the troops, in a radius of a few square miles in north miss; think about the inferior water, how many comrads we lost from sickness, how often we had to sleep hungry, march foot sore, & as a general rule cooly treated by the citizens, who seemed as void of sympathy for a Rebel, as a Pensylvania Duchman was when dressed in a blue coat! But as my old Father used to remark, I must give the "Devil his dues". I must make some allowance. The citizens were not responsible for the country being poor, the water being inferior, the soldiers hungry & footsore, or the health of the army being bad. No wonder they met a soldier at the door with frowns on their countenances & gave a short answer to his questions; you could not expect their faces wreathed in smiles or hear the sound of merry laughter within; when their country had been devastated by both armies foraging off them for several months, depriving them of every delicacy — if they had any — as well as substantial; houses sacked in many places & some families turned out doors, by their houses being destroyed when they happened to be in line of battle. I often thought this a sad affair & my heart went out in sympathy for them as they were fleeing from their own dear homes, almost distracted with sorrow & fear.

We often look back in retrospect of our past lives & note with feelings of regret some happenings of long ago, think & say how easily such things could have been avoided. Nevertheless as I pledged myself in the beginning, to write things just as they occurred, will endeavor, with as little "gilt edge" as possible to represent them, as we talked & felt at that time.

Campaign of Corinth

On the morning of the 2nd we didnot leave camp until 9 O.C. AM. Our march was in a southeasterly direction toward Corinth. You will readily recognize the fact, that we in our march had almost half encompassed Corinth & was near the Tennessee river, & when we changed our course from a north to a southeastern direction, it became self evident proof to us, that an attack on that place was contemplated as the Feds were there with a large garrison. Crossed the Tuscumbia river 10 OC. PM. on a temporary bridge constructed by our men, the good one having been destroyed by the "yanks", in order to check our advance, but we had a corps of men along for the purpose of constructing "quick" bridges, making roads etc etc, these were present at this time, & the troops were soon crossed in Safety. Slight skirmishing here the day before, but little damage done. Some fighting in front, in the direction of Corinth. Camped 9 OC PM — & suppered on sweet potatoes. Rather thin "grub" for a soldier on the eve of battle & after marching the largest half of the night, but we were accustomed to this manner of living — & many times we would have been without a bite to eat had it not been for 2 sweet potatoes. Camped again near Corinth, that dreaded place & the occasional roar of artillery in that direction made familiar "music" to our ears.

In 1854, surveys for two rail lines crossed at a right angle; Cross City, Mississippi, was established at the juncture of the Mobile & Ohio Railroad and the Memphis & Charleston Railroad. However, the editor of the local newspaper advocated a more favorable name and Cross City became Corinth (Heidler and Heidler 500-1).

Battle of Corinth

Battle of Corinth commenced Oct. 3rd. Early in the morning everything seemed to put on the garb of war. The sun was hastening up from his nights repose to give light while two hostile armies meet in deadly conflict, to pour out their warm hearts blood, in defense of what they thought was right. Father against son & son against Father, while Brothers would plunge daggers into each others hearts. Oh! I have often thought how strange it was, that an Alwise God, who rules all heaven & earth, would suffer such things to be. Some faces grew pale as the thought passed over them with a shudder! — Maybe my blood will help to color the field crimson; or I will not live through the coming battle. Oh! What a sad, sad, thought. Faces which but a few hours ago, were wreathed with smiles; wore a look of sorrow & gloom. Tongues that were chatting gaily or singing some pleasant; familiar chant, only a ~~fortnight~~ few hours since; remained silent. The commanding Generals were to be seen in groups, engaged in earnest & confidential conversation; couriers were galloping to & fro, on their panting steeds, distributing orders for the days programme; all was wonder, & excitement; the mind of every one was busily engaged upon the problem, the solution of which was near at hand.

According to orders our Captain had horses, guns, harness & men inspected, & everything in order left camp 8 OC AM. & moved forward toward the scene of action, crossed the Memphis & Charleston railroad 11 O.C. AM. The sullen roar of cannon was loud & frequent, in the direction we were going, indicating the near approach of the death struggle — still onward we pressed; hearts throbbing, as if to burst from their narrow sells; faces all flushed with heat & excitement; yet the countenance looked stern & grave, — while their actions displayed unmistakable confidence of a great victory. We moved up in front & halted for a few moments at the edge of a field in heavy timber where shell of all description & solid shot, attended with thousands of minnies, which went whizzing uncomfortably close to our heads, while the solid shot tore through the timber, throwing the trunks & branches all around & over us while the shells were bursting & scattering their deadly missles into our ranks. Yes, there we were, silent spectators, playing deaf & dumb "— as it were" — with a foe of a thousand fiery tongues. Stand firm! was the order & motto of all our company, except one cowardly scoundrel, who played sick while in the woods, & I guess is sick yet, for I never heard whether he got well or not. While standing in this position the roll of musketry was heard, a short distance in front, "Missouri Yell"! & Gates' regiment, charged & took the outer line of breastworks by storm with four pieces of artillery. Hurrah! for Gates. Lost only six men wounded. Wade's Mo battery was engaged, first Lieutenant killed one private & two horses wounded. Our battery one horse wounded. About 3 O.C. PM. our battery moved one & a half miles inside the first line of Federal breastworks, & took position on the brow of a hill in open field, while the shot of all kinds & description showered around us thick & fast. Our guns were planted in double quick time & returned the compliment, by giving them the best we had "in the shop", & as well directed as possible. We had a very warm & spirited artillery duel, of an hours duration, which terminated by the Feds giving up the contest, & falling back to their main line of work.

Jerry Cauley Wounded at battle Corinth

We had one man of our company, "Jerry." Cauley, painfully but not seriously wounded, by one of our own guns recoiling over his leg. He failed to step back far enough to clear the wheel, when the gun was discharged, & the ammunition with which artillery is loaded being so heavy, caused the guns to recoil or run back from eight to fifteen feet owing to the condition & situation of the ground. While the artillery engagement was in progress, the infantry were being formed & ranks closed up— their raising the yell, pushed headlong on the charge, away they go— & regardless of the immense storm of deadly missiles, hurled at them; drive their antagonists behind their iner line of fortifications. Oh! What a storm of everything calculated to destroy life, on the battle field, came whizzing, whirling & buzzing, over around & through our ranks, as we stood & listened to the boom, boom! Of cannon & volley after volley of small arms; every man at his post, ready — should our men be beaten back to hurl grape & canister into the ranks of their victors. This was far more disagreeable & eaqually as dangerous as to have been engaged. A great many were killed on both sides. The hotly contested field was strewn with the dead "Fed" as well as "Confed". Colonel. McFarland, 4th Mo Regiment, 3rd Brigade, was dangerously wounded. Brigadier Gen Green's horse was killed from under him in the charge. About 5 O.C. PM. a body of the enemy appeared on our left, about two hundred yards distant, rushing in double quick & moving as if to flank us. Times looked squally for a moment, we could almost count the buttons on their coats — but didn't take time though — we had to think fast & acting likewise, immediately wheeled the guns to the left, at the same time pouring a heavy fusilade of grape & canister into their ranks, causing them to "skedaddle", back into the woods in a greater hurry & with greater confusion than they made their debut — while we rent the air & made the woods ring with shouts over our little success. This little circumstance revived us very much; relieving our minds for a moment, of the dreadful slaughter of human lives going on. This in a manner closed the bloody strife of the first days battle of Corinth. & everything was favorable for a Confederate victory. Night soon intervened & threw its most sable curtain over the bloody field of strife, yet the sharp crack of the rifle in the hands of some lonely pickets, pealed forth to mingle with the low weak moan of the dying Soldier whose life was drip-dripping away. The field of battle became our habitation for the night, the earth our bed; the heavens our covering. All the Boys except a strong guard, with their blankets folded around them, threw themselves upon the ground & were soon wrapped in the arms of "Morpheus", where they remained almost lifeless, until their turn for watch arrived, unless they passed off to dreamland & imagined some foe lurking by their side, awaken themselves struggling to avoid his clutches. Drivers also assisted in guard duty. The sound of wheels in the Federal camp could be heard at all hours of the night; we wondered whether it was baggage being sent out, or batteries changing position, as if to strengthen the weaker points, however it was mere conjecture. We were very much encouraged over what we had gained & confident in the end, would come out victorious, & we earnestly hoped & was almost certain, the noise we heard was the enemy preparing to evacuate. This bivouac found us again as on many former occasions, without anything to eat & precious little prospects of getting any soon.

We were hoping to make another haul off the Feds similar to the one made at Iuka — only, on a larger scale. All the foregoing — yea — hours it takes to make up the words, acts & thoughts of a soldier's night on the battle field. Yes: if you could steal up by the side of the sleeping form, & catch his mind while snoring away, you would have volumes of unwritten history & Something more sublime than was ever penned by a Shakespear or a Byron.

Battle of Corinth

The first dawn of day on the morning of the 4th was ushered in by a reveille of artillery & small arms, breaking in upon the still morning air; reminding us that there was something more to be done; that the deadly strife was not yet ended; that our foe was yet confronting us; that the thirst for blood was not yet quenched; but what a glorious consolation it was, that while the battle raged furiously every Confederate soldier marched boldly to oppose the foe & offer his life as a sacrifice upon the Altar of his Country, thus showing to the world with what great veneration, he held the cause which had been so eagerly espoused. The cool breeze of an October morning was wafting back the smoke of battle from the former days slaughter, which was settling in blue streaks & ringlets in the eastern horizon, as if to vail in mourning the daily luminary which was just appearing, & seemed to hesitate, as if to forbear giving light for such a wholesale effusion of blood. Oh! It seemed an age before "he" dropped down behind the "trees" & smoke in his western home. It was a grand, grand, sight to behold the long lines of glittering bayonets, as the Infantry formed in solid phalax, to charge the almost impregnably fortified foe, & see the sullen, loud mouthed artillery, & cannoniers with spong staff & ammunition; & inserting the solid shot, Shell, grape, or canister, as the immergency of the case required, breaking forth in tongues of flame & smoke.

A sponge was made of "coarse, twisted woolen yarn and shaped like a bag." It was on one end of a wooden staff or rammer and used to remove gunpowder residue and eliminate any burning embers. Inside the gun tube, the sponge was "turned three times clockwise and three times counterclockwise" ("Sponge").

Such a grand display of human ingenuity & superior bravery causes one to worship at the shrine of the Goddess of war, & rejoice in a true spirit of patriotism, that he was one of the number who dared to do his duty. On!

On! went ~~the noble went~~ the noble men who dared to carry the bayonets into the enemies strong hold. The charge lasted one hour, then our battery was ordered to advance one half mile, to a hill; the same point from which we drove the yanks the previous day. Shells of all description flew thick & fast (we called them "gateposts & buggy wheels") from the immense size & fluttering noise they made, some of them seemed as long as I am, especially when passing over my head or plowing up the ground in front. They were striking & bursting around us in all directions, whirling, whizzing & buzzing at the same time the minnies were falling, it seemed as thick as hail, & looked impossible to remain a moment, lest we would be mown down as grass before the sickle. We took position regardless of the immense danger & fired a few shots, but were ordered to discontinue, on account of our advancing columns in our front.

Battle of Corinth

There were many dead lying around us — The Gray & Blue were mingling their life's blood together; Foes but an hour ago, under different commanders, & seperated by animosity & hatred, then side by side, united by the strong arms of death & under the one great commander in chief, whose mighty hand ~~could~~ did still the troubled sea. The sight of the stiffened corpse was sickening — the moan of the wounded, calling upon their passing comrads for help, was heartrending. To see the dying martyr waltering in his own blood & at the same time powerless to render assistance; caused one to think back, & while a cold shudder shocked the sensibilities, exclaim, My God! My God!! How long! Oh! how long! will this cruel war last? In addition to the dead, wounded & dying, Muskets — cartridge boxes — Knapsack — blankets — & canteens, were strewn in all directions, indicating a terrible death struggle. After remaining a short time we were ordered back to our old position; where we could do nothing but listen to the death knell of many a poor fellow. By this time the thousands of rifles sounded as if by one — & the discharge of the hundreds of pieces of artillery as one immense gun, as the charges of grape & canister plowed great furrows through our ranks as they moved on & mounted the breastworks. Although our position was somewhat remote from the main point of the enemies defense, we were not out of danger, stray shots reached us frequently. At 10 OC. AM the enemies left was driven in, & Gen. Price gave the orders forward, we being on the yanks right. The firing was very heavy booming of cannon incessant. The first & 3rd Mo brigades charged the enemies works, in front of the City, with same yell & deadly aim so characteristic of them; while forty pieces of artillery were showering grape

& canister with murderous effect into their ranks. But, still they go! on & on! they climb the works! Yanks run! the guns were theirs. The long sought for position was gained & victory almost ready to crown our efforts with success; When Gen Lovel who was in command of the reserve Corps, failed to arrive in time with reinforcements; the Missourians being completely exhausted & ranks so decimated, were compelled to fall back. This was a very unfortunate affair, & Gen. Lovel was censured with the loss of Second battle of Corinth. True the ranks of that noble band of Missourians were thinned out, but not without inflicting a serious loss upon the "yanks". It was very discouraging, indeed, to see the men falling back dispirited & gloomy; but they had done their whole duty! had played their part in the bloody drama, in a manner for which they deserved great credit & Missourians should never cease to venerate them. They were completely overcome with fatigue, hunger, & thirst, could not hold out longer without loosing all & thought a retreat far more credible than surrender or wholesale massacre. They came back in squads & commenced rallying in rear of the batteries. But, alas! Too late! the day was gone, we had to yield the prize to a well fortified foe, whose numbers were far greater than ours.

Battle of Corinth Concluded

Yes it was a prelude to another retreat from Corinth, that awful place where yankee legions abound, & many brave confederates had become, targets for their bullets, or victims of those miasmatic diseases which lurk in abundance around those swamps. Yes, their bodies filled many shallow graves there, without a friend to drop a tear or scatter a wreath of flowers; & doubtless ere this time their bones have dulled the plow share of the busy husband man. But thank God! the yanks were victims of the same causes of premature death. Our battery was ordered off the field in the afternoon. Gens. Price & Vandorn seeing no other alternative, ordered a general retreat. This caused great excitement & confusion among the troops & sometime intervened before order could be restored. There isn't anything, kind reader, more exciting than a retreat under such circumstances, & an occasion that requires greater courage on the part of the men & dilligence of the Officers, than to remain orderly while being hounded, by an overwhelming & superior armed foe. But, finally we got strung out & after marching until 5 OC PM, camped 8 miles from Corinth on the Ripley road. Rations very scarce for horse or man. Orders were issued to continue in the same direction the next day. Oh! if we could have just had a few waste crumbs from our Mother's tables such as the chickens & dogs used to get, would have checked our gnawing appetites. The casualties in our company so far as men and horses were concerned were one man & horse wounded & one man deserted, but our guns & gun carriages were all more or less injured & one gun disabled so asto render it unfit for field duty.

Second retreat from Corinth

According to orders our retreat was taken up on the morning of the 5th, & in the direction designated by our former days orders & commencement. The greatest obstacle with which we had to contend at that time was crossing the Hatchie River, which was but a few miles in our front & was pontooned for that purpose, but the "Feds" had thrown a considerable body of men around in our front, on the bank directly opposite where the bridge was constructed, who were bitterly opposing our right to pass over. About 10 O.C. AM. our uncertain march was commenced. Heavy cannonading & small arm heard in front. Our retreat seemed extremely doubtful, or at least in the direction we were moving, the avenue by which we desired to make our escape, in order to be near our supplies. The country was very unfavorable to us — very rough, & at that place the river formed a kind of peninsula, on the side upon which we were advancing, thus giving the enemy a direct as well as an enfilading fire. The men being so much torn to pieces after the two days battle, & so badly mortified over the defeat, put a more gloomy aspect on affairs, than perhaps would have been under ordinary circumstances. Our battery was ordered forward! Double quick, and soon arrived at the scene of action, halting in the road to await further orders; & I tell you the Feds gave us a very warm reception — "not as friends though" — It sounded as if the Heavens had opened for a few moments to pour out, Shell, grape & minnies, from the manner in which they hailed around us, & went tearing & screaming through the timber. The Boys all remained at their posts, but it was very difficult to keep the horses from breaking loose & running off — in timber was always worse than open field. The situation of the ground, rendered it impossible for us to gain an advantageous position — & our lives being in great peril — was ordered back to the rear, & we returned as quickly as we came.

Hatchie River

Our battery lost one man 4th corporal wounded & one horse. Gen. Caball was thrown from his horse & seriously hurt. The ground was contested with great animation by both parties, but the Feds having so much the advantage, in position succeeded in preventing our crossing at that point. This sudden check in our retrograde movement, caused great excitement, especially while remaining stationary — some thought the only alternative was surrender — while others remarked vehemently never! never! fight them as long as we had a shot — some of our company Boys, even had horses picked — said they would divest them of their harness — & become a command of their own — as a last resort, While this kind of programme was being headlined by us "high privates" — the General were holding a hurried consultation; for the immergency of the times, required immediate action. Vandorn was the Senior Gen. in command — but seemed very much puzzled as to the best course to pursue. Was very much excited & held to the idea that, it was almost impossible to escape by any other means than the first planned. Gen. Price said, give me full controll & I will lead the men out—Vandorn thought to shift the responsibility from his own Shoulders said — go ahead! Thus giving Price full management of the retreat — & I tell you the Old war horse looked more than "himself again", as he turned his weather beaten face to the rear, at the same time giving the order to countermarch.

Retreat continued

We went back about two miles & turned south on what was ~~what was~~ called the Boneyard road which lead us by a graveyard — perhaps the origin of the name & the amount of firing kept up at the pontoon bridge also in the direction of Corinth made us think that ere long — & perhaps then we were traveling the road to our "Boneyards". But Price had his wits at work, as well as his pioneer corps, & realizing the great responsibility resting upon him, as well as the truth in the old adage, "Necessity is the mother of invention", acted in accordance with its requirements, & after having both banks of the Hatchie river graded down with pick & shovel, crossed the whole army, baggage & supply train included, on a mill damn. A feat which was considered very dangerous as well as extraordinary.

Price crossing the Hatchie river on a mill damn

'Twas night when we crossed our guns, our way being lighted by fires made on each bank from large log heaps. While this crossing was in progress, the Old gray haired veteran "Pap", didnot stand on the bank & give orders, by simply a word or wave of his hand, but was on the damn working as a pioneer, filling up the holes with slabs, telling the drivers how to avoid bad places, close up! quick! etc etc.

After crossing we felt very much inclined to offer three long — loud — cheers for the noble old patriot through whose cunning & exertions we made our escape, but silence as near as possible was enjoined upon us, for fear of discovery. On this instance we didnot have a "real" Moses; we didnot have a pillar of cloud by day, to protect us, or a pillar of fire by night to guide us; as did the Isrealites, when fleeing from Pharoah & his murderous hosts of Egyptians, when leaving the land of bondage. But we had a good substitute — a noble type of manhood he was! Clothed with almost supernatural power for this emergency. We had a fire to guide our footsteps, & darkness to shield our movements from an enemy whose cravings for our blood, or capture, was equally as rapacious, as were the advocates of coercion in ancient times. After traveling a short distance we stopped by the roadside two or three hours about 2 O.C. AM on the 6th, without any thing to eat, & as little prospect of obtaining a full supply as had been experienced for several days previous.

Retreat Continued

Had been entirely without rations for two days. The Old Gen's hat was almost entirely full of feathers, from great renown, on former occasions; but this miraculous escape justly entitled him to another long one. We remained at this bivuoac until daylight, when we moved out on the Ripley road. The roads were extremely dusty; making the march very tiresome on the wearied men & horses; but we were favored by camping early 8 miles from Ripley 3. O.C. PM. also — with the privilege of cooking & eating supper, (or what ever you may call it, this was the only meal for sometime) one which seemed a little strange, as we had not been accustomed to such enjoyment for a while, & it was quite a task to get our faces clean enough to eat. "Tis said that every one is required to eat a peck of dirt during life — if that is all — several can excuse themselves to my credit — for I know that I have already consumed several pecks in advance of my allotment. The morning of the 7th found us again on the road 7 OC AM. plodding along the weary, dreary, uncertain road & after passing through Ripley 2 O.C. PM. & traveling five miles distant on the Pontatoc road, parked the guns in an old field. I didnot see those young ladies of whom I made mention of, as adorning the portico's, with their charming looks & golden curls, as we went north. I suppose they hid their beautiful faces in shame, not caring to witness our unfortunate retreat. The cause of our check, was the report that an attack upon our forces near Ripley with a large force of yanks was momentarily expected. Three Brigades of Infantry with sufficient artillery were dispatched with all haste possible to meet them. The trouble & excitement was all for nothing, the alarm was false, the troops returned, & our march was again taken up. Crossed the Tallahachie river & stopped at sundown to water, feed the horses & wait for our brigade (3rd Mo), then moved on until late in the night & parked the guns by the roadside, & after "wrapping ourselves" around some sweetpotatoes, a small ration of cornbread & broiled beef — laid down 2 O.C. AM. with orders to rise at 5 OC AM. Traveled 20 miles. We were so very tired that we could scarcely get to sleep, before being roused again, as the time for rising was curtailed one hour, as we had to move on the morning of the 8th at 4 O.C. AM. You would scarcely expect as man, kind reader, under such circumstances to rise up from his unfinished slumber, fall into line cheerfully & with a smile on his countenance answer to his name at roll call; yet we got our eyes open & "fell" into line in some shape, not always, without a "little murmur". Some of the Boys who were in the habit of swearing would utter a few "qualifying" adjectives. When we left camp that morning a very drowsy lot of men could have been seen, but our drooping spirits were very much revived when we received orders to camp 10 O.C. AM; & what pleased us still better there was some prospect of remaining until, the next morning — accordingly we unharnessed the horses & commenced cooking, as we left our former camp before having time to prepare breakfast. The Boys were busy around the bright messfires, preparing their frugal meal, when our hopes were all blasted, & from some unknown cause to me, (& perhaps to the man who gave it), an hour had scarcely passed, when the orders were given to hitch up & move out right away. We had something cooked & gathering our handsfull — crammed "red hot" — half done cornbread & beef down our necks burning as they went, at the same time loading the mess kit into the wagons, & making a few remarks about such "tomfoolery", that were far from being pleasant or complimentary, fell into our regular place, & all things considered made good progress.

Retreat Continued

Crossed the Tallahatchie river & camped a short time after night fall, in a cornfield — one consolation, our horses got plenty of feed, & sufficient time to eat it. Up to that time we had undergone many hardships, passed many days without a bite to eat & nights without closing our eyes for sleep, since leaving Saltilo to march upon Iuka; yet notwithstanding all this, the Boys were cheerful, there was always a joke to be passed, on a comrad, or a lively song to be sung by some one, on a march of this kind. They felt as though the best had been done, that could have been under the circumstances, & although, they had been somewhat out of humor & a little "wordy" at times — were consciencious in regard to the discharge of their whole duty as a soldier.

The Bugler roused the camp by blowing Reveille at daylight on the 9th, but we remained stationary until 4 O.C. PM, when the "machine" was again set in motion — & we were a tired lot of fellows, before reaching camp, on the morning of the 10th at 2 O.C. AM. The occasion for marching in this manner, so contrary to the habits & contraband to the health & happiness of the troops, was always a mystery unsolved by me, & perhaps a plausable excuse could not be given by those who issued the orders. This brought us to within 10 miles of Holly Springs Miss. a great watering resort & a place that was largely attended before the war. We remained in camp — which pleased us very much, for a cold rain commenced falling at 12 O.C. M & continued until night. We thanked the Lord, from the utmost depth of our hearts, that the prospects were good for an all nights sleep, for the first since leaving Ripley going to Corinth.

Retreat Completed

This was a gracious boon to us, & we were just in the right mode to receive such an one. The 11th day at morning roll-call, all the boys reported able for duty; & if you could have seen them around their messfires, eating a short time afterwards, would have been safe in judging them, blest with an appetite ample for at least double the rations they had. I was very much revived after a good nights' sleep, the air after the cool rain of the previous evening was very bracing, & being in a country where Chestnuts grew promiscuously & abundantly, & having a particular fondness for the fruit, took a tramp through the woods searching for them; but there were too many in the same notion that I was, to meet with very good or immediate success. however I was well paid for my trip as I tasted some fresh from the trees for the first in my life. Captain Landis received orders to take the guns to Jackson Miss, for repairs; as I remarked before in noting the casualties of our company after the battle of Corinth, our guns were all more or less battered up, & carriages shattered by shots of different descriptions from the enemies guns, rendering them unreliable & too weak for field service. Twenty one cannoniers were detailed to accompany them while in transit to & from the arsenal. The nights were cool but no frost at that time, which seemed rather strange to a North Missourian. The morning of the 12th was one which seperated the members of our company for a short time. This was not an occasion of great joy, I assure you, as we had been associated with each other so long, & in places under circumstances that were calculated to rivet the chains more closely, & had made us more than passing friends.

Holly Springs

According to orders received, we took the battery to Holly springs, & after loading it on the cars — leaving it in charge of the Captain & men detailed for that purpose, we the drivers took the horses & harness; & with the remainder of cannoniers, & baggage wagons, all under charge of our first Lieutanant, W. H. Weller, went south to camp 7 miles, on spring river, Where we found a very pleasant situation, wood in abundance & plenty of good & pure water near at hand. A rare treat for us. We anticipated a good time, & the record of subsequent events will show that our imaginings, were not over drawn. The 13th & 14th were spent lounging around in the sun like lizzards, passing the time as pleasantly as possible. Camp duty light, & plenty to eat & could sleep at pleasure, two of the greatest enjoyments of a Soldier. On the 15th our company purchased, Sixteen bushels sweet potatoes & turned them into our already overflowing commissary — this buying sounds a little queer, don't it? For we had been in the habit for some time previous, of getting them with out paying; just "reach over" the fence & take them; but when people were kind enough to bring them to us — were willing to pay.

False Alarm

About 11 OC. PM we were very suddenly aroused from our humble places of repose, & while we were perfectly bewildered as to the cause & rubbing our eyes open, the order was given to harness up, & be ready to move at a moments notice. This created a great excitement as well as discomfort. What could it be? The thought of being approached by an enemy, & as defenseless as we were at that time, was well calculated to produce a momentary demoralizing effect. But quiet soon established itself, when the alarm was found to be false, & we returned to our tents to finish our rest. The occasion of the trouble, was all on account of our acting brigadier Gen. getting a little too much "Red eye" & getting on the "war path". Some of the Boys offered up a few "prayers" (but not such as their good mothers taught them) that the next time he got full would explode before causing so much excitement.

Camp on Spring River Miss

The morning of the 16th was clear & bright, & after the drivers unharnessed their horses, & when the wreck, caused by the previous nights excitement was straightened around, all things wore the same monotonous appearance, yet I found plenty of employment through the day & one in which I took great pleasure. I wrote a letter to my old friends at Memphis Town. who so kindly took me from that murderous hospital, under their own roof, & nursed me with that kindness only eaqualed by Parental Care. Long & happy lives to such noble specimens of humanity is my heartfelt wish. I also wrote a letter home to my Dear Old Father. Although far away & very uncertain whether it would reach its destination, found great enjoyment in making the effort. The manner of writing as to quality & quantity was very much restrained not being allowed to write any contraband news & only one short page. This was pretty rough, but had to comply. About that time, I would have delighted very much in pouring out my thoughts on a half dozen pages — yes I could have filled a quire of foolscap & then not told half.

A quire equals one twentieth of a ream (24 or 25 sheets) of paper of the same size and stock. Foolscap paper measures approximately 13 x 16 inches. The term relates to the fool's cap with bells used as its watermark ("Foolscap"; "Quire").

Camp Near Waterford Miss

17th Fine weather continued, wood for cooking, & range getting a little scarce for our horses — moved camp one mile south on the river, stopping near Waterford Marshal Co Miss. This country was well supplied with all necessaries for a camp life. On the 18th one of our company Boys, Morgan & myself went out into the country on horseback to purchase Some butter, honey, or any other delicacies to which we were not accustomed, for our messes, but did not succeed in finding any thing but a bushel dried apples for which we paid $2.50. We were lucky enough to find one thing, for which we didn't have to pay — We "stuck our knees" under the table of a kind hearted Old Lady, & got a good "square" meal for the first in Miss, & returned to camp full to the "brim" of home like victuals. There was something noble about this old lady, quite different to some we found in our tramps. Our days ride was about 12 miles. so you can judge how scarce the articles for which we were hunting were at that time.

19th Sunday. I recorded it, for 'twas something unusual to know when the day come — This was the first time this day which was set aside so many centuries ago, as a day of rest, had been recognized by the name for sometime. When on the march we scarcely ever kept the day of the week, & I don't suppose I would have scarcely ever known the day of the month, had it not been for keeping a daily memoranda. When we were on the march one of the most infallible signs, or at least one from which the most convincing evidence could be gathered that such a day had again come around, was, the Darkies along the road all hanging on the yard fence, to see "de Soljers" pass; dressed in a clean homespun suit of cotton clothes, which they donned every Sunday morning.

Camp Near Waterford

This was a leisure, lazy day in camp — nothing to do but eat & lounge around in the beautiful sunshine of a mid autumn day, in the dear beloved sunny south, while talking to some Comrad of an event long since passed away, or if alone was thinking of the times, when I used to accompany my sweetheart to church, whisper a few words of love in her ears, & receive a bewitching smile as a sanction that my advances were favorably received; & often wished myself back to live it all over again; but alas! soon realized my situation, & with a sigh — almost uttered the sentence aloud, — perhaps ere this her heart's another's.

Camp 3rd Brigade

On the 20th the forage for horses becoming scarce in that section; the Stable sergeant was sent out to procure a better location, who returned in the evening with a favorable report; on the morning of the 21st moved camp 10 O.C. AM, one and a half miles farther down the river, turned the horses in a stalkfield — where there were plenty of corn, grass & water. A great relief, to have the horses where they could take care of themselves. Pitched our tents as quickly as possible, & in a few moments were all scattered over the woods hunting wild grapes & muscadines — which grew in abundance & were very delicious to taste. I ate about a "hat full" & returned to camp, satisfied for the time being. Our company formed a camp of itsself; some distance from the main army. Which was a great enjoyment; this was one feature in artillery to which I was very partial — we had more privilege in regard to camping, either on the march or when permanently situated — we were never crowded like Infantry or Cavalry. The name given to this general Rendezvous — was Camp 3rd Brigade. This name was given in honor of the 3rd Mo. Brigade. The 22nd day I spent in walking around — went to Waterford a station on the Memphis & Jackson railroad, & in order to find out what was going on generally, bought a paper — which stated, among other things that Gen. Bragg was falling back in the direction of Cumberland Gap Tenn. This news was not at all encouraging — but it seemed that such was the tenor, generally of the news from the

Army of the West. Some of our troops left Waterford. did not ascertain their destination. Thought, perhaps they were going to reinforce Bragg.

Our commissary department continued to fill us up with what we termed "luxuries," such as baked pork, pumpkin bread, sweet potatoes & beans, this was what we had on the "Bill of fare" for supper on the evening of the 23rd. This was good enough for a "home" Supper.

Camp Near Waterford

Our enjoyment was somewhat disturbed on the morning of the 25th by being cold & blustery — & still more so & greatly surprised, when about 2 O.C. PM commenced snowing & continued three hours — the wind blew very hard for a while, making it extremely disagreeable for all, & more especially for me, as my toes were protruding through the holes in my shoes, out into the snow, for the first time in my life. "Father" had been in the habit of furnishing shoes before my toes were "able to be out" — but he didn't happen to come around that time. I was only a boy there, but had to learn to look out for "No-one". The Old Citizens said that was an unusual cold "spell" for that climate & season of the year. This "snap" did not last long, the hard wind soon ceased, & by the morning of the 26th the snow had about all disappeared & this was Sunday again.

A Sunday's Ramble

The sun looked very bright as "he" ascended in the clear blue sky, while the cool bracing air was fanning back the fog & drying up the dew, which was dazzling in the sun's rays like so many diamonds. The morning was too beautiful to remain idle — & the forests too inviting for a ramble —to pass another day of "pleasure" like this one — in lounging around camp. I had but little trouble in finding two friends, who were as restless as myself, & we were soon engaged in earnest conversation — while strolling through the thick woodland & swamps, hunting for muscadines & grapes — then crossing the river & scaling the hills, helped ourselves to percimons & chestnuts until full & tired — "pulled" ourselves up — on an old rail fence to rest & "gass" awhile. This brought us in sight of a neat hewed log house, which appeared in the distance, across an old field — a unanimous consent & a soldiers "inquisitiveness", lead us in that direction - a short time intervened before the yard fence was reached, — hurriedly arranging our slouch hats, & ragged clothing, so as to appear as respectable as possible, mounted the low yard fence, & made rapid strides across the yard, closely pursued by three large dogs; stepping lightly upon the porch, made signals on the door for entrance, by rap rap-rap! After some delay by the Host; &

considerable uneasiness on our part — for the dogs were eying us with "blood" in their eyes — the door opened & we in obedience to the short invitation — "Co-min" by the man of the house, entered & seated ourselves before a bright blazing fire — in a fire place of huge dimensions. The room was very scantily, though neatly furnished, a bureau, clock, bed, a small mirror & a set of split-bottomed chairs made up the outfit. The old lady was seated in the corner, while the old man had just finished cutting from his "lantern" jaws a heavy crop of Sandy beard. All the persons we saw about the house, were one man & woman, who we supposed to be man & wife (about middle age) & I assure you, I have seen more pleasant & far better looking couples often. The man seemed very restless, & eyed us very suspeciously for a few moments, & without excusing himself, took his hat off the bed post — "Vamoused the ranch," leaving us with his wife. This very sudden disappearance, of our "host", created no little surprise in our minds — & a few sly glances & winks were passed between us — thought perhaps he had some "pals" hid out in the brush & would return by & by to try to take us in — but we didn't think of leaving with out a farther investigation. The Old lady who was looking through a large pair of spectacles, carelessly thrown across a "hook billed" nose of immense proportions, hurriedly arose, took her bonnet from a peg in the wall nearby; "threw" it on her noble "physing", pulling it well forward, to hide that grim look, which by many years practice had become indelibly stamped on her masculine countenance, & resumed her old "posish" in a low chair in the corner, at the same time using a snuff "swab" with great dexterity. This was very amusing to us, but we had to suppress our merriment. Many thoughts entered our minds, while the surroundings offered abundant food for conversation. Finally, one of the Boys ventured to break the spell, by asking the "Woman" if she had any dried apples to sell? Her words in answer were. No I haint! with as much emphasis, & as short as possible; at the same time "squirting" a big mouthful of tobacco juice extracted from the pulverized weed, behind the back log. This stumped the first querist & he seemed perfectly satisfied to remain quiet, & the second man thought to relieve him of his dilema, asked her, If she had any Socks to sell? Which she answered with another well directed shower of abbreviated monosylables. & to avoid any farther questioning, by her unwelcome visitors, added. I haint got nothing to sell! We haint got enough for the citizens let alone the Soldiers!!! The third man then spoke up, & said, boys let's return to camp this is no place for us, to which we all agreed & filed out of the door leaving the grim old Lady, "queen" of the household. The man did not appear on the scene while we were insight. I guess He thought us recruiting Officers, & fled.

Camp Near Waterford

The 27 found us yet in stationary camp & time of leaving uncertain. Nights cool & mornings frosty — but after sunrise a while — was pleasant. All nature had began to put on a dreary appearance the trees were stripping themselves of their verdant uniform, to don the cold & wintry garb, as if mourning for the loss which nature caused; the grass which sprung up as if by magic, & stretched its slender blades toward the Heavens, to lend its might to feed the hungry beasts & birds, has fallen prostrate to meet its inevitable fate — the beautiful flower & rose that so sweetly blooms o'er hill & dale, to distribute their delicious & mellow fragrance alike to all, upon the soft morning air; & nodded their tiny — downy heads to the passer by, were plucked from their tender stems, to nestle themselves away in the flowing golden curls of the daughters of Eve; or gave their short lives to adorn & perfume the homes of the rich as well as the poor, the pallace, as the most humble cabin — All! All! alike have bowed in the most humble submission & returned to Mother earth, the source from whence they came. Winter, would soon appear clothed with robes of ice & snow, in the North, while in our, adopted homes, the south, cold chilly rain will descend upon our unhappy & uncomfortable homes, making hard times for a soldier. But all such as this was mixed up in the life & adventures of one who took his chances on the tented field. On the 29th Sergeant Hance one of the men who went to Jackson, returned to camp, stated the guns would be ready for field sevice in about two weeks.

Bug washed out of ear

At that time, I was suffering from a very excruciating pain, caused from rising in my ear. Dr. Gough had shaved the hair from above & behind my ear, & drew a large blister by mustard plaster. He also provided me with a small, Syringe with which Caldwell had been washing it out for some time previous. The pain was very intense at times, would feel like the whole side of my head was decaying & for a night or so previous could not sleep — or rest in any position. But on the morning of the 30th the cause of the trouble was fully explained, when my Bro. was washing it out as usual. The bug which entered at Saltilo Miss was forced out together with a large quantity of corruption. This was the way the bug got out, that I had the Boys trying to "blow-out" at Saltilo. My ear although greatly relieved was very tender for some time afterward & the treatment with a syring & medicine was continued for awhile. but my hearing was never fully restored on that side.

Camp Near Waterford

Some prospects of paying the troops again, as our muster & payroll was inspected. Which caused all the boys to revive their somewhat drooping spirits — as it had been some time since "pay-day" & all our pockets were somewhat "Swinnied".

> **Sam draws a comparison from his background in animal husbandry. Swinn(e)y or sweeny is "atrophy of the shoulder muscles in the horse." To be sweenied, swinneyed, or swyneyed is to be "suffering from sweeny" ("Swinny").**

Nov 1st

On the 1st day of November Captain Landis returned from Jackson. We all gathered around him to hear the news, was glad to see him in good health & anxious to ascertain when the guns would arrive, felt as though we would like to see them again. Our duty was light & we endeavored to pass the time as pleasantly as possible. Bro. Caldwell & I took a hunt through the swamps for wild fruit & our labors were rewarded by the pleasure of finding plenty to eat. Our season of rest & plenty — or seperation from our guns, was lengthened out to a greater extent than expected but was highly enjoyed. Our Motto was, "Eat drink & be merry". for we could not tell how long our commissary would hold out good, or to what extent the brittle thread of life would be extended to us. On the night of the 5th about 12 OC M, all the Army, except our Company, received orders to prepare three days rations, & be ready to march at a moments warning. There being some prospects of a fight, as the yanks were advancing from the north with considerable force — the Infantry were issued fifty rounds of ammunition to the man. Before daylight the supply & baggage wagons commenced moving south in order to be clear of danger. It was a great surprise to us, to remain stationary & witness the long trains passing, & the teamsters applying the lash to the mule that dared to slacken his trace.

Moved to Near Abbeville

Couriers were galloping to & fro, while more or less excitement was depicted on the countenance of all. We thought there must be a wrong some where — were innocent as to the cause, & satisfied that we were not to blame. Every one who passed, would ask the question: What in the world are you "fellers" doing here, without guns, horses not harnessed &

yankees coming? The question was a "stumper" to us, & could only answer by saying, we had no orders to move. The trouble & delay was all caused by the negligence of the Courier who delivered the general moving orders, overlooking us. But when we finally received orders, no time was lost, we harnessed up & moved out, double quick, but the train had several hours the start, & we did not succeed in overtaking it the first day. We crossed the Tallahatchie river 10 OC AM. on the morning of the 6th. On the Southern bank we found some very formidable breastworks for infantry & artillery — which was of great value to defend the bridge & surrounding country. Arrived at camp about noon & found the wagons all parked & mules unharnessed. All of our Army remained near Holly springs to meet the enemy, who were supposed to be advancing in large numbers, to hear of them advancing was good news to our Gens. as they thought if we could succeed in drawing them some distance from their supplies, could fall upon them with such force & suddenness, a victory would be ours.

Camp Near Abbeville

At that time our camp was near Abbeville a small town on the railroad. On the 7th two Brigades of Infantry came to camp, while wagons loaded with supplies were sent back to the troops left to guard the rear. On Sunday 9th our forces fell back from Holly springs, to within a few miles north of the river. Gen. Price established his headquarters in Abbeville. Affairs for a few days, were a monotonous appearance, Forest's men amused themselves by hacking away at the Fed's Cavalry between Holly springs & Corinth. On the 12th we were still in camp, not much prospects of moving & but little of fighting. Had some rain, which was very disagreeable to me, as I was almost barefooted, & the prospect of drawing any shoes from the army quartermaster was very slim; but fortunately for me, I had some money, & that evening an Army Huxter stopped at our camp from whom I bought a pair of medium weight boots for which I paid him $35.00 in Confederate money. This I thought to be a very extravagant price — but he had "war license", you know, & his conscience left him, when asked the price of anything, that he thought the purchaser was compelled to have, & when he "struck" me was satisfied, a case of necessity had appeared — we soon traded — for I would rather by far, have an empty pocket book, than a bare foot in the cold mud. We spent several days in camp at this place, with but little change in affairs, of any kind. Had some Cavalry fighting near the Springs, with but little damage done to either side. The health of the troops was generally good, & as a rule when a Soldier was blest in that respect, was jolly & happy.

Return of guns

On the 29th our guns returned, on the cars, looking as nice as "new pins", & the Boys who went with them all fat & saucy. We were glad to see our old guns again, it made us feel that we had something to do — if military affairs had remained so quiet, as they were for some time after going into camp south of the springs on Spring river, we could have been well satisfied, but when we saw the other troops, drawing ammunition & moving to the front to meet the invading foe — while we took the back track with the baggage train; did not feel as though we were doing our whole duty — although obeying orders. We unloaded the guns & took them to camp nearby, & having orders to move farther south, busied ourselves making all needed preparations. Captain Landis Started to Atlanta Ga. After harness for the Artillery horses, also ammunition. Some skirmishing beyond the river. The Feds advanced very slowly & cautiously, feeling their way with a heavy advance guard of cavalry. On the 30th our forces north of the river, fell back to Ebenizer Church about eight miles north of our camp, where they halted & formed a line of battle, to resist the Feds who after recruiting with a large force, were now advancing in earnest, with all field arms represented. Our troops defended their position with great spirit & bravery — until convinced that further resistance, would entail too great loss; & knowing it would be very hazardous to contend against such overwhelming numbers; took refuge behind the breastworks on the south bank of the Tallahatchie river. The Feds did not follow up, & was well for them, as we were amply prepared to defend ourselves against great odds. One of Capt. Beldsoe's guns (Con. Mo. Battery) was disabled in the engagement. Our loss, all told was trifling. The stand made by our men at the Church, was only offered as a bait, to draw them into the net we have woven for their accomodation, & cripple them so badly they would not care to pursue us any father south. But they soon became aware that to attempt any farther advance on that road was impracticable, & commenced flanking, & our forces being so much less than theirs, were compelled to abandon the works, without being recompensed for our labors, as a means of defense.

Dec
Commenced Retreating

All the Infantry & artillery, left camp at daylight on the morning of Dec 1st, moving southward on the retreat. Our company was again left "out in the cold", & completely dumbfounded, as everything being on the move, &

we in camp & no orders to do otherwise than remain. I suppose we probably had been overlooked, on account of being without guns for some time previous, & camping to ourselves; but now that we were ready & willing to share alike with the balance on the advance as well as retreat, were feeling very much slighted. About 9 OC AM a courier came galloping up — informing us that we were in the rear except Cavalry.— This completely stunned our sensibilities, for a while & being under the impression, that we had been over looked intentionally — gave vent to our feelings, in words that were far from being praiseworthy exclamations, for the person or persons through whose negligence our delay was caused. But, talking would not move us, we had to act; & that quickly, & as soon as could possibly be done — the horses were harnessed & hitched, messkit & baggage loaded in the wagon; moved out through the mud & rain to follow up the army already several miles in advance. We had a great many impediments to contend with — some of the horses with which we recruited our company in the absence of our guns, had never been harnessed before — some never rode, & a great many wouldn't pull the "hat off your head", were continually balking & stalling on every hill.

Retreat Continued

The roads had become very muddy from being stirred by constant travel — cannoniers had to put their shoulders to the wheels in many places, while standing in mud almost knee deep. Times looked some what squally & very discouraging — the horses wouldn't "scare worth a cent" — if the Feds were in close proximity. This was pretty rough on us — after lounging around, & doing as we pleased so long — however we had done such work before & could do it again. Passed through Oxford Miss 8 O.C. AM. & our gun stuck in the mud on a hill in the edge of the Village, where we remained all night without anything to eat for horse or man & no place to sleep. The other guns being more fortunate, moved on one & a half miles before camping. The yanks didnot loose any time in following us up, as they arrived in the camp we left 2 OC PM, & we were mired to the hub in clay as tough as gumbo — only 10 miles from where we started. The morning of the 2nd was cold, & rain continued regardless of the poor condition we were in to receive it, & the half starved horses, shivering & stamping around in mud & water up to their knees. As soon as the gray streaks of dawn began to appear in the east, making sufficient light, we hitched up, & after splashing & prizing around in the mud quite awhile succeeded in getting out — moved to camp, where after eating a very small breakfast & feeding the horses, moved on with the rest of the battery —

having to contend with the same barriers as on the day previous, only worse — some times our horses balked on level road.

Crossed the Leochnapatopha river on an old rickety bridge.

> **Sam's brother Caldwell wrote in his diary about crossing the same river, but he spelled it Yocanapatafa. Contemporary maps of Mississippi do not register a river by either name. Fans of writer William Faulkner will recall his fictional Yoknapatawpha County was featured in a majority of his novels. Faulkner pulled this name from the lazy, muddy Yockneypatafa River found on the old maps of Lafayette County, Mississippi. According to historian Patricia Young of Oxford, Mississippi, the river has had many spellings, and no source exists that might name them all. The current pronunciation lightly stresses the "yock" sound of the first syllable. Sam's misunderstood the first syllable to be "lock." Mrs. Young stated that some events in the area still capitalize on the "antique, presumably Indian name, but today the river is called the Yocana River" ("Southern Roots"; "The Yocona"; Young).**

The river was very much swollen from continual rains & the side to which we crossed was low & swampy — rendering our travel farther very perilous & almost impossible, as night had already set in & the immense forest of tall cypress & dense fog that appeared; looked as if night had put on an extra robe of darkness. We had a small allowance of rice & mush for supper. All day & a portion of the night was consumed, & we only traveled 8 miles & we used all the strength, energy & management at our command. I know kind reader, you will sympathize with one confronted with such unavoidable obstacles ~~confronting them~~, while having but little to eat & clothing wet through making it impossible to get a good nights sleep, — if we had an opportunity. The morning of the 3rd was almost "lost in the fog" & drowned, when the light dawned upon us, in that dreary & dismal swamp — as it was yet raining; & we imagined ourselves almost too weak to make an effort toward moving — as we had nothing to eat. But we were soon brought to a realization of our predicament, & nerved to try it again — when Gen. Maurey, who was in command of the rear guard came upon us — informing the Lieutenant that we would be in the rear, unless a move was made quickly. His orders were immediately obeyed, but our progress was very slow, the horses were very weak not having had anything to eat since the previous morning. This was a trip long to be remembered by those who participated in the fatigues & dangers.

Gen. Dabney Herndon Maurey had been dismissed from service on the frontier for "treasonable designs" in June 1861. The next year, he was serving as Chief of Staff to Gen. Van Dorn in the Trans-Mississippi Department. He was appointed brigadier general after the battle of Pea Ridge and was serving with the Army of the West at the time of Sam's memoir entry (Boatner III 519).

The Feds had succeeded in throwing a small squadron of Cavalry on our left front, which harassed our movements for a while. A short time after dark, we passed within a fourth of a mile of a federal camp, & "you bet" we walked & talked light. Our orders were to move along with as little noise as possible, & as luck would have it, the ground over which we had to pass, under such cramped & dangerous circumstances, was a little down hill. Although moving along in a moderate walk, it seemed that we were almost stationary, but as the distence lengthened ~~out wider~~ between us & the light of the Federal camp fires.— My hair which had assumed an upright position, settled back to its propper place & heart resumed its usual vibrations. Passed through watervalley, a small railroad station, & camped nearby at midnight, after traveling 12 miles.

In 1847, the post office and stagecoach depot at Ragsdale's Stand, Mississippi, moved to William Carr's land and the name of the post office became Water Valley. The town is located in north central Mississippi in Yalobusha County, once the land of Choctaw and Chickasaw Indian tribes. Yalobusha is a native American word which means "tadpole place" ("Yalobusha").

Retreat Continued

Cooked & eat supper, or what ever you would term the name, which was a great enjoyment, & when furnished with plenty, was a privilege worthy of record. This left us but little time for sleeping, but we were like hungry children, slept better on a full stomach. A short engagement occured just before dark north of town, between a small body of the enemy & our Cavalry, which resulted in a defeat to the pursuers.

On the 4th our slumbers were brought to a sudden close, by the shrill notes of the bugle sounding reveille at 3 OC AM.— short nap eh?— & we had scarcely succeeded in getting our eyes open sufficient to cook & eat a few bites, until ordered to move on in our wild & troublesome career. It seemed so strange that we should always be on the retreat, or meet with defeat in every general engagement; while the Virginia army held their ground, & at almost every engagement, could inscribe another victory for the south on their banners. Had it not been for sending away troops at Waterford, to reinforce some other point, we could have held our position near Holly springs & avoided such a disagreeable & expensive retreat. And maybe we could have lettered our banners with victory! Most of the country through which our days march extended, was well adapted to cultivation, & some of the planters had a considerable quantity of last summers crop of cotton stored away in jin houses — & all of which, that could not be taken away, was burned — this lookd hard, to see the blue volumes of smoke, rising up all over the country, but was far better than suffer it to fall into the enemies hands. Passed through Coffeeville one mile & camped on a small creek. Some of the Boys as they passed, through town, provided themselves with a quantity of "rifle" whiskey, on which the most "greedy" ones soon got "gloriously" drunk. I called it rifle — because it took effect almost as quick as a gun. Some of them caused trouble for a while, but after tearing around until tired, coiled up to sleep & by next morning were alright. On the forenoon our rear guard repulsed the yanks at Watervalley, but little loss reported on either side as the Feds "Skedaddled" too soon.

Retreat Continued

Our horses being a little better accustomed to work & country more level, the distance traveled was greater than usual, traveling 12 miles. On the 5th the same old song, rain! rain! could have been sung very appropriately, for there seemed but little sign of a note being missed. Moved out 6 OC. AM, & our march met with but little drawback until the afternoon, we met a train of cars, where the distance between the highway & railroad was very narrow, the horses became badly frightened, & the road being crowded with men, came near crippling several, before they could be controlled, however, after mending a few trifling breaks in the harness, moved on as quietly as before down toward the Yalabusha river. The country was level & the larger portion in cultivation & the tastefully built dwellings dotted here & there denoted the inhabitants to be an industrious thriving people. The river was somewhat swollen by recent rains — making the point where we forded ~~it~~ about sixty feet wide.

Crossing of the Yalabusha river

While crossing, the horse on which I was riding, when in water about three feet deep near the middle of the stream — fell sprawling on his left side, as quickly as if he had been shot, & as flat as he could well be, the fall was so sudden & unexpected, that I didnot have time to think, before my left leg was firmly imbedded in the sand under the horse, & foot fastened in the stirrup, & to make my chances to escape more uncertain & add weight to hold me under the current, I had on an old jacket or two to keep me dry, which were already petty well saturated by rain before hand. The old horse was greatly fatigued by the long & muddy march of the last several days, & could scarcely regain his feet in the deep water. This was a dilema in which I never had any anxiety to be in again. I did a "heep" of thinking, but could not utter a word; all the good acts as well as mean ones, passed "like a flash" in panoramic view before my excited imagination; I thought sure my last bath had come, the last reckoning on earth was near; the end was fast approaching whether ready to meet it or not. 'Tis horrible to think of a watery grave. I can almost tell the feelings that one experiences — for I've been on the "edge" & "peeped over". The depth of the water rendered it impossible to get relief by placing my hands on the bottom & hold my head above water — but under the circumstances, all that I could do was to make an endeavor, for the old horse lay like a log, I began to think he surely had dropped dead — Finally — although but a moment — the time seemed an age — the old horse commenced struggling for breath, this gave me a chance to pull my foot out, & after kicking, splashing & clawing around for sometime, got on my "pins" again. The Boys were all too busily engaged in taking care of themselves, & didnot notice or realize the great danger that had befallen me, until I had relieved myself from the trap — one of them sprang to my assistance & lead me out as wet as a "rat".

The greatest damage that I sustained besides this wetting, was tearing the sole off one of my $35.00 boots. The old horse struggled to his feet & was lead to shore by one of the boys. A Louisiana artillery company, who always claimed us as their particular friends in camp on the march or in battle; had crossed a short time previous, & one of them had succeeded in getting a canteen filled with whiskey at Grenada a short distance from the river, & hearing of the misfortune that had happened one of his Mo. friends — came riding back toward the river, (by this time I was some distance from the crossing) enquiring, where is that man who got the "ducking"? He is one of our old stand by's! & I've got something that will do him good. He gave me the canteen from which I took a great big horn! which I assure you was taken with a relish — for I was very cold & numb, & returning the canteen to him. He insisted very much that I should drink more, remarking, It will do you good! Thanking him kindly for his generosity & freeheartedness — we seperated for that time, but met on several subsequent occasions, to add another link of friendsip to the chain which had been woven at Yalabusha ford. One of the boys went to the baggage wagon a short distance ahead, & got me a dry suit of clothes, which I donned in a hurry. After passing through Grenada, camped south one mile. During the day we traveled 14 miles. The circumstances at the river was unavoidable, yet very dangerous. It was only a mirical that I escaped as well as I did — & after the lapse of a quarter of a century — to bring back the scene at the Yalabusha, a fresh in my memory? Tis only necissary to ride a horse into deep water. I have always had an inclination to avoid that kind of water ever since. Considerable fight at Coffeeville – yanks badly whipped. This was a great satisfaction to us, although too far away to render assistance – only in rejoicing.

Near Grenada

On the morning of the 6th the sun shone out brightly for the first time since the march from Abbeville began. "Old sol" was a welcome visitor, every thing that was not thoroughly water proof was soaked & muddy. After breakfast I went to Grenada & had my boot mended, the damage caused by the previous days "wreck". This little city is pleasantly situated near the Yalabusha river a beatiful stream, when not fretted by excessive rain, which meanders, slowly along through the tall thick forests of Cypress & gum, as if selecting its course toward the Father of waters. After returning to camp 8 O.C. AM harnessed my horses, & the company moved on south overtook the Brigade 4 O.C. PM. Camped in comfortable quarters — Pitched our tents in an open field, suppered on sweet potatoes, pork, cornbread & burned corn meal "coffee". —

Cornmeal was one of a multiple number of items such as acorns, rye, potatoes, and chicory that could be roasted and ground as a substitute for coffee (Heidler and Heidler 1606-7).

Quite an extended bill of fare, & several times on our muddy march, which had just ended, would have been highly pleased to have been furnished one of the above named articles, and when the hour for retiring arrived — I did not wait for the bed to "come around" — but gathered a pile of leaves spread my blanket, & tumbled in, sleeping all night as soundly as a new born babe — felt as bright as a "bran new dollar" when awakened by reveille next morning — In fact almost imagined myself at home, everything being so much more comfortable & pleasant, than that to which I had been accustomed for some time. Moved eleven miles — this made our camp 12 miles south of Grenada, Caroll Co Miss. The 7th we remained in camp. Everything seemed to have put on a quiet appearance, especially up north a little ways — The yanks were as still as mice.

12 Miles South of Grenada

On the 8th a portion of the time was taken up in moving camp one mile down the river, to a nice camping ground. On the 9th we had a partial review. The first Mo brigade was the only infantry out. The artillery was represented by several batteries — ours among them. Maj Gen. Bowen was the reviewing Officer.

Gen. John S. Bowen was wounded at Shiloh, but recovered in time to participate in the Vicksburg campaign (Boatner III 75).

We had some ladies in attendance to witness our maneuvers, which I often thought was of great benefit to us — as their presence had a tendency, to make us more tidy in appearance & courteous in our manners. But, was almost inveriably the case, as on this occasion, some good looking ones appeared on the scene, & this always "melted" a soldier's heart right down; sometimes causing him to get out of line or step, a little & suffer a rebuke from an Officer for his carelessness. The 11th was a pleasant day, & something happened, which caused many glad countenances & full pocetbooks, in day time, & sad faces & empty "weasel skins" during the night.

An animal can be case skinned without cutting the pelt, but leaving it whole to form a pouch for carrying items. Weasel skins are small, making them a good size for carrying money.

We received four months wages ($48.00) But the circulation of the money was greatly curtailed before sunrise the next morning. Any one in camp at that time, could have satisfied themselves that this assertion is true, & could have substantiated the fact, by peeping in at the door of a tent — & seen by the dim light of a candle or torch — some of the Boys sitting around a blanket, spread on the ground — a pile of corn by each one, for chips — hats pulled down over their eyes "looking wise" — at a hand of cards before them — or "winking" at their partners — & occasionally you could see one, reach to the center of the "board" — & with the remark, that's my "pot" — rake in the stakes. Many poor fellows, would be "strapped" — not a cent of their wages left — in less than twelve hours after being paid off, & compelled to borrow or beg from a friend until the next payday, which you will notice from dates were "few & far between". To watch others loose their money was fun enough for me — to be a silent looker on in such cases — I considered the best policy; & I kept my pledge — they never got a cent of money from me in that manner. "Evil communications corrupt good manners." In like manner; a bad practice, desires company; when one is installed, another is ready for initiation — & when thoroughly engrafted, requires more nerve to abolish one than to ward off a dozen to which you are a stranger.

Camp Rogers Caroll Co. Miss 12. M. South of Grenada

This rendezvous was christened Camp Rogers, & you will observe from the further perusal of my records that we did a great many things while stationed here, which were not included in the regular routine duty of a soldier, & any one who has participated in the life consequent to a permanent camp or winter quarters of an army — I hope will not think me encroaching too greatly on the more noble qualities of a Soldier — or too pointed in my remarks when I assert, that there never was a better place to bring out the real disposition, & portray the most characteristic points of man's nature. I have often thought it opened the best field in the world for the study of human nature or would give the mind reader boundless scope to apply his science & cunning.

Many who had been brought up to early manhood by Christian Fathers & brothers & taught in youth to know the duty — & follow in the path of morality — had an evil disposition acting as an under current which had only been kept in subjection, by the constant surroundings of Christian influences; now in the absence of such, broke forth in ungovernable bubblings, to satiate their greed in all the vices & immoral surroundings. Some were ignorant, indolent, filthy & of a general shiftless nature, & when their life as a Citizen previous to the war could be ascertained, "nine times out of ten" the lives they lived on the tented field, was a perfect duplicate; may be a little worse for perhaps in times of peace they had been accustomed to being cared for by some kind relative. A Soldiers comfort, (if he had any) depended largely on his own doings.

Camp Rogers

We had not been in camp a sufficient length of time to commence drill — yet several days rest afforded us considerable recuperation, from our long arduous march, & we had began to grow restless — many things sugjested themselves to ward off the monotony of camp life, & for a little recreation on the morning of the 12th one of our company boys, Charles Marent, proposed that he, Caldwell & myself take a hunt. To which we willingly consented; & after Marent had procured an old condemned army musket, the old "piece" used as a company safeguard to keep at bay, "fighting hogs", Caldwell & I with an ax — started off through the swamps at a lively pace — at the same time annoyed by the taunts & jeers of our messmates — with such expressions as "Fishermans luck" etc etc. After we had left the camp some miles in our rear, & becoming some what foot weary from tramping around through the swamps & marshy lands of the Yalabusha river, sat down on an old moss covered log to rest, for a few moments but our rest was of short duration — One of our party espied a young coon playing around in some grape vines hanging from a tall cypress tree, a short distance from where we were seated.

A Coon Hunt

We were soon at the tree, when Marent put the "Old trusty" musket to his shoulder, & as the deafening roar of the immense charge of powder reverberated through the swamps, Marent attained his equlibrium & the smoke cleared away sufficiently to see — discovered one coon tumble to the ground. The firing was kept up until three of the "ring tailed" monsters of the hen roost, were on the ground & the fourth lodged in the vines. Not knowing to what extent the tree was inhabited by these midnight ramblers — concluded to fall it ~~the tree~~, as it was too large to climb; Shed our jackets, & by turns plied the ax, after more than an hours hard chopping — the top commenced wavering, & in the absence of dogs two of us stood picket with uplifted clubs & glaring eyes, while the third used the ax with all his might — but to our great surprise when the tree fell, the war was over, our game was all dead, the old ones were gone. After resting a short time Caldwell & I suggested a return to camp. Marent being more disposed to ramble — was not yet satisfied — said he would take the gun & hunt for a short time, while we if preferable could take the four coons & ax, & return to camp. The last half of the evening was pretty well consumed, thick clouds o'erspread the sky, from which a fine mist was descending through the tall boughs of the cypress, from which was dangling the moss in long silky shreds, to meet the immense fogg rising from the surrounding swamps & ponds of stagnate water, where the toad wallowed in filth & slime uttering his shrill screams, to mingle with the sweet melodies of the lonely whippoorwill as he perched himself on the branch of a weeping willow near by. Well, we seperated & according to the previously arranged programme, divided our burdens as eaqually as possible, and started as we supposed in the direction of camp. Our travel was uninterrupted for some time; the distance between us & the coon tree seemed to be increasing very fast, we feeling so much elated on our success in so short a time, hastened on to tell the good news to our comrads — not taking the time or precaution to survey the surroundings until sometime had elapsed — in fact "Old Sol" had just about consumed all the time allotted him, to complete the days journey; we began to think we had traveled far enough to be near camp, finally we stopped & held a hurried consultation, the sound of axes as the men were preparing wood for the evening meal could be heard in the distant camps — the sharp notes of the bugle sounding stable call, the neigh of the horses & bray of the mules mingling in one confused mass, rang in our ears; finally we heard a noise! one we seemed to recognize as a familiar one, & said, That's our company!! let's go that way; so on & on our wearied limbs carried us, & the echoes as they proved to be, came no nearer. At last, after several miles travel, we very reluctantly came to the conclusion, that we were lost, & as such cases generally terminates, under such circumstances, after an other vain attempt to find our way, came up to the Identical tree for which we had fallen to get the coons. Well, kind reader were you ever in a cypress swamp? if ~~you~~ you never have been — when ever you see one, you will not be so much amazed, at two North Missouri Boys loosing their way who had never seen one previous to that — I tell you every tree looks alike, the huge roots of one is an exact duplicate of its neighbor which stands in close proximity, the thick undergrowth interwoven with muscadine vines & briars of all kinds, have a great tendency to misguide the already confused traveler.

Not Yet found

We were seated side by side on the trunk of the old coon tree, conversing in earnest under tones, in regard to our bewildered situation. But having become habituated to disappointments, by our experience in "rough & tumble" life — had about concluded to spend the night, listening to the hoo! hoo! Owl, or the lonesome song of the whipporwill. We did not need a Mothers lullaby then to put us to sleep, or a feather bed on which to dream — no! Hush! What's that? I hear someone's foot steps coming through the brush! They are coming toward us! — in an instant later, the familiar voice of Marent, was heard in greatly surprised tones, as he exclaimed W'y Boys! I thought you had gone to camp? We thought so too! but didnot quite make the trip was the subdued reply. At first we denied the real cause of our predicament, saying we just thought, we'd rest until he finished his hunt. But our countenances betrayed us, & his looks showed that our story was disbelieved — & believing in the old adage — "an open confession good for the soul" acknowledged that we were lost. However we were cautious enough to obligate him not to tell the boys in camp. After a short rest Marent remarked, let's be going boys; night is almost upon us. We staggered again to our wearied feet to follow our deliverer, with feelings intermingled with joy & doubt. Joy, because our friend had come ~~to~~ in the moments of despair, & proposed to lead us, out of this troubled situation as Moses did the Isrealites when under Egyptian bondage. Doubt, as to his ability to do so, as we had experienced eaqual confidence within ourselves, but a few hours previous, when we started out for camp. But we were soon aware that he knew just what he was doing, & where he was going — having been reared in the south was more familiar with the swamps than us. A short time after night fall, we wearily trudged into camp, & piled the fruits (four coons) of our days hunt before the mess fire; & you ought to have seen the surprised look & glaring eyes of our mess mates, remembering their prophecies & fun at our expense when we left camp on the memorable coon hunt — true — we were "wet" but had plenty of game "all the same". The boys were all willing enough to assist us, & the coons were soon skinned & dressed ready for the "pot". But those best posted in regard to the character of such meat, thought best to let them hang out all night in order to get off — the "coon smell". So the cooking was posponed until the morrow. For our noonday meal on the 13th the coons were cooked in the most magnificent style our limited means afforded, with sweetpotatoes & brown gravy. I had often heard ~~of~~ the old darkies at home, talking about what a delicious dish — "de possum & sweet-taters" were (I always took their word for it) but we had coon & "taters" & "you bet" we helped ourselves until the skillet was sopped dry; as we had almost uncontrollable appetites for "something fresh". This was my first mess of coon, & I guess will be the last unless I am caught in "Rome" again.

Camp Rogers

Our commanding officers, thinking it probable that our "stay" at this place would be indefinite, thought it advisable to move camp — & on the 14th we moved camp about half mile, to the edge of an old field, in a beautiful grove of scrub oak & hickory — plenty of good wood & water for mess purposes nearby. The major part of the army was also reviewed — our battery did not attend, as our horses, needed rest more than exercise. The principal portion of the weather, since our retreat closed, had been wet & gloomy, many days the sun did not appear at all. I remember one of our men by the name of Phelps had a mule which he drove to one of the company baggage wagons, while here tied to the picket rope, would go forward as far his halter would permit, then back in same proportion, until the mud & slosh was more than knee deep, then his driver would give him a fresh place, for a similar repetition. It was very amusing to me, & strikingly strange, to notice with what exactness & regularity he plied his avocation. I suppose the mule had become accustomed in former days, to this almost continual motion by being used in some Planters cotton gin, as in antebellum days the majority of that class of machinery was driven by the tread wheel power.

> **A traditional tale gives credit for the invention of the cotton gin to Eli Whitney's witnessing a cat clawing a chicken through cracks in the walls of a coop and retriving a paw full of feathers. The word gin is drawn from the word *engine.* Originally the small gins were powered by hand and horses or water wheels powered the larger ones ("Cotton gin").**

Although the weather for several successive days was very unfavorable overhead & underfoot — the troops were becoming extremely restless, a great many were not content with coon hunting or fishing, saying too much work for such a little pay; would slip up to a chicken roost when night had pulled down her sable curtain, while the owners of the fowl were asleep & use their utmost cunning to change their roosting place without interrupting the rest of the slumberers; or occasionally drag in a hog, without giving value-received, sometimes one of the boys would find some bacon that he thought was cured sufficiently for use, or a pit of sweet potatoes holed up for family use, frequently ~~then~~ pick up & walk off with a bee hive. These occurrances were becoming too common, & the citizens made complaint to the commanding Officers, & they decided to give the men something to do & issue stringent orders to punish every man who committed a crime, according to the gravity of such offense. The whole army commenced drilling. Our company had field drill in the forenoon & park drill in the afternoon five roll calls every day, & every man had to be in ranks to say here, or have an awful good reason for his absence filed with the orderly Sergeant, or messmate.

On the 24th we had a grand review of the army at this place. Our horses, shoulders were in such bad condition, we did not attend in a body, a few of us attended as spectators, "by permission". Pres. Davis & Gen.

Joseph. E. Johnston were the special visitors & reviewing Officers; who were well pleased with the general appearance of the troops. A eulogy from such dignitaries as these was very encouraging. The nice appearance was not so surprising, for we had been warned a few days previous to the advent of these noble old patriots. Long life to such Leaders, was the unanimous Shout.

Gen. Joseph Eggleston Johnston began a feud with President Jeff Davis in July 1861 over his status in the Confederacy. He was relieved of duty and replaced by Robert E. Lee after being wounded at Seven Pines. He returned for duty in November 1862 as commander of the Department of the West. Johnston's promise as a commander failed to bring results, as he repeatedly surrendered ground the South could not afford to lose. In 1891, Johnston died of pneumonia ten days after braving the bitter cold at William Tecumseh Sherman's funeral procession. He had refused to wear a hat out of respect for his former foe (Boatner III 441; Flagel 239-40).

Some preperation made for Christmas. There was some whiskey – as a great many thought the day "too dry" with out a "wee drop" to stimulate the inner man. Our mess "went dry". The company commissary went to Grenada where purchased a gallon of "pine top" (as we called it) for which he paid $40.00 Confederate money, & after testing it a time or so, started on his return to camp very jubilant over the "heep" of fun that he had corked up in the "little brown jug". He had not traveled very far until all of a sudden he was halted by a man on horse back, with gold lace around his collar & cuffs, sabre dangling by his side, who proved to be the Provost Marshall, & notwithstanding the earnest pleadings offered by the owner of the jug — the whiskey was poured on the ground. Well if you'd a been there or any where near when that commissary returned to camp — you would have imagined he had the contents of two jugs in him, from the manner in which he used ungrammatical quallifying adjectives to express the great disgust he had for that inhuman Marshall.

The southern slang term "pine-top," meaning cheap illicit whiskey, was first recorded in use in 1858 (Harper).

According to the *American Heritage Dictionary of the English Language*, a provost marshall is "the head of a unit of military police."

Christmas

The morning of the 25th was ushered in by an early roll call. We awoke from our dreams of happy days gone by, to roll our eyes up & spy the old familiar weather beaten tent. We could scarcely realize that this day was another anniversary of our Savior, that we had once been accustomed to celebrate the birth of one so grand & precious to all the world; our surroundings were so different, as in past days although we had gathered up sufficent "grub" for an extra feast, yet the little stockings filled with candy & nuts dangling from the old mantle, for the little ones; that bunch of firecrackers stuck away under the pillow of the sleeping boy, the tingle of the sleigh bells, the merry laughter of the happy girls & boys, as the panting horses went plowing through frost & snow — no this could only be imagined as an absent pleasure. But instead of being permited to get up at will, were awakened from our dreams, by the familiar notes of the bugle sounding reveille — & if we did not make our appearance almost immediately, the orderly sergeant would poke his head into the tent door & yell out wake up! roll out!! tumble out!! or any way to get out & fall into line. Well we wore out the day as best we could, eating, lounging around telling stories — the man who could "spin" the longest & funniest, received the "head mark". When night came on, we cleaned off a piece of ground as the boys used to, for a marble yard, & as most of us were familiar with the old style cotillion dance, concluded to amuse ourselves a while by what we termed "stag" dancing. We had a kind of "one horse" fiddler" belonging to our company by the name of Phelps (by the way, he was the man who drove the restless mule of which I gave a desciption) & he too was a decided mimic, sometimes he would make a hand organ of himself, by using a portion of his person as a crank, imitating the music with his voice, at the same time yelling, ten cents! admission.

Christmas Dance

Our dancing "hall" was soon lighted up by some dry wood prepared for the purpose. Phelps tuned up his old greasy violin — the choice of partners commenced, those acting as girls, wore something to denote their "sex". A short time intervened before the set was pronounced full, & at the first stroke of the bow, then the call rang out, "all hands up & circle to the left"! to see the broad smile that played across the countenances of those rugged boys, spoke of the great joy within & how glad they were to live in imitation of Christmas at home. I often think how well my poor friend Welch (who afterwards died at Atlanta Ga) enjoyed this occasion. Music had a great power over him, & dancing his favorite amusement. Our fun extended in to the morning hours — we had to hurry to catch a short nap before roll-call.

On the 28th Sunday morning, orders were given to review. One regiment 3rd Mo. Inft. commanded by Col Gowe, stacked arms & refused to go out. They claimed that too much of that kind of business had already been done; they were tired of reviews, drilling & tight reins; but the officers couldn't see it that way. Gen. Greene made them a long, pathetic & Sympthetic speech, earnestly pleading with them to return to ranks & be good soldiers, & not soil the fair name & fame so dearly won on the many bloody fields. They all responded except Co. A. who were marched to Gen. Price's headquarters — when the Old Veteran came forward His bald head gleaming in the sunlight; with the inquiry — what's the matter here? The cause was soon explained, & the power of speech was again tried at some length, by that noble & chivalrous old soldier, with the same result as before. As a last resort with tears almost approaching, a heart filled with sorrow to overflowing. he made this proposition. Those of you who wish to return to your regiment & be good & obedient soldiers; step to the right! those who do not, step to the left — & I will have the last of you shot, in less than ten minutes!! They all knew that "old Pap" ment every word he said — & stepped quickly to the right, & marched back & took their respective place in the old regiment.

Camp Rogers

Although the time for which they had enlisted, run over a few days, I donot suppose any of them ever entertained the idea of quitting the service, & to show a disposition to mutinize at that particular time, was looked upon as very disgraceful — a stigma upon their fair name & all Missourians that ages could not obliterate. Another reason for regretting such a move, the reports received from all parts of the Confederacy were very favorable, the brightest side of the picture, was before us; many being impressed with the belief, that e're the lapse of another year, the south would gain a lasting victory over her enemies.

Although this was ~~the Sabbath~~ Sunday, a day set apart, as a day of rest, by One who created all things, was one of great commotion in our camp, when things in general had attained their common equilibrumn, after the excitement of the morning — chaos was again produced about 3 O.C. in the afternoon, by the reception of an order to cook three days rations immediately & be ready to move at a moments warning. This afforded another wide field for speculation & excitement, but we always had a few "smart alecks" around the camp, who could tell us just what it was done for, the destination of the army etc etc. Well — after an hour or so of bustle & "pot slinging", the order was revoked — immediately a broad "grin" lit up the countenances of all the boys, & the remainder of the Christmas holidays passed as agreeable as the first.

Camp Rogers

During our stay at this camp, a great many men were sworn into the confederate service, for three years or during the war — for which each of them received $50.00 bounty. As a kind of slur, this transaction was termed selling out to Jeff Davis, but we were already in his possession, this only compelled us to remain as long as hostilities continued.

1863

Enlisted for 3 yrs. or during the war

Bro. Caldwell & I did not view it in that light, & although the time had expired for which we had sworn to serve the south at, Vanburen Arkansas, yet we having fully determined to remain in the south as Soldiers — on the 2nd day of January 1863, took the Oath & "pocketed" the money, which came in good play to buy peanuts & sweet "tater" pies. A short time prevous to Christmas, most of the messes in the company built log cabins — the walls of small — gum, pine & ash sapplings & covered with boards made of cypress — which was made very comfortable by the addition of a huge — mud & stick chimney — which took up the principal portion of one end. Bunks were erected for beds at the sides, of small poles, making a sleeping, as well as a culinary & dining apartment.

Small Pox

It seemed that while we were camped here, we were doomed to excitement, if it was not one thing it was another, but one that created the greatest consternation, was the smallpox scare — this was one of our most dreaded enemies, & one of the best safe guards in the world to private propperty, against the depredations of a soldier, ~~in the world~~. But luckily for us there were but few cases in the army. Col Gates of Buchanan Co Mo. was one of the subjects — he was moved to a safe distance from the army, & carefully attended to by Dr. Gough until out of danger, The principal part of the troops were vaccinated, Several of our company boys had very sore arms from impure matter.

Smallpox vaccine made of pure pus from one individual's active smallpox scab was scratched into another's skin with a needle to induce a mild case of the disease. Large numbers of soldiers were vaccinated to prevent epidemics (Rutkow 16).

Col. Elijah P. Gates enlisted in 1861 in St. Joseph, Missouri, as a private in the Easton (Missouri) Guards. Within six months, he had risen to the rank of colonel, serving until the fall of 1861 under Gen. Sterling Price. On January 1, 1862, the entire guard was transferred to the Confederate States Army to serve under General Beauregard at Corinth and remained east of the Mississippi during the rest of the war. General Price once said Gates was the bravest man he knew. Gates' first capture was at Big Black River; he escaped to be captured a second time at the Battle of Franklin. There, Gates was wounded in both arms, but with the reins in his teeth, he stayed on his horse to continue leading his men in battle. Gates escaped a second time following his capture at Franklin. He was captured a third time at Fort Blakely, Alabama, at the last infantry battle of the war, which was fought on the same day Gen. Robert E. Lee surrendered at Appomatox. According to Robert Mershon, great-grandson of Colonel Gates, a legendary story credits Gates with attempting to generate an insurrection among the prisoners being transferred by boat across Mobile Bay from Fort Blakely to Mobile, Alabama.

"Gates' hope was to take command of the boat," Mershon said. "For him, the war was never over." (Mershon).

Gates was incarcerated at Ship Island three weeks before Gen. Richard Taylor's surrender in early May 1865 and returned to Buchanan County, Missouri, where he resumed farming. Elected sheriff on the Democratic ticket, he served four years before being elected treasurer of the state of Missouri (1877-1881). He later retired from the transfer and bus firm of Piner & Gates. Colonel Gates died March 4, 1915, and is buried at Mount Mora Cemetery, Saint Joseph, Missouri (Bailey; "Col. Gates").

The some what drooping spirits of the boys were raised again on the 12th by being called to Paymasters head quarters & receiving two months wages. This awakened the "poker" feeling in the old sports of the company, & immediately on returning to quarters, the money commenced changing hands over the "board," & continued the remainder of the day & all night.

1863 Jany Camp Rogers

On the 20th there was a change of Gen. Officers ordered, which was quite at variance with the feelings of the troops generally. Price, one who was honored & loved above all other Missourians, was placed one grade lower, to command a division in Gen. Bowens stead, & Bowen took command of the 1st Mo. Brigade — where he was hated. Bowen was a good soldier, but was very haughty, overbearing & aristocratic, which rendered him very unpopular with his men.

Gen. John Stevens Bowen recovered from wounds received at Shiloh and participated in the Vicksburg campaign. (On the 8th of May, John C. Landis would be named Chief of Artillery, Bowen's Division. Sam and his brother Caldwell were part of Landis' unit.) Following Bowen's capture at Vicksburg, he was paroled to Raymond, Mississippi, where he died ten days later of dysentery contracted at Vicksburg (Boatner III 75; Heidler and Heidler 258-9).

Brig. Gen Greene, our kind old Gen. was given command of the 2nd Ark. brigade. We disliked very much to part with him, he was so generous, so plain in his manners, & always willing to share eaqual hardships with the lowest private. All our horses, mules, & brigade wagons, were sent thirty miles south on the Yazoo river — Where forage was more plentiful. The army having remained at this place so long — corn & hay were very scarce & stock becoming very thin. It was a case of necessity, in order to recruit them sufficiently to move the artillery & wagons. When a change in officers was made, a change in tactics was considered indispensible, In order that the effects of power & military rule might be noticed.

In our company we were on duty three days out of four — nine of our men were detailed daily as guards. This was one of Bowens orders. We knew that he was aware of our dislike toward him, & thought the extra detail of guards a little price of spite work toward us.

Left Camp

On the morning of the 25th orders were received to cook three days rations immediately. No point of destination mentioned. Supposed to be Port Hudson 200 miles south of Vicksburg on the Miss. river. Additional orders were afterward received to move on the following morning at 7 OC AM. Our horses were also ordered back to camp immediately. All were very eager to ascertain an idea of our future, for a while. But amid all our bewilderment & anxiety, in regard to the unexpected order to move, our hearts were made to rejoice & shouts went up from all interested, as if cheering for a great victory; when our beloved Gen. Greene returned & took his former command (1st Mo Brig) Gens. Price & Bowen resumed their former places. When the hour appointed to move on the 26th arrived the Infantry marched out to the music of brass — band — fife & drum, in the direction of Grenada. T'was late in the afternoon when our horses arrived, & it was not thought expedient to leave camp that evening. This was very satisfactory, for we had lingered around our old cabins so long, they had become to feel like home.

On the morning of the 27th when we were awakened by reveille — & rolled out to answer to our names, the weather was cold & blustering — but this did not cut any figure in the case, or change any orders, we had to move out 5 OC AM & follow in the direction the infantry started the previous morning.

March to Grenada

The boys faces were all pretty long, & expressions of regret were frequently heard — being compelled to leave our comfortable camp, & an abundance of good wood & water near at hand, to face the cold rain coming from the north & wade the roads very muddy. The march was a slow & tedious one, had some new horses that did not like to work, & the old ones had rested sufficiently to make them foolish, but just about the time the chickens were going to roost, & night had began to pin her curtain down, we pulled into Grenada & parked the guns in the north edge of the Village, near the cemetery. When the hour for drawing rations arrived one of our mess went to the company commissary, & on his return was very much surprised to see him with bacon & flour, the first we had drawn since the capture of Iuka.

On the 28th, we remained in camp, & I was feeling very much worse of the wear as our baggage wagons got stuck in the mud; some where between Grenada & the camp we left & failed to reach us with either blankets or cooking utensils, we were compelled to sit up all night, around some scant smoky fires to keep from freezing. We hooked wood from the cars as long as possible — & as a last resort commenced on the picket fence around the grave yard, when we left there the spot that marked the last resting place of so many dear departed ones, was turned out to the commons. But it was a case of sore necessity — this as a matter of course didnot affect the dead, & I am sincerely of the belief, that it was a great contribution to the lives of those who were unfortunate enough to be there.

Grenada

A short time after dark, we loaded our guns on the cars, ready for transportation south. Caldwell & I were two of the guards detailed to stand picket over the horses that night. and I tell you it was a cold & disagreeable ~~that~~ night, some rain was falling with a driving wind from the north. & not being very well clad was shivering with cold, tramping back & forth on our beat to keep our blood in circulation — A man approached us with some bottles — which he said contained a quart each of the very best Kentucky peach brandy, & as we reasoned under the present circumstances & unfavorable weather — a little of this pure "stuff" wouldn't go bad. A bargain was soon made for a quart, for which we paid $10.00. After testing it slightly. concluded it was too good & quantity too great to be all for us — so one of us went down to where the company was quartered nearby, to bring up two of our special friends & messmates; an old Irish man by the name of James. Scully — who was "niver" known to refuse a "wea droph of the crathur" & Tom. Boone our company "songster" — Well, a fellow didn't have to knock either of them down to make them take a pint; they were soon on hands & we passed the bottle from one to the other remarking — we must drink it all — until the contents were drained to the dregs — & bottle mashed into a thousand pieces.

A BBC Northern Ireland internet site defines "crather" as "a drink of poteen." ***The Art of Drink*** **defines poteen as "a high proof moonshine [illicit whiskey] made from grains." John M'Lean writes in** ***Notes of a Twenty-Five Years' Service in the Hudson's Bay Territory*****, "I presented him and his companions with what is always acceptable to a shanty-man, a liberal allowance of the 'crathur,' to enjoy themselves withal" ("Crathur"; "Fionn McCool"; M'Lean).**

We had taken the medicine — as prescribed by ourselves, but it did not produce the effect desired — Instead of being pure peach brandy, as represented, — it was the worst of "pine top" whiskey — that had never seen a still house, unless it was a "moon-shiner's". Well, now for a description of the effects on the different subjects. I was about half sick any way — & my stomach full of old strong bacon, of which I had partaken of freely for supper, & in less than fifteen minutes after helping to drain the bottle — the whiskey together with everything I had eaten, were on the ground before me. This relieved me, & I could join in with the balance of the company in laughing at the boys — whose "medicine" stayed with them. Caldwell & Boone made fun for the company the greater portion of the night. Scully sat down by the fire, with his old pipe in his mouth — stem about two inches long — & after a few dry jokes dropped off into a "snooze" & woke up as sober as a "judge" the next morning.

Bivuac at Grenada Continued

On the morning of the 29th all the guns, half the horses & all the men except ten, left on the 9 OC train (Caldwell included) could not ship all at the same time on account of the scarcity of cars. That night while seated on a chunk of wood by a dimly blazing fire, I took from my pocket a small memorandum, which I always carried with me & wrote on one of the dirty pages; We are left in rather a precarious situation, having sent our rations & baggage on the first train. I am sitting up by the fire to night — not having anything to keep me warm lying down. Feeling bad. We passed several nights in this manner, nodding & shivering around the fire, until completely overcome & worn out, & drop over into a confused mass similar to so many hogs, & sleep as best we could until morning. The Officers, said they were under the impression, that the remainder of the company would soon follow the first shipment, was the only consolation received for our ill-treatment.

Grenada

The 30th found us still lingering & waiting with less prospect for leaving than ever before — as orders were given not to ship any more artillery until ten thousand Infantry were sent out.

Feb. 1st

On the 1st day of February I felt so much indisposed. I thought it impossible & very injurious to my health to remain in camp, with such treatment, as that to which I had been subject for the last several days — & through the kindness & instrumentality of Lieut. Harris, I got permission to stop at the house of an Old Citizen of the Town, the same one who had been sharing his liberality with Lieut. On the 4th we had quite a snow ranging in depth from two to four inches. An occurrence very unusual in that country. This made it extremely disagreeable & trying on the poor soldiers, many of whom were compelled to remain at the depot without blankets. I often wished the boys were all situated as comfortably as the lieut. & myself. We were living fat, & sleeping snugly in a feather bed. Had plenty of Rio coffee (although very scarce in the country at that time) beef steak, milk & butter — Wasn't that luscious living for a soldier. On the 7th 9 OC AM the horses & remainder of the men were shipped, southward bound, on a train of flat cars; the Lieut. & I being on the "puny" list — concluded to wait for a passenger.

When the morning of the 8th dawned, I was very sorry the time had arrived for us to return to camp — not that I wished to shrink from my duty as a soldier, but the change from good comfortable quarters, to none at all, in such very disagreeable weather had rendered me unfit for camp duty. I would have remained a few days longer to recruit, had it not been for being without a change of clothing. We were very kindly treated & well fed. About 9 OC AM. the Lieut. & I thanked our newly made friends for the care & protection given us during our stay, & after procuring a pass to Jackson Miss. boarded the train & was soon passing the mile posts at a rapid rate. Arrived at our destination about 3 OC PM. Found the company camped near the depot; which was very gratifying to me, not feeling able to walk far. On the morning of the 9th after cleansing my body & swapping my dirty garments for cleaner ones, was very much revived, & thinking in all probability, we would not remain long, & being anxious to veiw the Capital, in company with some of the boys, took a stroll through the principal streets of the city. Business of all kinds seemed to be flourishing, but prices were very exorbitant. The street venders appeared to have the greatest amount of customers. On every corner there was a huxter stand, covered with pies, cakes, "goubers" & percimon beer.

Goubers are peanuts.

Our camp was also flooded with old negro women & boys, selling half moon "sweet-tater" pies — 25 cents a piece. A thin slice of potatoe without sweetening, crusts about half inch thick without shortening — & so tough would almost give one the lockjaw to chew them. Nevertheless we paid our money & swallowed them down. "Anything for a change." On the morning of the 10th orders were given to move on the day following. In the afternoon we loaded our guns on the cars. The drivers were also started by highway with the horses under charge of a Lieut. Destiny said to be black river bridge twelve miles east of Vicksburg.

Jackson to Edwards Station

On the 11th in obedience to orders received, mounted the cars 6 OC AM to follow in the direction designated. Traveled fast but very rough the repairs of the road bed having been badly neglected. but our distance was cut short a little — we stopped at Edwards station one & a half miles east of the bridge. Unloaded the guns & camped in a little flat meadow, in the edge of an old field. Horses arrived late in the afternoon. Had a very hard rain at night, which flooded our tents, coming with such a dash, we did not have time to ditch — our usual manner of protection in such cases. We had to "hang" ourselves & blankets on the fence to dry.

12th during the day we moved camp one & a half miles down the river (Big Black) where near its banks on a beautiful slope to the south, we parked the guns & pitched the tents in regular military order. Plenty of wood & water near at hand — two very much needed & essential articles to a solders comfort & welfare. It was also adjoining the plantation of an old rich southerner, whose meadow near by supported a considerable drove of hogs, & a report also gained circulation in camp that he was in the habit of & delighted in dividing — his surplus milk & butter with the soldiers — in fact one of the boys went up & got some. We soon noticed that he was watching his hogs very closely. When at home, & in his absence posted a half grown negro boy on the fence, with a double barreled shot gun, at some convenient place, to act as a safe guard against any intruder. A reconoiterring party of the company was organized, & sent out on the 13th & a plan of action soon decided upon. The 14th was a rainy muddy day & nothing going on in camp to attract any particular attention, & being in full view of the drove of hogs — some of the boys got very hungry for pork — concluded to try the old man's liberality — in that line — having ascertained, that he was absent, & noticed that the negro, with the gun had become a little negligent — was over the hill a little out of sight — the thought struck them that now was the "golden" opportunity — A few ears of corn were procured from the company forage wagon — a slip gap made in the rail fence, corn strewn along inside & outside (but "mostly" outside) the gap — the hogs being hungry for corn were easily decoyed from their enclosure, & gap in the fence fixed, so as to avoid detection, at the same time a careful vigilance was kept for the negro with the gun, & house which stood on a hill about one hundred yards distant. Well, three of the hogs were driven over the hill with sticks in a hurry, killed, & secreted under some brush, until night came on, when they were skinned & prepared for the kettle. If the Old gentleman ever suspected us of getting his hogs; we never found it out — in fact we were not very inquisitive on that subject. There was a vast amount of rain fall, at this season of the year, which caused the river to overflow its banks in many places & submerge the crops of corn & cotton on the low lands. One of our boys rescued an old darkey, who in attempting to cross the river above, the skiff was capsized by coming in contact with drift wood. He was clinging to a tree top, in the water.

After a few days, everything moved along in the common humdrum of camp life, & almost half a month dropped out of existence into the "wastebasket" of time, before I was aware of the long interval between dates in my records. On the 4th day of March, while basking in the beautiful rays of the sun — like a lizzard — suddenly realized that spring in the beautiful sunny — sunny — south was with us; drear winter had again disappeared, & the tender bulbs & flowers were opening, while being fanned by the balmy breeze & warmed by the soft mellow rays of a bright southern sun.

Dear land of sunshine & flow'rs,
What more can, we do for thee?
To show that great love of ours!
And set thy, good people free.

It was rumored on good authority that Gen Price starts for the Trans. Miss. department soon, & it is said he will take command in the field, Gen. Kirby Smith the Department.

Gen. Edmund Kirby Smith, a math professor at West Point and botanist before joining the Confederate States Army, was severely wounded at the Battle of Bull Run. Then in October 1861, he was commissioned major general and given command of a division under General Beauregard. In March 1862, he assumed command of the Department of East Tennessee. The month before Sam's reference, General Smith had gone to Richmond to assist with the reorganization of the army, and in February 1863, he was sent to the Trans-Mississippi Department (Boatner III 769-70).

"Old Pap's" familiar face, & bald head, which he uncovered so often in passing us, will be greatly missed on this side the "Father of Waters". The quietness of our camp was occasionally broken, & we were reminded that the war was yet going on, by the firing now & then of our seige guns at Vicksburg & reply of the Federal fleet, our men were firing at long range, when the yankee gunboats appeared around the bend above the doomed City. Their fleet made several attempts to pass, but were unsuccessful, our land batteries gave them, such a warm reception being strongly fortified & well mannered.

Marching Orders Toward Grand Gulf

On the 9th we were somewhat surprised — & not very agreeably either; upon receiving orders to march the next day in the direction of Grand Gulf. The infantry of the first Mo Brigade moved out this morning. in command of Gen. Bowen again. Gen. Greene was transferred to the 2nd Mo brigade, likewise Gates' regiment & Maj. Samuel's Battallion. This change was of similar character, as one spoken of only a short time previous, & one which produced results of similar character. Men didnot like to change officers so much, but Vandorn was running that part of the business. On the morning of the 10th we were awakened by the bugler sounding reveille at 4 OC & 30 M AM. & we were a "powerful" sleepy looking set of boys, when we rubbed our eyes open & hurriedly fell into line. Our morning meal was prepared & eaten as hastily as possible, horses harnessed, hitched & we moved out 7 O.C. AM. As usual it consumed more time the first morning, preparing to leave a regular camp, than when marching every day. I left this place with a heavy heart, for it was the most pleasant & convenient camp, we had since crossing the Miss river. And I regreted very much at having to be deprived of my regular ration of milk to which I had been accustomed almost daily since our arrival here. Traveled southward, on what was called the Telegraph road. The day was a very dismal one & our progress was slow, as most of the time was consumed in traveling, five & a half miles. We had reveille at 5 OC on the morning of the 11th & moved at 7 AM, marched one mile & went into camp again, on fourteen mile creek, The bridge being broken down & water too high to ford.

March 14 Mile Creek

This creek was said to have been named by Gen. Andrew Jackson, when he crossed his army at this ford, on his march from Nashville to Neworleans in the winter of 1814 to fight the Brittish troops at that place. Some of the boys enjoyed the delay very much, riding up & down the creek, in some skiffs that were kept here, by some of the citizens as pleasure boats, or for crossing the stream above or below the bridge in times of high water. The morning of the 12th found us still waiting on the banks of this ever memorable stream, which was yet too deep to ford, the depth having only decreased one foot the previous night.

Early in the morning Capt. Guibor came up with his battery, & seemed greatly surprised at us waiting for the water to fall; & immediately put his men to work — preparing a raft out of a portion of the old bridge — & after a vast amount of work & noise, knocking & splasing around through the mud & water, completed a rough structure, on which he effected a crossing late in the afternoon & camped three miles from the crossing. Wade's battery was yet ahead of him having crossed before the creek became swollen. The 13th we had reveille at 4 OC. & moved a 6 AM. The water having resumed something similar to its natural stage, we forded it easily — the cannoniers crossed on Guibor's raft.

March to Grand Gulf

Our travel was uninterrupted & progress good. Passed through Eauka, a very small insignificant place, in fact the surrounding country was too poor to support a town of any larger proportion — neither did the appearance of the inhabitants, denote any great amount of prosperity or Industry. About the middle of the afternoon, marched through, Rocky springs — & the same deffinition can be given of this Village, as applied to the preceding one — only worse — as we were passing through, I was thoroughly convinced that the Town was eaqually as hard as the first part of the name. We were greeted with songs as an imitation of singing, from some of the most outlandish, ignorant, ugly, half-civilized creatures in the form of women, I ever saw, at the same time throwing bouquetts of every description at us — A member of our company received one composed of dogfennel & jimpsonblossoms. Their songs were numerous, but by no means facinating, all of which were pretty much the same tune but different words. After leaving this place six miles in the rear, passed Wade's battery camped by the roadside, & four miles farther on we came up on Guibor's battery camped, & we also stopped for the night 5 O.C. P.M. after traveling thirty miles. So you will see Guibor didnot gain anything over us, by building the raft — but we formed the resolution before leaving the creek. Our days march was over the roughest country, I had seen up to that time. The hills were so very steep, the farmers could not plow straight over them, consequently they went round & round, which made an endless row from top to bottom. No wonder the girls were so ugly, no doubt their shoes were run down, if not their feet — similar to the "Arkansas Women". On the morning of 14th reveille was blown at the usual hour, (4) & moved at daylight. Our order of march was Guibor in front of us — Wade in the rear. Country very rough — I often wished on this trip to be an artist — to sketch the country & road over which we traveled.

According to the *American Heritage Dictionary of the English Language*, dogfennel is a weedy plant found in the southeast United States. Jimson weed is a coarse poisonous plant. The trumpet-shaped large blossoms can be white or purple ("Dog fennel"; "Jimsonweed").

March completed

A few strokes of his brush, would add greatly to the interest of my records, & illustrate more fully the pen picture, I have endeavored truely to present. I have often wondered how the Palmetto tree — chanced to grow in this unsightly country — yet near Grand Gulf — along the small streams leading to the river it flourished, rearing its green foliage; above the tall cane, opening its snowy white blossoms — to fill the valleys, with their sweet fragrance. It's a lovely tree — its' beauty unsurpassable — & its name of great worth to the south. We camped 4 O.C. P.M. one fourth mile from the Miss. river, after traveling sixteen miles

The palmetto tree can be any of several small palms having fan-shaped leaves, which can be stripped and used in weaving ("Palmetto").

Winkler's Bluff

On the 15th our battery moved a short distance, & placed the guns in position, on a high embarkment called Winklers Bluff, near the mouth of Big black river, where it intersects with the Miss. river, which is in plain view, & pitched our tents & picketed the horses a short distance in the rear.

Our position ~~w~~ was also about one & a half miles north of Grand Gulf. Our mission here was, to prohibit the yankee gunboats & transports from passing up Big black river. Rumored that one Federal Gunboat passed our batteries at Port Hudson & is expected up here any time. The country which surrounded our situation here, was very rough, the majority of which was covered with a luxuriant growth of canebrake about forty feet high. The timber was enclined to be scrubby, & but little sign of the woodman's axe — no habitation nearer than the Gulf — which was only a small trading post & boat landing. If you will excuse the expression I think it was the most Godforsaken country I ever saw. The chief Inhabitants, were snakes & bees — & they had to be industrious & use a great deal of economy to make a good living.

Winklers Bluff

On the morning of the 19th while I was hunting my horses (as I was driver at that time) over the hills & through the canebrake, was instantly & greatly surprised, by the sudden roar of artillery at Grand Gulf, less than a mile from where I was ~~at~~. The occasion of the artillery duel, was Wade's battery firing at the yankee Gunboat Monogahala & Sloup of War Hartford. Wade's men fired rapidly & struck the boat several times; but this didnot check their course, as they moved leisurely up the river, taking time only to fire a few shots. No damage done on either side. I ran to an elevated position near by, to catch a glympse, of the conflict — but could only see the boats after passing our batteries, steaming up the river. Those were the first yankee gunboats I ever saw.

At least three boats had the same name of Monongahela. However, one was dismantled in 1854 and the other burned in 1859. The one Sam sees at Grand Gulf was a side-wheel packet (coastal or river steamer) with a wooden hull built in Pittsburgh, Pennsylvania, in 1863 (Way, Jr. 329).

At least three boats also had the name of Hartford. One was grounded in 1855. Another wasn't built until 1869. The one Sam saw was a stern-wheel packet with a wooden hull. It was built in Cincinnati, Ohio, in 1863. At the time Sam saw her, she was patrolling between Port Hudson and Vicksburg, blockading supplies badly needed by the Confederate army. In 1864, she was converted into a gunboat and renamed SIBYL ("Hartford"; Way, Jr. 208).

At that time our men were working hard to strengthen the means of defense at that point — and by the 20th had added six more siege pieces of large caliber — maned by Confederate states regulars from Louisiana. This encouraged us very much; & not knowing at that time how formidable a Gunboat was constructed, thought our defense sufficient to prevent any more passing. While these things were transpiring with us, matters of still greater importance were going on elsewhere — on the morning of the 25th the following account of a Gunboat fight at Vicksburg — was received at Gen. Bowens headquarters. Four boats appeared above the town & commenced shelling our batteries. They soon attempted to pass, when a terrible conflict ensued, in which one of the boats was sunk on the spot & all her crew was drowned; two of them succeeded in passing — one of ~~them~~ which was disabled so that it drifted down the river unmanigable –

the crew attached a slow watch & made their escape, but the boat didnot burn, it was the ram Monarch, one of their most valuable boats. This news was very satisfactory & encouraging to us — we were very much in hopes they would be sunk or disabled in passing — for if they succeeded were liable to drift down upon our position & give us a shelling.

> **There were at least two packets christened Monarch. The one built in 1844 was dismantled in 1848. Sam saw the side-wheel packet with a wooden hull built in Cincinnati, Ohio, in 1853 for Capt. John A. Williamson and others. She sank at Louisville with her cargo, bound for New Orleans. Following repairs and another disaster, she was sold in April 1862 to the United States government and converted into a ram, becoming part of Colonel Ellet's Ram Fleet. She saw major participation in the Battle of Memphis and at Vicksburg. Following the fall of Vicksburg, she was dropped from the naval list in 1864 ("Monarch"; Way, Jr. 328-9).**

We continued to strengthen our fortifycations on the Bluff. On the morning of the 31st the smoke from yankee gunboats was plainly to be seen, was supposed to be about fifteen miles up the river, & from the appearance of the smoke ~~was~~ were evidently moving down toward our position. They came down within ten miles of the Gulf & anchored until night, during which time their marines were pillaging the country on the La. side, & killing beeves, for rations to last them, until a junction was formed with their fleet below. We were kept constantly posted – in regard to their movements, by our signal corps & couriers. I tell you we were watching with eager eyes every movement & litening intently, to grasp every flying report, concerning the movements of the enemy, up or down the river. At 7 O.C. P.M. our cavalry picket, sationed at Hard times landing on the La. side, sent up a rocket the designated signal, to warn us of the approach of the Gunboats — But a few moments intervened before the booming of cannon, with deadly roar, broke in up on the still night; echoing from bank to bank & dying away in the hills & valleys, to interrupt the wearied trooper whose preperations for a nights dreams should have begun. Our whole company was immediately aroused, raised a hideous yell, ran in haste to the edge of the bluff, where we stood almost motionless, abated breath, throbbing hearts & gazing anxiously to catch a glympse of the coming battle; not knowing but what we might become participants. It was a moment of great suspense; the stars in the Heavens sparkling, & the pale faced moon looked no less beautiful, while casting her soft rays upon the broad bosom of the Miss, assisted by the bright flash of the Federal guns, we could only indestinctly see the din of battle; at the same time our land batteries replying; afforded a grand & magnificent specticle for the looker's on. Yes, it was a grand sight to us; but some poor fellows had to die martyrs upon the soil of the beloved south. The Gunboats passed down, sustaining only a trifling damage. The Hartford received two ineffective shots in the stern. When they were opposite the lower batteries, one of Capt. Wade's guns burst, caused by one of his men inserting a shell, the fuse end toward the powder. The explosion wounded every man around the gun, & killed two men in an adjoining battery, (Capt. Guibors) Our men deserved great credit, for their noble defense.

April
Winklers Bluff Harrison's Feast

On the 1st day of April some of the Boys belonging to my mess, crossed Big black river in a skiff, on a hunt & foraging expedition, took a gun & an old colts revolver, thinking they might find a "wild" hog or calf, but when they returned in the afternoon they reported large game scarce. One of them had a rabbit, & a young man by the name of George. Harrison from Hannabal Mo, had a stick across his shoulder to the end of which was suspended a large rattle snake. We were very much surprised to see him walk into camp, with this poisonous reptile dangling down his back; but were more astonished when he skined it, & after dissecting in small bits, proceeded to fry in bacon grease, & as fast as done, eat with a great relish, regardless of the curious eyes & smutty remarks of his mess-mates. I happened to pass by while he was enjoying his "feast", & by invitation took a bite. I thought if he could eat a whole snake with such unconcern – a small piece wouldn't hurt me & I tasted it through curiosity. Harrison after eating this unusual "mess" — rubbed himself & remarked — he was ready for another "rattler".

Caldwell was confined to his bed, here with Erysipelas, was very sick for several days, but through Dr. Gough's medicine & my careful nursing — was soon on the convalescent list, & in a week or so again ready for duty.

The cause of erysipelas was not understood in Dr. Gough's time. Also called "St. Anthony's Fire" or the "Rose," this disease was later understood as an acute, inflammatory disease caused by streptococcal bacteria (Rutkow 26).

Our bunks at this place were a little better than usual, being made of the cane stalks were some what springy, & the leaves stripped off placed on top was a very good substitute for a bed — especially in the absence of a better one. Yankee cavalry & Infantry could be seen marching down on the other side the river.

Winkler's Bluff

On the morning of the 4th the 1st & 2nd regiments of the first Mo brigade under command of Col. Cockerell, crossed the Miss river below Grand gulf, to meet a force of Federals under command of of Gen. Frank Blair of Mo about five thousand strong — who were committing all manner of depredations ~~on~~ to the citizens & on property in that section of country — but our men were soon compelled to retrace their steps being confronted by a superior force, & laboring under great disadvantages. On the 5th considerable cannonading on the La. side. The Feds were advancing in large numbers & shelling the woods as they advanced, for fear of an enemy in ambush. This massing of troops was kept up for several days. Early in the morning of the 9th just before I had arisen from my "couch of cane". While looking out at the coming light — I spied one of my mess, pass by the tent door, with three pieces of bacon on his back, which he claimed to have captured by the "slight of hand", off the Dott, a small steamer that had tied up near by, so as to be protected by our guns. This fellow had an eye to "business", & knew the meat would come in good play — for we had been out of beef for two days, & only half a ration of cornmeal. This was getting to be very dry close living, & it was ~~very~~ but natural for us to assist our, fellow man in hiding this extra "draft" of rations.

The Dot was built in 1862. It is not known if she had a side-wheel or stern-wheel paddle. The following year on May 17, 1863, the Confederate forces used her to ferry across the Black River and then set her afire. She was found by the Federals near the railroad bridge at Bovina, Mississippi (Way, Jr. 132).

On the 20th we were reinforced by the second mo brigade — a regiment & battallion of Miss troops. To receive an addition to our numbers always gave us great courage. On the 21st the smoke of ~~sev~~ seven gunboats & two transports, were visible up the river. They came down to Hard times landing, about three miles distant, remained a short time, & returned up the river to their former places.

On the morning of the 22nd the smoke of the gunboats still in sight, & seemed to be moving down the river. In the afternoon they hove in sight at "Hard scrabble". The first turned the bend & halted, until the others came into line; as if to make a simultaneous attack on our forces, & after firing a shot or two went back a short distance.

These maneuvers were all done very leisurly, & with great precission. These movements were made, to attract our attention, & at the same time a direct attack, from that point was not then intended. It was thought; & the supposition was based upon good ground, they were massing their troops in some other quarter while this was going on.

Our officers thinking perhapse, an attack was intended, concluded to strengthen our position. A small transport, the Charm, was immediately dispatched for a raft of logs lying in the gulf — to blockade the mouth of Big black river, & prevent them from advancing too near our station. Soon after the boat had tied on to the raft, the Feds commenced firing, & the load was cut loose, & the charm. made good speed up the river, out of danger. No damage done. The yanks fired twelve shots & went back — our batteries were polite enough to return the fire — but fell short.

The Charm, a wooden hulled, side-wheel packet built in Cincinnati, Ohio, in 1860, was one of two steamers (the other was the Paul Jones) that ferried Col. Francis M. Cockrell's troops across the Mississippi from Vicksburg to meet General Grant's forces. She delivered large guns brought by train to Grand Gulf and then moored near the railroad bridge on the Big Black River. Following General Grant's success at the Battle of Champion Hill, the Confederates attempted to protect the crossing of the river for General Loring's troops in the Battle of Big Black River on May 17, 1863. Sam was seeing the Charm only a month before this confrontation, which would result in the Confederates burning the Charm and the Paul Jones to prevent their capture. In August 1962, divers located the wrecks of both boats and salvaged many souvenirs (Way, Jr. 81-2).

23rd Soon after dark last night, our Capt. & five men went to cut the levee on this side of the river & below Grand Gulf to prevent the enemy from landing troops, but they could not accomplish much, as the water on the outside, was almost as high as the river, but they worked faithful all night & a portion of the morning of the 23rd was gone before they made their appearance in camp.

They reported yanks in large numbers on the La. shore — the general impression is — we will be compelled to fight before many days. One section of Capt. Low's Mo battery (ten pound rifle guns) arrived to receive a portion of the shelling from the gunboats which we daily expected. On the 24th we were again reminded, that our "pests" were still on hands, by them firing several shots — no harm done.

Nigro "Hoedown"

We had a force of darkies, at work for several days, strengthening the works for our battery. And amid all our trouble & anxiety, we didnot forget to have our fun out of these old negroes — at night after their days labor was over, & we had a chance for a little recreation. We would get a few of those "Old sons of Ham" out & after Phelps (our Grenada fidler) "rosined up" his old greasy bow, a few words of encouragement would start some of them to dancing, while the others did the patting & singing — & once the "ball" was rolling, was no trouble to keep going; & I tell you, this was fun let loose — for us. One of the number, styled himself "Old Kaintuck". His foot was about fourteen inches long & was bow-legged besides. He had one peculiar step to perform in dancing, by dropping upon one knee & rocking his toe on the ground. This performance always caused a big laugh among the boys, — & a hurrah for old "Kaintuck" — when the old nigger would almost kill himself. We amused ourselves the fore part of several nights in this manner.

Winkler's Bluff

Last night several of the boys & myself, went out after tattoo roll call, to cut a couple of bee trees — which one of the company had found, but didnot know whether he had the oldest claim, or somebody else — but we were disappointed as the first tree was already cut & robbed of its "sweetness". The "Doe Boys" (Infantry) had done the work. We then proceeded to the other, near by, which had shared the same fate. And to say we were very badly disappointed, doesn't express half — but had to "grin & bear it" — could do nothing but hang our heads, talk as low ~~as low~~ & as little as we could, return to camp — & if possible, slip into our tents with out being observed. The idea of being "sold out" so bad — was enough without the jokes & criticisms of our comrads. To day those yankee crafts were yet to be seen — we could also see troops, marching down the opposite side of the river — some crossing over to the Miss. side, below Grand Gulf – out of range of our land batteries.

In the morning of the 29th there was very heavy bombardment at the Gulf. The second section of our battery — the one to which I belonged — moved to the breastworks near the Gulf. The Gunboats & transports, that had been almost constantly in our view, for some time past; moved down & passed by the Gulf — regardless of the shot & shell, that we hailed upon them, with great rapidity & decission. It was very discouraging — to see our shots hit the object at which they were aimed; rebound & fall harmless into the water. These boats added great strength to the fleet — which could be seen on the morning of the 30th about three miles below, where Federal troops were crossing in large numbers. It would have been very indiscreet on our part, to have evacuated Grand Gulf at that time; yet our force was not sufficient to hold it, & at the same time prevent the enemy from gaining a footing on the Miss. side. It could be readily observed we were steadily loosing ground — a battle, soon — would be the only alternative, & if defeated; a hurried retreat in the direction of Vicksburg, the stronghold of the Army of Tennessee, would be a natural consequence.

May 1st

We had passed a month & a half in the hills near Grand Gulf — & May — beautiful May — the most lovely month of spring — in my dear old home, Mo; the one in which all nature seems aglow with the decorations of an alwise Creator — although more advanced toward decay — in this sunny clime — still retains a portion of the sublimity which nature intended. But we cannot remain stationary longer & enjoy these glorious gifts — we must be up & doing — our country is appealing for help, & we must lend our might, to defend the most noble cause for which man's life was ever sacrifized. The Federals after crossing a large force at the landing four miles west of Port Gibson Miss, attacked Gen. Green's brigade, 2 O.C AM, & drove him about two & a half miles. He was surprised by a superior force, in the thick woods & being dark caused some confusion. But was soon reinforced by the first Mo & Baldwin's Miss Brigade. & the advance of the enemy was immediately checked & held at bey until daylight. The second section ~~our~~ of our battery received orders at daybreak to move to the scene of action immediately. The guns were at the breastworks at the Gulf & horses at Winklers Bluff. They were harnessed in double quick, & but a short time intervened, until they were hitched to the guns & moving at a rapid gait.

The major route to Port Gibson extends from Grand Gulf on the Mississippi River to Fourteenmile Creek and the

battlefield in Raymond. The Old Port Gibson Road, also known as the Old Natchez Trace, is about fifty miles long; along this road, many of the historic sites related to the Civil War no longer exist (Drake).

Battle of Port Gibson

Our route was a circuitous one, the country being too rough, to admit of a direct course. When we arrived within six miles of the battle ground, a courier came riding in a dead run, his horse foaming with sweat — breathing heavily — grasping in his hand, a dispatch from Gen. Bowen, to move up as briskly as possible. The sharp crack of the enfield — mingled with the sullen roar of the cannon, only added fuel to the flames which were already burning within us.

The Enfield rifle musket weighed 9 pounds, 3 ounces, with bayonet and fired a bullet similar to the minie. It was extremely accurate at 800 yards and dependable up to 1,100 yards, which made it highly popular with the Confederate soldiers (Boatner III 266).

The cannoniers were mounted on the caissons & limber chests, the poor horses spurred into a sweeping gallop; & with scarcely a break, this pell mell speed was kept up, jostling & jolting over rocks, ruts & bridges, until we arrived near the contested grounds, & placed our guns on a bald hill ready for action 11 OC AM. Soon after planting our guns, the Federal skirmishers made their appearance, only a short distance in our front, & sent a few minnies whizzing too close to our heads to be agreeable, but they quickly disappeared, when we fired a few shells at them. But the firing brought to our opposition, a more formidable foe. A battery of rifled guns appeared on a hill about eight hundred yards in our front & opened fire with their long shells & solid shot, tearing through the timber & ground near our position. Almost as quick as thought we turned our guns upon them, but they had a great advantage over us, having four guns, & we only two, & ours being howitzers could not use solid shot — But we made things as warm as possible, for them until our infantry advanced compelling them to fall back. This uneaqual duel lasted about one hour. We remained in position & continued shelling at intervals most all day, when ever a body of the enemy appeared. About 5 O.C. in the afternoon, when we were resting in place, the Federal sharpshooters crept up a small ravine, under cover of a thick undergrowth near our position, & commenced firing — trying to pick off our cannoniers. We had for our support, some raw

Miss skirmishirs, & we could not get them to advance, to drive these "dare devils" from their hiding place, & our Captain ordered us to open on them with grape & canister — a few rounds made them "skedaddle". But we were only relieved a short time, as our firing, brought back to the same position, our old enemy, the four gun battery which had opposed us in the morning — & I tell you they "poured" shot of all descriptions into us thick & fast. We replied until our ammunition was exhausted— leaving the field about sundown. Our company loss, was one man Wm Yarbrough mortally wounded, one horse killed & one wounded. I have often thought our loss here, small, & our escape a miraculous one, when the character of our position, is taken into consideration, & being exposed to the enemies bullets about seven hours. The force in opposition to us, being far superior to ours, in order to avoid loosing too many men & gaining nothing our whole force soon after we left, fell back across the Bayou pier river near Port Gibson & burned the bridges, to check the advance of the "yanks"; & by so doing hold them in check on the south side, until we received reinforcements — which were hourly expected.

Cannon is a simple term to describe a complex array of all firearms larger than small arms such as rifles, muskets, carbines, and revolvers. The term includes the basic artillery piece, the Napoleon, as well others such as 6- and 12- pounder guns, 12-, 24-, and 32- pounder howitzers, the 12- pounder mountain howitzer, the 10- and 20- pounder Parrott rifles, and the 3-inch Ordnance gun. Cannon can be rifled or smoothbore, made of brass or iron, be breech- or muzzle-loaders, use different types of fuzes, and use ammunition of various calibers. Nine common calibers are solid shot, grape (usually nine iron balls strung together), canister (tin can filled with cast-iron or lead balls or slugs), shell (any projectile containing a bursting charge of powder), and chain (two balls connected by a chain) or bar shot (two balls connected by a bar) (Boatner III 119-20, 135, 354, 738, 766-67).

After feeding our horses, received orders to return to our old camp at Winkler's bluff. where we arrived late in the night, hungry, sleepy & tired. But our condition was good, compared to the sufferings of our poor jovial comrad Yarbrough, who was lying at the hospital weltering in his own blood mortally wounded, & afterwards died, without a friend to smooth his ruffled brow, in his last sad hours. On the 2nd we remained in camp. I was feeling very sore & tired from my previous days travel & engagement. The first section of our battery was sent to the bridge at Bayou pier river, late in the afternoon, for picket duty. The raft of logs over Big black river near where our guns were planted, had been almost completed. There was a large force of men at work for some time past, & when the structure was nearing completion, it looked as if the purpose for which it was intended, was little needed, for there wasn't a gun boat to be seen, & the signs of the times denoted a speedy evacuation of the place. The reinforcements for which we had been looking so long had not appeared.

Evacuation of Grand gulf

The morning of the 3rd our camp was aroused at one O.C. AM, & ordered to move immediately. This created great confusion, to be awakened from our slumbers, at that unusual hour, to be confronted with the startling intelligence, that the enemy was in force near by. No wonder we felt a little dismayed at the thought, of being pursued by an enemy far superior in numbers & equipments, hemmed by water on two sides, & a very rough mountainous country on the other, leaving our only means of escape in the direction of the foe. However as soon as possible we hitched up & moved out, although our progress was very slow; having sent the best horses with the other guns; those we had left, didnot care to pull & wouldn't "scare worth a cent"

After going south & east a short distance, turned our course in the direction of Vicksburg. Retreat was the order of the day — & with an enemy close upon our heels. All the Siege guns at the Gulf were spiked, carriages destroyed & magazines blown up, in which was stored a large amount of ammunition; the explosion of which made the earth tremble for miles around. This was a very sad gloomy time indeed, we had remained in that vicinity a sufficient length of time, to accumulate considerable munitions of war — some of which were very valuable to the south, but it was better policy on our part, to apply the torch, or cripple them in such a manner as to render them valueless, in assisting our enemies to destroy us.

Retreat From Grand Gulf

We crossed big black river at Hawkinson's ferry, on a pontoon bridge & after going one & a half miles camped, for the night at sundown. When the rear guard of our army had crossed the river & was tearing up the bridge, the yankee cavalry dashed up & fired upon them. Our men returned the fire with shell & minnies, driving them back & completed their work of destruction. Loring's Division & the first section of our battery brought up the rear. Our mess killed a hog & cooked a piece for supper, fresh pork was always acceptable & pleasant to a Soldiers appetite. On the morning of the 4th we were awakened by an early reveille, & were soon trudging along our weary & uncertain journey.

During the day met the long looked for reinforcements, with the help of which, could have forced a hasty recrossing of the Miss. at the battle of Port gibson & saved the wanton destruction of property at the Gulf & a hasty retreat. But at the time we met them, their services were not needed, as the enemy was several miles in our rear. Arrived at Brown station on the Vicksburg & Jackson railroad 11 O.C. P.M. Oh My! but I was tired & hungry, not having had anything to eat since the night before. Good thing we "filled up" on the hog wasn't it. During the day, & almost half the night we traveled thirty miles. The 5th we remained in camp & I cannot tell when I enjoyed a rest more for I was awful tired.

Camp at Black River Bridge

On the 8th moved two miles east & camped near the railroad bridge, which spaned Big black river, where we had a very pleasant situation. Captain Capt. Landis was appointed Chief of artillery Capt. Bowen's Division. While we were stationed at Grand Gulf Bowen was placed in command of a division. We remained very quiet at this camp, & it seemed that military movements, came to a "stand still" so far as we were concerned, until the 11th we had quite a commotion, but turned out to be a false alarm. All the batteries were ordered out; but some of them didnot succeed in getting across the river, before we were met by a courier from Gen. Bowen & ordered back to camp. This circumstance brings to memory, a large camp kettle filled with rice, which my mess had on the fire cooking as rapidly as possible & when the order to move was given, not knowing but that we would perhaps, be absent all day — & loose it all — which at that time was a great rarity — sooner than run any risk — concluded to eat it half done & redhot, at that, so we hurriedly filled our tin plates, at the same time mixing a liberal quantity of Neworleans sugar with it "sloshed her down". Well the excitement of the next hour was sufficient to put the mixture to boiling within us, & upon our return to camp, there were several first class cases of Cholera morbus — I amongst the number. I was extremely fond of rice previous to this time, but my appetite was not so good afterwards. Especially "hot."

Cholera morbus, a term no longer in scientific use, was an acute inflammation of the mucous membrane of the stomach and intestines, which generally occurred in summer or fall. Symptoms included severe cramps, diarrhea, and vomiting ("Cholera morbus").

There being no bridge at this point except the one used by the railroad — two small transports were anchored in the river, & a temporary construction was made on which we crossed infantry & artillery. The Federals instead of following directly after us, came up the road which we traveled on our march to grand Gulf, & on the 12th our pickets attacked them near fourteen mile creek & finding them in force was compelled to fall back.

Black R Expedition

Our battery was ordered to take position in the breastworks, which had been constructed about one & a half miles on the east side of the river. The guns were placed in position & drivers returned to camp with the hordes — but had scarcely unharnessed them, before ordered out to assist in hauling cotton bales, with which to construct hospitals. The breastworks were in an open field of low level land extending back to the river, & it was very necessary to construct protections for our wounded & the Surgeons while administering to their temporary wants. The infantry also took position in the works, & notwithstanding a battle seemed imminent, there was a large force of negroes busily engaged in extending the line. I don't know whether "Old Kaintuck" was one of the number or not, times were too squally for that kind of sport. On the morning of the 13th the horses were again ordered out to the guns, & preperations made for an immediate advance. When any of the boys had mischief in them, or an ill feeling existed between any of the members; on an occasion of excitement like this — was sure to crop out; or if some one was proud of his authority — was more apt to show it plainer than at any other time. There was one of that kind; belonging to one of the guns in the first section, by the name of Hall, he was very aristocratic & overbearing. One of the boys got tired of his abuse — & he & Hall commenced fighting — a third one by the name of Paul. Brenin — a very small man — also had a grudge — & picking up the trail hand spike of one of the guns — struck Hall a stunning blow up on the head, knocking him senseless & fracturing his skull, opening the scalp four or five inches from which the blood ran freely. He was taken to the hospital & his recovery ~~was~~ thought to be very doubtful; but I understood afterwards, he made his way back to his home at Saint Louis Mo, had his skull trepaned, & was living at the close of the war.

Campaign of Big black

The infantry commenced advancing at 2 O.C. AM. ~~the~~ artillery at daylight. When we arrived within two miles of the enemy at fourteen mile creek, a line of battle was formed & all the necessary preliminaries for battle made. Some skirmishing in front. We remained in line of battle all day & night. One the morning of the 14th a few regiments of infantry were sent to the front, in search of the enemy, but returned after a few hours absence & reported no "yanks" in sight, & upon the reception of this news, we broke ranks & went into camp. My mess took up quarters in an old negro cabin. It seemed that the excitement of the two weeks previous, had completely unballanced some of the boys; — being without regular rations, & a great — deal of the time — none at all, shifting from place to place, without gaining any visible advantage made them very nervous & feelings easily ruffled. Two of the drivers on one of the guns, became involved in a quarrel — when one gashed the other in several places, with a pocket knife, inflicting dangerous wounds, which sent another one of the company to the hospital. These occurrences were very unfortunate & caused our Capt to say some ugly words. Among other things — he said, for them to "hold their temper", quit fighting among themselves, & he would insure them plenty of fighting in an other direction in a few days. Our wagons containing baggage & cooking utensils were ~~also~~ ordered up — the prospect of getting a warm meal revived us very much. On the following morning (15th), wagons arrived, & according to orders cooked rations ready for marching. About 4 O.C. PM commenced advancing on the enemy, who ~~was~~ were reported in force at Raymond.

Battle of Bakers Creek or Champion Hills May 16th

Our march was kept up until 11 O.C. PM. when we halted & laid down to rest the remainder of the night, leaving the horses harnessed. On the morning of the 16th, we were not aroused by the bugle call — as in camp; but by the quick grasp of a hand on your shoulder, & a low voice — Wake up! Wake up!! there is going to be a battle here pretty soon! the yanks are not far off. We were not aware of being so close neighbors, to our most inveterate enemies — nevertheless it was too true — the battle cloud, was — hovering low, over us, ready to pour forth its deluge of blood. The time had come — & now I will record what happened under my observation, at the Battle of Baker's Creek — or Champion Hills.

Skirmishing all around the lines, commenced early in the morning. We immediately repaired to a hill near by, & unlimbered ready for action — a hasty examination, of gun, spunge bucket, & staff was given & everything pronounced ready — Shells were inserted & the ball was opened. The enemy soon appeared in the center of our lines, in force, &

we were ordered there. Our battery & Wade's took position in an open field. We were immediately opposed by a Federal battery of parrot guns, & they fired very rapidly & with great precission hurling their shot of all descriptions in our midst. I could do nothing but hang to the reins of my horses, which were rearing & snorting, at the smell of powder & screach of the shells. Part of the time we had to sit on our horses. This is a trying position & I tell you a fellow thinks of everything at once. We had a very spirted duel of more than an hours duration, & we made it too hot for the "Feds," & they had to "get up & dust". We lost four men killed out of the first detachment. No's 2 — 3 — 4 & the gunmen. This mischief was all done with one shell, besides injuring the gun. The shell passed through the body of No. 2 then burst & killed the others. This gun had to retire from the field, as did the other gun of the first section, having been crippled also.

Our Capt. "Landis", displayed great, courage, in this engagement, & gave personal supervision, directing the guns. He sat up on his horse, while the shells flew thick & fast around him, one shell from the enemies battery burst under his horse, which only seemed to make him more erect in the saddle, & he continued to direct the movements of the guns with his same unconcernedness. The roaring of artillery mingled with the sharp crack of musketry, was heard on our left; the yankee legions were driving our men from the field, & the enemy having disappeared in our front, our division, Bowens, was ordered to their assistance, & our arrival was none too soon to check their wild career & save our men from being captured.

Battle of Bakers Creek

Our section of Howitzers & Wade's battery took position on a slight elevation about seven hundred yards from the enemy, under a perfect "hailstorm" of minnies & cannister. We prepared for action immediately & opened fire with shell, grape & canister. Bowens Infantry pushed forward, on a charge, with a wild yell & deadly aim, drove the enemy back one mile. Victory seemed almost ~~almost~~ ready to crown our efforts with success; but the Georgia troops on the left failing to do their duty & keep in pace with the advancing columns; the missourians were compelled to fall back or be captured, & having to retrograde in this manner, many brave spirits were left wounded & dying on the field, exposed to the tread of an infuriated & almost heartless foe. During the engagement at our second position, I received a bruise, from a spent canister ball, from the enemies guns, ~~between the leaders of~~ upon my left knee, which numbed my leg for some time. When the shot first struck, I thought I was badly hurt — but upon closer examination, found no blood, remained at my post, arriving at the conclusion, that my case was not dangerous; only leaving a black spot & causing me to be lame for several days. It was stated the Gen. Loring, whose division was held on reserve, urged Gen Pemberton (our commander in chief at that time) to permit him to take his division to our aid, when we were compelled to retire, & upon Pemberton's refusal — he denounced him as a traitor to our cause. Retreat was inevitable, & with an expansion of disappointment on our countenances; proceeded on our perilous retrograde movement, fired into from all sides, by every modern means of destruction in the hands of a victorious enemy. Oh! how disheartening it was; the thought, that brave men had to yield to an enemy, on account of the timidness of a brigade who failed to do their whole duty, in time of danger, & when needed badly as a support. These men were braver in camp behind a plate filled with grub than any where else.

Gen. John Clifford Pemberton, a veteran of the Seminole War, Mexican War, Indian fighting, and the Utah Expedition, refused a Federal colonelcy in April 1861, to accept a lieutenant colonelcy C.S.A. commission later the same month in Virginia. Placing Pemberton in command of the Department of Mississippi is considered one of Jefferson Davis' major mistakes. The forthcoming Siege of Vicksburg would bring out Pemberton's mediocre generalship. He would even be suspected by some of treason (Boatner III 631).

Retreat from Bakers Creek

Gen. Loring's division was left to bring up the rear, Soon after leaving our position. Brigadier Gen. Tilman of Miss was killed by the explosion of a shell from the enemy, while marching near us. To act orderly in a retreat, requires more nerve than to engage in battle; a brave man ~~is~~ writhing under the disgrace of being defeated, becomes sullen & careless in regard to the surrounding danger & a coward becomes disorganized — runs pell-mell over everything, or seeks shelter until the approach of the enemy, & becomes a prisoner. The road frequently becomes blockaded in front, causing delay — while the shells & minnies from several thousand guns, whizzing & bursting over & around you — the excitement becomes very great — the only aim is to get out of the way.

We made our way as best we could, according to orders, to the intrenchments near Big black bridge, where we arrived 8 O.C. PM. On the morning of the 17th when the gray streaks began to appear in the eastern horizon & a blood red sun was struggling to peer through the smoke of the previous days battle, one could see the glistening bayonets of our infantry, & smoke bedimed cannon in the breastworks, awaiting the coming enemy. Our section not having any ammunition, was ordered to the west side of the river, where we cooked & ate breakfast, & to enjoy a warm meal was very nourishing. The yanks kept in hot pursuit, & skirmishing commenced at sunrise; their advance, was slow, but sure, soon succeeding in driving our picket line behind the works & the deadly conflict was on again in earnest, & many brave men poured out their warm hearts blood, upon the altar of their country.

Fight at Big black Bridge

About 9 O.C. AM. the Federals charged our left, & was beaten back with heavy loss. Thinking this to be our weakest point in the fortifycations, they again massed their forces, & making a furious charge on the same point, succeeded in breaking our lines. The unbroken columns of blue coats as they advanced one after another; was too much to withstand & under a very galling & destructive fire, our lines gave way & commenced falling back. The boom of cannon & rattle of musketry, was taken up, as if by magic all along the lines. To fall back, was the only chance; but to hold the enemy in check while our troops were crossing the bridge, was the task to which we had to direct our immediate attention. The Artillery men at the works did some noble fighting — defending & firing their guns, until the enemy mounted the parapets; then abandoning them, not having horses with which to move them, Gen Pemberton having ordered all of them left on the other side of the river previous to the engagement. This looked like a very lame piece of Generalship — or being confident of a victory. In the mean time our section having received ammunition, but not in time to take a hand in the general engagement, planted our guns on a high bank west of the river, & opened fire, & continued to shell as rapidly as possible, holding the advancing columns of the enemy in check, until most of our men crossed the river, on the transports used as a bridge, & which were burned — having been thoroughly saturated with turpentine, a few minutes previous — the work of destruction was quick & effective.

Evacuation of Big black

Several men found it impossible to reach the bridge — swam the river & made their escape – others less fortunate were drowned, or forced to surrender — some were killed while swiming & found a watery grave. We lost about half the Second mo. brigade — which was on our extreme left, which made their chances of escape more perilous, & twenty pieces of artillery.

The remainder of our days work, plan of operations, & directions to move, was readily seen. Our last resort was to fall back, behind the intrenchments around Vicksburg; & leaving a sufficient force to protect the rear, & destroy all valuables, which could not be moved, or liable to fall into the hands of the enemy — we moved on — arriving at the modern "Gibraltar" of America 5 O.C. PM.

We had long looked upon this as a final resort, — a city of refuge, & a formidable defense; yet we were almost confident of our final overthrow, & notwithstanding we felt secure behind the works, was confident our doom was sealed unless liberated by help from the outside. We were somewhat despondent, having been defeated in three successive engagements recently. But we thought "While there was life there was hope."

Siege of Vicksburg

Now my kind reader, before we enter into this Siege of Vicksburg, which commenced on May 18, 1863 — I will ask you to bear with me in my feeble effort in trying to give a partial history, or in other words, a description of that portion, which came under my observation, or that I know to be true; of that memorable event. If I was a writer of tragedies; I could draw a pen picture that would flood your eyes with tears & make your heart sick to read, & then leave more than half untold — or a poet I could have found an endless chain of pathetic & heroric scenes, to fill a volume like ~~of~~ Shakespear; the Philanthropists' could have had a boundless field, to extend their love to the human family, when they chose to show such gratitude at the risk of their own lives, — & thank God we did have many there, who dared to offer themselves martyrs, to care for suffering mankind. In order that you may receive the full benefit of this description, & appreciate the motive I have in giving a short outline of the dangers, miseries & extreme sufferings at this place, you must enter into this living sepulcher with me, remain forty five or six days, & imagine if possible ones feelings, when hemed in on three sides by almost a million Bayonetts, in the hands of that many men, besides numerous cannon of all calibers & kinds dealing out their deadly discharges, some of which passed from one side of this narrow prison to the other, & on the fourth side by the Miss. river, the opposite bank of which was bristling with mortars of huge dimensions, & the men operating them seemed to be greatly delighted while shelling the City, & disturbing the midnight slumbers of the citizens in town, as well as the soldiers in camp.

Siege of Vicksburg

On the morning of the 18th we moved our guns to the breastworks, on the east side of the City, about the center of the line of fortifycations, leading around the town intersecting the river above & below the City. After remaining a short time, we left the guns in charge of the cannoniers, returning to camp with the horses in the northern suburbs of the City. I was greatly astonished when viewing the breastworks in rear of this place, & wondered why it was called one of the strong holds of the south; & I assure you felt very insecure on returning to camp. The ditch for infantry was about three & a half feet in depth & the same in width, only one line, & no embankment on the outside. The parapets for artillery, were not more than half as high as the muzzle of the gun, affording no protection for the cannoniers above the knee. Had it not been, for the walls that nature placed here when the universe was constructed, & centuries previous to the founding of this City; the defenses prepared by man up to this time, would have been but slight obstructions as a hindrance to the advance of an overwhelming enemy — such as hounded our rear at that time — & if their movements had been such as characterize those of brave men, we would have been forced to an immediate surrender, or a wholesale massacre. Our men went to work with 'ax, pick & shovel, & in less time than ~~a fortnight~~ forty eight hours, our lines were greatly strengthened; The experience of the past in that line, made us almost experts in building fortifycations. The enemy moved up very cautious giving, us ample time to make our works strong.

May & June
Siege of Vicksburg

However, this work was kept up during the entire time of the Siege. Any point around the line, that was considered weak was built up until our defences were almost impregnable — or at least Grant's forces never entered until the white flag was hoisted by our men, with a view of a general surrender.

After a few days, on visiting the City I found all kinds of merchandise & provisions, scarce & selling at exhorbitant prices, however this state of affairs had become in a great degree general all over the South, but in this City was especially so, having been superinduced, by the prospect of being cut off from the outside world for sometime.

The citizens seemed so much frightened at the constant booming of cannon, they were very much discouraged & miserable, only traveling the streets when compelled & then almost running, half bent & dodging from side to side; trying to escape the destructive mortar shells, which were falling in the City night & day, plowing the streets up in many places & tearing houses to pieces, the occupants in many instances becoming victims of this wanton & inhuman destruction. The principle of attacking defenseless men women & children, destroying private property — so characteristic in the Federals from the beginning to the close of the rebellion, was so inhuman & despotic, that the hatred toward them has been so indelibly stamped upon the mind of every Southerner, that time with all its changes will fail to eradicate.

Siege of Vicksburg

The longer the Siege continued the greater, the danger became, a great many of the business houses & dwellings were deserted; the residents having dug large caves in the towering hills east of the City, into which they fled for safety, many of whom were buried alive, by the explosion of one of those large mortar shells after entering the ground over them. These shells, thirteen inches in diameter frequently fell in our camp, & when they entered the ground, before exploding, the excavation made was sufficient to admit the burial of a horse. Darkness was no hindrance in this business, the shelling was kept up the entire night; the fuse ~~in~~ burning in the shell as it descended on its mission of destruction, reminded one of a falling meteor. But these imitations were very frequent visitors, & when an explosion occurred in mid air, the light was very brilliant for some distance around, but in an instant the density of night resumed its former stage & we poor fellows could only shrug our shoulders in fright, while listening to the fragments hailing around us.

During this time our boys at the works were having frequent artillery duels, with the enemy, occasionally loosing one of their number killed or wounded. We drivers were a short distance to the rear; where we attended to drawing the company rations, cooking & taking them to the men at the works. A large majority of the horses with which we entered Vicksburg didnot live through. Those that were not killed by the enemies bullets, perished for the want of feed & proper attention. Our water facilities were scarce & of the poorest quality, having to drink from seeps & mud puddles, many of which were "flavored" by the drainings from the carcass of ~~a~~ dead horses. In fact, to talk about a place of safety, was an absurdity — there was no safe place; where the balls from the enemies guns didnot reach us; desolation, hunger, thirst, disease & death were our constant companions.

Siege of Vicksburg

Our camp was situated near a cemetery; a city of the dead, the occupants of which had died in peace & prosperity; in the midst of loving friends & relatives, who tenderly laid their remains away to rest, & amid tears marked on the marble slab at the head of the grave. This is to the memory, of Father, Mother, Brother, Sister friend. But alas! how different was our situation; when sitting on the camp stool, or ground, lying in our tent — or attending to our duty, while these deadly messengers were hailing around us from all directions — half sick — half clothed — half starved, gloomy, wondering who would be next — maybe it's ~~me~~ I; And while these dark forebodings were hovering over us — many a poor fellow passed into eternity without even a friend, to drop a tear, grasp his hand, or smooth his ruffled locks from off his blackened brow; no coffin — no shroud, many times not even a blanket, a few clods of the valley, scarcely enough to hide from view, was his final resting place. Our camp was situated on the west side of a very precipitous hill, the bottom of which was dug until purpendicular, for four or five feet. where the majority of the tents stood. One of the boys who had been on duty at the works, came to camp & laid down in one of the tents to rest, & while asleep received a wound from which he died. There were many men killed in camp daily. We were annoyed by the whistling minnies & bursting of shells over our heads & in the midst of our ranks during the day & the deafning roar of the mortar shells at night. The scream & buzz of the parrot shells from the yankee land batteries, could be heard tearing through the air over us, & plunghing into the waters of the miss. river. Many! very many! of our brave men were killed, but the hopes of the remainder were brightened on several occasions, every eye gleamed with the brightest anticipations of victory, every cheek was flushed with renewed ambition; all thoughts of despair would be cast aside; every mind filled with a joyous hope; on which was indelibly stamped, die before give one inch. But the cause of all this excitement, & refreshing of our languishing hopes — was only vague rumors, that were frequently circulated, that Joseph E. Johnston was at Jackson Miss — only fifty miles distant, with an ample force at his command, to assist us in cutting our way through the enemies lines, & be free again. But this long looked for help — never arrived. For every hope, we had two disappointments; — for every joy, two sorrows — for every pleasure a half dozen miseries, & for every feast a hundred fasts, & I could go on & ennumerate many more happenings to illustrate our condition — but 'tis enough, to say, the City was doomed, the Angel of death, in the shape of those yankee leaden missles, had been hovering over the occupants for forty five long weary days — our provissions were exhausted, surrender or starve, was the only alternative;

Gen. Joseph Eggleston Johnston's feud with President Jefferson Davis, over his status in the Confederate Army, led Davis to refuse consideration of Johnston's war plans. This mistake ultimately led to General Bragg and General Pemberton's defeat at Stones River, Vicksburg, and eventually Chicamauga, and Chattanooga (Boatner III 441).

July

Accordingly on the evening of the 3rd day of July, the white flag was hoisted, & arrangements made by which we were made prisenors of war, the following day, & Grants million victors marched in & took possession of the handfull of their vanquished foes.

My eyes are still dimed with tears!
When I look back in pensive mood;
Although my locks are gray with years,
I yet can see that field of blood.

Surrender of Vicksburg

The firing ceased all around the liens on the evening of the third, & when the surrender was announced, although, not unexpected; Yet we were not prepared to receive the intelligence, with the same nonchalance as an idle rumor, which was often circulated in camp. The minds of all seemed to be enveloped in the most profound study, the eyes were cast downward & hearts filled with sorrow. The wharf was soon filled with yankee Gunboats & transports. The "Grideron" (Union flag) once loved but ~~now~~ then hated, unfurled to the breeze, & almost touching the muzzles of our silent siege pieces, which had been our safeguards for so long, & scarcely a ~~fortnight~~ night had intervened since they were belching forth flames of fire & shell, to aid in the overthrow of its hated bearers. Salutes were fired in all directions, by a hundred guns; as if the whole south had been conquered. But I thought at the time if Grant had known the true state of affairs — how near our commissary was drained, munitions of war consumed & our garrison reduced to a mere "handfull" of impoverished Veterans; would have ordered the salutes discontinued & flags at half mast. Instead of capturing a Bonanza — his prize was on its last legs, & badly crippled at that. However, on they came, & the streets formerly occupied by our own Citizens & Soldiers, soon seemed alive with Federal Officers & couriers, galloping in all directions. The Confederate Soldiers & Citizens became spectators & witnesses of their own downfall, forced to look upon their dread scenes or hide their eyes in shame.

Oh! Joy where did'st thou flee?
In this dark hour of Sorrow.
And hide thy sweet face from me;
To not appear the Morrow.

Surrender of Vicksburg

Tears of sorrow & fear rolled down the furrowed countenance of the aged Mother, as well as the Father whose locks had become gray from the cares of many years. The once blooming cheeks of the maiden looked pale with fright, while her eyes were bathed with tears. And the little Boys inquiry, as he hung on to his Mothers dress, & his Parents answer might be best illustrated in the following rhyme.

Oh! Mother why do you look Sad?
And Father's eyes with tears are wet?
Our homes were taken by the "Rad",
And filled with yankee bayonett.

If Grant could have captured this place when he first surrounded it the ~~loos~~ loss to the Confederacy would have been much greater & saved a vast amount of men & money to the United states. Notwitstanding; it was a death knell to the South; the key stone of the western department had dropped out; the flower of the army of North Mississippi was captured, the heaviest siege guns of the Confederacy was gone; & who was to blame? Some said that Pemberton was. A remedy could have been offered when it was too late, the great calamity could be avoided, if repeated again — but the fatal dose had been swallowed; the consequences were upon us — & all that we could do was to bow our heads in sorrow & succumb, to fate. The Garrison & city under command of Gen. Pemberton was surrendered to the United states forces under command of Gen. Grant, with the following stipulated agreement.

Surrender of Vicksburg

The garrison were to be treated as prisenors of war, paroled, & sent under guard, out of the Federal lines, Officers allowed their horses & side arms.

Privates their blankets & clothing, also a sufficient number of wagons for the transportation of baggage, cooking utensils etc etc. For the benefit of those who donot know the nature of a Parole, I will insert a copy in this book. This was given me when Caldwell was able to leave the hospital.

Vicksburg Miss July 24, 1863
To all whom it may concern, Know ye that

I. Sam. B. Dunlap, a privat of Landis battery, Bowens Division, Vol's C.S.A. being a prisoner of war in the hands of the United states forces, in virtue of the capitulation of the city of Vicksburg & its garrison, by Lieut. Gen. John. C. Pemberton, C.S.A. commanding, on the 4th day of July 1863, do in pursuance of the terms of said capitulation give this my solemn parole under oath—

That I will not take up arms again against the United States, nor serve in any military, police, or constabulary force in any Fort, Garrison or field work, held by the Confederate States of America, against the United States of America, nor as guard of prisons, depots or stores, nor discharge any duties usually performed, by Officers or Soldiers against the United States of America until duly exchanged by the proper authorities.

This was signed by me, also Captain C. A. Catlin — 101 — Reg 1 — Ill. Vol. Paroling Officer.

As I did not write a detailed & lengthy description of all the events during the Siege, I will now refer to some of the most important ones that took place & of which I have correct dates. On the 19th, 21st, & 22nd, of May the "yanks" made a desperate effort to break the lines, on our right & left, & were repulsed every time with great slaughter, the ground in front of our works was litterally strewn with the Federal dead, that they were compelled in their flight, to leave on the field, to decompose in the rays of a hot southern sun, & on the 25th Gen. Pemberton sent out a flag of truce, solicting Grant to bury his dead. The truce was granted & the dead were buried, which afforded us great relief, & more especially our men who occupied the lines where the charge was made. The stench arising from a dead body of any kind is very oppressive, but that of a human peculiarly so — & in this case, the odor arising from these dead bodies had become so very offensive, that our men could not endure it longer. The 27th our upper batteries sunk the Federal gunboat Cincinnati.

The Cincinnati, a United States gunboat with a wooden hull, was built in Mound City, Illinois, in 1861, by James B. Eads. Records indicate she was sunk as a result of a battle

> **above Fort Pillow on May 10, 1862. Commander Stembel was wounded by a minie ball through his mouth, but he recovered. The Cincinnati was raised and returned to service. When Sam saw her, she had joined the attack on the Vicksburg batteries, where on May 27, 1863, she was sunk for a second time. Raised in August 1863, she served until decommissioned in 1865 ("Cincinnati"; Way, Jr. 87).**

About the first of June we commenced to live on one half rations — this for several days — consisted of eaqual parts of corn & peas ground together. But this was soon pronounced unhealthy by the Physicians & discontinued, which was a great relief & satisfation to us.

This mixture tasted very good to us, provided we could have it always arranged to eat while warm. We drew such a small quantaty for a days rations, the waste would have been too great to make three mixings — or in other words too much would have stuck to the pan & "cooks hands" — & another reason — it was impossible for the men to leave the works. We had to divide the bread while in the dough — "so many" buiscuits to the man — if we had not adopted this plan, a few of the fastest eaters, would have gotton two or three rations. You could have "knocked a Bull" down with one of these buiscuits when cold.

Review of the Siege of Vicksburg

I often hear the remark — "a person don't know what they can do until they try." Or they don't know how much they can stand, until forced by circumstances. All the adages & old sayings, were fully demonstrated by the lives we lived during this memorable siege. It looks unreasonable that a man could live on one pound of rations per day & at the same time perform the duty of a Soldier, yet we did it for some time — & it sounds a little "fishy" no doubt, to talk about a man living on mule beef — nevertheless we did that too, — for several days previous to the surrender, & was very glad to get it — for it was mule beef or starve. I tell you my experience is, a man in his right mind, will do anything, or eat anything to save his life. We didn't need any narcotics to put us to sleep, all we required was a full stomach & a chance to ly down. Nor did we need anything while at this place to cause us to want to eat more we were always hungry — the best appetizer in the world! On the 9th of June beef gave out — (not our mule beef) — but our "blue" texas beef, & you couldn't get enough tallow out of a whole steer to grease a pair of boots.) & we received one fourth pound of bacon in its stead — also half pound of corn meal, the same quantity of peas & rice per day. On the 18th our rations were cut down to one fourth pound of bacon, the same of rice, peas & flour, making in all, only one pound of rations per day. The quantity was so small, we cooked the rice until thoroughly done, mixed with the flour & baked in the shape of buiscuits, which were very carefully divided by the cook. The bacon was cut in small slices to correspond with the number of men in the mess, cooked with the peas & both were divided as the bread. This bread was similar to the other mixture, which I have here to fore described — better eaten hot. Some of the boys would eat the whole amount at one meal — saying, they would rather have one meal a day than three pieces.

Review of the Siege of Vicksburg

On the 22nd Caldwell was taken sick with flux, & his case being considered somewhat dangerous, he deserved better treatment than could be given in camp, I was granted the privilege of going with him as a nurse to the field Infirmary, which was situated south of the City, at a point that was considered the least dangerous; although the shot & shell found us occasionally — a hot shot burned Tom. Boon's foot while lying sick in one of these hospital tents. Rations at the hospital were also short & of the poorest quality for the sick. As the siege neared the close, some of the "Feds" & "Confeds" became very good friends, In several places around the works, when there was a short cessation of hostilities, the pickets of the opposing armies, would meet, on half way ground & exchange sugar for tobacco & coffee. We had an abundance of Neworleans sugar, but had but little tobacco, & no coffee, the Feds being scarce of sugar were glad to make the change. As for tobacco, it didn't matter with me, as I never used it in any form, but could use the coffee. In some instances, by talking from one picket line to the other, found an old acquaintance or relative, arrangements were made & a meeting consumated. According to the stipulations of surrender the garrison were to be paroled, but about half of our company as did several more of our army, prefered to take their chances in a northern prison to a paroled camp in our own lines, & the choice was given them — but most of them bitterly regretted it, long before release came.

Review of the Siege of Vicksburg

They entertained various views in regard to the matter — some thought they would be exchanged sooner — but the yankee's said they would sooner feed, than fight them. others said they could make their escape — go home, or return to the ranks. But they were not exchanged until the early part of the spring of 1865 — when the war was almost over. Some few made their escape & others enlisted in the Federal Army in order to get out of prison.

On the 8th day of July, all those who went to paroled camp, except the sick, wounded & nurses at the hospitals, marched outside the Federal lines in an easterly direction.

There was some good jokes told about the troops on this march. They had been hemed up in a pen so long, when they got out — were like a bird turned out of a cage. Corn was in roasting ear, & to take time to cook it, before eating was out of the question, with some. It was told to me after I arrived at the paroled camp, by one of our boys who was a good joker — that one fellow, a Mississippian, was so hungry for corn, that he ate twenty eight ears & died with the twenty ninth clinched in his hand, about half of which was consumed. Another went to a house & asked the lady for some buttermilk. She said she was out, had given the last bit, she had on hands to the soldiers. Being badly disappointed, hesitated a moment — then asked her — When are you going to churn again? About next Wednesday — was the reply, which was about four days in the future. This didn't daunt her visitor in the least, who was so lean you could almost see through him, staggering over toward the chimney corner — said — I must have the milk & I guess I'll just make my pallet down in the corner & wait. But I don't know whether the fellow got the milk or not. By permission I remained with Caldwell at the hospital, his health not being restored sufficient to walk.

Ham Hillix's Death

During the Siege our company lost Six killed & Six wounded. One of the killed was a young man, named Ham. Hillix a resident of the same neighborhood from which I came. He was a lasting friend; a good jovial companion, & in his death the south lost a true & tried soldier. He was mortally wounded, while lying behind the breastworks asleep, by the explosion of a shell directly over our works, from a federal battery, directly in front of our guns. Soon after our men marched out, the Federals moved up & camped near our quarters, & they treated us very kindly — gave us plenty of good rations, which was very nourishing & acceptable after our long fast.

Charles Hamilton Hillix, son of James Hambleton Hillix and Ann B. Walker, was born abt. 1838 in Woodford County, Kentucky. According to Gaines Hillix of Marietta, Georgia,

the 1860 Missouri census indicates Ham was living in Buchanan County, Missouri, with his sister Cora and her husband S. Barbee. Ham Hillix is listed on Capt. John C. Landis' Muster Roll, April 30, 1861, serving under Gen. D. M. Frost. According to Gaines Hillix, the family believed Ham was killed at the Battle of Shiloh, but he was later able to determine Ham was killed in the siege of Vicksburg, Mississippi, in June of 1863. Sam's memoir does not record the exact date of death, but his brother Caldwell Dunlap's entry in *As The Mockingbird Sang* confirms Ham Hillix was killed at the redoubt on June 23, 1863 (Hillix).

The Federal Pants

I was guilty of a trick here, a few days after the "Feds" went into camp around us, that every time I think of it, makes me feel mean just a "leetle bit". The spring from which we carried water, was at the base of a very steep hill, about one hundred yards from our tent. One day I concluded to go down to the spring & get a canteenfull of fresh water — after filling it, I noticed some blue pants, belonging to the Federals, hanging on a fence near by, which enclosed a small patch of corn, on which an old negro woman had hung them to dry after washing. And after taking a careful survey of the surroundings, as I thought, — & a short parley with my conscience, concluded that a pair of them might fit me — so I went to the opposite side of the enclosure, climbed the fence, crept through the corn, as slily as possible & pulled a pair off the fence. I did not take time to think or notice how plainly I could be seen, from the high hills on either side of the valley, & the corn being so low my movements were easily detected. But I rolled up the pants, stuck them under my arm, & walked back to camp as leisurely, & with as much unconcern as possible. I had scarcely entered the tent & made a hasty examination of my bundle — when one of the boys said Yonder comes an old negro woman! And if he had said Yonder comes your "Box"! I would not have been more dismayed, than I was at that remark. In a moment the tent door was darkened by a large negro woman of the "old fashioned" type with the remark. Oh yes massa, I saw you git dem pants! I Seed you pull dem offen de fence! I was a watchin you all de time. I handed them to her with the remark, Take your old pants! They are the wrong color any how; & a hole in them at that. But it wasn't on account of the color, or hole either, that made me return them as quick, I was too anxious to get rid of the old negro without attracting the attention of the "Feds" with whom she threatened me. I could have soon dismissed the subject from my mind, so far as I was individually concerned, but there were several of the company present, who didnot forget it soon.

Receiving Parole

On the 24th all the men at the hospitals, who were able to travel received paroles, & several that were not able whose homes were in Alabama, Georgia & the two Carolina's, being so anxious to reach their friends took the desperate chances, died on the trip & was buried in the Gulf of Mexico. Caldwell & I received ours. Although we had been well treated by our new companions, our minds were very much brightened up, when we were informed that we would soon be sent to our friends. The Federals having decided to send us around by water, late in the afternoon of the 30th we were marched up to the wharf under guard of a squad of Federals, & about 9 O.C. P.M. went on board the steamer Continental, said to be the largest boat on the Miss. river at that time. We remained at the landing all the next day, & I could not avoid feeling very restless, as the guards were negroes & the first I had seen with Federal uniform on, & knowing the treacherous nature of that race, from past experience, would not have been astonished, at any time to see them bayonett one of the boys. I was really glad when the hour of departure came, which was on the evening of the 31st 8 O.C. P.M., we bid adieu, to the City of hills, & started for Mobile Alabama. The great suspense which had held us so spellbound, was broken & we felt greatly relieved, as we plunged through the darkness upon the broad, peaceful waters of the Miss, & would almost break forth in extacies of delight; when the thought would approach us. This City is gone! gone; & can only be redeemed by the blood of our Countrymen.

The Continental was a side-wheel packet built at Shousetown, Pennsylvania, and finished in Pittsburg in 1860. She was 282 feet x 41 feet x 8 feet 5 inches with four boilers, each 44 inches x 30 feet, and her engines were 26 feet x 9 feet. Her paddlewheels were 34 feet in diameter and had 14 foot buckets. She was pressed into service as a troop carrier early in 1862, was in service in Grant's Tennessee River campaign, and became a hospital boat at St. Louis in 1864. She was dismantled following a sale in December 1873 (Way, Jr. 109).

August
From Vicksburg to N.O.

Farewell! Farewell! to the City of hills!
Thou hast been our abiding place so long.
Although thou hast caused us many ills.
To leave with sighs, is better than a song.

The trip down the river was a very pleasant one indeed, during the daytime, we enjoyed the scenery along the banks very much. A goodly portion of the night was passed away very agreeably wasting & eating irish potatoes, which we "jayhawked" from barrels, of which the boat was well loaded. We were not quite so bad on the potatoes as, the fellows were on corn & milk, we had gotten filled up a little, on Uncle Sam's rations before leaving the Hospital. We arrived at Natchez Miss in the forenoon of August 1st. I thought of the tune called "Natchez under the hill" when we landed as a portion of the City is on the level running back a short distance from the river & the other is on the hill.

"Turkey in the Straw" is one of the earliest and most popular American folk or minstrel songs. The melody harkens to an 18th century British tune, "The Rose Tree." A variation was performed on stage as "Old Zip Coon" in New York in 1834, and its popularity spread across America. "Natchez under the Hill" is one of multiple variants of the original song with similar tunes, but also had other titles such as "Another Little Drink," "My Grandmother Lived," "There was an Old Soldier," "There was a Little Hen," and "Haymaker's Dance" ("Music").

But we didnot stop long, only a short time to discharge some freight. Passed Port Hudson about sundown, which but a short time previous was one of the strongholds of the South. But the die was turned against us, the bank of the river was yet bristling with guns, that were manned by the blue instead of the Gray. Also passed Batonrouge La. 9 O.C. PM, didnot make any halt — & in the forenoon of August 2nd tied up at the Wharf at Neworleans La. As soon as we stopped, the news spread like wildfire throughout the City, that a boat had landed, laden with paroled prisoners from Vicksburg, & as many of the residents had friends & relatives at that place — the thought struck them, maybe, Father's there! Or the bereaved wife, maybe Husband's there! Or the loving Sister, I know Brother's there! for he certainly would come this way. Well! I go & see was the conclusion.

At Neworleans

Very soon the landing which was clear of houses for some distance back — was packed to almost to suffocation, with an almost impenetrable mass, of men, women & children, gazing with eager eyes at the men on board — thinking they might recognize a familiar face — in that fragment of their disarmed defenders, who were hanging over the railings, looking with eaqual interest, at the sea of upturned faces. But to look & look, again & again! Was all that could be done. The citizens were kept back by a heavy guard, who frequently used the butts of their guns in shoving them back, they were placed there as soon as the boat landed. None of the Citizens were permitted to come on board, & but a few Confederate Officers to go ashore & they not outside the guards. I being from Mo, didnot expect to see a relative or particular Friend; but I thought it was enough to melt the heart of a Demon, —if as hard as adamant, would shrink under the pleadings of those patriotic men & women, who so pathetically hung around those guards, that could scarcely prevent them from rushing on the boat, at all hazzards. The crown continued to increase, & as a natural consequence the excitement became greater. The guards would frequently make motions, as if to use the bayonett, & such a thing would not have been unexpected to me, at that time, as the City was under the controll of "Spoon. Buttler" (Ben. Butler of Mass) He got the name of "Spoon Buttler" from stealing silver spoons from the residents of Neworleans. The crowd finally became so great, the guard was increased. A Battallion of cavalry, 1st Texas (so called) was ordered down & a battery of four guns planted at a convenient range.

Union Gen. Benjamin Franklin Butler was criticized heavily for having issued General Order No. 18 on May 15, 1862, which became known as the "Woman Order."

> **As the officers and soldiers of the United states have been subjected to repeated insults from the women (calling themselves ladies) of New Orleans, in return for the most scrupulous non-interference and courtesy on our part, it is ordered, that hereafter, when any female shall, by word, gesture, or movement, insult or show contempt for any officer or soldier of the United States, she shall be regarded and held liable to be treated as a woman of the town plying her avocation.**

The Mayor of New Orleans was arrested when he protested on behalf of the New Orleans citizens. Butler was criticized by Prime Minister Palmerston of the British House of Commons and across the northern states. However, Butler held fast, and the United States government did not revoke his order, but his action ultimately led to his removal from New Orleans in December 1862. Sam was writing about Butler's continued control of the city well into August 1863. After the war and after several election defeats, Butler did become Governor of Massachusetts in 1883 and then ran unsuccessfully for President the following year (Boatner III 109-110; 945-46).

Neworleans Continued

I understood afterward that, the battallion was composed of the roughest men that could be found, & didnot claim Texas as a place of nativity more than any other state. The name was only given as a slur. They had the lassos but the purpose for which they used them was a disgrace to any state or any people. The cavalry came galloping down & formed about fifty yards behind the infantry guards — in rear of which the citizens, were ordered — to go immediately. They didnot receive the order as imperitively as it was intended, by their inhuman persecutors. They moved a few paces, then turning around, to cast one more long lingering look, with a hope they might yet see some dear one. But these acts of endearment, didnot attract any sympathy from their cruel abusers; on the contrary it only kindled, the venom within their vile souls, they were only too eager to ply their dirty work. The order to charge was given, when these cowards — with the look of a fiend, Spurred their horses into a gallop, plunging into the midst of this surging crowd, riding over all who failed to get out of the way. They quickly fell back behind the line which they were ordered. But this didnot stop these fellow's devlish work — on they went! riding over women & children, the screams of whom was only music to their nefarious ears; beating men in the back with their swords, as they ran for dear life, lassoing the poor negroes & dragging them upon the ground.

Neworleans

In this manner these heartless soulless; infamous unprincipled hounds, amused themselves, & even when the sun went down, & night put on her sable robe; as if morning over the condition of these poor unfortunates, the shrieks of women & children could be heard in all directions. While lying on that boat endeavoring to close my ears against such unholy proceeding thought to myself. Oh Heavens! how long can this be tolerated? How long can such dogs be allowed to crow & rule over as brave people as live in Neworleans? Late in the evening when one of these fellows, was pursuing a man & beating him in the back with his sabre at every jump — thinking to escape his adversary — made a quick turn around a street corner — & the fellow wheeled to follow him — when his horse fell flat upon his side. Us fellows on the boat, had become silent spectators of the dreadful scenes; Standing erect, with abated breath, throbbing hearts & clenched hands; wishing that we had our old guns again, to turn loose a few charges of Grape & canister upon them. But when the horse fell with that rascal, we could not retain our silence longer, & before realizing our situation, raised the old rebel Huzza. This infuriated the Infantry guards in our immediate front, who presented arms, & threatened to shoot every last Son — of — a — b — of us, if we did that again. I heard some of the hammers click, & I would not have been surprised in the least, if they had executed their threat for they were employed to act as Imps of a Devil in the shape of Ben. Buttler. This is strong language, but I think a person could use all the vile epithets of the english language, & they would then prove inadequate, in heeping the abuse upon Buttler & his dupes, at Neworleans, which they so richly deserved.

Neworleans Completed

On the morning of the 3rd after the gray streaks of early dawn, had disappeared & daylight was again upon us; the Heroic Ladies, not daunted in the least by their former days ill treatment & disappointment, were again upon the scene, with baskets upon their arms, & crowding around the Federal officers; earnestly pleading, to be allowed, to bring them on board. But no! the Yankee's heart softened not — . His feigned excuse, was, they might bring on something contraband. He heard their cries & expressions of grief! He turned a deaf ear to their sighs, lamentations & sympathetic prayers! He saw floods of tears rolling down their cheeks, as an evidence, that their hearts were melting away with pure love & affections, for the dear ones who espoused the glorious cause, at the shrine of which she often knelt & prayed, with a devotion that none other than a true woman could. Yet, he still retained that stolid indiference, & with a heart as hard as adamant — positively refused to allow them the privilege. But finally said they would "send" them on by some of their own Soldiers. Although this didnot afford them the same pleasure as delivering the baskets, themselves. Yet in doing this, felt that they had accomplished a great deal. The Blue Coats were kept busy for a while, & the boat was strewn with articles of various descriptions. (Nothing contraband, though; as the baskets were carefully inspected before being sent on) Some clothing, provisions of all kinds, brandies, wines etc etc & also some ice & watermelons. We had an abundance to last us until our arrival at Mobile.

Neworleans Completed

Long will I remember, the kind ladies of Neworleans!! And long will I hate the cowards that abused them. In the afternoon a steam ship pulled up by the side of the Continental, & we were ordered to "pick up our beds & walk." Caldwell & I took our position on the upper deck of the Ship, & about the time the sun was disappearing in the western horizon & early twilight was coming upon us — the whistle was blown, anchor pulled in, & the ship was soon riding the waves with its cargo of human freight. The noble ladies yet lingering in clusters around the wharf, who had given us such a kind reception up on our arrival, waved an affectionate & last farewell with their handkerchiefs. And when their yankee tyrants saw this harmless proceedings became enraged, charging amongst them, a repetition of their old proceedings. This was the last scene that appeared to us, to blacken the escutcheon of "Spoon Buttler" & his band of outlaws.

From Neworleans La. to Mobile Alabama

Soon after leaving Neworleans, Caldwell & I spread our blankets upon the upper deck of the steamer, which was covered with a coat of pitch & sand, & with the stars shining down upon us, was soon wrapped in the arms of Morpheus — this was delightful — the cool breeze off the salt waters, but a few miles in advance — caused our slumber to be sound & rest unbroken. When I awoke on the morning of the 4th the ship was riding the rugged waves of the Gulf of Mexico. I rose to my feet, but found it difficult standing — tumbled down on my blanket again, & remained the greater portion of the day in a sitting or reclining position. Nothing could be seen but the water beneath & Heavens above which seemed to meet, but a short ways ahead. The rolling billows as they slashed against the sides of the rocking vessel, the white foam, tossed from one to another, or flying high above them; settling back only to be carried higher into the air again by the mad waters; was well calculated to frighten a boy like me, who had never been out of sight of land before.

Voyage Continued

Several times on attempting to rise, my head commenced swimming, &

feeling sick at my stomach; curled up on my blankets again trying to glue myself, if possible to the deck, which I imagined had gotten a great deal — smaller & slicker, & in this manner I kept from vomiting. I had often heard of sea sickness — but this was the first time I had seen it demonstrated. The deck was covered with the "remnants" of Vicksburg — several of them not being very well when they started — could not restrain their appetites, & gorging their stomachs with the good things of Neworleans; the rocking of the ship, brought ~~on~~ on sea sickness in earnest. And it was a distressing sight to see the poor fellows hanging on to the banisters, with a death grip — vomiting overboard. Some of the weaker & less fortunate ones, had to "holler" "New york" — etc etc etc too — before reaching the outside. Just such another nasty mixed up, conglomerated mass of filth, you never saw as a portion of the top of that vessel, presented when we arrived at our destination. There were several on board who should have remained at Vicksburg — but as I remarked before — were so anxious to get home; by the assistance of their friends flattered themselves that they could stand the trip, but being so weak, could not stand the rough waters of the Gulf — died from severe attacks of vomiting & purging — was wrapped in their blankets by the Sailors & without ceremony buried in a watery grave. This was a heartrending sight indeed — but this is an old custom among seamen & one which is rigidly enforced.

Voyage Completed

I have often thought it would have been a just punishment of Ben. Buttler & his crew to have been forced to sour this vessel from one end to the other, while the people who they so unmercifully abused at Neworleans stood guard & seen it well done. Passed through the Federal blockading fleet on Mobile bay under flag of truce 11 O.C. AM. Steamed on a short distance until a signal gun was fired by our troops from Fort Morgan. The meaning of this signal was to halt, which was promptly obeyed. Only a few moments intervened, before the Confederate Steamer Dick-Keys came along side the vessel which we were on, ~~&~~ & we were transferred, from the Federal to the Confederate Steamer on the waters of Mobile Bay. This was a joyous occasion, I imagined a great burden had been lifted from my shoulders — I knew that I was free again, my shackles were once more loose, & I was again sailing under our own beloved flag.

The Dick-Keyes, also known as Dick Keys, was a stern-wheeler packet with a wooden hull. She was built in Cincinnati, Ohio in 1853. She was captured by the Confederate fleet off Mobile in May 1861 and sold into private ownership.

She was later chartered to assist in blockade running out of Mobile and served as a transport at times between the forts and the city of Mobile ("Dick Keys"; Way, Jr. 128).

Arrived at Mobile Alabama 11 O.C. PM. & all that were able to walk went on shore & took up quarters in a large ware house near the wharf, those too sick to travel remained on board the boat the balance of the night. True our habitation to which we went wasn't a very sightly one — but I would have sooner slept there, than in a palace in the Yankee lines. This trip from Vicksburg Miss to Mobile Ala. although only a few days were consumed in making ~~it~~, was one full of momentous events, which will be remembered as long as one who witnessed it, lives. I am frank to acknowledge that I colored my description of that fiendish outrage on the people of Neworleans, pretty high; yet if you could ascertain the whole story of their doings at that place, would find unwritten volumes of dark deeds too infamous to blacken the pages of history. We only remained at this warehouse a few days. but during our stay had an abundance of good wholesome rations furnished us by the good ladies of the City. On the 6th with a view of getting out into the country to "rusticate & recuperate", Caldwell & I procured a thirty days furlough from the Officer in command of Paroled prisoners at this place. The greater portion of the 7th we spent in promenanding around the "Town". This was one of the most wealthy & fashenable cities of the South, the streets of which were, decorated by many beautiful women, who were very kind & courteous to us. All kinds of merchandise & provisions offering at high figures, but business was not very brisk as the principal portion of the customers bought only as necessity demanded. The advance in price & scarcty in commodities, were the only inconveniences to which they had been subjected up to this time. The true ravages of war had not come upon them. Their streets were yet paraded by their own soldiery, who always met them with a smile or salute — they were not subject to daily insults as were their friends in the Sister cities Vicksburg & Neworleans.

The streets were broad & beautifully arranged — fringed on both sides by nice shade trees, & yards in front of the stately mansions, tastily ornamented with orange, pomegranate & all kinds of evergreens & beautiful shrubs, of which the southern clime is a natural producer. Alabama is my choice of all the Southern states, & if in my writings I get a little "one sided" you need not be surprised. As, I always, was partial to the ladies, & I do think that Alabama contained more, kind hearted good looking, affectionate women, (& men too) than any other Confederate state through which we traveled during the war. I make this little deviation from my subject In order that any one will not be surprised at me pronouncing frequent encomiums upon their beauty, intellect and symetrical development at any time.

From Mobile Ala. to Demopolis

Having heard that the paroled camp had been established at Demopolis Ala, & being anxious to see the old company boys again, on the afternoon of the 8th procured tickets, by way of Meridian Miss, on the Mobile & Ohio railroad. Late in the evening the train pulled out, & after an allnights travel, just as day was breaking the engineer blew the whistle for Meridian & we were soon treading Miss. soil again, however the train on the branch road leading to Demopolis was on time, & but a few moments of the morning of the 9th were consumed before we were on the way to that place. I will not trouble you with a description of Meridian & surrounding country at this time, as I have quite an experience concerning them to relate hereafter. This railroad at that time did not intersect with the one at Demopolis, & a short time before that place was reached, took passage on a small Steamer, on the Tombigby river, which acted as a connecting link between the two stations. Arrived at our destination about 10 O.C. AM.; were very much disappointed on approaching the camp; as most of our old friends were gone. But when the cause of their absence, was explained, were held blameless. They had gotten furloughs & gone to the country. This town is beautifully situated on a high hill overlooking the Tombigby river in the midst of a rich & productive country; inhabited by a people whose souls are filled with patriotism to the South, hearts full of love & gratitude, for a Confederate Soldier, & always ready to extend a helping hand, to promote his comfort; or aid the cause for which he was fighting.

Paroled Camp at Demopolis Ala

These noble people had come to camp with their fine carriages; loaded the boys in, taken them to their houses, & bade them "eat drink & be merry".

The morning of the 10th was nice & pleasant, & after a portion of it had been passed off in lounging around camp — some of the boys proposed a walk up to town, to which I readily consented, after tramping around the streets a while — an other proposed to go into a barber shop & take a shave.

My first Shave by a Barber

Nature had not yet endowed me with much beard, only a little white "fuzz" ornamented my chin & upper lip, with snow & then a beard with sufficient, stiffness to cause the razor to "rattle". But I concluded to go through the motion, rather than stand the ridicule of my companions, who were several years my senior. So, after considerable instructions from the "chin scraper' in regard to the position in which to hold myself — to "be natural", & so on etc etc. the "job" was soon performed. Well; there is nothing peculiar about shaving, or having it done; but this was my first shave by a barber, & the remark he made impressed it deeply up on my mind. After replacing my old cotton (southern wool) hat, settled the bill, & started out, with the thought. I'm a man at last! My "feathers dropped", When he said — call 'round again, — your face is a good one to sharpen my razor on! This raised quite a chuckle with my companions; & I often wished I had left off the shave. The camp being so near deserted by the Soldiers, & we having been accustomed to so much stir & excitement, for sometime past, & realizing that the time for which our furlough was given, was rapidly passing & not reaping the benefit in the direction intended, decided to seek a more quiet retreat in the country.

A trip to The Country

And with that motive in view, on the morning of the 11th boarded the cars & traveled in an eastern direction, to Taylor's station thirty five miles, on the Demopolis & Selma railroad, & as we had no particular point of destination in view, the surrounding country good; dismounted & struck out on foot in a northern direction, to enjoy for the first time a furlough, & the thought of spending it in the country, filled out hearts with ecstacies of delight. My Brother & I had not traveled far before we came to a house, where lived a gentleman whose name was Pool, who after understanding the nature of our errand, made us welcome, but said he regretted very much that he could not keep us longer as he was on the eve of a move to Marion Alabama, on account of his wife's health. This was Perry County. When we entered & took the chairs offered us on the porch, the gentleman after eying us for a short time very closely — asked — What are such boys as you doing with confederate uniform on? How did you happen to enlist so young? Where are you from, any how? How old are you? His surprise seemed So great, & questions so fast, that we could scarcely answer one, before interrupted by another. Told him we were Paroled prisoners from Vicksburg — Also informed him that we were from North Missouri & had enlisted in the Confederate service in the spring of 1861. The last answer surprised him more than any. You Boys!! Why by George! you fellows could turn yourselves loose here if you ~~are~~ were a mind to, & never be bothered by the recruiting officers. We looked younger than we really were being small in stature, smoothe faced & pale from the long confinement & siege from which we had only been liberated a short time. Or maybe my "first shave" at Demopolis, might have had something to do in the matter.

In the Country

During the first night we remained at Mr. Pool's. I was attacked with disentery, very severe griping & every indication of a bad spell. But my newly made acquaintences, gave me medicine & treated me so kindly, that I was able to be up & around after a few days. When a person is at home, surrounded by friends & relatives, ~~we donot~~ he doesn't appreciate the value of the old adage — "A friend in need is a friend indeed." True; I had an untiring Brother at my side, but he needed something with which to comfort me, & these good people saw my need & willingly contributed. The acts of such friends at a time of need like this, will always be remembered by those worthy of receiving them. On the 15th having been informed by our worthy Host, that he would not remain at that place but a few days longer, suggested that Caldwell hunt another house to go to, as soon as I was able to travel, also directed him to a Mr. Pope's about two miles distant. After a few hours absence, he returned & said every thing was alright. Which was awful good news to me, as I didnot wish to return to camp, as sick as I was at that time. My improvement was slow. But having gained sufficient strength to walk around some, on the morning of the 18th concluded to make our way to Mr. Pope's. Mrs. Pool having gone to her new home — we bid her worthy husband good bye, & thanking him for his kindness & hospitality; started for our prospective abiding place.

First trip to the Country

The walk fatigued me considerable, but was very much revived, when met at the door by the kind lady of the house, who with a smiling countenance bade us enter & make ourselves at home. Showed us into a nicely furnished room with a well selected library of good books, & told to read any one we wished. Mr Pope was not at home — he belonged to the state Ala. Malitia, & only made ocasional visits home. Caldwell went to Camp on the 19th & was gone several days, & during his absence I was very lonesome, & in order to pass off the time as pleasantly as possible, employed a portion of the day in reading, then walk around over the place until wearied, & while sitting on a fence resting which enclosed a small pasture, in which was a herd of goats, & they being something new to me, found great amusement in watching them romp & play. — but they were not quite as familiar as those at Saltilo Miss. There were several fig trees in the garden, laden with their delicious fruit ready to be plucked — & as I always was a dear lover of that fruit when dried, concluded to try some fresh from the tree. The flavor being so rich, could not eat but one or two at a time, at the beginning — but being told by our worthy Lady friend, to keep trying — they were harmless, & would soon get so we could eat all we wanted — also said when fresh from the tree were very healthy.

I was not slow in taking her advice, & before I left could have almost eaten a "hatfull", without suffering very much inconvenience. She also had an abundance of sweet potatoes & buttermilk — & we didn't have to wait until "next Wednesday" for a churning either, this was better than all the medicine & I tell you — when I left there — looked as if I had an over dose of clover.

Mr. Pope's Residence

On the 22nd, Caldwell returned from camp, & Mr Pope came home from the army on a short pass. He treated us with a great deal of kindness & respect, took us out buggy riding over the country, the soil of which was very good, yielding abundant crops of corn, cotton, potatoes, tobacco & garden vegetables to reward the labors of the husbandman. While here we took the cars & spent a portion of a day in Selma Ala. a very flourishing little City. The manufacturing interest was very extensively manipulated, but chiefly in the interest of the Confederate government. We frequently hunted squirrels through the timber on the river bottom a short distance off — the woods also abounded in choice wild plums & muscadines, of which we partook with the greediness of a child. Although there were no young folks there, we enjoyed ourselves very much. It was a very quiet place, sometimes we could scarcely realize that the war was yet going on, not seeing any troops or hearing any guns, as we had been so much accustomed, in former days, was a great, great relief, yet in a moment of deep silent thought, would start; as if arroused by the sullen thundering of the loud mouthed cannon or the rattle of musketry. Notwithstanding, we had already been in the country the greater portion of a month, our time was passed as pleasantly, it seemed but yesterday since we left the camp at Demopolis, but a hasty examination of our furlough, revealed the fact, that the period of time over which it extended had about expired, & as punctuality had been our motto heretofore, desied not to be lagging in this instance.

September
First return to camp

Accordingly on the morning of the 5th of September, we bid our kind Protectors a friendly adieu, with thanks for their many kindnesses & hospitalities; while they in return were extending their wishes for good health, the preservation of our lives, & safe return home at the close of the war, & with reluctance turned our backs upon this comfortable home, made our way to the Depot & were soon passing the mile posts at a rapid rate, – the train soon pulled up at Demopolis. When we arrived in camp found several of the boys sick & quarters unclean. This uncleanliness, to a great extent was occasioned by so many being absent & remainder becoming careless in regard to their habits & diet. The day following our return, was sunday, & to act something after the fashion, of our antebellum days, attended Church in Town, but there were so many more in the same notion we could not enter the house.

Second trip to the Country

After remaining in camp for a few days, without any particular duty to perform, & no news in reference to our exchange, we again became restless, having lately tasted of the sweets of home like life, made us more anxious to return to the country, & with that view made application to the Officer in command of the Post & received a four days pass, & on the morning of the 10th jumped on board the cars, traveling in the same direction as before, but farther on to Marion junction, & after changing cars, traveled to within five miles of Marion Ala., dismounted at a way station, & struck out on foot in a western direction, after traveling about one & a half miles, night overtook us, & we remained at the house of a Mr Morgan. On the next morning when we informed him, what brought us to the country, what we were doing, & where from, pursuaded us to remain with him, & spend all the time our pass called for, to which we very readily agreed, as all the surroundings, suggested an abundance of "old fashioned" comfort. The dwelling was slightly on the antique style, & from appearances, had stood the storms of many summers. The family consisted of a widow lady past middle age & one Son who had turned on the second grade of Bachelordom, also a large lot of negros.

The morning of the 13th we were still enjoying the hospitality of our friend Mr Morgan & it being ~~the sabbath~~ Sunday, his usual custom was to spend a portion of it in divine worship, & by request I accompanied him to church. I assure you, it seemed to me that I was out of place, seated in a carriage by the side of these people with their "store clothes" on, when I had on my old dingy faded uniforms, but they took in the emergency of the occasion — & said, the clothes are right if the heart is right, & with that assurance I enjoyed myself finely. On our return trip was overtaken by a carriage filled with ladies; friends of our worthy Host, & after a short friendly chat, they insisted very strong on me accompaning them to their home, only a short distance, & take dinner, & as the Ladies always wielded a great influence over me, I was not long in yielding to their urgent request. Suffice to say I enjoyed myself exceedingly well, especially in the society of two young ladies, & I have often soundly abused myself for not recollecting their names.

At Mr Morgan's

I being a stranger, they treated me with more courtesy than could have been expected, & more than would have been given, under ordinary circumstances. But those war times were very extraordinary, & any clean respectable looking Confederate Soldier, was at home in the finest furnished parlors of all true Southerners, I tell you all false modesty & style were banished, & the noble ladies were seen & met everywhere dealing out acts of kindness & mercy. If the men had filled their sphere as well as the women, the south would have come out victorious. The 14th we spent a large majority of the day, on a plasant visit with Mr Morgan to his Brotherinlaw's. This of itself was a very agreeable circumstance, one worthy of record, especially in a soldiers life — but that wasn't all — every time this date came around, made me one year older. I was now entering on my twenty first year — the time all boys consider themselves free — but the cruel war still raged with increased fury & barbarism — & the time of my servitude was uncertain, — but thanks be to God, I was not serving as a slave, my service was voluntary — & the yoke I was wearing was my own choice. We often rejoiced that circumstances, threw us into Mr. Morgan's company, as he was a whole souled jovial fellow — & spent all of his time during our stay, in visiting his neighbors with us & hunting squirrels, of which the woods were well stocked. There was but little hunting done as the war had about drained the country of able bodied men. On the 16th we received the news that the Vicksburg prisoners had been exchanged — & also a request for all of them to return to paroled camp as promptly as possible.

Furlough Concluded Paroled Prisenors Exchanged

This news was not unexpected — but we had become very much attached to our new home & associates, & would have been more than glad to have had the ~~time~~ period extended — a short time any way.

This was our second parting from newly made friends & country pleasures, & as a matter of course was worse than the first. But the time had arrived for us to return to our duty — & in obedience to the summons, on the morning of the 17th it again became our painful duty to separate from our country friends — a comfortable & happy home, to return to our post of duty, in the tented field, & endure the hardships privations & uncertainties of such life.

Return to Camp
Exchanged Sept. 17 - 63

Oh! what a great change & whether altogether agreeable with our feelings or not; it behooved us as good & true Soldiers, to return to our post of duty, regardless of all these thoughts & pleasure desires. Arrived at Demopolis 2 O.C. PM and found everything putting on military airs again. Wagons were busily engaged in hauling enfield rifles, with which to arm infantry of the first Mo. brigade. The infantry were also being payed off. On the 18th the remnant of our company was paid off, which was money very welcomly received, as it had been a long time between "showers."

The infantry continued drawing arms. Our camp was very quiet until the 22nd, when all was astir & months filled with glorious good news from Bragg's army in Tennessee, who was reported as fighting the "yanks" for two days, & driving them before him in every engagement. During this time we were having a good old lazy time lounging around camp, doing nothing, waiting for our guns (cannon). But not so with the infantry, they had daily drill, & dress parade every evening about sunset. This proceeding was something new in that part of the country, & the Ladies in large numbers, from the town & surrounding country attended to witness it every evening; & I tell you, their appearance on these occasions, was a great stimulant to the boys. While here there was also a brass band, made up of Missourians.

In June 1862, Gen. Braxton Bragg took command of the Army of Tennessee from General Beauregard, but failed to distinguish himself as a competent leader in high command. He was ultimately relieved by Gen. Joseph E. Johnston and became a military advisor to President Jefferson Davis. He frequently suffered migraine or sick headaches, thus, despite his genuine patriotism, his service was ineffective (Boatner 78).

Camp at Demopolis

At this time the army in all the different branches was busily engaged in organizing, & some not having arms, in order to get them back into their old channel, & ready for active business, & that they might have exercise & something to pass off ~~them~~ time, we were frequently called out on review. On the 24th there was brigade review in the morning & division in the evening, conducted by Brigadier Gen. Cockerell; It was estimated we had one thousand men in ranks. 25th we had division review again, by Lieut Gen. Hardee, a brave noble looking old gentleman. The Review grounds were again ornamented by quite a number of Ladies, who were always very acceptable spectators. Also had plenty of music by the band which was a great addition to the days programme.

Col. Francis Marion Cockrell commanded the 1st Missouri at Vicksburg; he was commissioned brigadier general in July 1863 and served under Gen. Samuel Gibbs French in the Atlanta campaign. He ended the war in Mobile, Alabama (Boatner III 161).

Gen. William Joseph Hardee was commandant of cadets at the United States Military Academy at West Point. He was on leave when his home state of Georgia seceded, and he resigned twelve days later to join with the Confederacy (Boatner III 374).

While we were at this place we had preaching in camp by the army pastor at night; which continued some time. Although his sermons were very interesting & feeling; well calculated to touch the heart of the hardened sinner; his labors were only rewarded by a few mourners, upon the "anxious seat". He had a very good audience & a moderately attentive one, in the immediate vacinity of his stand. But on the on the outskirts of the crowd & under the sound of his voice, monte banks were running in full force, & poker seven up & euchre, were played, & not for passtime either, they believed in the old axiumn "Money makes the mare go".

Seven Up (also called Old Sledge) is an American card game spun from an old British card game known as All-Fours. Variations such as Setback and Cinch developed, and today the popular descendant is Pitch (Jacoby and Morehead 277-78).

Euchre is the American form of the old European Triomphe game. The origin of the name is unknown, but the play is extremely simple. Each player is dealt five cards and attempts to win more than half the tricks (Jacoby and Morehead 264).

Camp at Demopolis

The description I have given, sounds a little harsh, but 'tis nevertheless true — as I have remarked before, many thought entering the army, gave them free license, to enlist in all immoral acts, & the more they could practice, with the least exhibition of shame the better.

As for myself I always took pleasure in attending divine worship wherever & whenever a chance afforded itself, & I never played at any game of chance for money. As the saying goes — it takes all kinds of people to make a world; & as the Confederate army was principally — in fact all of that portion, volunteers, made up of men from almost every state in the united states, would naturally be composed of all classes. Not having anything particular to hold me in camp, & beginning to feel somewhat restless on that account, on the 29th I procured a twenty four hours pass, & went to the country near Uniontown Ala. on a visit. This was not very far from the place we spent our first furlough. Spent the time very pleasantly at Mr Watts residence, in face I was so much charmed, by the music on the piano & the young lady who made it, that the time for which my pass was given, had gone & another twenty four hours besides. She played & sang the southern airs so sweet, & with so much enthusiasm, it was a great luxury to be a silent listener. I always was a dear lover of music, & had a "whole heep" of respect for the gentler sex.

1863 October
Camp at Demopolis

The 1st day of October was a rainy day, & returning to camp I got considerably dampened. The remnants of Landis', Wade's, & Guibor's old batteries were thrown into one company. Perhaps a short explanation in this connection, would be beneficial in order to afford a better understanding.

These three companies went into Vicksburg, with almost a full quota of men, but their ranks were thined out, by death from disease, as well as the enemies bullets, missing & those who went to northern prisons, that we could not draw guns for every company, & to recruit from the infantry, would reduce, their already weakened ranks too much; & as a natural consequence, the army that came from the trans mississippi department, had all suffered the same reduction & it was not necessary to have as much light artillery in the field as before. Capt. Guibor being the senior officer of the three companies, was honored with the Captaincy, & the consolidation was called the first Missouri battery Confederate states of America. Our Captain was turning somewhat on the shady side of life. But he was full of energy, kindhearted & generous in every respect, yet he was a strict deciplinarian, had enough french blood in his veins, to make a complication of daring & bravery that was very difficult to excel in any man. But unfortunately for himself & us he was not blessed with health & physical powers sufficient to be with us all the time. This Consolidation made one of the best artillery companies in the confederate army — & to note the facts as I record them, in regard to their daring bravery on so many well contested fields, & true devotion to the southern cause, from this period until the last act of the bloody drama was performed, will be sufficient proof that my assertion is not an exagerated one.

Camp at Demopolis

On the morning of the 2nd we moved camp about half mile north to the fair ground & commenced duty as soldiers, that is standing guard etc etc, but could not drill as we had no guns. This move gave us shelter, in the absence of tents, but wood was rather too far off, as we required a great deal in cooking — remained here several days, during which time having an opportunity of sending a letter through the lines, by our mail carrier Grimes, wrote one to father, it looked very much like a game of chance, but I knew a fond Parents' desire to hear from a son, & rarly ever let a chance however uncertain escape.

The weather was cool & pleasant — but Caldwell could not enjoy it very well as he commenced chilling. On the 9th we again moved camp, this time one mile south of Demopolis, to a nice cedar grove, & plenty of hickory, oak & ash timber to burn for cooking purposes, also good water handy. Several of the company boys sick, partly caused by not having sufficient shelter from rain, & the heavy dews so common in the south. No guns yet & not having any tents, on the 10th Caldwell & I built a shanty of cedar poles, halved. We left one end open & made it just wide & high enough for two to sleep in comfortably, & after putting in a liberal quantity of dry grass, on which we spread our blankets, made good sleeping quarters. On the 13th the Missourians were very interestingly entertained by a short but very forceable speech from George. Vest who was representing the fifth

Congressional district of Mo, in the Confederate congress. A southern man never listened to him speak, without going away filled "brimen" full of enthusiasm for the cause he so ably & fearlessly advocated.

> **George Graham Vest was born in Frankfort, Kentucky, in 1830. He was a graduate of Centre College, in Danville, Kentucky, the same college Sam's older brother Wallace attended before the war. Vest began practicing law in 1853. When Sam listened to him speak, Vest was serving in the House of Representatives of the Confederate Congress (February 1862 to January 1865), after which he returned to the practice of law. In 1877, Vest moved to Kansas City and, two years later, was elected as a Democrat to the United States Senate. Vest died in 1904 and is interred in Bellefontaine Cemetery, St. Louis, Missouri ("Vest").**

In the afternoon of the 16th the first Mo & Ala. brigades were reviewed by Gen's Johnston & Hardee. The long line of infantry was formed, & as these two grand old Patriots, started on horse back in front, a salute from the artillery was fired. Cheer after cheer greeted the noble gray haired veterans who had faced the foe on many hard fought fields, & all eyes were rivited upon them as they rode with uncovered heads up & down the lines. Although the troops had been called out on review so often that it had become monotonous & tiresome, yet on this occasion, they returned to camp feeling well recompensed for their trouble. Our company was divided into four detachments, to be ready for the guns, & sergeants were appointed over each. Also commenced drilling, but could not go through the whole maneuver, not having guns. While here we foraged the surrounding country pretty extensively for sweetpotatoes etc etc, and in this case there was no dodging — when your time came around, you had to go —, as there were regular details made from the mess, when articles were needed, or when the "bag" was empty the next in turn had to fill it. This of course was an arrangement among us privates, this was not in accordance with military tactics, it was some thing the officers had nothing to do, or knew nothing about. The mission upon which one of these details were sent, & time allotted them to perform their duty, never commenced until after tattoo roll call.

Camp Near Demopolis

One night several of the boys from different messes, went out on a tramp for potatoes, & after a long weary fruitless search for that highly esteemed vegetable, becoming tired & disheartened, turned their course toward camp, they had come but a short distance, when they overtook two old Negro men, carrying a sack full of peanuts each, upon their shoulders which they expected to sell to the soldiers, & no doubt they were out without permission as the boys conjectured & the idea that the darkies had stolen them while their masters were asleep, was readily accepted & one of the party suggested they capture them, in which they all agreed; raised the yell, at the same time rushing up on them, the old darkies did not run far before they became so bably frightened, ~~they~~ dropped the peanuts & fled begging for dear life.

About midnight the boys strolled into camp, minus the potatoes for which they had gone, but thought the peanuts beat nothing. On the afternoon of the 17th all the troops at this point were again reviewed. It was about 1 O.C. PM when they were found in the streets of Demopolis. At this time another more noted figure accompanied the reviewing Officers. This noted person was Pres. Jeff. Davis, & as this was the first time it had been my good fortune to see him, I scrutinzed as closely as possible, his tall slender form, as he stood almost erect in his stirrups, while passing our position in line. Although one eye was gone, the remaining one which set well back under a high projecting forehead & firmly knit brow, had lost none of its brilliancy. As the Pres. accompanied with Johnston & Hardee passed; — each regiment seperately gave three long loud cheers, in praise of the illustrious trio, with whose presence they had been honored. This occasion also brought out a great many of the citizens. We also drew twenty one horses & harness for a four gun battery. This amount of horses, was scarce one third enough; as it required fifty six to haul the guns caisons & mount the Commissioned & noncommissioned Officers that should be mounted.

In her memoir, *Jefferson Davis Ex-president of the Confederate States*, Varina Davis described a fever which brought on acute inflammation of Davis' left eye and threatened ulceration of the cornea. She recounts his sleeping three weeks during the day, arising only after dark to walk about the house. At that point, Davis could not tolerate bright light nor see at all. On August 22, 1852, Davis wrote a letter from his home in Palmyra, Mississippi, in which he referred to a letter he had recently received. He stated he was unable, because of ophthalmic disease, to write an answer at an earlier time. Mrs. Davis later described Davis in the winter of 1859 wearing a blindfold during another convalescence period. She wrote, "Mr. Davis grew slowly better, the unimpaired eye cleared, his throat had been for some time pretty well;. . ." (469-71; 581-2).

Camp Near Demopolis

On the 19th the first Mo brigade, in obedience to orders received the previous day, to move in the direction of Meridian Miss, marched out early with elastic step, but murmered considerable at the idea of returning to a state, where a cold hand, had heretofore been extended, which was emblematical of a heart, seemingly without a soft spot for a southern soldier. A portion of Miss had been used as a battle ground & that part was badly torn up, but that should not have affected the whole state. True there were a great many good people in miss. but they were scattering when compared to Ala. When a minstrel troop or anything of the kind happened around, some of us generally went to pass off the time. On this occasion we went to Demopolis, to witness a panoramic view of the battle fields of Bull run, Oak hills & Lexington. I was unable to decide whether the scenes of the former two were correct or not, but I didn't see any of "Old Paps" hemp bales, in the scene intended to represent the battle of Lexington Missouri. All this looks well & shows off to a good advantage on "paper". Yet one cannot gain the faintest idea, of the real danger agony & destruction of life, by simply an eye seeance of this description.

Camp Near Demopolis

We also received orders to move at the same time the brigade did, but to our great satisfaction were countermanded on the 21st. We had a nice camp, had gotten things a little "fixed up," & we naturally detested the idea of following in the direction taken by the brigade. We had various duties to perform in the absence of our guns, & amongst them a very sad one on the 23rd. I was one of a detail of sixteen men, sent out as infantry, about five miles in the country, to perform the last sad rites over the remains of a Lieutenant. Lee of the fifth Mo Infantry. After his body was lowered in the grave, we fired one volley of small arms, over the open grave to represent the arm of service to which he belonged, & after hiding from view the rough coffin with the "clods of the valley" all that was mortal of this noble young soldier & officer; made our return to camp about dark through the rain. It was a great honor to be burried in this manner, & one which comrads delighted to extend to one of their number, when overtaken by the grim monster death, if so situated. Many poor fellows who fell in battle were not buried at all, & many more even if covered was not sufficient to hinder the hogs & buzzards from mutilating their bodies.

Drew guns

On the 27th we drew four twelve pound Napolean guns. These were smoothe bored brass pieces, for shooting solid shot, shell grape & canister. This lifted the great suspense to a certain extent, under which we had been laboring for sometime past, but our outfit was not yet complete as the caisons had not arrived. Well, as I said before we had our regular details to forage for sweet potatoes; I had already filled one appointment, on which we struck a field containing fifteen or twenty acres, of fine yellow yams, & soon grabbled our gunny sacks full & returned to camp without being molested.

Camp Near Demopolis

They were very fine, the soil & climate made an abundant yield of extraordinary size. But the old planter noticed that some one had been making inroads on his potatoes, & he began watching the patch, & when the time for my second trip came around, things began to be a little ticklish, nevertheless we concluded to try it.

A fruitless Sweetpotato raid

Having a fellow in the company by the name of Tom. Burgess who volunteered to lead us. He said that he could fool the old man — & with that assurance we gathered our sacks, he taking a bridle, as a blind — & all trailed off through the darkness. After traveling about two miles & a half, we arrived in a thick woods that was near the potato field. Now boys said our leader, I know we are close to the place we started for, & addressing us in a tone scarcely above a whisper; you all stay here & be as still as "mice" & I'll go out & see if the old man is watching. This idea of sending out a "feeler", we had gained from our experience in military tactics. If we had all gone into the field in a body, our purpose would have been readily detected, & in all probability some of us hurt. Burgess hung the bridle upon his arm, climbed the fence & proceded very slowly & cautiously through the field, traveling as though he did not know~~ing~~ where he was going, acting as if he was badly bewildered, wandering aimlessly about through the patch; finally came near where the old gentleman was secreted behind a small pile of rubbish, who raised up with a double barreled shot gun in his hands, Saying halt; who comes there? & demanded of Burgess his business out there at that late hour. These rapid interrogatories & the appearance of the gun, only unhinged our leader ~~only~~ for the time being

— as he was always ready for any immergency; told the defender of the patch — that he had been looking all day for some horses that had strayed away from camp; had lost the direction since dark, was completely turned round, bewildered — in regard to the course to take! The Old gentleman asked if he was hunting the camp near Demopolis & being answered in the affirmative. was very particular in giving directions to his deceptive stranger companion, so that he could return to camp & take the rest of which he professed to be so much in need. Thanking the old man very kindly for his information, Burgess came back to where we were; bewailing the ill luck, with which he had been encountered, & after a short consultation, beat a hasty retreat to camp, with empty sacks & tired limbs — crawled into bed as easily as possible to avoid, being noticed by our comrads. There were a few sleepy looking fellows, fell into line the next morning at reveille roll call, & I imagined all the rest knew where I had been & how badly I got left. About this time we commenced drilling on the guns — which after a few lessons became familiar again. This was our first drilling since sometime previous to our incarceration at Vicksburg. We also cleaned (which we termed policed) off the company grounds — with brush brooms.

Camp Near Demopolis
Nov 1st

On the 29th having been notified of the arrival of our caisons & battery wagon, took the horses to the depot at Demopolis & hauled them out to camp. Having drawn our full quota of horses a few days previous, this after so long a time, made our outfit complete, so far as our required weapons of warfare, were concerned. On the first day of November, we received orders to move to Maridian Miss on the 4th Inst., as a portion of the troops had already preceeded us several days — this order was not unexpected; but we fondly hoped that the order would be countermanded.

Inst. is an abbreviation of instant and refers to the current month. This term is not commonly used today.

On the morning of the 3rd moved the guns down to the boat landing at Demopolis, & leaving a guard with the guns, the others returned to camp, with the horses, to await transportation. On the 5th agreeable to orders received, broke camp, & moved down to river, where we remained all day & night. And to make our position a very disagreeable one, rain commenced falling 3 O.C. P.M. & continued the greater portion of the night. The only shelter we had was an old leaky transport tied up at the landing. We regreted very much to leave the camp, where we had subsisted to a great extent, upon the fruits of our night raids, for articles we did not draw from the company commissary. We all made a promise within ourselves, to pay the farmers for their sweet potatoes when we come back, "in a horn";

On the morning of the 6th feeling very drowsy & bad, from the nights experience I had passed on the old boat which leaked awful, it being an impossibility to find a dry place large enough to spread a blanket, & feeling the need of a good warm breakfast, went up to the hotel in town, where I indulged my appetite, as long as I thought agreeable with the patience of the land lord, & when I pulled my knees out from under the table, I felt as if my proportion had become greater & I know my strength was very much increased.

Demopolis To Meridian

About 8 O.C. AM the Captain of our old leaky craft ordered the cables pulled in, yelling at the same time all aboard, & we were soon floating down the Tombigby river, on the transport called Marengo, as the distance was short our ride didnot consume many hours, & we hardly had time to warm ourselves in the sunshine, before our frail conveyance ~~was~~ anchored at McDowel's landing.

At least two packets with wooden hulls, one a stern-wheeler and the other a side-wheeler, were named Marengo. The one built in 1844 in Louisville, Kentucky, was lost in a collision on August 24, 1848, at Clarksville, Mississippi. The other one, built in 1855 in Brownsville, Pennsylvania, made the Cincinnati-Memphis run in the spring of 1860 and the Pittsburgh-New Orleans run in the spring of 1861. However, Way Jr. reports she was dismantled in 1862 and that her machinery went into the building of the Armenia. In November 1863, Sam reports "floating down the Tombigby river, on the transport called Marengo." Information on the stern-wheeler packet Armenia built in 1862 in Brownsville, Pennsylvania, reports her engines came from the Marengo. It is unclear whether the Marengo that was lost in collision in 1848 was raised at a later date or whether the second Marengo described was dismantled at a later date (Way Jr., 31, 307).

The wharf was not in very good condition for handling artillery, which occasioned considerable delay in removing the guns from the boat, to the cars, as it was 2 O.C. PM before the signal was given by the conductor & the locomotive steamed off in the direction of Meridian Miss. Traveling by rail in the south at that time was very dangerous, & as a general thing very slow, On this trip we got several pretty severe shaking's up, & lost one gun & caison on the way, which fell off the cars. This caused an extra detail of men & an extra trip for an engine & flat car, but the lost was soon recovered & brought up with but little damage. Arrived at Meridian 8 O.C. PM. The men feeling considerably worse of the wear from the previous night, gathered their blankets in haste & were soon sound asleep on the platform around the depot. On the morning of the 7th unloaded our "tricks" & moved out to camp about one mile from town. The surrounding country is generally rough, soil thin on upland & was covered with a heavy growth of pine timber, interspersed with scrub oak & some ash & hickory. We received tents after dark, the long looked for & often promised, arrived at last, but not before they had been greatly needed, & those who were vested with the power of distributing them, had been given many an old fashioned "Cussin" for not sending them sooner.

Camp Bowen Meridian Miss

This was not surprising when all the surroundings are considered. Turn a lot of men loose in the fall of the year, in the cold rains which invariably accompany that season in the south, & the best of them will become fretful & abusive. If they had not used all possible means in their power to keep themselves warm & dry — as Caldwell & I did in building the little cedar shanty, & many others likewise — the mortality in our army from exposure would have outnumbered those slain by the enemies bullets. On the 8th tents & messes were divided, & the tents ~~were~~ pitched in military order. This camp was named Camp Bowen, in honor of the deceased Gen. John. Bowen, who died a few days subsequent to the surrender of Vicksburg. His widow who is yet living was with him during the siege, & a faithful nurse at his bedside at the time of his death.

On the 9th we grubbed all the stumps in the company & parade grounds, & policed them thoroughly. The idea of soldiers grubbing stumps may sound a little amusing to the readers of now-a-days, but we took as much pride in having our quarters clear of stumps & rubbish — when we had a prospect of remaining some length of time — as the majority of farmers display in clearing their fields of them, & whence clean, but little labor was required to keep it that way. On the 12th the first mo. brigade was again reviewed by Gen Johnston. From information gained from Officers who were situated so as to form an idea, & news paper reports all favored a prospect of winter quarters, & some of the infantry commenced building cabins, also some of the messes of our company.

The matter of erecting shelter other than tents, was left wholly to the discretion of the men, if they prefered lying in their tents & save the extra labor — alright, but the majority of our company built cabins, whenever a chance offered itself. About this time clothing, was issued, & I was lucky enough to draw a pair of pants & one shirt — the pants were always so long & large in the legs for me — I had to alter them before they would look any ways decent, & in this manner, I became handy with a needle before the war closed. Clothing was always so badly needed, by the troops before it was received, that I was as much pleased to get a new article to wear as, I once was proud of new boots in wintertime, & almost as well pleased over a new pair of pants — as I was of the first pair I had when a little boy. — I went to bed without them — but on awakening in the night — put them on & returned to bed. On the 18th my mess finished a cabin constructed after the same plan of the one at Grenada, & about the same material — except we made boards of pine instead of cypress. This put us in shape to enjoy Soldiers life very nicely, yet this comfort didnot make some of them any more obedient, if any difference it had a tendency to the contrary, & seeing this disposition making, its appearance — the Officers began to draw the reins a little tighter, & for a while it was a daily occurrence to have a man bucked, or tied up near the sentinels post, and often the offense committed would be of the most trivial character.

Camp Bowen

I remember on one occasion a man was bucked for disputing a corporals word, this was an unusual occurrence between noncommissioned officers & privates. This consolidation of batteries, gave us a company of men who were hard to beat, but we had one or two Lieutenants, who I often thought banked a little to heavy on old regular, military tactics, & at times were very overbearing. This camp was beautifully situated near the summit of a hill, on the side which gradually sloped to the south & west — the immediate ground occupied by our tents & guns had once been cultivated, but from appearances had been turned out to the commons for some time, surrounded on three sides by timber, the majority of which was pine. To demonstrate the thoughts & feelings that take possession of a soldiers mind & heart in a strange land, I will give you a verbatum copy of my notes of the 23rd.

23rd

A variable day was passed & night came on, which shrouded the camp in darkness; the night was well nigh gone; the pale faced moon had already passed her central spot in the heavens, on the nights tour, & was looking down upon the earth from a thinly clouded sky, the bright guns reflecting her sparkling rays, as they fell softly upon them; when the sentinels beat become my post of duty. All things seemed hushed & silent; nothing was heard to break the dead stillness of the night; save the lonely Sentinels voice, in the surrounding camps, as he said halt! Who comes there? To the Corporal as he approached with the relief guard, the lonely, sad & monotonous song of the whippoorwil, in the far distant valleys; or a Southern breeze softly murmering through the tops of the majestic pine, which bowed their lofty heads toward the earth, as if reverancing the creator of all things. Though far far, away in a distant land, where the cruel ravages of was have bound me; my thoughts yet wander back upon those dearly cherished scenes that occurred in childhoods happy day around my own dear Father's hearthstone.

Camp Bowen

Such thoughts as these frequently filled the minds & hearts of the soldier, but he was too manly to mention them, or drop a tear in sympathy with his feelings — in presence of his comrads. The only alternative was to hunt some lonely place & with pen & ink — or pencil, transmit them to paper, or when lying upon his couch tossing his aching head from side to side, upon a pillow made of his clothing, canteen or a chunk of wood — could then bid them come near & be his companions while the eyes can be bathed in silence from floods of tears, the upheavings of a pentup soul. The 24th was made especially memorable to one man of the company, who was bucked for not giving his horses the proper attention. Perhaps in this connection, it would be well to explain the meaning of bucked as used in the army.

This was a punishment, & although one I never received, I looked upon it as one very severe & degrading — well calculated to cow the most obstinate nature of the strongest man. It was done by tying a mans hands together with a string, & slipping them over his knees, so as to admit a small stick, under the bend of his knees & over the arms, thus forcing him to remain in a sitting position. While camped at this place, we devoted a great deal of our time ~~n~~ to drilling, we had one entirely new feature, introduced, which was very interesting, & one which was well to be instructed upon, in case of an emergency. That ~~was~~ of mounting & dismounting the guns, changing the wheels etc etc. which was all done quickly by numbers & without any discord, as every man knew his post, & where to take hold at a given command.

Camp Bowen

It was astonishing to see how easily & with what dispatch those heavy guns & carriages were handled by six or seven men. On the 27th we went out on field drill, which gave me rather too much exercise for the amount of B__l beef & cornbread we got for a days rations. If any one could have mustered up courage enough to have made a motion, for more rations & less drill — I am sure a vote of thanks would have been tendered him. Yes; & resolution would have been passed to that effect, if we had not been afraid of getting the punishment the fellow did for maltreating his horses. When the rations began to run short, some of the boys always commenced scouting the country round, to see what could be found, & some times this was done when it was not really necessary — but seldom ever, for a Confederate Soldier was rarely foundered on something to eat. The locating was generally done in the day time, but the object in view in most cases was allowed to remain until after night. That part of the country had already been visited by the Soldiers prior to our advent & everything that could be "picked up" had about been "cabbaged" upon — hogs in particular were so scarce that people who had any, almost kept them in their dwellings — & as some of the boys said almost slept with them. On one occasion, some of the boys while out scouting, dicovered two large "porkers", weighing about four hundred pounds each, in a small pen which joined up to the kitchen, of a house in the suburbs of Meridian, & outside of camp limits; the end of which made one side of the pen.

Camp Bowen
Two Hogs Captured

The hogs were put there, in order that the owners might keep a close vigil upon them. To capture them unobserved, by any one outside their own confederates, was a desperate undertaking — nevertheless a few of the most daring ones of the company, concluded to run the risk at all hazzards. So one dark night after the camp had become silent, & but few of the fires remained to give a flickering light; the only noise to break the stillness was the sentinel as he passed back & forth upon his beat, humming low some sweet melody of long ago — & the folks at the house feeling secure in the possession of their swine, had dropped off into a sound sleep. Arming themselves with such implements for butchering as they had, slipped away from camp with as light a tread & silent lips as possible. The party were soon at the place & when one advanced & while in a recumbent position, noislessly pulled down one side of the low rail pen, & allowed the hogs to walk out at leisure, some of the boys being stationed on each side, to continue them in the direction desired, which lead off through the timber & down into a deep hollow, some distance from the house. The hogs had been raised "pets" & being very gentle, killing them without noise was an easy undertaking, the skin was soon stripped from their bodies — intrels secreted under some rubbish, & after cutting the hogs in pieces were carried to camp. This meat was divided with several messes. Now that we had it, the next thing was to fix, it secure, as ~~we~~ we expected the old gentleman to miss the hogs, as soon as he got up the next morning. The meat was placed in vessels, holes dug in the ground, in the corners of the cabins, & after covering with something to keep clean, the earth was replaced, & packed in such a manner, detection was almost impossible. We slept the remainder of the night, & tried to look ~~as innocent~~ as innocent as possible the next morning. Any how, we looked & acted so much that way, we succeeded in fooling the old man; who as predicted came to camp, on the "war path", made complaint to the Officers & demanded of them a search of our quarters. They went with him to every cabin & tent belonging to the company, & after a careful but fruitless hunt, finding no evidence of the lost swine, hung his head in sorrow & vexation, bending forward on his return home to relate the sad news to the family. I have thought since, this was a little bit wicked, but I'll tell you, a hungry soldier, would never pass a chance to take something to eat "on the sly". I didnot help to steal these hogs — but I knew they were stolen & assisted in secreting the meat, & I guess you can call me an accessory. About this time we had drill or inspection every day & some times both.

Camp Bowen
Inspection of guns Harness Clothing etc etc

On the 28th harness & guns were inspected. The guns were new & as a matter of course would not likely need any repairs, but the cannoniers had to keep them bright & everything in its proper place. There were two objects in view, in regard to harness. One was to ascertain if they were in condition to stand a campaign if called out immediately, & another was to see if they were kept in proper shape. It was the duty of a driver, when in permanent camp to keep his harness as clean as possible, & hung up off the ground, in a shape so if required to handle them after night, could do so quickly, & without tangling or confusion. Another was to keep a close watch & in case they were broken, or weak in any part, to take them to the company Saddler, whose business it was to mend them. A direliction of duty in this respect upon the part of the driver, frequently caused delay on the march or trouble in battle. But while in camp, if known to intentionally neglect his duty; was reprimanded & sometimes severely punished. There were many men in the army, who had never harnessed a horse previous to the war, those had to be learned, & any mistake made through ignorance, was indulged as patiently as possible. On Sunday 29th company inspection again; this time it was the men, their clothing & quarters. This was generally done by the Captain, or Lieutenant. The men were formed in line in front of their guns; their clothing & person closely scrutenized to see that they kept clean & in proper shape, after which their quarters received, if possible, a more severe criticism. This was all very essential & right; had they not done this our camp would have soon been alive with "graybacks", as some men always waited to be ordered, or driven to do everything — but eat. But I will say in this connection, & in behalf of the very many deserving ones — the idea of wearing greasy clothes, & a face to compare, had almost been banished in toto, from our army, long before the close of the war — unless unavoidable. This being the ~~Sabbath~~ Lords day, the day on which we, when so situated, shaved & cleaned up generally — & when at home went to see our " best girl. We did the former part of the business — & feeling full of mischief, several of us engaged in an old fashioned wrestling match — in which I came near dislocating one of my shoulders; the pain was so great that the night was more than half gone before sleep came to my relief. Our camp was frequently filled with wild rumors, which we denominated "Grape vine" news — this cognomen, was generally applied when received from a source which was not considered authentic or of a very unreasonable character.

Camp Bowen

On the 30th we had an abundance — & to spare of this kind. It was reported the yanks had captured & shot to death seven hundred men of Gen Stephens division, for taking up arms before being legally exchanged — this sounded a little "fishy," & we knew could not be so — unless the enemy had lost all honor; also it was the talk of the camp, that Gen. Bragg's army in Tennessee was falling back — the latter report was not altogether surprising, as he was opposed by a force of men far superior in numbers & arms, to his. Such rumors as these were well calculated to make men wild, & when coupled together created a great excitement for awhile — but later dispatches failing to confirm them, the usual quietness again prevailed.

Sam was referring to Gen. Clement Hoffman Stevens when reporting what he believed was erroneous information. At the time of Sam's entry, Stevens was leading a South

Carolina militia regiment. General Stevens had been severely wounded in September 1863 at the Battle of Chicamauga and was mortally wounded at Peach Tree Creek in July 1864 (Boatner III 796).

December 2nd 1863

On the 2nd of December, the whole company, sick, lame, blind & lazy, — were fallen into line & shoes inspected, by Brigadier Gen. Cockerell, which he found of a very inferior quality — & rather short in quantity, in fact about two thirds were almost a total "wreck". You can make the estimate, & judge, with regard to the truthfulness of my assertion — as an order was given for fifty pairs, & at that time we only had about Sixty five or seventy men, all told. Good thing — wasn't it — the majority of us were from North Mo. the winters there being so much colder, & we had not been in "Dixie", a sufficient length of time, to become climated — the ground didn't feel so very uncomfortable to our feet, but the pine burrs & gravel, got away with us occasionally. The 6th was Sunday again — which in a general sense, means a day of rest. Yet it was seldom ever enjoyed in that manner by a Confederate Soldier — if it wasn't fighting, there was a forced march, or something else on hands. This time, it was "something else" — was what we termed battery inspection. The horses were harnessed & hitched to the guns, drivers mounted as if ready to move, & cannoniers of each detachment formed in front of their respective guns. This was done to see that everything; men, horses, harness & guns were ready for service in the field, & also to have everything in readiness for the review, which had been announced for the following day. Accordingly on the morning of the 7th soon after finishing a hasty breakfast of "blue beef" & cornbread; boots & saddles were sounded, & the order for review was given. Every fellow tried to look his best, gave his hair an extra combing — gave his mustache – (if he had any) an extra comb — concealed the holes in the "bosom" of his pants as best he could. — Any how — we were soon on the reviewing ground, & it was a grand sight to see the infantry keeping step with the drum, & cannannoniers in their respective places, all flags unfurled to the breeze, upon which were inscribed in large letters, the names of the numerous battle fields, on which their noble carriers had supported them. It was also very gratifying to be greeted, while passing in review, by the smiling countenance of our beloved old Gen. Joseph. E. Johnston. After the duties of review was completed Gen. Cockerell drilled the infantry for a short time in presence of Gen. Johnston which he applauded very highly. There were a great many ladies present, & almost a regiment of "brass mounted men". This was the nickname given to Commissioned Officers — some of whom wore a great deal more gold lace (or brass lace) around their coat collars & cuffs than necessary. Some were not satisfied with the insignia; would add gold lace (so called) around their collars & cuffs, until their appearance denoted more outside show than anything else — hence the above "ornamental" name. There were a great many supernumerary officers at that time, having been thrown out by consolidating companies after the exchange at Demopolis, & had so far failed to have a position assigned them. About this time our meat rations became very scarce again & of the poorest quality. There were "lots" of the beeves butchered for our use, that there would have been required a great deal of frying, boiling & skimming, to get enough tallow from one, to grease a pair of boots — The bubbles of grease, sparkling upon the water of a five gallon camp kettle of this beef when boiling — looked in comparrison similar to a teaspoonfull, poured into a hogshead of water, the meat was almost blue & of a gluish nature. Some of the boys swore — if it was thrown against a tree would stick. but we never tried it though — it was too scarce — but it wouldn't stick to our ribs, worth a cent. The more we ate the lanker we got, & no wonder we again began to scout the country for & threaten the "mudlarks" (hogs) It is only those who shared with each other — this beef — corn "dodge" — & burned corn meal for coffee, that can imagine ones feelings — when fed upon this kind of rations. This was our regular bill-of-fare — occasionally we made a variation by "pressing" in a few articles.

Camp Bowen

The 8th was dark, gloomy, & being hemed in the cabin by rain, passed a portion of the day, writing a letter to Father & Mother — having a chance of sending it through the lines, by a Mrs. Baron of Saint Louis Mo, who proposed trying to run the gauntlet. This means of corresponding was very uncertain to the sender as well as dangerous to the carier. Yet knowing the great anxiety of the dear ones at home, to hear from me, grasped every opportunity however uncertain. Farther on in my days records, I wrote; the country was very poor, people ignorant, & pine the principal timber, & "gals" very ugly. Yes; the practice of snuff-dipping — alone was enough to make them homely — & that was almost a universal practice amongst the women of all ages in that part of the state. On the 10th feeling some what in a letter writing mood again — wrote one to Cousin, James E. Moore, a soldier in the transmiss army, was also once, an old neighbor of mine in North Mo. The time of our departure from this place, seemed yet indefinite, & the company commenced building stables for the horses, to protect them from the cold chilly rains; not having much to fill, their insides, concluded to shelter the outside, & make up the deficet, as much as possible. And in order to have a regular system of this work, a certain number of men, were sent to the woods daily, under a supervisor to cut timbers. The life of a Soldier was filled with many sorrows. When one joy appeared upon the arena, to be crowned with glory — there were always two sorrows or disappointments appeared in opposition.

Camp Bowen

On this occasion it was the burial of Lieutenant Lonsil of the first Mo regiment, on the 13th, who died at a house a short distance out in the country. The procession that followed his remains to the cemetery nearby, was long & mournful — a great many of his old brigade attended, as well as several citizens of Meridian. The solemnity of the occasion was made more impressive — by the brigade band which lead the funeral cortege, while playing the dead march. On an occasion like this, if there is a soft corner in a soldiers heart, it is reached. This brought vividly to mind, the uncertainties of life, & the certainty of death, & we having so many more chances to fill an immature grave, as our worthy young comrad did — than to live out the alloted age of man — made those of us who trusted in the supremacy of an alwise ruler of the universe; feel sad very sad! while participating, in the last solemn, exercises which hid from the eyes of man, the mortal portion of our friend & brother.

After the usual ceremonies at a soldiers grave had been performed, the crowd despersed, citizens returning to their respective homes & soldiers to camp, all lamenting the loss by death of a true-hearted Southerner & good Soldier. Late in the evening of the 14th I came in from the woods feeling very tired, having been chopping board timber all day, with which to cover the stable. Our boards were very uneven in length, not having a crosscut saw — but after a few days hard labor, our rough stables were completed.

Camp Bowen

As I remarked before, our rations were scarce & of poor quality. The day was fast approaching, upon which in former years we had become accustomed, to having a feast; & in order to live somewhat in immitation of the past, concluded to send two men from our mess, to the country for Christmas "tricks", such as butter, eggs, dried fruit etc etc, which were great delicacies for a Soldier. On the 17th they procured a three days pass, a wagon & team, & after collecting an eaqual amount of money from every man in the mess, struck out in the direction, they thought had been the least visited by the troops.

The weather was cool & frosty, feeling somewhat chilly to the citizens, but very pleasant to me. I should have said in connection with the party sent out for Christmas articles, there were also men sent from other messes in the company, making four or five in the squad altogether.

Camp Bowen Hogs Captured

The shades in the afternoon of the 20th were beginning to lengthen out fast — suggesting to the boys, with whom we had entrusted our contribution, to make preperation for the great anticipated feast, that the last day in the evening, upon which their pass terminated, was fast coming to a close, & having succeeded in purchasing, about all the articles for which they went, was within five miles of camp on their return, when seeing some "mudlarks" running "loose" in a field near by —although very exultant over the success, with which their efforts had already been crowned, & returning while having within them a conciousness, that their dealings had been so far honorable & just; yet the sight of the hogs, caused an evil spirit to come over them & not having anything in that line — concluded that some of them would be a very valuable addition to the already extensive collection, & if they could capture them, without price, or attracting the attention of the owner —so much the better —. So gathering an ax & gun, which they had in the wagon, soon had three dead & loaded in the wagon; but not before the last one squealed, which attracted the attention of a small boy, who happened to be a silent spectator not very far distant, But the boys minds were so much enveloped in capturing & secreting their ilgotten spoils, that they failed to observe the movements of their little unwelcome guest, who was running in hot haste, to inform his Father & was near the house. A hint to the wise is sufficient, & our boys having an idea what was coming, made their way to camp as quickly as possible, & with a view to escape identity, left the driver alone with the wagon, hastened on as rapidly as possible to the companies quarters. The Old gentleman saddled his horse & made pursuit as quickly as possible, succeeding in overhauling the wagon just before reaching Genl Cockerell's head quarters, & upon ascertaining that he was the general supervisor of the post, laid his grievances immediately before him. But a few moments intervened, before the wagon appeared, & moved along —as if to pass, but being pointed out to the Gen. by the nervous old farmer —was promptly halted & a guard placed over it. The General soon found out, where the wagon belonged, & another guard from the Infantry was sent to our company for the other Boys —who were captured & taken to the guard house near Cockerells quarters for~~e~~ safe keeping during the night.

Cockerell's Punishment For stealing Hogs

The manner of punishment was soon decided upon by the Old General, & I assure you his punishment was always sufficient to the offense. Which was, for the Boys to march in front of the Brigade — with the hogs upon their shoulders, boards about ~~about~~ six inches wide & two feet long tied across their backs, with the words written in large characters upon them Hog thief. Also were compelled to pay the owner of the stolen swine one dollar per pound for the meat. This was an enormous price, yet we were very willing to pay it —if the boys could escape the disgraceful punishment assessed — & the Farmer seemed well satisfied with the remuneration; but Cockerell would not recall one Iota of his former orders, & owing to this seemingly unfair punishment, after the old gentleman's reconciliation, the performance was discountenanced as much as possible. About 9 O.C. AM. on the morning of the 21st —the infantry of the brigade, was formed in line as on an occasion of dress parade, the prisoners brought out —boards tied across their backs, with the unenviable inscription upon them, & ordered to Shoulder, — hogs! Forward, March—! The course designated to march extended in front of the already formed line of infantry — followed by three fiffers & drummers, playing Yankee Doodle — (which was rogues march for the south, in war times). The Boys performed their part with the same degree of nonchalance which was characteristic of them when passing in review — when review was the order of the day. Cockerell was badly fooled — thinking it would be a great source of merriment to the infantry, who he imagined would break forth in wild huzza's; but their sympathy for the men overballanced their joy, & they almost to a man hung their heads in sorrow, which was very agonizing to the General. Our company camping grounds were some distance from the brigade, but our situation was such, that we could have seen the performance plainly — had we not been in our Shanties by order of the Captain.

Camp Bowen Hog Capture Completed

The boys completed the punishment meted out to them & delivered the hogs alright — the price was promptly paid — & they were soon ready for the "pot." Pretty dear meat — wasn't it?

On the 23rd & for several days following, we had considerable confusion & comment, in our company — caused by having seventeen guards detailed daily from our ranks, this put each man of the company of duty three days in a week. For some time we had been missing bridles & halters. from the stables — & with a hope of catching the thief — this unusual extra guard was placed on duty. This was a great punishment of the innocent to catch the guilty — but such was the orders — & we had to obey.

Christmas Day A feast

As the day approached for which our boys had procured the already named delicies, & thinking the supply was yet insufficient — & in order to have something to add merriment & jollity to the occasion, on the 24th sent a man from our mess, with money to procure Some whiskey — in which undertaking he proved successful, but being very fond of a "wee drop" himself, partook of the "overjoyful" too freely — so much so, that he & the whisky became so far seperated, that he did not get any to camp — except what he had in him & not even that amount, until the next morning. But as it happened he made a good exchange. Having lost the "grog", thought our disappointment, occasioned by him returning without anything — & to save his own credit, came in with two thousand fresh oysters. This was quite an addition to our already extensive bill-of-fare, & one too, which was not so susseptable of evil consequences as the one that he lost. But people in those days, thought it the next thing to impossible to pass a Christmas, without a "social jug" — & any reasonable person can readily offer an excuse for a soldier, seperated far from old friends & relatives, to have a desire to cling to the old tradition. Our Christmas eve was passed in happy thoughts & dreams of long ago, & when the roll was called on the morning of the 25th every countenance was beaming with anticipations of a joyous day, which they fondly hoped was in store for them. It was amusing, as well as interesting on an occasion like this, to see the amount of interest taken, & great skill displayed in preparing something "extra," & when the means with which we had to prepare it, are taken into consideration, 'tis only a wonder that we succeeded so admirably.

Shortly after the noon hour a rough table was prepared, upon which was spread a bountiful supply, of Oysters, roast turkey, pork, butter, potatoes, fruit etc etc, upon which we feasted until our appetites were more than satisfied. Feasting, was our principal enjoyment during the day, & as our old company fiddler had dropped out of sight, the night was passed without any "stag" dancing, which was indulged in so pleasantly, one year previous at camp Rogers. The remaining days of the old year were passed, without any happenings worthy of note, except the 31st which was cold & rainy in the forenoon, terminating late in the evening, in snow, the first for the winter, but was of short duration, & disappearing almost as quickly as it fell. Some of the old men of the surrounding country came into camp, shivering under the heavy folds of their long overcoats, which had scarcely been doned before during the winter, complaining of it being the coldest day for several years.

1864

Jany 1st Camp Near Meridian Miss

The curtain has again been run down at the close of another year of bloody scenes, the last farewell has been uttered, the last hearse containing the remnants of 1863 has been driven; the last sad cortege has passed with its many mournful hearts & tear bedimed eyes; the pall bearers have taken their stand for the last time; the closing prayer has been repeated for the last time; the grave has been filled & monument erected, with an epitaph written in blood, So we can only turn away with mournful hearts, with emotions of a pentup soul, &, with a deep unbidden sigh of disappointment & with trembling lips, exclaim Farwell! Farewell? Farewell!! Thrice repeated since this cruel war commenced, & yet no tidings of peace have appeared. No star in the dim future rises up to guide our pathway & lead us on to victory: Not even a flickering light appears in the dark & dreary future to beckon us on to peace. No! 'tis midnight to us but some one sees, & we can only hope on, fight on, & endure all, as we have in the years of carnage just past. Yes brush away the tear that has unconciously appeared, "Swallow back" the welling up in our bossoms & hope that ere another time comes around like this; before we are pained with another sad adieu, victory will have perched upon our dearly loved Southern Confederacy; & peace happy peace will have produced its sweet fruits all over the land. Time will bring around all things, we can only wait & offer ourselves as martrys upon the altar of our beloved south. As I remarked, our future seemed to be a sea impenetrable darkness, yet we had confidence in ourselves & commanders to so great an extent, as to warrant the assertion, & rekindle the hope that our cause would finally triumph. Our private mess commissaries had again been replenished, so we feasted on roast chicken & many other unusual articles for a Soldiers table as a New years dinner. The "old folks" used to say, if a person had plenty to eat on that day, they would continue to have an abundance the year round, but this adage proved to be all fiction with a Soldier — or atleast one that wore the Gray. We remained in this camp longer than usual, which was the occasion of a great deal of restlessness among the mess, causing a considerable amount of mischief to be done by those so enclined. Camp life is very monotonous, especially winter quarters, & one who has a turn in him to be dishonest, it is sure to crop out. I have already given you an account of the manner in which the boys coaxed the hogs, off to the Slaughtering place, & the way some fellow got away with halters & bridles, now I have an instance of horse stealing.

Near Meridian

On the night of the first, Gen. Cockerell's horse was stollen from his stables near head quarters, by Lieut. Digman of the first Missouri Infantry regiment. Soon after the discovery was made scouts were sent in all directions, our company contributing some help to join in the chase. We had one man by the name of "Tom" Burgess, that was an extra scout, & one of the best foragers in the world, especially for himself. The reading of a Private Soldier's "ups & down's," the record of daily events & occurrences, the duties performed, the life we lived, the kind of weather, the appearance of the country over which we traveled, ~~by~~ the class of people who inhabited it etc etc, may become monotonous & tiresome to the person who takes the time to read them; but the intention of this little narrative, & the aim of the writer, is to present a true picture, giving the plain unvarnished, impartial truth in the case, with as few higheroglyphics & embellishments as possible — written too with the same vim & courage that were so characteristic of the average Southern Soldier at the close of the war. This is no love story, nor a story drawn from imagination; but a record of events that actually transpired. As a matter of course my time to do guard duty came around in the regular rotation with the rest of the boys of the company. The third day of the month was Sunday, my detail came & regardless of the rain that was pouring down I had to pass back & forth on my beat infront of the guns.

This dreary weather continued until the morning of the 6th about 1 O.C. AM when snow commenced falling & continued until daylight. This Sudden change caused an extra demand for fuel, the troops gathered their axes, & one not knowing the cause, or acquainted themselves of the presence of an army, would have imagined themselves in the midst of an immense clearing & an army of wood choppers. Trees were felled in all directions, & the rude wide fireplaces in the open shanties were soon blazing with warm & cheerful fires, the small hardwood timber was getting very scarce & the falling of a large pine was not unfrequent. but we Suddenly were brought to a realization that our stay at this comfortable camp was soon to be terminated, when the first, third & fifth Mo. Infantry regiments received orders 11 O.C. PM. to cook three days rations & be ready to move at a moments warning; Their destination not generally known. The move was some what unexpected & a little mystereous, considering the weather & condition of the roads. And in addition to the gossip that was taking the rounds of camp, the surprise was still greater when on the morning of the 7th 'twas ordered that twenty rounds of ammunition be given to each Infantry man, & the artillery supply was also restocked. The whole Brigade soon received orders to leave, two regiments left on the 7 O.C. AM train & remainder on the 5 O.C. AM on the following morning. The parting from their cabins, though the covers were uneven, walls rough & rugged, the chimneys of mud & sticks; where they had passed in social chat, many happy hours together (if there be such in a Soldier's life) was almost as trying to them at this time, as the parting from their loved ones at home, when they resolved to cast their lots in the uncertainties of war. But such partings are common in this life, although the oftener repeated the less exertions are required to controll our feelings; yet the impression is visible & another wrinkle is added to the already careworn brow.

In the forenoon of the 8th our company received orders to cook three days rations & be in readiness to move at 5 O.C. PM, & with as much haste as possible the skillets were soon hot, & the cooking of corn "dodgers" commenced. We had only made a beginning ~~on~~ of filling the order, when it was countermanded & time changed, until 7 O.C. AM on the morning following, this was some trouble & caused us to eat a cold supper, & I tell you "them dodgers" when cold were very hard.

Breaking Camp at Meridian

About 4 O.C. P.M. the horses were harnessed, guns taken to the depot at Meridian & loaded on the cars; the horses & all the men, except a guard over the guns returned to camp. This caused many glad hearts, especially to those who had the opportunity of spending another night in their cabins. The Infantry of the Brigade left in the morning, destination said to be Mobile Alabama, & purpose for which they were sent was announced, to quell the disorderly conduct of two or three Ala. Regiments that mutinized because they were not all furnished furloughs to go home & spend the christmas holidays; indeed some were so anxious they actually threw down their arms & started without leave or license. Our boys didnot sympathize very much, the remark was often heard, & in a very sarcastic manner too: "Poor home sick critters"!

Mobile, Alabama, founded in 1702 by Jean Baptiste le Mayne, was named Mauvilla for the site inhabited by the Mauvillas, a Muskogee tribe. The first Spanish explorers originally spelled the name "Mabila" ("Mobile").

Well, after it was all past, & we could consider the matter in our more sober senses, their actions in the case could be overlooked to a certain extent. The majority of the persons composing these regiments had not been in the service long, never had been in battle, they were made up of boys, young & old men, who had remained at home as long as possible, were very anxious to shun the duty as well a the dangers of a soldiers life, only volunteering to avoid being conscripted. As a rule, when you compel a person to perform a duty there isn't much good in it, more especially when forced to do soldiers duty. In such cases their acts are invariably void of patriotism. On the morning of the 9th our horses were ~~carred~~ loaded on the cars early & about 9 O C AM. bid adieu to our cabins & Meridian & started to Mobile Alabama. After a run of two hours the train stopped at Enterprise Miss.

From Meridian Miss to Mobile. Ala

This was a nice little village & we enjoyed our lay over of half an hour very much; when the train which caused our waiting passed on; our journey was continued, although very slow for railroad travel. The road bed was very much out of repair, not having received much attention since the ravages of war had visited that locality, & the lives with which it was freighted at that time were too precious to endanger them by fast & reckless traveling. However our slow progress gave us ample time to take notes & observe the country, the principal portion of which was level, a thin sandy soil thickly covered in many places with a tall pine forest, intermingled with scrub oak, hickory, ash, woven together, with Muscadine & grapevines, Some of the country on our route was very sparsely settled, & the manner in which the dwelling were constructed, the surrounding etc etc didnot denote much thrift among the inhabitants, but like "Arkensaw" had plenty of the dear little ones. Arrived at our destination about midnight but didnot unload anything until morning, we snored away on the flat cars until the gray streaks of early morning had all disappeared, & "Old Sol" had commenced his days tour, & a few of the early morning hours of the 10th passed before the guns were unloaded. But this was a job of short duration, after which the horses were soon dressed in their leather uniform, hitched in their respective places & guns moved out to what was called Camp Cummings near the suburbs of the City, & about 4½ miles from the bay in a northern direction. Upon our arrival found the Brigade comfortably quartered; which was very different to our prospective situation. We had only two houses (formerly negro cabins) for the company — Swamp water to drink, wood of poor quality & scarce in quantity. Country very level & sandy. We found the Gen. Maurey had been very busily engaged since his arrival in hunting for the mutineers & succeeded in capturing sixty of them & had scouts to scouring the swamps for more.

Camp Cumings Mobile Alabama

Near our camp were many swamps, which afforded a good hiding place for all those who wished ~~to~~ refuge from the outside world in their dark & lonely recesses. The disagreeable weather which began before our departure from Meridian Miss. continued with but little cessation until the morning of the 14th when the rising sun once more showed his glittering head, "peeping up" through a cloudless eastern sky, making the whole face of the earthm, which was covered with water, glow in beauty & splendor, all hearts leaped for joy. The time had been so long since the sun had been permitted to shine upon us, we felt good, & imagined all else looked & were as happy as we. Yes & this fine morning suggested to the captain that a general clean up would be beneficial, as well as "ornamental," & by his orders the whole company turned out & policed the camp & park thoroughly. Well; this was a new country to us, a large & flourshing city in antebellum days adjacent to our camp, & the curiosity seekers were soon on the tramp to find something "fresh," & the consequence was on the 16th several of the company Boys were digging stumps as a punishment for going to town without passes. We had very stringent orders, yet some for the sake of a little fun would break over, regardless of the stump digging or any other punishment. On the morning of the 17th we were apprized of the fact that it was Sunday by the tolling of church bells in many places in the city, the deep & mellow tones of which were wafted back with a cool morning breeze, reverberating among the stately buildings, along the wide & beautiful streets; dying away upon the still waters of the Bay near by, or hiding away in the tall pine forest as the soft southern sea breeze was singing a lullaby in their lofty boughs.

Sunday In Camp & a ramble

The morning was all that could be desired; was as lovely as ~~wast~~ its name was renowned. The mid morning sun shone brilliantly from his exhalted place in a deep azure Sky, lighting as it were the pathway of the citizens as they bent forward on their way to the different places of worship to kneel at the shrine of that Almighty one to whom all shall atlast bow. This caused a sadness to creep over me, reflections of long ago stole in & took possession of my mind, my heart was full. I looked at my clothes, which were greasy & ragged, not suitable to mingle with the fashionably dressed people of a wealthy southern city, so I banished my thoughts in that direction; worse still if all else would have been right, before going; would have been compelled to get a pass from the captain. I soon became restless & very much dissatisfied sitting by the lonely & smoky campfire. A walk was suggested, & with four others of the company took a ramble around the breastworks to the Bay. To follow the meanderings of the works & scrutinize the many different interesting objects as they presented themselves for our consideration as we passed along, soon dispelled the sadness that held us spell bound in camp.

'Twas truely delightful to sit down upon the beach, so beautifully & artistically strewn with shells of all descriptions, watch the small vessels floating leisurely over the waters whose occupants were busily engaged in dredging for oysters which were caught in abundance. (While here at Mobile I saw my first live oyster & ate the first before being canned, & I soon learned to like them.) The enjoyment was so great. So many new & interesting scenes Springing up to attract our attention, we became unconscious, that the day was passing very rapidly, & the consquence was, when we became aroused to ~~of~~ the fact, it was necessary to make a hurried return to camp, in order to answer to our names at retreat roll call, & avoid a job of stump digging as our camp had a few left.

The day was not passed without some evidence that hostilities had not entirely ceased. Several guns were heard in the morning in the direction of Fort Morgan.

The United States began establishing coastal fortifications along the shores of the Gulf of Mexico in 1817. Fort Morgan, designed by French military engineer Simon Bernard, was constructed over a fifteen-year period (1819-1834) to help defend Mobile Bay. Fort Morgan gained fame on August 5, 1864, when Rear Admiral David Glasgow Farragut's Union fleet of wooden ships and ironclad monitors began an attack on Mobile Bay. Rear Admiral Farragut lashed

> **himself to the mainsail of the Hartford to get above the heavy smoke of battle to see what was happening. The sinking of one of his monitors, the Tecumseh, stalled the rest of his confused fleet. It was here one of the war cries destined to be remembered was first heard when Farragut shouted, "Damn the torpedoes! Full speed ahead!" (Bennett; "David Glasgow Farragut").**

The yanks were firing at a vessel laiden with supplies for the South, (Called a Blockader) But unfortunately for us, while trying to run the gauntlet, grounded & was a total loss; while we regreted our loss very much, it was equalized by the consolation that our enemy didnot reap any particular benefit. On the 18th all the troops at this place were reviewed by Gen. Maurey 2 O.C. PM. The order in which they marched was good, bodies erect, lines Straight, Step steady & with the tap of the drum. But no wonder the music from the different bands was magnificent & very stimulating — and still another reason for our steps being more elastic on this occasion, was both sides of the street, yards & balconies were thickly crowded with citizens; the greater portion of whom were ladies, whose smiles, songs & waves of their handkerchiefs, increased our encouragement, as well as to lighten the duties of camp life. That night I got a pass & went to the Theater, which was a rare thing, a great treat & something that caused me some enjoyment & mirth for a short time. On the 19th by order of Gen. Maurey his compliments were read to the first Missouri Brigade while on dressparade, praising them for their fine, cleanly & soldier like appearance on the day previous. The Newspapers of the city came out in large editorials, doing us great homage by saying that we were the finest troops that ever honored Mobile with their appearance.

Camp Cumings Mobile Alabama

Everything was quiet until the evening of the 22nd at retreat roll call, when we were somewhat puzzled by an order being read for our company to report to Major Truehart who commanded a battallion of artillery.

Review on Government Street

On the afternoon of the 23rd 2 - O.C. PM all the troops at this point were reviewed by Gen. Maurey on Government street. This point was a good selection & a beautiful place for a military display, very suitable for an army to pass in review. The street was very broad, from whence I suppose it took its name, in the center was a row of shade trees, as well as on either side beautifully shaped by the pruners knife, extending from one end of the City to the other. The large business houses spoke highly of the wealthy owners along this main thoroughfare, the dwellings so artistically erected whose inmates had beautifully decorated the front yards with such a varied selection of ornamental shrubs & flowers, told us of the once happy homes. This review was much more interesting than the previous one, as several regiments had arrived to swell our number. These occasions always attracted a large crowd, & the bright eyes of the beautiful maidens, reflecting the light from a warm heart, whos great love for a southern Soldier was dealt out in sweet smiles & words as we passed them, causing us to make new & better resolves, & be more devotional to the cause which we had sworn to defend — There now! I have passed another eulogy on the Ladies. I can't help it! It seems perhaps to one not knowing the importance of these reviews, that the occurrence was too frequent, & in fact it was too frequent for us. But the meaning was two fold

First it caused a man to keep his person ~~l~~ clean & clothing as tidy as possible. Another a General could better ascertain his available force. The arrival of troops was a daily occurrence, & many prophesied a battle imminent & to be fought in that locality soon. Yet many times such prophecies were uttered & as many more went unfulfilled.

Capturing a "Swine"

I have already given you an account of the scarcty of hogs at Meridian Miss. the means used by the people for their safe keeping, & the adroitness displayed by the Soldiers in their capture. But I have an instance while camped at Mobile ala. that caps the climax so far. Hogs were very scarce there at the time of our short sojourn, in fact almost, none. Those who happened to have a pet pig, resorted to almost any means to protect ~~them~~ it from the solders.

Capture of Hog

Pens on the ground, however near the kitchen door they might be, proved insecure; & as a last resort the use of elevated ones were adopted. A short time after our arrival at this camp, one of the busy bodies of our company while passing through the suburbs of the city near our camp on a "lark", Spied a small "porker" near the kitchen apartment of a residence in one of these elevated pens, & immediately his mouth began to "water" for a slice of the rare meat. His wits were put to work to devise some means to capture the prize, & I assure you he was not long in devising a plan that proved successful, (as he was "up to snuff") so when night came on, & the occupants of the house were sleeping soundly, he with two or three of his most venturesome companions, succeeded in capturing & killing the hog without discovery.

Mobile Ala.

On the 25th our Old Captain Guibor whose health had failed, so as to render him unfit for field service, was relieved for the present & our Senior first Lieutenant Walsh promoted to his place. This was something unavoidable. and greatly regreted by the company. Walsh, was a nice man & brim full of style & military tactics yet a little despotic. For some time subsequent we were ill at ease, the kindness & unassuming qualities so characteristic in our old gray haired Captain could not be forgotten. Men admired a plain sociable commander. On the 26th our camp once more began to put on the appearance of permanency, as several of us were placed on detail to cut & haul logs for building cabins. This was quite a surprise as well as a big undertaking, as we had considerable distance to go after the timber. On the morning of the 29th the order was given out for inspection of artillery by Brigadier Gen. Shoup & Major Truehart, & as one of the chief characteristics of our company was punctuality in all places & on all occasions, was on the review ground at the hour appointed.

Brig. Gen. Francis Asbury Shoup served under General Beauregard and Gen. Thomas Carmichael Hindman at Prairie Grove and Mobile. He was General Johnston's Chief of Artillery and no guns were lost under his command on the Atlanta campaign. General Shoup became an Episcopal minister after the war (Boatner III 758).

Inspection & Field drill

About that time a very heavy rain set in, we remained in place one hour, & no others coming returned to camp, completely drenched, & in anything else but a good humor. Several indulged in abusing the practice of inspection, & those of the company who were in the habit of expressing themselves in superfluous qualifying adjectives, were extremely lavish in their use. We had performed our duty, by obeying orders, & were fixing to "hang ourselves out to dry", the drivers had scarcely finished unharnessing when to our great surprise & displeasure, boots & saddles ~~was~~ were again sounded by the company bugler & we had to return to the review ground. But this time, the different companies appeared & inspection was soon over, after which we engaged in a general field drill of some length.

This was very exciting as well as dangerous, once while the horses were trotting, the cannoniers mounted the ammunition chests & had scarcely become permanently seated, when by order of the Captain the horses were forced to a sweeping gallop, & one of the rear wheels of the caison upon which Bro. Caldwell, another companion & myself were seated, struck a stump almost overturning, throwing us some distance, & with great force, "splash" in the mud. As I happened to be on the under side & our middleman a six footer, was forced to favor a sprained leg for several subsequent days. If I had ever learned to swear, I certainly would have risked a "few" on that occasion. But I said Dog-gon-it & limped on. My partners came out without a scratch.

Murphy's Potato & honey hunt

We had a man in my mess, by the name of Louis. Murphy (Nic named Polk) who enjoyed something to eat better than any man I ever saw, & especially something different to our every day camp diet. He was particularly fond of sweetpotatoes & honey. One day while prospecting through the country a few miles from camp, discovered a place that had the appearance of a cave where sweetpotatoes had been stored by a family for ~~the~~ winter use. They were kept in that country by piling up on top of the ground with a slight covering of fodder & dirt. The night following after tattoo roll call, with a gunny sack under his arm; retraced his steps to the mound to make a closer inspection, & there wasn't a very long time intervened before he came cralling into the tent wagging a big sack full of the long red fellows. Some of the boys roused up & asked him if he got any, & "Polk" answered back — Yes! I — I — g — d thats what I went "fur". One very prominent characteristic in him, was liberality — he always divided his spoils with his messmates. He was so successful on this raid, in getting what he went "fur", besides making his escape undiscovered, that but a few nights intervened until his appetite began to desire a change from "Blue" beef & cornbread to something sweet.

Murphy's Exploits continued

He had discovered some beehives, not very far from camp; had also become apprised of the fact the old gentleman the owner there of with his dog was on guard, but he said if a "feller" never tried to do anything, he was dead certain to make a failure. So one night about the same hour he chose to "Jayhawk" the potatoes, "Polk" took a bucket & knife, struck out through the woods & darkness to bring in his booty. After a short ramble & a few moments spent in reconnaisance, the course to pursue was arrived at — that all things were quiet, especially in the locality—, the old man & his dog were surely asleep — & in the language of the revivalist —then "was the accepted time", & suiting his thoughts by actions, crept stealthily up in the shadow of the bee gums & from the direction he imagined — least liable to attract the attention of his antagonists — & with as light a hand as possible, lifted one of the hives from the bench & started off through the brush as fast as possible, the dog being awakened by the noise, pursued close to "Polks" heels, yelping every jump for some distance, agged on by the old man — who by this time had become aware that something was going wrong. The racket & shaking up caused the bees to swarm out so thick on ~~him~~ Murphy, that he was compeled to drop the gun. He fought his little busy antagonist in silence for some time. The dog soon returned to his kennel the old man thinking it only a false alarm soon became quiet, & the bees had about suspended hostilities — when Murphy concluded to return to the gun, which he had dropped during the escapade a short distance in the rear. After removing it a little farther from the house, he filled the bucket with nice honey & returned to camp, as happy as a "rooster with his first spurs". When daylight came the old man discovered his loss, but never found the Gaines.

Sunday Thoughts

The 31st day brought around Sunday again & a repetition of the signals for the assembling of those who were enclined, or so situated as to join in song & praise to their great Redeemer could be heard throughout the city. After the dense fogg (so common in that country) had disappeared, the day was truly delightful & the Sun shone forth in splendor from a cloudless sky. The fresh morning breeze from off the Bay, though nice & pleasant, carried to our ears the deafning roar of cannon from the fortifications at Fort Morgan. It was dreadful to think, that we could not enjoy one more sunday as we once did; 'twas awful to contemplate the feelings that passed over a person when these harsh sounds broke upon the sanctity of the day which was given to all as a day of rest. It caused one to become somewhat Melancholy for the time, especially one so far away from his native state & home as myself. If seated would drop his head in his hands — while his mind wandered back & dwelt upon scenes & thoughts of long ago — or if disposed to write would be apt to express his feelings in words similar to the following, as did the writer of these records on this occasion. Oh! could I wield the pen of a Homer, a Byron or could command the language of a Webster, I might then attempt to describe my feelings toward that dearest place — home. My thoughts are still brilliant & my hopes are not yet blasted; I look forward to the day with gleaming eyes, when peace happy peace, will crown our efforts with success & we will reap the rewards of our labors so richly deserved, while at our again happy homes. We can only wait, time is Swiftly passing, when the Sun went to "sleep" in his western home at the close of the day — the first month of another ~~day~~ year passed down to history.

February
Mobile Prize drill

On the 2nd day of February we had something very exciting in the shape of a prize drill between a battallion of infantry from each of the following states, Mo. La. Ala & Miss, The drill was well executed & every maneuver in Infantry tactics was admirably performed, every inch of ground was contested with great spirit by the champions. But the Missouri Boys carried off the prize — Which was a very costly army flag. We were frequently reminded during the day, that Fort Morgan was yet besieged by yankee gunboats. On the 3rd all the Infantry & light artillery of the army stationed at Mobile were formed around the inner line of breastworks Surrounding the City, so the amount of troops required to fill them could be estimated. About 10,000 or 12,000 were present. It was supposed the object of this move, was to ascertain how many troops would be an efficient guard in case of an emergency. In the afternoon orders were given to the first Mo. Baldwin's & Quarrell's Miss Brigades, to march in the direction of Jackson Miss.

On the morning of the 4th we received orders to cook four days rations, & be ready to move on the following morning at 6. O. C. After cooking rations, about 3 O. C. PM. boots & saddles was blown & we were soon on the way to the Depot. But when we arrived, the announcement that no transportation could be furnished caused us to return to camp. In the evening of the 5th 3 O.C. the horses were again harness, wagons packed with our baggage & mess kit & a move toward the depot commenced, & by 4 O.C. of the same after noon everything was loaded on the cars & we bid adieu to Mobile.

From Mobile to Meridian

Traveled or tried to travel all night; our progress was very slow, as I stated on our downward trip, the road was very rough & many places almost impassable, at one time our train stalled in the midst of a swamp, & in order that we could be enabled to continue our journey, were compelled to carry water to fill the tender & wood to fire, that sufficient steam could be raised to reach the next wood & water station. We had but little sleep or rest, in fact I deemed it the best policy to keep wide awake, as I was expecting every "minit" to be the next, & I always thought it horrible, to be killed while asleep. When daylight came on the morning of the 6th I found myself only 56 miles from Mobile, & as tired as if I had walked the whole distance. The nearer we approached the end of our journey, the better we found the condition of the road & speed increased accordingly. Arrived at Meridian about 3 O.C. PM, found the citizens as well as Soldiers excited, having heard the "Feds" were at Jackson Miss, in force with a view of extending their jurisdiction farther in the interior.

The country had been occupied by our army so long, every thing almost in the shape of Something to eat for either man or beast had been consumed. Starvation was almost staring the poorer class of citizens in the face, & when they contemplated the approach of an inveterate enemy, whose villainous disposition was best satiated, when driving the helpless women & children of the south from their homes & afterwards apply the torch, 'twas natural for them to become dismayed & hang around their friends to implore their protection. The guns were left on the cars, but the horses were unloaded watered & fed — this place was said to be our destination when ordered from Mobile, but the signs of the times denoted a short stay. We all remained at the depot during the night, sleeping as best we could around the platform, on the cars or where ever room enough could be found to "curl up".

Meridian

Clothing was issued to us during this temporary halt. which was badly needed at that times & always accepable to a "Reb." It was nothing uncommon to see the "bosom" of a fellows pants threadbare — or a "flag" at half mast hanging out. Some of us learned to patch. The drawers & jackets given us here had buttons on them made of wood, & some of the boys remarked, would be useless to kick now, for Jeff. Davis had the "dead wood" on us at last. "Necessity is the mother of invention" when the south decided the manufacturers of buttons were cut off — but she was determined to become self supporting as near as possible, hence the adoption of wooden buttons & homespun suits for the ladies.

On the morning of the 7th 10 O.C. AM. the horses were loaded & we all jumped aboard the long train pulled by the "ironhorse" bound for

Morton Miss, a station on the Vicksburg & Meridian rail road, we traveled with but little interruption. Arrived at the point for which we started 10 O.C. P.M.

False alarm at Morton Miss

Nothing unloaded but the horses, provisions, cooking utensils, & according to orders three days rations were cooked. What was left of this night after preparing our "grub" was devoted to sleep, — & I assure you that wasn't much. of our rations of all kinds had been as plentiful as sugar, our haversacks would have been overflowingly full. Just before leaving Meridian the Boys saw some Neworleans sugar "laying around loose" & concluded to take care of some it — a charge (as they termed it) was made, a capture effected — & using an army phrase, we got "oodles". Early in the morning of the 8th a report reached us that the yanks were eight miles in our front & advancing in force. We immediately unloaded the guns, harnessed the horses hitfched in & marched out about 8 O.C. AM. in the direction the enemy was reported. Each man was allowed only one blanket, the ballance of our baggage was ordered sent back to Meridian. Fine thing that we were in a warm climate or some of us would have frozen. The baggage was sent ~~by way of~~ in wagons by way of Hillborough. Afer we had gone three & a half miles toward the front, were brought to a left-about & marched back one mile, & formed in line of battle, — but didnot remain in this position long, until the order to advance was given, we then moved up again one mile, 'twas said to gain a better position. This maneuvering & diladallying, looked to a "high private" like myself, that somebody didn't know what they were doing — but we immediately unlimbered in the woods ready for action~~s~~ & at the same time feeling confident that we could hold our position against great odds, as we had the first Mo Brigade for our support. About 3 O.C. in the afternoon skirmishing commenced one mile in our immediate front, between our cavalry & the enemies advance guard.

Morton Campaign

At the crack of the first rifle every man in the company was at his post, & eagerly watching as if trying to catch the first glympse of the advancing foe. This kind of a dilemma was a very disagreeable position in which to be placed — & according to the experience of all old soldiers, whether "Fed" or "Confed" required as much if not more nerve to retain an equilibrium, as in the midst of an engagement. Our forces at this time & place consisted of all the artillery & Infantry of Gen's Loring's & French's

Divisions. About 4 O.C. PM the first & only shot from Artillery was fired by the yanks, from a small rifled piece & the ball fell near our position. For a short time a battle seemed imminent. To tantallize our antagonists, the Mo & La. bands commenced playing Dixie, Bonnieblue flag etc etc. & continued for some time. The yanks ~~made~~ made no reply. This was the first time that I ever heard music on the open field near the rank & file, when expecting a battle. It was very stimulating indeed, & the effects were plainly visible — every man looked to be in good spirits & anxious for a fight.

Retreat from Morton Commenced

The firing of Shapshooters ceased at sundown, & about one hour after dark, when the large campfires which we made were burning at their brightest around the entire line of battle; our forces commenced to withdraw, as silently as possible. And the time was not long until our whole force was on the retrograde movement.

The fires were left burning as a blind, to hide our movements from the enemy, & I suppose they were completely surprised as they didnot attempt to follow us until near daylight, & then found our position deserted. We marched until 4 O.C. AM. on the 9th when we stopped for a short time to feed & sleep a little. This was tough treatment to what we had been accustomed, & I tell you it put a rough edge on us in a hurry. This was always a mysterious move to me. I never could see where any benefit was derived — I suppose it was intended to draw the enemies forces from some other point, but if it did we were never any the wiser. On the morning of the 9th about daylight the Feds reached Morton, in search of their mysterious adversary — but by this time we had left that town about twelve miles in our rear — we had "dropped back" a station or two down the railroad. About 10 O.C. AM our march, or fall back was resumed. Passed through Hillsborough a~~s~~ small inland village of little importance, & continued in an eastern direction until after night fall, when the order was given to stop to feed & rest. This would have been good news very thankfully received, if it had been a rest for all alike — but some had to guard while his comrads slept, & others had to cook to keep from starving. I was one of the cooks that night, & I failed even to get a short nap.

Retreat From Morton Continued

But the time allotted for this purpose was of short duration, as we again fell into ranks on the morning of the 10th about 1. O.C. We were a tired sleepy lot of fellows, & our countenances bespoke bewilderment. The remainder of the morning was consumed in travel, made good progress & little occurring worthy of note. The mists in the eastern Sky had cleared away & the sun had been "up" about an hour, when we arrived at Newton station on the same railroad upon which we made our advance a few days since, but several miles in rear of where we made the "Sham". Cooked breakfast & rested all day, & "you bet" we enjoyed this for it didn't come around very often. Soon after dark we commenced loading our guns, horses & traps on the cars, & by 10- O.C. PM everything was in readiness for another nights travel. This looked a little funny — but I suppose somebody was trying to bewilder somebody else. About 11 O.C. the train pulled out destination said to be Meridian. Before starting Bro. Caldwell & I made preparations for a nights sleep, by spreading our blankets on the rear chests of a caison, which was loaded up on a flat car. As our supply of bedding was "few & far between", our nest was easily prepared & we were soon wrapped in the arms of Morpheus.

This was the only sleep of any consequence, or the only opportunity offerd since leaving Mobile. The rocking of the train over the rough road only made us sleep the sounder & Snore louder, infact when we awoke on the morning of the 11th about 8 O.C. we were at Meridian, & unconcious as to the time of our arrival. It would have puzzled an expert, almost to have told to what tribe we belonged. The boys almost imagined some "gentlemen: of Color had sneaked in on them for a ride. To say that we were "beautiful" specimens of humanity doesn't express half. Our eyes were as red as fire, faces as black as "niggers", hair matted together with smoke fine chunks of coal & cinder that scaped from the smoke stack of the engine. As soon as we got our eyes pulled open sufficiently to realize our dilemma, made way to a pool of water near by & cleansed our rugged countenances.

Arrival at Meridian

Stopped at Meridian all day — letting the guns remain on the cars — somewhat mystified as to farther movements, but would not have been surprised, if at any moment the order had been given us to return to Mobile. Such was the gossip that passed around the "knowing" ones; However about 7 O.C. P.M. the Idea of another trip to that City was banished from our minds; by receiving orders to unload the guns & move out to camp a short distance north of Town.

The Feds were yet pursuing, reported a considerable force at Chunky river about four teen miles distant.

The confluence of Chunky Creek and Okahatta Creek forms the Chunky River, a tributary of the Chickasawhay River. Chunky River has flowed through east-central Mississippi under other names such as Chanki River, Chunkey Creek, Chunkey River, Chunky Creek, Ectchangui River, and Tchanke River. The waterway was officially named Chunky River in 1963 by The United States Board on Geographic Names ("Chunky River").

The Old Lady's Eggs

Becoming restless during the day while lounging around the depot awaiting orders & desiring a change of diet, "Bob", Welch, Caldwell & Myself concluded to go to a boarding house & get a "square" meal (as we termed it). We saw one not very far distant, with the sign hanging out. Boarding — Meals at all hours! Which from outside appearance had seen better days, & upon entering the building, found the inside & hostess (an elderly Lady) in a corresponding mood. Everything told the tale of war & its ravages. We ordered "Grub" for three.

She bade us, be seated, & after many appologies about not being "fixed" to keep boarders as she'd like to be — disappeared in the kitchen. During her absence the time was passed as pleasantly as possible, which was about half an hour, which seemed an age to such hungry fellows as us. But she reappeared & announced — dinner! & I assure you we were not long in getting our knees under the table. The "bill of fare" was a slim one — No. printers ink wasted in delicacies. But among other things, the land lady tried to cook some eggs, & I suppose from the way they looked, there wasn't any grease about the house. They were brought in after commencing our meal, & placed on the table with the remark —These eggs "don't" look very straight, but I guess they'll eat Straight! We soon straightened them. This remark of the Old lady, passed around the mess fire the remainder of the war. When anything was cooked & not as intended, the person who did it was reminded of the "old ladies eggs".

Temporary Camp at Meridian

In the forenoon of the 12th we moved out north of town one & a half miles to camp. Orders were received to keep three days cooked rations on hand all the time. This kept us with a haversack full of cold, hard — corn — bread & beef so dry & hard that a man would almost choke, unless — he had a cup of corn-meal coffee or water to wash down with the beef was almost as void of tallow, as the Sahara desert is of water; you would have had to stew up a whole beef to get enough to grease a pair of boots. The order was also given to send all clothing & blankets to Demopolis Ala. except one change & one blanket to the man. This left us in good shape for traveling — so far as baggage was concerned — & we were not liable to be troubled with a full stomach. On the 13th I cleansed myself thoroughly & put on clean clothes — first opportunity for some time — which made me feel & look like some other, "Boy", & was thinking how nicely I could enjoy a rest of a few days, when a sudden disappointment crept over me, by the sounding of Boots & saddles at Company Headquarters, about 12 M. The order was quickly obeyed by the drivers — & cannoniers soon had their guns in order — but didnot move until 3 O.C. PM. when we bid adieu to Meridian & I hoped for the last time while the war lasted. We had been there so often, & seemingly nothing was left; had stripped the town & surrounding country, of everything to eat so completely — that I as many others imagined it the most God-for-saken place in the South. Passed through Marion a small town & station on the Mobile & Ohio railroad & camped after traveling one mile. The army marched in the direction of Moscow another very insignificant place situated on the Tombigbee river. All rolling stock & army supplies of any kind, that would be of benefit to the enemy — were sent farther south, for safe keeping.

Gen. Polk's Meanderings

This kind of maneuvering denoted that we were loosing ground somewhere, & was very discouraging to us, as well as the citizens, who frequently asked, if we were going to turn them over to the mercies of the Enemy. Our company was attached to a Battallion of artillery commanded by Major Storrs. On the morning of the 14th we had Reveille at 5. O.C. & soon after moved out on the road, where we remained stationary for some time waiting for Gen. Loring's Division & baggage train to pass.

Our march was very slow & tiresome. The cannoniers were kept on their feet & drivers on their horses ready to march but didnot go far. Passed through Old Marion, a small town 1 O.C. PM two miles from Marion station; also through "Old Town" another unimportant place, & after traveling two miles camped for the night. Cooked three days rations. We also crossed the state line between Miss & Ala. & bivouaced near the border in Sumpter county Ala. During the day heavy firing was heard at Meridian, our men drove the yanks back sustaining a trifling loss. On the 15th we broke camp & moved out one hour by sun in the morning. All the baggage & cooking "kits" sent forward in the direction mapped out for the army to march, — this was always a signal of danger in the rear & it looked as if the yankees were determined at that time to make us fight — & if they had, would have received a glorious thrashing, for we were some what weary, hungry & awful wet, the rain had been pouring down upon us for three or four hours — could not run — & was just in the right shape to fight anything that came along.

Gen Polks Campaign Continued

The roads were soon worked up into a thin slush over our shoe tops, & such another dirty set as we were, is seldom ever seen. A person would have had to be a very close scrutinizer to tell whether our clothes were made of mud or cloth. The rain had made rivers out of small branches, & the Infantry when nearing the banks would raise the yell & wade through. We cannoniers got to ride over most of them, but had to dismount as soon as the opposite bank was reached. Our battery & first Mo Brigade brought up the rear, but didnot have an occasion to use any ammunition. Feds quiet. Passed through Gaston a small town & camped near the edge about dark, & unlimbered ready for action.

Whiskey was issued to the troops — one "snort" to the man. I thought this the right thing at the right time, & would have been willing to swallow a "wee bit" more of the "crathur" if it would have dried my clothes.

Crossing Tombigbee

On the morning of the 16th our camp was again deserted, & line of march taken up. As it was customary to take it "by turns" in the order of march, our battery was in front that day. The roads were soft — in many places the wheels of our guns sank to the axle & the cannoniers had to put their shoulders to ~~the wheels~~ them. Came to a halt at Lewis ferry on the Tombigbee river about two hours by sun. Found but little done toward preparing a way to cross, but Gen. Polk our Chief commander of the exploit, put his wits to work, & with the assistance of a large force of men, soon constructed a pontoon, out of the bows of three small steamers & four flat boats. Our company were the first troops to cross about 7 O.C. PM. & found camp about one & a half miles distant.

Gen Polks' Campaign Continued

The night was chilly & unfortunately for me was on guard. The 17th our company remained in camp. Gen. Loring's division passed by our camp going south in the direction of Demopolis. On the 19th we had Reveille at

5 O.C. AM & moved out at daylight, in high glee because we were nearing the place where we had so much pleasure while parolled prisenors. When we arrived within one mile of Demopolis our messkit was again unloaded for the night. This was about 2 O.C. PM & after a travel of nineteen miles.

The weather was cold & winds high mixed with a little snow, which made it very disagreeable, as we had no other wood to burn but green pine & that not very plentiful, also Swamp Water to use for cooking & drinking purposes. But these inconveniences were offset to a great extent, by making a junction with a portion of our goods, which were sent from Meridian Miss at the beginning of this campaign. Found my blanket all "OK" which was a great comforter during the cold snap — our tents were yet "non-est". Two days 19th & 20th our company remained in camp, & as there wasn't anything particular happened to attract my attention, tried to solve the problem that we had been working at for the last seven or eight days; I endeavored to study out the advantage gained by our circuitous march. I asked myself the questions. Was it intended as a retreat. Was Gen. Polk afraid to try to cope wih the enemy upon open field? If so why make this round about march — when more than half the distance could have been saved by coming through? There was a motive in it; & I guess He knew — the why's — but I didn't.

The 21st was a pleasant day & being the first one of this kind for sometime, I was anxious to note it. We were also made aware of the fact that Sunday had come again by the chiming of bells at Demopolis being carried to our ears by a cool refreshing breeze, kindling in my bosom a desire to join the crowd going to church — but "business before pleasure" — our Division Commander Gen French, thought a review necessary & we had to obey his orders.

Demopolis Alabama

Gen's Hardee's corps & Cheatham's division were ordered here from Gen. Joseph E. Johnston's command at Dalton Ga. & on the 22nd troops from the latter command commenced arriving.

> **Gen. Benjamin Franklin Cheatham first commanded his division in Polk's corps, then Hardee's corps. He succeeded Hardee as commander during the Franklin and the Nashville campaign. After the war he returned to farming and public service (Boatner III 147-8).**

The infantry of our division (French's) were ordered to cook three days rations, but met with a considerable drawback — as the commissary couldn't give them but one ration of meal. On the morning of the 23rd our division & Loring's crossed to the west side of the tombigbee river on a pontoon, camping near its banks & adjacent to Town. We found an abundance of good water, Hickory ask & oak wood. The Steamers at the wharf & bank of the river were crowded with ladies while we were crossing, & thinking our movements denoted an advance upon the Enemy — used all kind of expressions ~~to~~ calculated to nerve us for the task — such as push on you braves & drive the vandal hords from our midst!! You will not suffer then to Sack our homes & lay waste our country. etc etc. The boys answering their implorations. We will — We will & no never! On the 24th we remained stationary, but were greatly surprised when Hardee & Cheatham received orders to return to Dalton Ga. 'Twas also rumored the Feds were advancing upon that place, which occasioned their return, & on the 25th Johnston was fighting them there. Our rations were very scarce at this time, but the Officers didn't care for that, their only thought was to give us exercise, & one of the Lieutenants (McBride) on the 26th went out in search of a suitable place for field drill — & as we expected found a good one. The 28th was Sunday & we had to get on our clean clothes, tie up our sundown shoes, ready for battallion inspection by Maj. Storrs.

Demopolis Alabama

But of all days the 29th was received with more shouts & glad faces than any which had been numbered for some time. Our tents were brought back, causing great satisfaction, but our hearts were made gladder still, by receiving two months wages, & commutation for clothing, which should have been drawn. I received one hundred & twenty four dollars — This was rich for a soldier — or atleast I felt that way — for my pocket book was again badly "sweenied" & had been for some time.

March

The 1st day of March was made memorable to us, by a general rumpus at company headquarters amongst the Officers, in which some of the participants got considerably worsted. There had been some whisky drawn by the company commisary for medical purposes, & the Officers sampled it pretty freely — so much so that some of them became noisy & on the "war" path. Lieutenant McBride & Dr. Moore our company Surgeon, engaged in a very abusive quarrel, which finally ended in blows — but were seperated before much damage was done — McBride coming out best man. This enraaged Dr Moore so much that he became more noisy &

abusive than ever — so much so that Maj Storrs who had been attracted by the racket, ordered him bucked & gagged for awhile. This disagreeable affair created a great deal of excitement in the company but night came on & closed the disagreeable & discreditable scenes. The Dr was the most guilty one & the next morning repented in "sack cloth & ashes" Saying served him right, & all was again Serene. On the 2nd our tents were pitched in military order, which was quite a surprise to us, as we had predicted a short stay. The weather was cold & disagreeable for a Southern climate.

Camp Near Demopolis

In the afternoon of the 3rd I was very much interested, in a speech made by Govenor Watts of Alabama, near our quarters, to the Missourians. He applauded them for their heroic valor upon the battlefield & good conduct on the march & in camp. Eulogized them in the most flattering terms, for the great patriotism displayed — by forsaking home, friends & their own native state, to fight the bloody battles in a far distant country.

Gov. Thomas Hill Watts, upon graduation from the University of Virginia, established a successful law practice and became a successful planter as well. Although he had professed strong support for the Union in the 1850s, in 1860, Watts owned 179 slaves. Ultimately, he became one of the signers of the Alabama secession ordinance. Following his defeat in 1861 for governor, he joined President Jefferson Davis' cabinet as attorney general. In 1863, as the newly elected governor of Alabama, Watts faced all the challenges the war had wrought in his state, although he remained positive about the South's military position. By 1864, Governor Watts recognized his limitations and chose not to seek reelection, finishing his term in 1865. Sam heard Governor Watts speak optimistically, as he was prone to do, despite the fact by now Watts' constituents held little hope for victory ("Thomas Hill Watts").

On the 5th we were very much gratified by our Old Captain Guibor returning to the company & taking command. He appeared much better from his seat, & we all received him with a hearty shake & a wish that his health might permit him to remain with us through the struggle.

Capt. Henry Guibor, a Mexican War veteran and a graduate of St. Louis University, first led his State Guard and later his Confederate battery with the competence of a skilled

commander. Most of the cannoneers in his First Missouri Light Artillery were veterans of the Missouri Volunteer Militia, the Southwest Expedition and the Southwest Battalion, and Missouri State Guard. Their combined experience was unequaled by any of the Confederate artillery units prior to the war (Tucker 94, 154).

On the 6th one hundred & fifty yankee prisenors arrived, who had been captured in north Miss by our cavalry. On the 7th all the troops at this point were reviewed by Gen. Polk, also all the Ordinance & baggage wagons were on the field with teams hitched. This was a new feature, but I suppose, a very essential one. These reviews always brought out the ladies, & on this occasion the hillsides around the grounds, were covered with some of Alabama's fairest Daughters. It was a grand time, but the days programme was cut a little short — the troops & spectators were hurried home, by the appearance of heavy clouds in the east, unnecessarily though, the rain was light & of short duration.

On the 9th rain fell hard & steady all day. The ground occupied by our camp, was so level, that we were forced to gather the spades & commence ditching to keep from being "swamped". The water got so deep around our tent & kept falling so fast that we could not cook supper. This brought to memory the overflowing, while in our tents asleep at Memphis Tenn. But we didnot sleep long when the water came in upon us. The 11th was friday, the unlucky illfated day, & by the superstitions is always consider~~ated~~ed unlucky to commence anything on that day unless it ~~can~~ could be completed. This is the day upon which the Savior of all mankind was crucified, which noted event was the origin of hangman's day, or I suppose the reason why all criminals who deserve death punishment are put to death on that day, & the day didnot pass, without being observed in the vacinity of Demopolis.

For hundreds of years, Friday has been known in all countries as Bad Friday. Being born, being wed, washing blankets, cutting fingernails, and planting potatoes on Friday are examples of bad luck superstitions that have grown up around this day of the week. Journalist Robert Lovinger includes in his long list of Friday superstitions that it is unlucky to begin something on Friday, unless it is finished the same day. In some cultures Friday has been the day criminals were executed, thus the term "hangman's day" (Lovinger; Radford 126-7).

Federal Spy Hung

The noted Federal Spy McGibbon was hung at the old fair grounds at 11 O.C. A.M. He was a brave man, but no doubt according to military usages, deserved his punishment. He stepped upon the death trap with an unshaken tread & unflinchingly faced his doom.

We had now become settled down in the every day humdrum of a permanent camp duty. Most of our time was consumed in rollcalls, drill & inspections, alternating field & park drill — sometimes mounting & dismounting the pieces. On the 14th one Soldier (a Miss) was shot for desertion, two Arkansian's were sentenced to share the same but were reprieved by order of Gen. Polk. This seemed like an awful punishment, for anything short of murder or rape; yet for a man to throw down his arms & desert the cause, he had pledged himself to defend at the risk of his life, was very degrading, & a crime which had to be met with the most severe punishment — or our ranks would have soon become greatly depleted & our army without decorum.

Flour raid at Demopolis

On the 16th we had cold bleak winds, which reminded me of march weather in north Mo — but my blood was kept warmed up by drilling. About this time our rations were running pretty low, & becoming worn out upon the scanty supply of corn meal, one of our companies "private" foragers, concluded to take a "Sashia" & see what could be picked up in the way of something to eat. A body of Texas troops had lately moved into the vacinity & camped not far from our quarters, whom he saw had a wagon load of flour, & also noticed a guard with a bayonet in his gun ~~was~~ watching it.

Sam's reference to a "sashia" appears to connect to our current word "sashay" which can mean excursion, jaunt, junket, expedition, or outing ("Sashay"; "Synonyms for Sashay").

After taking an "absquint" of the surroundings, returned to camp & reported his find. The programme was soon mapped out, & it was silently a greed to make a general raid on the flour that night. — So when darkness had trimed the earth in mourning, & the camp was at its stillest — one from almost every mess in the company, quietly stole away through the night, & when within a short distance from the wagon, all stopped but the leader who went forward, ~~who went forward~~ to see what had become of the guard, & finding him sound asleep upon the sacks, signaled his companions forward — climbing in placed a sack upon each ones shouler, who all beat a hasty retreat back to their own quarters. This put us in possession of the flour — the next thing was to hide it. Some of the messes buried it under their mess fires, where they cooked, for a day or two, mine buried a sack under our bed of leaves in the tent, sleeping over it. The Texans missed their flour of course — a search was made — but, 'twas like the "Old mans hogs at Meridian. "No good". As luck would have it — we drew a few rations of flour about this time, & by mixing the Texas "rations", had an abundance for some time. I made my first attempt at lightbread making here — but didnot succeed very well.

Saint Patricks Day

The 17th was Saint "Pathricks day in the morning". The Officers of the army concluded 'twould be too bad to let it pass, without a good time; some demonstration at celebration as in days of yore. So according to arrangements previously made, were to have a grand picnic ~~in~~ on the Black warrier river on the South side of the Tombigbee.

The Black Warrior River, a tributary of the Tombigbee River, is in central Alabama. The largest city on this river today is Tuscaloosa ("Black Warrior River").

Officers Picnic At Demopolis

As this was an Officers affair exclusively — the Ladies were all invited as a matter of course. They even had a committee appointed to wait at the depot for the incoming train to take care of the visiting fairsex, but were sadly disappointed upon its arrival, to see but few alighting. The "Brass mounted Men" as we termed them attempted something grand, but made an almost complete failure. Having been given out for some time, that it was exclusively for the Officers, was I suppose what "killed" it — which caused a great deal of hilarity amongst the private soldiers — twas meat "too sweet" for us.

Grand Review

On the 19th we had a grand review, & early in the forenoon troops commenced crossing to the south side of the river to the review grounds, also carriages came teaming in from the surrounding country, laden with citizens, mostly women. About 12 M the troops being all in their respective places, were given the command attention! Then came Gen's ~~Pol~~ Polk & Loring down the lines upon their beautiful chargers in a sweeping pace, being cheered by the men as they lifted their caps while passing every stand of colors. When they arrived at the review stand — the command was given. Pass in review! By companie's, right wheel! forward March!!

Immediately the music commenced by all the bands, affording a grand sight for the lookers on — twas magnificent to see how straight the lines were, bodies erect & knees bending as one. The first Mo received the praise for being the best drilled troops on the ground. After the review, Senator Curry of Alabama, made a speech to all the soldiers in which he gave us great encouragement, by saying one more years fighting would give the South her Independence — which caused great applause. But subsequent events soon showed that he "saddled" the wrong horse.

Jabez Lamar Monroe Curry was elected to the U.S. House of Representatives in 1856. When Alabama seceded from the Union in January 1861, he was named to the Provisional Confederate Congress. After 1863, he joined the Confederate army and following his appointment as lieutenant colonel, 5th Alabama Cavalry, Curry led his regiment in Alabama during the last part of the war. He later became a Baptist preacher and was also involved in education, establishing a public school system across much of the former Confederacy. Shortly after the war Curry wrote, "Perhaps there is no problem of greater gravity before the American people than the just and wise solution of the race question...," believing "It needs the calm, patient, thoughtful, intelligent foreseeing and forcasting study of our best men and women." In 1899, the Jabez L. M. Curry Elementary School was established in Birmingham, Alabama (Goodrich 225; "Jabez Lamar"; "Jabez L.M.").

Demopolis Alabama

For several days there was a great deal of rain fell; so much, the pontoon across the river was removed to avoid washing away. The weather was cold & high winds, & on the 24th the river was reported as rising five or six feet every twenty four hours. On sunday 27th we had inspection again 9 O.C. AM. The day was beautiful, & in contemplation of the ugly ones just passed, was almost beyond description, which I suppose put a rambling notion in the boys heads & the consequence was three of them were put under guard for absenting themselves without leave — But the day & night following rain fell in torrents with but little interval, overflowing several tents, & if it continued much longer, the river would have been out of its banks, & then all that couldn't swim would have had to climb a tree. About this time Confederate money was depreciating in value very fast, & the army suttlers commenced discounting the old issue thirty three & one third per cent on the dollar. So you see it took a "heep" to get a little.

> ***The American Heritage Dictionary of the English Language*** **defines a sutler as one who follows an army and peddles provisions to soldiers ("Sutler").**

In the fore noon of the 30th orders were given French's division to move in the direction of Lauderdale Springs Miss. & on the 31st preparatory to the comtemplated move, all the tents were sent by rail to that place, & the preference was given to the men, to send their knapsacks in the same manner, or carry them upon their backs, as transportation could not be furnished by wagons. Everything in readiness our company moved out 11 O.C. AM. in a north western direction. The country was hilly, & roads being muddy our progress was very slow, only traveling six miles. Passed through Belmont a small village & camped near by, & after a "short" supper "flew up" on the ground to sleep, with a slight sprinkle of rain in our faces.

April

But we were very agreeably surprised when awakened at daylight on the morning of the 1st day of April, & found the sky clear with prospects for a nice day. This was all fools day, & jokes passed around freely. Several of the Boys took the Captain very much unawares by approaching his quarters & addressing him in this manner. What will you have captain? Meeting with a surprised look & the answer, Nothing sir! Would turn to go back to his own quarters & the answer April fool! April fool!! could be heard from a bevy of "boys" who had sent him.

From Demopolis to Lauderdale Miss

Left camp 8 O.C. AM. The country over which our march extended was hilly & sandy, not very indicitave of prosperity; notwithstanding this during our days march passed some nice residences. After camping drew one days ration of flour, for the following day, & as we didnot have any meat, was forced to fall back upon our "good old" standby corn "dodge", retiring hungry & considerably out of humor. On the morning of the 28th had reveille at daylight, moving out at 8 OC., our Brigade in front. Orders for the cannoniers to stay with their guns, caused by some of them straggling, or dropping out into the country to get something to eat the day previous. Marched over some good country.

Also, through Livingston Ala. a nice pleasant town of about one thousand inhabitants; the streets of which were as usual, crowded with people the principal portion of which were women & children. Bivouaced 2. O. C. PM. Sunday 3rd had reveille at the usual hour, & moved out 7 O.C. AM. This didnot feel like sunday to us, neither did it look that way only by the appearance of the people we saw along the road, & especially the darkies, who had donned their white homespun cotton shirts & aprons as was their custom every time this day came around.

Passed by two small towns; a rickety dwelling or two, blacksmith shop, stable & well constituted the buildings & conveniences of either place. The country was very undulating, sandy & covered with a tall thick pine forest. Camped about 2. O. C. PM two miles from Lauderdale Springs. Lauderdale Co. Miss. Once more upon the soil we had trodden so much, & under whose sod many brave Missourians had already been laid, & would probably envelop many more, before the cruel & devastating war was ended. Some of the boys got "boosy" on whisky found along the road (In this part of the country there was a great deal of illicit distilling done by— so called — moonshiners) & one of them became so noisy & abusive toward the Officers, had to be bucked & gagged to "cool him off".

Lauderdale Springs Miss

The morning of the 4th broke camp at 8. O. C. passed through Lauderdale springs & Station near by, & after going two miles camped in a piney woods. The town & station were considerably injured & disfigured by the torch in the hands of a raiding party of the enemy, a short time previous to our arrival. Several houses & the Depot were burned. Oh! what a cruel set of Soldiers those "Feds" must have been, or they would never have resorted to fire in this case. As usual, when there was a prospect of remaining in camp for several days, as it was in this case, had to clear off a place to park the guns. My mess cut up a good supply of oak wood, taking the advantage of the scarcty of that kind of timber. Having some dirty clothes on hand, on the morning of the 5th went out into the country a short distance from camp, to find a washerwoman, but failing, returned & helped to police camp, also the tents having arrived assisted in pitching them in regular order.

A Ramble

To while away the time in the evening, with two companions concluded to take a ramble. After passing out into the country one or two miles, advanced toward a house we saw in the distance, which was soon reached, & a knock or two upon the door, roused the inmate (women) who invited us to come in, & be seated. The proprietress was a very plain looking lady, & had some visitors of the same stripe; all scrutinizing us very closely, & after several questions, as to who we were? What we were? What was our business? Where from & so on, becoming satisfied that we were friends & our intentions good, settled down into a social chat. The filthy practice of snuff dipping was participated in, to an alarming extent by the women in this section.

Lauderdale Miss

We had not been in the house long, before the snuff box with a home "spun" brush in it, made by chewing a small stick, was passed around, of which the women all partook, as did my companions — they said — to be sociable. I didnot use the "weed" & was excused — Spit! the gee Whizz!! I believe they could have hit an inch auger hole ten feet — as they never failed to land it behind the back log — in the fire place, from their places in the circle. Suffice, to say we returned to camp that evening with "much" experience.

About this time there was considerable dissatisfaction in the company — Some thinking the Officers too tyranical, & too fond of showing their authority. Indeed it looked that way — for we had just completed a march of several days, taking things "rough & tumble" sleeping without tents & living on scant rations. We felt wearied — could have enjoyed a little pleasure & rest; But instead of this, had us policing camp every day. This caused the boys to make some ugly expressions & say a great many things. I rounded up by writing in my notes; Would to God! that I was once more free from the tyranical oppression of such Officers, that I might bid defiance to all such tribes. This sounds a little harsh — but it only demonstrates, to what pitch a man's feelings can be worked up to, when he thinks some body is imposing upon him unnecessarily. And among other things we had to bother us while camped here, had a good deal of rain & my mess had a leaky tent.

Camp at Lauderdale Furloughs Issued

On the 7th by orders received, the Brigade commenced issuing furloughs, at the rate of one for every ten men able for duty. An order was read at retreat roll call, to furlough at the same rate, all those who would reinlist for the war — & those who would not — to be furloughed according to order No - 3 — that is one for every twenty five for duty. The question of reinlisting for the war, caused a great deal of excitement in the company — especially among the hotheads. The furloughs were for 10 days. At retreat roll call on the evening of the 8th some of the leaders made motions which were seconded to reinlist for the war. & not let this the first Mo battery, be the last in showing to the world! our intentions to fight the great struggled through. I called all such proceedings foolery, "Tomfoolery" & worse than nonsense. As for my self, I had been sworn in once for during the war, & deemed it unnecissary to multiply oaths, for the sake of having a better chance at a short furlough. I as several others concluded to take our chances under order No 3. On the 9th a portion of our company reinlisted, & we all drew for furloughs — some under the new & others the old order. I got a blank.

Camp policing still went on, rain or shine & occasionally our camp was visited by the ladies. The 10th was another sunday & to while away a few hours, went to church at the Springs, & was very much surprised to see but few in attendance, for the day was very beautiful — the sun shinning with great power from the Heavens, distributing his sparkling rays — with eaqual brilliancy, upon the trees & flowers, which had already unwrapped their tiny leaves, to greet the gentle April Ƶ zephyrs, passing by & welcome with gladness the warm rays of a spring sun. Returned to camp in the evening feeling very much refreshed by a walk, away from the smoke & noise of the army.

This was a poor country, as is always the case when the major part of the timber is pine, & the people with few exceptions, were generally in harmony with the country. To drive away the monotonies of camp life, & get up something new; on the night of the 11th the men of our battery & Hoskin's Miss battery — engaged in a sham battle — our arms being pine burrs lighted. The burrs presented quite an exciting & picturesque appearance, as the boys hurled them through the air at each other; resembling sky rockets, as the long blaze followed after them. This queer warfare was kept up with great zeal for some time; but it was finally decided by the Mississippians surrendering to our boys. Hoskin's battery was in our battallion at that time; & were associated with us upon many subsequent battlefields.

Camp near Lauderdale

On the 13th all furloughs issued under the late order, one for every ten were revoked, by order of Gen. Polk. This cooled the fellows off somewhat, who were boiling over with patriotism a few days previous.

On the 15th went out on a fishing excursion, with several of the company boys. There had been some fishing done with the hook, & not meeting with much success, we went to a pond or old slough, & in order to make a wholesale catch of it, attempted to drain it, & after working hard all day with spades & shovels — failed, returning to camp late in the evening — with fisherman's luck — a wet _______ & hungry besides.

Once again Sam holds true to the promise he made to his father and doesn't use the words he sometimes thinks, thus he draws a long line to represent the word he had in mind.

Catching Deserters

During our stay here, several infantry companies of the Brigade, were employed in searching the swamps for deserters out of the Miss. ranks, & most of the time their labors were rewarded by bringing in two or three daily. On one occasion when the boys caught four, & were taking them to the Provost Marshalls quarters — were followed by a lot of women, young & old, who called them all kinds of ignominious & ugly names that ever defiled the tongues of the gentler sex. Capping the climax, by saying that we missourians had been driven from our own state at the point of the bayonet, & come down there to tear away from them, their husband's Son's & brothers. Oh! I tell you, they were mad, awful mad! But they should not have blamed the Missourians — they were only obeying orders.

A Mississippi Sweetheart

On the 16th I visited the country again, this time as I told the boys before starting — to find a Mississippi sweetheart. When I had traveled out into the country, least frequented by the troops, & about four miles, stopped at the residence of a Mr. Givens. It being about the noon hour was invited to come in, stay till after dinner to which I very readily consentend — & as luck would have it, when dinner came on the table was ornamented by a good looking young lady, who after the meal, invited me into the sitting room, where a few hours were very pleasantly passed; returning to camp late in the evening feeling greatly flattered at the success of my first adventure of the kind in Miss. On the 18th French's Division was reviewed by Gov. Clark of Miss, who being a cripple rode around the lines in a carriage attended by his wife & Daughter, also Gen. French & staff on horse back. As the Gov. appeared upon the ground, was received by a salute of nine rounds from Hoskin's Miss battery.

After the Union forced the surrender at Vicksburg, many Mississippians were discouraged and wanted to negotiate with the Union to end the war. Charles Clark disagreed and became the anti-peace candidate for governor. During his term (1863-1865), the Union occupied Jackson, and he was forced to move the state capitol to Macon, then Columbus, and then back to Macon. Following the surrender of the Alabama and Mississippi troops on May 6, 1865, Clark ordered the return of the capitol to Jackson. Upon his arrival there, he was arrested by the Union military commander and imprisoned. Clark was eventually released and he resumed the practice of law until his death in December 1877 (Sansing).

The citizens of the country for several miles around assembled to witness the grandest Sight of their lives — this being their first opportunity to see troops on review. Among them were quite a lot of good looking girls — flying around in their home spun costumes; but their good looks & fine appearance, were greatly marred, by the masterly manner in which they used their snuff "Swabs". On the 19th orders were given to move in the direction of Gainsville Ala. on the following day; & preperations were made to increase speed as much as possible — by sending the tents, all clothing, except a change, & one blanket to the near by rail. On the morning of the 20th camp was broken 10. O.C. AM. & line of march taken up in a northern direction on the Gainsville Ala. road as directed the previous day. We traveled about twelve miles over dusty roads, through a poor country, & piney woods, camping in Kemper Co, Miss. near the state line. We had reveille at 4. O.C. AM. on the 21st Breakfast cooked, eaten & things packed in the wagons in short order, & a move was commenced at daylight. Quite a contrast in the country, compared to that we had left behind — that over which the days march of twenty miles extended, being low level, soil rich & well adapted to the products of the climate.

From Lauderdale to Gainsville

We again stopped to rest our wearied limbs about 2.O.C. PM in an old field, three miles from Gainsville, Sumpter. Co. Ala. Camp roused 22nd 4.

O. C. AM. moved at twilight, & but a short time intervened between our departure from camp & arrival in town, as usual having heard of the approach of the army, — every nook, corner & elevation was crowded with people, who looked on in amazement. We found quite an interesting place, Situated on the west bank of the Tombigbee river, about Seventy miles above Demopolis.

We were delayed some time in preparing a way to cross the river. Our troops presented a fine appearance, marching through the streets, & as customary on such occasion — bands playing & banners floating in the breeze — completely overwhelming the citizens with surprise & admiration, causing them to burst forth in loud Huzzas, remarking — the south could never be subjugated as long as such men were in the field. Never. No never! Our battery crossed about noon, & parked the guns on the opposite banks.

You may have doubtless thought me paying too much tribute to the Missourians — in these records, because one myself. Yet I have not put on any embellishments, about the public eulogies pronounced upon them; in fact I have only given you a mere outline besides I have not numbered the many courtesies shown them personally. Here we had an instance of the respect in which we were held by the people of Gainsville — by giving our Brigade a party at night. There was a general invitation extended, but there wasn't a great many private soldiers attended — the Officers showed a disposition to monopolize. There were a great many Officers very plain, while, there were many more, bigoted & hateful, not caring to equalize themselves with the common soldiery.

From Gainsville to Tuscaloosa Ala

On the morning of the 23rd left our position on the banks of the Tombigbee at sunrise —, while the ladies were standing in groups on the opposite shore, expressing their good will, by waiving their handkerchiefs — which signal was answered by the boys, with long & repeated shouts — making the woods & valleys ring. Marched in a northeast direction through a good country, & after traveling sixteen miles, camp at Pleasant ridge Green. Co. Ala. 2. O. C. PM. a small town but nicely situated, upon a ridge to suit its name. Our march through that country, caused great excitement amongst the citizens, who assembled in groups at every cross road & town. The artillery, especially was something wonderful to them, being the first they ever saw, their querries in regard to the manner of using them, etc etc, were very many indeed. 24th had Reveille at daylight, moving out at 7. O.C. AM, regardless of the falling rain. Artillery in front, roads mudy, &

country to the opposite of that over which we had lately passed, it being very hilly. Camped in a deep ravine, Pickens Co. 2. O. C. PM after a march of sixteen miles. On the 25th we were aroused from our slumbering couches at day light, & proceeded on our uncertain & tiresome march, as the sun was appearing in the eastern horizon. Country poor & inhabitants generally ignorant, who seemed completely bewildered at our appearance. One old lady who had been looking on in silent astonishment — remarked as our gun was passing, Don't that beat you!! I never "knowed" before that they ever made as big a thing as that out of brass! Having but little obstruction, made good progress, & after traveling eighteen miles camped 12. m. in Tuscaloosa Co. Ala seven miles from the town by same name.

Tuscaloosa Ala

On the morning of the 26th we were again on the move at sunrise, but after traveling three miles, halted until the infantry passed, who marched through Tuscaloosa in columns of companies, bands playing as usual & cannoniers in rear of their respective pieces. The streets on both sides were densely crowded with ladies, who strewed our path with flowers.

God bless the women! If every mans strength had have been in the contest — as were the hearts of the noble ladies of the south, our cause would never have been lost. Camped two & a half miles east of Town, & as gossip had it, some signs of remaining several days. Not having tents, on the 27th commenced building arbors, to keep off the burning rays of the sun, & offer some protection from the rain, & according to previous practices, commenced policing camp, which was kept up on the 28th & guns also parked in regular order. Had a hail storm in the afternoon, & as we were in poor fix to receive it, caused considerable inconvenience.

On the 29th we had review of our division in Tuscaloosa. There were several Generals present, one of them was Maj. Gen. Hodge of Jeff. Davis staff, who pronounced the drill of the first Mo Brigade uneaqualed by any troops in the Confederate Army.

Gen. George B. Hodge alternated at the beginning of the war between serving as a private and in the Confederate States of America Congress. He rose in rank and was ultimately appointed brigadier general in 1863. However, the Senate refused to confirm this appointment until August 1864, after which he commanded the District of Southwest Mississippi and Eastern Louisiana. Following the war, Hodge practiced law and maintained involvement in politics (Boatner III 403-4).

This was a broad assertion, but I guess he was posted; as he was in a position to know & had seen all the troops. This was a great satisfaction, as well as stimulation — However less review, — more "grub" & rest would have been far more acceptable to us. "Tom." Harris of Mo made a speech to our Brigade on 30th at 4 O. C. P.M. His talk didn't amount to much was short full of stories, witticisms & vulgarisms.

Thomas Alexander Harris was born in 1826 in Missouri. Following his service in the Mexican War, he was elected as the Representative from Missouri to the Congress of the Confederate States. At the time Sam heard him speak, Harris was nearing the end of his three year term (1861-64). Harris died April 9, 1895, and is interred at Cave Hill Cemetery in Louisville, Kentucky ("Harris").

Camp Near Tuscaloosa

We had a nice camp, which was visited almost every evening by the ladies, & those of the company who could afford "lead harness" entertained them while they remained, showing them the guns, ammunition, friction primers; the manner in which they were used etc etc. while we poor lads with our old dingy uniforms on, stood back & looked on or sneaked away in our tents — but as goes the world, where brains fail — brass prospers, & too many women are captivated by outside appearance.

May
My first Vote

The first day of May was Sunday, but a gloomy one & some rain. On the 2nd an election was held by the Missourians, for the purpose of electing seven men to the Confederate congress from their state. Here I cast my first vote, & if you will take the trouble to count, was a little too soon — but I was anxious to vote, the first time, to see if it would make a "man" out of me.

At this time, Sam was only twenty years old. He would not be twenty-one for four months and thirteen days.

One of the men on the ticket was George. G. Vest — who was elected & I am voting for him yet. Orders received by the Infantry of the Brigade, to be ready to march on the next morning at ~~5~~ 5. O.C. Our company didnot receive any. According to orders the Brigade left at sunrise, in a northeast direction — their business was to drive deserters from a swamp about forty miles from our camp. They were not allowed a change of clothes, no cooking utensils only one skillet for every ten men — ten days rations of meal & twenty of salt. Some of the swamps in this part of Ala, as well as those in Miss. were great hiding places, for deserters & men who were dodging, to keep from being conscripted. This was one great cause of our defeat, & very discouraging to troops from other states. Had they all enlisted, or even those who did — had remained in the ranks & fought like men — the work of the Historian, would have been quite different.

On the 4th by order of Gen. French, the company was turned "out of doors", or atleast the only protection against the suns rays, or rain — was taken from us. We had two tarpaulins for every section, one of which we were using in lieu of a tent. This was taken from us, rolled up, put away & the other hung over the harness. We immediately commenced building arbors to sleep under — also over the guns & caisons; when about half completed an order came to move camp on the 6th to near Utah Springs Ala. where forage was more plentiful. This occasioned quite a surprise, yet a very agreeable one — as we were more than anxious to abandon the work. As soon as the nature of the order became known, loud huzza's took the rounds of the company. I thought French's order, depriving us of our shelter, very unnecessary & inconsistent — & looked as if He placed more value upon the tarpaulins, than human comfort or lives. However a great many Officers cared but little who else got wet — so their heads were dry — as they generally had tents. On the 5th the order to move on the following morning was again reiterated, & Six days rations of meal, bacon, salt & soap issued; but when the hour set for moving arrived — the order to go to Utah was countermanded, & an additional one read to remain in tact, but to hold ourselves in readiness to move at anytime — as the Federals were said to be advancing upon Johnston's position in north Georgia — 'twas thought our forces would soon join his army. On the morning of 7th we were somewhat hurriedly roused from slumber, when breakfast was cooked & eaten in doublequick time — scarcely half hour intervening, before our very pleasantly situated camp was left, & we were marching on the Montavallo road in a northeastern course. The country over which our days march extended, was mountainous, rocky & almost wild. The few houses we passed, were log, many of which were without chinks or daubing. The country looked as if a great deal of hard labor & very close economy, would be required to obtain the necessaries of life — I tell you it looked like hard times & worse coming. The day was warm & roads dusty, making our march very wearisome.

About 3. O. C. in the evening, after a travel of Seventeen miles our camp was pitched in the most God forsaken country, I ever saw, & we had to use water for cooking & drinking purposes, from standing & bad smelling pools.

From Tuscaloosa to Montavallo Ala

The morning of the 8th was ushered in by a very early reveille — 3 O. C. AM. — after some hesitation, such as stretching — eye rubbing Etc. I rolled out of my slumbering "couch" — hurriedly threw on my clothes, & fell into ranks to answer to my name. This was hurrying matters a little more than we had been accustomed to, for some time past — but every fellow was allowed about five minutes in which to dress — & when he did fall into ranks was required to be full dressed not with one "gallas" down barefooted & hat off. If he did appear in that shape — was severely reprimanded — but more often punished. Left camp at daylight.

In the late 1700s, men and women began wearing braces or straps over the shoulders with one-button attachments to hold up breeches, pantaloons, trousers, or peasant shorts and skirts. Known as *galluses* or *gallowses* in England, *suspenders* in the United States, and *bretelles* in France, they changed in the mid-1800s to two-button attachments. Sam's spelling appears to be a variation of one of the English words (Yarwood 48).

Passed over a poor country — not much adapted to cultivation as farms of any importance were very scarce. The manner of the people denoted but little thrift. — Crossed Shoults' Creek — quite a stream — at Scottsville — a small town — yet of considerable importance to the South — affording two good sized factories — which manufactured some goods for the army — The work was done by young ladies — who turned out to witness our passage — whose appearance, words & smiles, had a great tendency to drive away our tired feelings. We "tied" up again for the nght about two miles from town — after a days travel of fifteen miles, Bibb. Co. Ala. On the 9th the hour for reveille & moving, was about the same as had been adopted on previous mornings. & our line of march — crossed the Cahaba river at Centerville — a small unimportant village. Surrounding country rough & rocky. A few miles distant crossed Six mile creek at Six mile town — but was hardly worthy the name of town — a few dilapidated dwellings, a storehouse of the same "stripe" — with quite a sprinkling of negro cabins — constituted the buildings. We had a very agreeable rest of three or four hours here, during which time Gen. Ross' cavalry passed, & again our march was continued, which lead us by the Iron mines.

Gen. Lawrence Sullivan Ross served as a captain under Sam Houston in the Texas Rangers, later enlisting as a private in the Confederate army. When Sam saw General Ross, Ross was commanding his brigade under Gen. Joseph "Fightin' Joe" Wheeler. Following the war, Ross oversaw his plantation, was sheriff, served as a state senator from 1881 to 1885, and was president of Texas A. & M. College until his death in 1898 (Boatner III 708-9).

To Montavallo Continued

Camped 5 O. Co. PM five miles from Montavallo — & almost as far from water. This was very inconvenient — as water was a Soldiers best friend, but a stop with a chance for a little rest was a great pleasure, as well as a necessity. I was very much wearied after the long days march of twenty miles, through the thick dust — with the warm rays of a southern sun beaming down upon my back. I was almost overcome. On the 10th had reveille at the usual hour & our march continued at sunup. Arrival at Montvallo. Shelby. Co. Ala. 8.O.C. AM. — situated on the Va. & Ga. railroad — parked the guns near the Depot, so as to be handy to load, & as cars were scarce, the horses were sent under charge of a Lieutenant & the drivers, by highway to Blue mountain — at which point it was our intention to join them as soon as transportation for the guns could be had. During the evening, we had a very heavy rain fall, inconveniencing us very much — as our means of Shelter was, only as we could catch it — so most of us caught the rain —, But were kept pretty well warmed up; & "dried out" to a certain extent, by the wires bringing glorious news from our side, all around — Virginia, Johnston's army at Dalton Ga. & the Trans miss department. But had a little too much sound of the "Grape vine" — to be true. The 11th was spent in bivuoac —with a cold drizzling rain falling upon us. This was extremely disagreeable — but being no room for "dodging" had to "grin & bear it." Transportation for troops was very slow coming — but we managed to get our guns loaded on the cars a short time after dark; where they remained until 3 O.C. in the afternoon of the 12th before orders were given as — to pack our tricks upon the cars, ready to leave — & then a lapse of two hours intervened before the train pulled out.

From Montvallo to Blue Mt

Traveled along very nicely until dark, a halt was made at Lime station; where a delay of about twenty hours was caused by the up trains being behind time. Schedule time was a rare thing in war times, especially in transporting troops — as the amount to be sent & destination were not known at all times. Our delay was quite lengthy — but I spent the time very interestingly — watching some old negroes make barrels, while others filled them with lime; at the same time making fun for us, singing plantation songs, etc etc.

Women Fight, at Lime Station

But the climax was capped, about 3. O. C. in the afternoon of the 13th about the time our train was ready to pull out; when our attention was attracted by a small group of the citizen of the Village, in which two middle aged women figured most prominently, & from the demonstrations they were making & language used; a combat was near at hand — which was soon opened by one slapping the other in the face with her hand — at the same time calling her some very ugly names. But before any hair pulling commenced or further licks passed — a man interfered & stopped further demonstrations, endangering life or limb. — But a war of words between the maddened adversaries was still heard when we departed. These were white women — but not the "upper crust". The cause of the trouble was a "family affair" — or one in which two neighbor families were implicated.

One accused the others daughter, a blooming "maiden" of about Seventeen summers — who was standing near — of doing things & keeping company — not becoming any lady — especially a girl of her age.— But we didnot have time to inquire into the truthfulness of the acusation. It was rich enough, as it was — & one which caused a great deal of merriment & funny remarks — Such as Give it to her! Hit her again! Ah! I wish that "gal" was mine, Etc. Made good speed, but after crossing the Coosa river, a short distance from which we stopped at a station by the same name. Country very broken & rocky — looked as if 'twould crowd a person to make a living in times of peace, much less in war. After the train for which we waited passed down — the word "all aboard" was given, & our northward course was again commenced.—

Blue. Mt

Arriving at Blue mountain, ninety miles from Montavallo, & terminus of the railroad, about daylight on the morning of the 14th & found the horses waiting. The guns were soon unloaded, breakfast cooked & eaten — after which we moved out about four miles to camp, & remained the ballance of the day.

From Blue Mt Ala. To Rome Ga

On the morning of the 15th had Riveille at 3.O.C. & marched early in a northeast direction, on the Rome. Ga. road. Passed through Jacksonville Ala. ten miles from Blue mountain 8. O.C. AM. a very nice little village. Affairs began to look like, a battle was imminent, & from the manner in which our forced march was kept up, it was one in which we were destined to figure.— & our march was made more burdensome & tiresome by being compeled to carry our knapsacks — upon our backs — not having but one wagon to the company, for transporting cooking utensils, rations. etc etc. Marched up wills valley & down Tarripen — a spur of the Blueridge mountains, being the dividing ridge between them. Our days march alas extended through crossplains & Gigy — two small villages. But we stopped about 1. O.C. P.M. to rest, feed the horses & cook supper. This perhaps will sound singular indeed, to the reader — we could not always find water at the proper hour for meals, & as this was an occasion, governed by emmergencies; were bound to make good time, regardless of usual time for cooking, & rest. Our line of march was again taken up about 3. O. C. of the same afternoon, & continued until dark. I was greatly fatigued from the twenty five miles travel, & gathering my blanket — with the earth as a bed — no other covering but the Heavens, the stars sparkling brightly, & the soft beams of the pale faced moon — falling upon my way worn brow — was soon sound asleep. But the allotted time was short, our rest was again broken at 3.O.C AM. on the 16th & our march continued at daylight. You will notice in many places on this march I neglected to keep the counties. I was so near worn out for rest & sleep — that in many cases I could scarcely sum up courage enough to record the names of the towns.

Rome, Ga

Crossed the Ala. & Ga. state line. Passed through Cave-Springs Ga. & over a very mountainous Country, arriving at Rome Ga. 9.O.C. PM. very hungry, sleepy & tired — but ~~were~~ was some what brightened up, by a prospect of an other short ride on the cars. This was a very trying march on us, & one on which many poor fellows became leg weary & dropped out of ranks — to report for duty after the lapse of several days. Everything was loaded on the cars on the morning of the 17th so that we left Rome A.M. bound for Add~~d~~air Station — at which place we arrived, in the afternoon 3.O.C.

Add~~d~~air Station
Formed a Junction with Joseph. E. Johnstons Army

Some fighting about two miles north, soon after our arrival our guns were unloaded regardless of the rain, pouring down, & a position taken in line of battle, abut one fourth of a mile north east of the station, on a hill in an open field. There was no general engagement, but skirmishing, was kept up a short distance in our front until dark — close enough to our position to hear the minnies whistle passing around us.— This was the first since Morton. Miss — but 'twas the same old "song".

Georgia Campaign

About 9 O.C. PM. when the shades of night had settled thick over the earth, & while the campfires were burning briskly, our army silently withdrew — falling back in a southeastern direction, & about twelve miles, to Cassville Ga. This distance could have soon been made, with a small body of troops; but we had a large body & a late junction of two commands, rendering our movements very slow & keeping us on foot all night, & until 7.O.C. AM on the 18th. Troops came in at a lively rate all day, & took position in line of battle on the adjoining hills, among them were the first Mo. & Ectors Miss. Brigade — They met & repulsed the Enemy near Rome the day previous.

Gen. Matthew Duncan Ector fought at Richmond, Stones River, and Chicamauga before being sent to Mississippi in 1864. Later, during the Atlanta campaign in Georgia, Ector lost a leg while leading his brigade. Following his recovery, he served with Hood in Tennessee and surrendered at Mobile, Alabama, on May 5, 1865 (Boatner III 260, 559).

Cassville Ga

There were but little demonstrations of a hostile character during the day; a few stray shots from the artillery, & a skirmish or two between our & the enemies cavalry, was about all. About one year had intervened between the time of our arrival at Add~~d~~air station & our entering Vicksburg, & when the latter is compared to the campaign which followed, the hardships of one, are almost — if not eaqual to the other. But to return — our company was greatly surprised, at the sound of boots & saddles soon after dark, damaging our supper, which had commenced cooking — but about the time cooking was stopped & some of the utensils put in the wagon, the order was countermanded & one issued to remain in position until further instructions. Our supper was a little mixed — but was like the "Old lad~~ys~~ies eggs" — soon straightened. Although discommoding us some — the change was very agreeable, as we were very desirous to get a nights sleep & rest. The breaking of day on the morning of the 19th found us on the field near Cassville. The forenoon was principally taken up by Gen. Johnston, placing his troops in the most effective positions around the entire line of battle — which extended ten or fifteen miles from east to west & across the Chatanooga & Alanta rail road.

Georgia Campaign

This line was our principal means of supply — was our main hold to defend, & the great prize which the yankees, were endeavoring to capture & destroy. About 8 O.C. AM the fracus was opened by our artillery — the firing was slow, but kept up all day — with a slight musketry. About 10. O.C. AM. our battery took position in the third line of battle. About 4.O.C PM our whole line of battle was withdrawn, one half mile to secure a better position. The move was scarcely begun, before it was observed by our antagonists — & the new position was hardly reached before our old one was occupied by the enemy, who seemed eager for a fight, & about one hour by sun a brisk fire of artillery & musketry commenced by both armies all around the line. The solid shot & shell from the enemies guns passed over, where our company was held in reserve, occasionally one bursting near us, making it a very unpleasant place. Hoskin's Miss battery took position on a hill a short distance in our front — but did not remain long — yet the time was very damaging to them — having one of their pieces disabled — also a Lieutenant & two privates wounded. The men of our company came out all right but had one horse wounded.

About dark cannonading ceased — but the sharp crack of the skirmishers rifle was heard — the dim light of the moon giving him a chance to continue his deadly work. Soon after night fall — all the cannoneers of our company, went up on a hill with picks & shovels, a short distance in our front, & commenced throwing up parapets for the guns. Mr "Yank" soon spied us & our job was made a very disagreeable one — by their minnies whistling around — but fortunately no one was hurt. When our work was about half completed — orders came to suspend & another retrograde movement commenced. The reserve artillery & infantry moved at 11-30-O.C. PM. leaving ample force to guard the rear. Agreeable to orders received our battery fell back about ten miles, which took us to the south side of the Coosa river — & also consumed the greatest portion or another night in travel & bewilderment. On the morning of the 20th the drivers received orders — early — to harness up, & the guns were moved down the river in a southwestern direction, two miles, the object being to feed & rest.

Near the Coosa river

The men were very tired & horses hungry & jaded. A short time after noon, heavy firing was heard in the rear the direction from which we came the night previous. At 4 O.C. PM. our company according to orders — went back near the bridge & took a left hand road — leading a little east of south. This was a little risky as we had but one road to pass the bridge leading ~~winding~~ along a low bottom — overlooked by a prominent hill on the opposite bank — & liable to be occupied by the foe at any moment. The cannoniers were ordered to mount & drivers soon spurred their horses to a gallop. At this time our troops were all across the river — & the two bridges railroad & highway, were in flames. The Federals could not yet be seen, but could be very distinctly heard a short distance in the rear, coming in hot pursuit. After we had passed what was thought to be the danger line — the cannoniers dismounted & the usual gait assumed.

Allatoona

Camped at Allatoona station 8.O.C. PM. ten miles from the bridge. After a good rest, left camp on the morning of the 21st — but only to move out about two miles — where we received orders to cook three days rations. Every thing seemed to be quiet — as there were none of the enemy, reported on the south side of the bridge or rather where it had been. The rumor was current, that an advance was contemplated by Johnston. The troops were all in good cheer & confident that "Old Joe" would soon turn the scales in our favor; When our rations were issued that evening — one ration to the man of real coffee was given us — which rated as a great stimulus, & of such rare occurrance — that I took time to record it. The 22nd was Sunday & in imitation of the day of former years, all was quiet in our front, so far as firing was concerned, Most of the day.

Georgia Campaign

Our army was reinforced by five thousand troops under Gen. Flyn & with hopes of a good nights rest — but the happiest dreams & fondest hopes were often broken — as in this instance, a sad disappointment, came over us when roused in a hurry about 10. O. C. P.M. & ordered to load our messkit in the wagon, which according to orders, was sent to the rear, — but the hurry soon passed over, & the same old hum drum, of watching — waiting, expecting & catnapping — again came in to stay a while. This case as in many similar ones, seemed cruel & uncalled for — but in a campaign like this, & where we were opposed by such great odds — every point along the line had to become self supporting — for had one been weakened to strengthen the other — our lines would have been broken — & disorganization followed. We remained in kind of quandary until 8- O.C. AM the 23rd boots & saddles sounded & a move commenced at 10. O.C. — went back a short distance to the rear of our position, to Antonio a small Village — taking a left hand road leading to Atlanta Ga. The day was very warm & roads dusty, making our march — notwithstanding it was only ten miles — very tiresome. This retrograde movement may seem a little singular, to one not acquainted with the facts in this campaign — as the feds were not troubling our front — we were ready & anxious for an attack there — & as this running fight grows older will see — they made several desperate attacks upon our center, & were as often repulsed with great loss.

Georgia Campaign

But Sherman's army, as I remarked before — out numbered ours by such great odds — when a direct attack failed — a flank movement was resorted to — causing us to fall back to protect our supplies, & save the men from a wholesale butchery or capture. We were aroused by a reveille at 3- O.C. AM. on the 26th & about daylight our march continued in the same direction of the day previous. Country mountainous & covered with huge boulders — but abounding with good water — which was of great worth to the army. It was also well adapted to warfare — for one army could scarcely gain a position — but what the other could gain an opposing one eaqually as good.

We again went into bivuoac, by the roadside 11. OC. AM. after a travel of twelve miles. Some cannonading was heard late in the afternoon about six miles to our right & rear. The immense dust was settled by a heavy rain at night. We were called up on the morning of the 25th by a reveille at 2. O.C. — but didnot move until daylight — & then only traveled about two miles until ordered to file out into a cornfield — where we remained until midnight awaiting orders. Oh! What awful suspense —

listening to the roar of cannon not far distant — with occasional musketry — & expecting orders all the time to take a hand. To rest was impossible — & sleep a stranger. Some heavy firing on our right, east of the railroad. The Federals were so anxious to drive our men from that position — that three attempts were made — three desperate charges — but were as often defeated — with heavy loss — while our loss was trivial. Soon after dark firing ceased all around the lines, & about this time a heavy rain set in, continuing three or four hours.

Georgia Campaign

At midnight we received orders to go back six miles & take position in line of battle — where we arrived 3.O.C. AM. 26th & unlimbered our guns ready for action, on a high hill in an open field — Where our view of the country for several miles round was "only" interrupted by Shearmans Army & it looked as if all yankee-dom had been "emptied" out — a few miles in our front. But we felt secure against great odds, when Cockerell's & Ectors brigades were our support.

Near Lost Mountain

Our position was near Lost Mountain. Skirmishing was commenced on the right by Gen Hood's corps, at Sunrise, & kept up at a lively rate until noon — when the first shot from artillery was heard. Most of our men had very good temporary breastworks. A short time after dark our battery commenced throwing up works — but our progress was very slow, as the ground was extremely hard — & considerably mixed with rock. Our work was continued all night — giving us a good chance to listen to the lively skirmishing — which was kept up all the time upon our right, & right center — & when the sun rose on the morning of the 27th the artillery joined in the chorus & continued all day — About 11.O.C. AM skirmishing commenced all around the line.

Our company had been engaged for several hours cutting the large timber, in front of our position, to avoid the directing & obstruction of our shots — But at 2.O.C. PM. were instructed to discontinue, & a move of one mile to the left ordered. No's one, two & four guns were assigned a position upon a high elevation — & no. three the one to which I belonged, was planted in a valley, so as to sweep it — in case of an approaching enemy. Everything was in readiness, ~~in readiness~~ in less time than it takes to describe it, & a confidence of holding our position brightened up the faces of all the boys.

Heavy firing was heard on the right both musketry & artillery. Our new possition was held in peace & quietude, until midnight, when orders came, that we were needed on the right, to operate against a flank movement of the enemy. About one hour before leaving our position — the Feds charged our men upon the right — on open field; but were repulsed with great slaughter — leaving their dead & wounded, to the number of eight hundred or one thousand in our possession — & one hundred & forty four prisoners.

Georgia Campaign

This was quite a prize & a very encouraging victory. Well we trudged along through the darkness, over logs, ruts, brush, hills & hollows — our pathway being occasionally lighted by a bursting shell over our heads from the enemies guns — also kept dodging from the "zip" of the minnies — arriving upon the scene of action about 3.O.C. AM of the 28th — but too late to take part in the battle. After a short pause the order to counter march was given — but took a circuitous route toward the right & rear. About 9.OC. AM stopped for a short rest — which was appreciated "muchly". At 12.O.C our ramble or "wild goose" chase was again taken up — & continued until 4. PM when we found ourselves only one & a half miles from our old position. This is similar to the manner in which persons act when lost — but we were not — or at least as I said before the yankees found us frequently with stray shots. In this march of twenty miles — almost a day & night were consumed & we were about worn out, as this was the third night in succession without sleep. I tell you this looks as if it would have worn out a "wooden" man. But just hold on a while, my dear reader — this isn't a "drop in the bucket." Sharpshooting between the skirmish lines of both armies — continued regardless of the hour or condition of the weather, also occasional artillery. At dark we were ordered to relieve a battery at the ditches, that couldn't stand the pressure.

They would not fire when ordered. We had to move along a narrow road through the timber, which was rough & the night being dark, rendering it very difficult to keep down the noise & avoid attracting the attention of the enemy.

Georgia Campaign

Before arriving at the place, met the men who we were going to substitute, who received several derisive remarks from our boys — Saying in return — you fellows needn't crow yet! You will soon play out! which was answered back with a ha! ha! — Not much "Mary Ann"! Arrived at the works 10- O.C. PM. & very quiety rolled the guns in to position, & eaqually as quietly removed the ammunition chests from the carriages, & placed them in the redoubts with the guns,— after which the drivers were sent with the carriages & horses to the rear a short distance to a safe position. But we didnot do all this without being bothered by the enemies sharpshooters — for their distructive work was kept up all night. Not far from midnight, ~~or a~~ or about the time we had become settled in our "nests"— the yankee pickets charged in our front, rousing us — & were soon ready for business — but were soon — handsomely repulsed. Bully for us!

Taking the Place of another bat

After we had arranged things as best we could — & matters settled back to the old channel— we again laid down to catch a few snatches of sleep, & on the morning of the 29th — the sun had already peeped up from his eastern home, & shining in the boys faces as soon of them were yet sleeping — I arose from my humble couch of "dirt" while the minnies were whistling & buzzing over the parapet — reminding an "Old Vicksburger" that he was once more besieged. And after the smoke & fogg, had cleared away — so that I could get a good view of our position, & lay of the country surrounding — I didn't wonder much at those fellows saying, enough — if they had any shaky places at all about them. We were situated in a low level place, with an old field of the same character in our rear, & running back about two hundred yards, & a mans life was at stake when, that piece of ground was crossed. The position occupied by the enemy in our front, was considerably higher than ours.

But regardless of the advantages in the enemies favor — we determined to hold our position if possible — & use our guns when ordered. Outside the Sharpshooting — everything was more quiet during the day than usual. —

Georgia Campaign

About sundown the feds fired a few shots from artillery at our position — but we didnot return the fire, having orders to the contrary. After dark, we commenced to strengthen our works — but were driven off by the enemies sharpshooters. At 10 O.C. PM the yanks made a general charge on our left — with infantry; at the same time using their artillery — with good success firing over their heads — but made another failure — with the loss of a great many "blue coats. During the engagement, a shell from the enemies gun, burst over the works of our battery — wounding two men Dickenson & Taylor.

The Feds didnot seem satisfied & at midnight another charge was made at the same place — our boys repeating the dose with similar results. This seemed to put a quietus on their movements for a few hours — but the first dawn of day on the morning of the 30th was ushered in by a reveille of artillery intermingled with some musketry. A great bluster & noise, but no damage done. If we could have had the ammunition to waste, they did — we could have made much more racket than we did — & would have taken a delight in replying to them on many occasions where silence was kept. I suppose their idea, was to scare some body — or hide a movement, somewhere around the lines. Sharpshooting & cannonading was kept up at intervals all day. At 4. O.C. PM orders were received by our company to prepare to move at night, & in accordance to instructions — after dark, thinking everything, as still as we were liable to catch it — commenced moving — which was a slow process — having to carry the ammunition chests about a quarter of a mile to the rear — to avoid noise & discovery by the yanks. When two had been taken out, instructions were received to let the others remain in the works until further orders — we immediately returned to our guns, & "flew up" for the night.

Georgia Campaign

About noon on the 31st we spied the enemy throwing up works for three additional pieces of artillery, directly in our front. A volley from our four guns & three others were fired into them, & repeated seven times to the piece — but this only stopped their work while firing. About 1.O.C.PM. our battery fired two rounds to the gun, at the Federal skirmishers in our front, who had gotten so near as to be very annoying.

Our first letter from Home

Just as the smoke of battle was settling around in the valleys, & the twilight was putting on the tinge of darkness — Brother. Caldwell & I were made joyful by receiving a letter from our home in Mo, & being the first since leaving — our hearts were more than gladdened — to find out that our dear parents were yet living & had something left to live on. We read it & re-read it, many times regardless of the whizzing & buzzing of the minnies flying around us. It was a great encouragement to know too that we yet had a home — but at that time & under the circumstances, could scarcely ever expect to ~~ever~~ reach it again. Our comrads were being picked off — one by one — & we often thought — maybe — my time will come next.

June 1st

After sunrise of the first morning in June, I aroused from my bed to again listen to "zip" of those "blue yankee pills" hunting a victim — which when taken according to their senders directions, meant instant death — or disablement for life. At 8 A.M our battery opened upon the parapets in our front — with four second shell & fired fourteen rounds to the gun — the yanks took their "medicine" very quietly — not remonstrating much until we ceased — then commencing an awful fucillade of solid shot & shell for half hours duration — throwing dust in our faces continually — but most of them passed over, taking effect in an old hewed log house directly & immediately in our rear.

Shells were exploding projectiles that were fired by cannons. In order to make them explode at the proper time, timed fuzes were used. Shells were usually timed to explode in the air, allowing shrapnel to deploy upon the enemy (i.e. Francis Scott Key's "bombs bursting in air").

They continued at intervals all day — we treating them with silent contempt.

This manner of artillery dueling became very prevalent before the close of this campaign — It was not unfrequently the case that one party remained silent while the other was firing — unless in a general engagement. Federal pickets charged ours on the left — & while attracting our troops attention by these light attacks — it was supposed they were massing their forces in our front preparatory to a charge. In the forenoon of the 2nd the sharpshooters were about all that made much racket. My friend, who ever you are? You may be getting tired of reading the names of skirmishers & Sharpshooters so often — but if you had been keeping notes of this kind, & writing many of them, while these fellows were making their bullets whistle around your ears — you could scarce refrain from saying something — you would have considered your days records incomplete — & I expect most of you would have said some ugly words. Some of the boys who swore sometimes used to "dam" them a little.

From time to time, Sam has referred to his "kind reader." Here he seems to move to a deeper level of friendship with his readers in anticipation that his future readers will be

interested in even the details of his experience. There seems to be no question in Sam's mind that his words will be read by others; however, he gives no indication as to how far in the future he sees this extend. Considering all the individual diaries were destroyed and only the composite, this memoir, survived, Sam's expectation is made possible for as many as have interest through the publication of *Fishing on Deep River*.

The Old Brass Clock

About noon rain commenced falling & continued three hours, filling the redoubts six inches in water — wetting our blankets & "grub" — after the rain ceased the water was bailed out with buckets. Our parapet resembled a hog wallow — & we looked like a new breed of swine — or atleast we had the mud on us all right. But it didn't matter if our blankets got wet — or our beans & corndodge filled with sand; the minnies might whistle, the cannons send forth their missils of destruction, & the fortunes of war tremble in the ballance; but there was an old brass clock, in the house, I have heretofore described, that ticked away regardless of the shattered condition of its protector — several of the logs had been torn in two by cannon balls, & roof almost demolished. This house had been occupied by a family, until the line of battle was placed, & in their hurry to get out of danger, left the clock fastened to the wall, & after we had taken the position some of the boys happened to notice it, & kept it wound up every day — & when our "pests" in front were not making too much noise — the striking could be plainly heard from the works.

Georgia Campaign

The morning of the third about 9. O.C. skirmishing commenced more rapidly than usual — at noon we saw some of the "Fed" Sharpshooters leaving their pitts in a run — & our Infantry boys noticing their escapade, peppered the balls into them — lively greatly accelerating their speed. Late in the same afternoon federal transportation wagons could be plainly seen from our position, moving to our right. The prevailing opinion at that time — was they were massing their troops at that point to make a flank movement. The weather was somewhat foggy & gloomy — late in the evening — had a shower of two hours. As the yanks had become a little more quiet in our front — some of us concluded to risk a nights sleep in the old house — rather than ly in the mud — & listen to the tick — tick — tick! of the faithful old clock — tended greatly to drive away the blues during our wakeful moments. The rain again commenced falling before daylight on the 4th & continued until 10- AM. filling our trenches again with waters — but the sharpshooters managed to keep their powder sufficiently dry — to pop away at every head seen above the works — & many times by random just to keep their "hands in." Whisky was issued, at the rate of one pint to every six men — this warmed up the inside very "muchly", but didn't dry our blankets, clothing & grub. Late in the evening moving orders were again received.

Georgia Campaign

Soon after dark the guns were rolled by hand as lightly as possible, & ammunition chests carried to the rear a sufficient distance, to be safe to hitch on the horses — our tread was light — commands were almost given in a whisper, & executed as noislessly as possible — for well might they be — had our actions been discovered — it would have been but the work of a moment — to have swept us from that open field with their artillery — & many valuable lives would have been sacrificed, while unable to defend ourselves. All things were soon ready for a march. The second section, the one to which I belonged brought up the rear of French's Division. The rain continued falling — the night was drak, & so many traveling, had worked up the roads into a thin "loblolly" about eight inches & many places knee deep.

Lost Mountain

Oh! what a time we had, & what a night was spent — the whole of which we were on our feet, arriving at Lost Mountain 7 O.C. on the morning of the 5th only nine miles from where we left the "old clock." After stopping — one days ration of cornbread was cooked. The report was not long reaching our ears that the Feds were advancing. About noon the drivers were ordered to harness — & in this manner we were held in suspense for one hour — then instructions came to unharness & graze the horses until further orders. It was enough to make any one who had a drop of human kindness or sympathy in them feel sorrowful, while on this fall back or running fight — to see the large fields of wheat almost ready for the reaper, corn & rye, trampled underfoot, — farms laid waste — fences burned, houses burned or torn to pieces with the cannon ball — while their occupants frightened almost to insensibility — fled in destitution for safety. But no one could help it then; The fate was ineveitable — & people of that section could only have been recompensed by the complete overthrow of Sherman's Army. Many, very many times on this campaign — My heart was made more than sad — Yes could have wept some, if that would have relieved the poor women & children — I saw huddled together by the roadside, with out food — home — father or Husband. Oh! what a cruel war! & what a fiend Sherman must have been, to apply — or cause the torch to be applied — that rendered so many innocent victims homeless — & farther on, to his men (if they could be called men) to gratify their beastly passions — while the noble & pure women of Georgia, yielded up their virtue at the point of the bayonet.

Near Lost Mt

On the morning of the 6th had reveille at sunrise. Troops came in fast, formed in line of battle & commenced throwing up breastworks. The situation of the troops at this time — was — Hardee's corps on the right — Hood's the center & Polk's on the left. About 8.O.C. A.M. our company commenced throwing up parapets for the guns. After we had gotten the work under good head way — our division (French's) moved to the right to a new position, & were ordered back to the rear of it — a short distance to camp — & our place in line of battle taken by Loring's Division.

In the afternoon in company with some of the boys, went up on Lost mountain to get a view of the surrounding country. The scenery was beautiful to look upon — but the smoke from campfires — & burned powder, hindred one from seeing very far with the "naked" eye. The smoke from Federal campfires could be seen in the distance, while the noise of the ax — & rattle of wagons & artillery moving could be distinctly heard. Our men worked hard all day — throwing up entrenchments — not much fighting done. Had our usual shower of rain. The 7th we were on reserve. About 11 O.C. AM. all of Polk's corps moved to the right — to counteract the movements of the Feds. who were continually moving in that direction. Our battery moved six miles & parked the guns in an old field, four miles from Marietta Ga. Cobb. Co. also in rear of Hood's corps.

Georgia Campaign

The weather was dark, gloomy, & some rain almost every day. This made it very disagreeable, roads almost knee deep in mud — our clothing was always wet, mudy & blankets the same way — making a bad bed, even when we had an opportunity to sleep. On the 8th Hoods corps commenced passing our position early in the morning — going to the right, which seemed to be the main point, of the enemies attacks. About 10. AM we according to orders began throwing up redoubts for the guns, & if they had been completed according to instructions, would have been almost impregnable. The dimensions given us were, eight feet high & Sixteen feet wide. Gen. Cockerell sent a large detail of men to assist us in the work. The reason mainly, for ordering such strong works built, was, the situation, was a very inferior one for artillery. Generally quietness prevailed around the line, during the day. On the 9th we were aroused from our slumber at daylight, to work on the breastworks, & after laboring faithfully — having them almost completed — had to move on. At 4 O.C. PM our corps. (Polks) commenced moving to the right —

Boots & saddles sounded & we were soon on the move with them. We took another position about one mile to the right & south of our former one. We were well pleased with the move as it gave us a very advantageous position. Sear's Miss Brigade was assigned for our support.

Before joining the Confederate army in 1862, Gen. Claudius Wistar Sears taught mathematics and engineering at the University of Louisiana. Wistar fought at Chickasaw Bayou, Fort Pemberton, Port Gibson, Baker's Creek, and Vicksburg. He was appointed brigadier general March 1, 1864, and led his brigade under Gen. Samuel Gibbs French during the Atlanta campaign before illness curtailed his participation during July 1864. General Sears fought in the Battle of Franklin and lost a leg at Nashville, Tennesee, where he was captured. Following the war, Sears was a professor at the University of Mississippi (Boatner III 729).

Our rainy weather continued. Some cannonading on both wings of the army late in the evening when the morning of the 10th came around, prospects of a fight seemed very prominent — it looked as though, the "rose which had been trying to bud so long, would soon be in full bloom. Early in the morning, skirmishing with artillery & small arms commenced about five miles in our front — gradually drawing near — so when night came on, they were within two or three miles of our position. In the afternoon we threw up our works higher & made embrasures — but they were not very substantial, the ground being completely saturated by rain. The morning of the 11th was another gloomy one — but as soon as the fogg cleared away — skirmishing commenced, & by 2.O.C. PM. they were advancing rapidly down the railroad one mile to the right & east of our position — Late in the evening our detachment had to make another redoubt, commanding a deep ravine running to our left & front — our position here was in the edge of an old field, & where the breastworks made an elbow, or almost a square turn to the left for a short distance, &

owing to the situation of the ground in front & this deep ravine running up close on the left — made it very hard to defend, & was very destructive to our company afterwards. At 4. PM orders were received by all commanders of batteries, to have their horses harnessed & be ready to move at any time — but were unharnessed soon after dark. Late in the afternoon a few shots from artillery were exchanged, about one & a half miles in our front. When I awoke from slumber on the morning of the 12th — found the rain still pelting down — almost drowning out the noise of the sharpshooter for a while. About 9.O.C. A.M. firing with artillery & musketry was again heard at the railroad — the artillery soon ceased — but the pop — pop — bang — bang — of the rifle still went on, regardless of the rain, which poured down all day & night. The night was extremely dark — but one picket fired at the noise of the others gun & oftener at the flash — it was all guess work, but frequently some one got hurt. 'Twas not an infrequent occurrance to fine a lone picket dangerously wounded or dead in his pit.

Georgia Campaign

When the order was given to get up on the morning of the 13th the same old "seven & six" greeted our ears —rain & picketfiring. About 2.O.C.P.M. rain checked & artillery firing commenced & continued until after dark. The early morning hours of the 14th brought the noise of artillery & small arms — the occasional buzz of a shell or scream of the minnies, passing over our works, warned us of the close proximity of a dangerous foe.

Gen. Polks Death

Gen. Canty's division & Sear's brigade moved to the right & Gen Polk who had a short time previous been given command of a corps — with the rank of Lieutenant General — was inspecting the line of breastworks occupied by his Corps — when he was struck by a solid shot from a yankee rifled gun — passing through his body, causing instant death. This was a great loss — at a time most keenly felt, & his servises greatfly needed. He was a good, plain, brave noble, highminded man — & the loss of such an officer at that stage of the war — was another death blow to the Confederacy.

Gen. James Cantey had moved to Alabama following the Mexican War to oversee his plantation. While there, he received his commission in 1861 as colonel with the 15th Alabama. Following his appointment in January 1863 as

brigidier general, he led a brigade, then a division, and then in the Atlanta and Tennessee campaigns he again led his brigade. General Cantey returned to his plantation after the war (Boatner III 121).

About noon, heavy skirmishing in our front — & the Feds were made to "skedaddle" — but we thought it policy to strengthen our works, as it was reported, the yanks were advancing in the same direction, in three lines of battle, & as another signal of approaching danger — & a contemplated hurried move, the horses were ordered harnessed & hitched to the limbers & caisons (which were in our rear a short distance). Notwithstanding the great bustle & excitement that existed, our men all seemed anxious to receive an attack, & confident of successful defense. We were tired of being held in suspense & would have been glad for the decisive hour to have arrived.

Georgia Campaign

The 15th almost completed a month since we took part in this campaign — the middle of June had come, & with as little prospect of a settlement as the day we entered upon it — the armies were grinning at each other like two caged lions — only matching a chance to take advantage, at a time & point, when & where least expected. A free exchange of shots was on the days programme & was carried out to the letter. Early in the morning the yanks commenced shelling our lines with rifled guns & continued all day — in the after noon the same was heard upon our left — & late in the evening picket firing was heard a short distance in our front, & the familiar — zip —zip —of the minnies, whistled too close to our ears to be agreeable. Gen. Loring being the senior Maj. Gen. took command of the corps at Gen. Polk's death. Our nap was frequently interrupted during the night by the sharpshooters rifle. During the night the line of infantry immediately on our left had been moved back a short distance to gain a better position, — & on the morning of the 17th when it was discovered by the enemy, thinking it meant retreat — & a victory for them; followed up, after the fleeing "Rebs" — as they supposed — shelling the woods as they advanced — but were soon checked in their mad career, & brought to an unexpected halt — by running up on Hardee's corps well fortified — who gave them a warm reception & a very sudden reverse.

Georgia Campaign

At 4.O.C. PM the Feds charged our pickets on the right — but after a contest of an hours duration, our boys came out victorious — at sundown our pickets in front were charged, also on the left, & the yanks were compeled to stand back — but sharpshooting was kept up all night. We had but little rest or sleep —illy fitting us for the trials of the 18th which was destined to be one upon which, much blood was to be shed & many lives offered up on both sides.

The Battle of the Alatimo Farm

Our position here was on what was known as the Alatimo farm, & the engagement of the 18th was called The battle of the Alatimo Farm. The dwelling was near the first position occupied by Hardee's corps but after he fell back to a new one — & the general engagement commenced, was in the Federal lines, & our battery fired shell into the building to dislodge their sharpshooters, who were trying to pick off our cannoneers.

About 7.O.C. AM. the Feds taking advantage of the rain & dense fogg, charged our pickets with a large force; the skirmishing of Walker's Ga. division, on our immediate left, gave way after a slight resistance — causing the skirmish line in our front to fall back to the ditches or be captured. This inspired the Feds with renewed confidence, who advanced in line of battle, to within two hundred yards of our works — when a galling fire of musketry & artillery was simultaneously opened into their ranks, causing them to waver & fall back in confusion —

Georgia Campaign

Our battery gave them a few rounds of grape & canister; but soon reformed & occupied the deep hollow, near where our works made an elbow — which was occupied by our battery. This gave them a position, which we could not reach with artillery, or small arms, & one from where they enfiladed our works, doing great damage during the engagement. I believe if a hat had been held above the works, ten minutes — a hole for every minute would have been shot through it — for the balls came across that corner all day like hail. About 10. AM the enemy advanced in our front, to within eight hundred yards — & commenced planting a battery of four guns — we immediately opened upon them with shell — causing them to fall back under cover of the hill in double quick time.

Battle of the Alatimo Farm

Had all our adversaries been situated so as to snake a direct attack

— could have defended ourselves against great odds — but those fellows in the hollow, keeping up a continual crossfire — & being in a position from which they could not be dislodged — without a great sacrifice of life — was a great source of annoyance, though the entire engagement. A cold rain with a driving wind was falling all day — which drenched us to the skin, chilling us through & dampened our ammunition — although we used every means at our controll to keep it dry. Some of us held a piece of canvass, while others prepared the fuse — notwithstanding — several of our shells fell in the yankee lines unbroken — caused by the fuse getting wet. About noon the Federals regardless of all our remonstrations — succeeded in planting a four gun battery of rifled pieces, at the same place from which we had driven them in the morning — they had thrown up works during the interval — as soon as they got in position — commenced hurling their solid shot & shell at us — with great rapidity & precission — battering down our works — scattering the fence rails we had on the inside to hold the dirt, in every direction — knocking the poles out of the embrasures — & the works becoming so soft from continued rain — shots frequently coming through.

Georgia Campaign

At one time when we ceased firing a few moments, one of the boys by the name of Young, was lying stretched out, close up to the works upon some rails, propped up for a temporary bunk & to keep out of the water — which had formed in pools on each side of the embrasure — when a ball from a ten pound Parrott gun, came through, striking him on the back of the head, & ~~him~~ he & the bal both rolled off into the water — The force was too near spent to do much damage — but the boys rushed to him as quick as possible & pulling him out, was greatly rejoiced when finding him only stunned & was soon able for duty.

Battle of the Alatimo Farm

We kept up an almost constant fire, in reply to them all day. Lost two men killed & three wounded on the gun to which I belonged. One of the killed was "Ollie." Simms of Saint Louis Mo. who came near falling upon me — shot through the head with a minnie — death was instantaneous. He was tall — & wore a red cap, making a good mark for the sharpshooter — was brave but a little too reckless at this dangerous place — contrary to the entreaties of us all, to not expose himself unnecessarily — frequently sticking his head above the works — & say —

look! look! See! see! the "blue coated devils"— they are right at us! — pointing to the deep hollow near the corner of our works. One of the wounded of our gun — "Fred." Garlichs of Saint. Joseph Mo. perhaps might have escaped — or atleast been more ok had he taken care of himsef — when he could. We had a small fat mule that helped to pull the battery forge — killed some distance in rear of the works (where the horses were) — in the morning — & Fred found it out some way, & being a fellow full of curiosities & always hunting up something fresh or odd — concluded to try a slice of mule beef, taking a knife & going back about three hundred yards to where she was — cut a large slice from the hindquarter — came back to within a few feet in rear of the gun, kindled a fire & proceeded to broil it on the coals. The boys kept telling him, to look out or he would get hurt — but passed it off with a jest — saying they were not shooting at him — or they couldn't hit him — at the same time gnawing away on his beef — but he did quit before his meal was completed — a minnie ball struck him on the ankle — luckily though, with only force enough to bury its-self in the flesh. He came hopping back into the works, in a hurry swearing every jump. The wound was not dangerous — yet very painful & will cause him to limp as long as he lives. We held our position until ordered to evacuate — but it sometimes looked as if the Feds would come over the works, in spite of our desperate defense.

Battle of the Alatimo Farm Concluded

This was a dreadful days battle all along the lines. Our company lost during the days engagement, three killed & nine wounded. The battle raged with unabated fury until dark, & then preperations were made for another fallback. I was truly glad when our time came to leave that position — as we had lost so many — & under the circumstances it was impossible to defend ourselves longer without hazzarding the lives of the remainder of our men. It was not the intention of our Generals to let the yanks occupy that ravine — but the pickets of Walker's Ga. division got scared so badly they didnot stop until the main line was reached, & could not be induced to make an attempt to drive the yanks from it, & we could not command it with artillery as was supposed — the depression being too great. Soon after dark we silently withdrew our forces — falling back two miles to the Kennesaw Mountains, & established a new line of battle, running from Northeast to Southwest. The roads were extremely muddy & some rain falling — making our nights march a very arduous one. Arrived near the mountains at day light, & parked the guns to await orders.

In the entry above, Sam describes what he terms the Battle of Alatimo Farm. No references to this name have been found, but an historical sign posted on the site of the nineteenth-century farm of Ruben Latimer, currently occupied by The Marietta Country Club, describes the battle that took place there where Latimer and his wife Sarah, along with their children and eleven slaves, raised livestock and grew cotton and food crops.

In June 1864, Gen. Joseph Johnston's army built a series of earthworks across the Latimer farm to impede the movement of Gen. William T. Sherman's army toward Atlanta. Early on the morning of June 18, 1864, Col. Fredrick Bartleson's 4th Army Corps attacked the First Missouri Brigade led by Gen. Francis M. Cockrell and drove Cockrell's Confederate troops back to their main line of earthworks. Their counterattacks and artillery barrage failed to dislodge the Federals and General Johnston withdrew his troops to more defensible positions on Kennesaw Mountain (*Civil War Action*).

Georgia Campaign

Many times I thanked God that we were out of that death trap — & rejoiced that I could once more stretch up full length without running the risk of getting my head knocked off. But this didnot last long — for as soon as day dawned on the 19th our evacuation was discovered by the yanks, & they immediately followed up, & at 10.O.C. A.M. commenced throwing shells over the mountain. At noon our battery took position at the base of the Mountain on the west side — so as to defend a valley in case of a charge. Rain poured down very hard for three or four hours — followed by showers all day. About 2.O.C. P.M. we were relieved from our position by, Ward's Ala battery — ordered to the rear a short distance, to the south side of Little Kennessaw Mountain to rest, & Serve as reserve.

Near Kennessaw Mt Ga

We enjoyed it "hugely" for a short time, & could have taken a great deal more with a relish — had it not been for our hated followers. Captain. Hoskins went up on a hill near the mountain — to take position with his battery — but being discovered by the Feds — who gave him such a warm reception with twenty two guns — was compeled to abandon it for awhile. This also occasioned a great disturbance with us — as we were in line with their contemplated position — the yankee shell flew thick & fast around us — as we were in line with their contemplated position — a very uncomfortable one. Fortunately, none of our men were hurt — but one horse was wounded.

At this time our company was in poor shape to travel over the rocks & pricley pears, which abound in that country — as atleast one third of them were entirely barefoot, or their toes ~~sticking~~ sticking through their shoes. However but little attention was paid to the condition of their feet, they stuck to their posts as Veterans of Old, hoping for a better time — But it never came to the south!

On the morning of the 20th we were yet on reserve, listening to the roar of distant cannon — & the fragments of shells — stray minnies buzzing & whizzing over our heads, & not unfrequently dropping among us. The familiar rattle of the sharpshooters rifle could also be heard in the distance. Our position was truly a demoralizing one, for reserves could not retaliate — but compeled to remain in place, & receive the shot & shell from the enemies guns — which being aimed at our forces on the Mountain, descended upon us at an angle of about forty five degrees — & 'twas only a wonder that we made such a miraculous escape.

In reserve Near Kennessaw Mt

Two of our horses had their legs shot off, rendering them useless — which were knocked in the head, to relieve them of their misery — & two others slightly wounded with minnie balls. The majority of this country at that time was covered with heavy timber — mostly pine — mountainous — rocky & well watered — farms of any size were also scarce. At 10. O.C. AM No two gun of our battery, was ordered to take position on little Kennessaw Mt & after a great deal of hard pushing & pulling, it was planted & opened fire about 1. P.M. waking the Feds up from rather an unexpected quarter — who seemed to be enjoying themselves splendidly — Some were scattered over the woods — lounging in the shade etc etc — & in one old field, were drilling skirmish drill — while others were cooking & eating. But, this business was soon stopped — a few shots caused them to scatter in all directions, in search of more genial quarters. The gun fired twenty two rounds as fast as possible & in any direction the largest group could be seen & reached — had one man by the name of John. Harney wounded in the heel by a minnie ball. We got a few more strong shots under the hill.

Georgia Campaign

Soon after dark the other guns of our battery, & one section of Hoskins, received orders to take position on little Kennessaw, with our other piece. There were two Mountains here — one of which was called Little Kennessaw, which was one half mile in height — the other on the east — Big Kennessaw three fourths of a mile high. Eight hundred Infantry were detailed to assist in pulling up the guns with ropes — as the elevation was too steep for horses to climb. We succeeded in getting the pieces in the desired position at midnight — & the pioneer corps were put to work immediately throwing up works.

Kennessaw Mountain

Had another showery day — which was not unusual on this campaign — but we were not like the old "darkey" "more rain more rest." — had to work night & day, rain or shine. When I awoke from slumber on the morning of the 21st the rain was falling in my face — & the fogg so thick, the valleys on either side were invisible. It looked as if we were stranded upon an Island, in an immense sea — I almost imagined myself back upon the Gulf of Mexico. I soon rubbed the skim from my eyes — & after taking a small allowance of corn bread & bacon for breakfast, proceeded to assist in strengthening our works. We had a good high & dry position — "when it didn't rain," and after the morning mist had cleared away a good view of the Federal lines of infantry & batteries planted could be had. On the south side our wagon trains & smoke from the engine at Marietta, about two & a half miles were visible — while on the north — in "yankee dom" the same greeted the eye, but a few miles distant, & upon the same ground, which but a few days since was occupied by our own Soldiery. Our forces destroyed the railroad as fast as they fell back — & the Feds rebuilt it as fast as they advanced. The yanks fired several shots from ten pounder parrott guns — supposed to be about nineteen hundred yards in our front — no damage done. This was the thirty fourth day of the running battle & about the twentieth of rain. Or at least we had been with Johnston that long.

Georgia Campaign

On the morning of the 22nd the sky was clear & being the first for several days — was worthy of record, & it was a beautiful sight to behold the Sun as he mounted the eastern heavens, & lighted up the weeping earth & gave new life to all animate objects. It was a grand view that presented itself in the valley below & north of us, but calculated to cause a thrill of horror to pass over us — when realizing it was swarming with a well equipped foe, thousands & tens of thousands strong — only too eager to leap upon us & crush us to the earth as a lion does his prey. At 10. O.C. AM we greatly surprised "Mr" Yanks — by opening upon them with six guns from the top of the Mountain — also from other positions simultaneously — & as our movements didnot attract attention from any particular quarter, we directed our shots promiscuously — alternating at wagon trains — working parties — Generals head quarters etc; Yelling as loud as possible, to see them dodge & scatter in every direction. This was a "picnic" for us, & too good to last long. The yankees didnot return a shot at us fellows on the mt. but directed their shots at the batteries on our left. About 3.O.C. PM our section, two guns moved twohundred yards to the left — to get a better view & a more direct fire upon the enemies artillery — we fired seventy two rounds from our gun as fast as they could be inserted — when it became so hot as to be dangerous — & had to cease firing until it cooled off. Between three & five. O.C. PM for the first time in my life, was a silent spectator of a bloody battle.

Georgia Campaign

The contested ground was almost due west of our position, & in ground much lower than we were situated. It was the most grand superb & magnificent scene that ever presented itself before my eyes — hundreds of pieces of artillery were belching forth volumes of flame & smoke, keeping a constant roar, echoing their deadly sounds through valleys over mountaintops & mingling with the cruel rattle of the rifle. I stood silent — completly awe stricken — occasionally peeling my hat down — which seemed to be creeping off my head — from my hair standing on end.

Kennessaw Mountain

Soon the scene was vailed in obscure darkness so far as we were concerned, by the immense smoke which ascended rapidly — making the sun appear as if eclipsed — still the incessant roar went on, & on until darkness put a stop to their mad career. The battle was a bloody one, but scored another grand victory for our Side. At every new position taken by Johnston on this campaign, one or two & some times three, desperate efforts were made by Sherman, to dislodge him — but he always made a failure attended with heavy loss, while Johnston's was insignificant. Not a cloud appeared during the day to obscure the sky — the first time within a month.

During the day & night, the gun to which I belonged fired one hundred & thirty shots. About 7.O.C. PM we fired five rounds, causing the yanks to extinguish their lights. About midnight, we fired five rounds more — & I imagine our yankee brethren, roused from their slumbers rather unexpectedly. There was a great deal of labor & loss of sleep, firing as many shots & in the manner we did — but had but little opposition only from sharpshooters — their work never ceased & their supply of ammunition seemed inexhaustable.

Georgia Campaign

The sun had already risen on the 23rd when my Brother & I rose from our bed — which was a large flat rock — from which we cleaned off most of the prickly pears — however enough were left to stick us occasionally — Thousands of blue coats with their glistening bayonets could be seen over in "yankee dom" taking position in line of battle. Some sharpshooting — but the calm of the morning, was not disturbed by artillery until 7.O.C. AM. when our battery fired eight rounds — to which the Feds replied from several directions. About 10.A.M. our gun was moved back to the first position in the breastworks. We immediately proceeded to carry up a good supply of ammunition which was quite a task — as it could not be brought up in any other manner than in our arms. About noon the yanks commenced tantallizing us, by firing an occasional shot from their artillery about nineteen hundred yards in our front — & at 3.O.C. P.M. our Maj Storrs, thinking it was intended as a banter — Said, Boys can't you silence those fellows?

Artillery Duel on Kennessaw Mt

The answer was — we will try. & at it we went — with our four guns & two of Hoskins battery. The duel although very uneaqual was quite animating — they having more than ~~five~~ ten guns to our one. The roar of artillery was incessant — & the yanks kept an almost solid sheet of shot, shell & fragments of shell raining over & around us. After firing one hour, our gun was running short of ammunition, & ordered to cease — But the enemy kept a hail storm of their deadly missils in the air.

Brother Caldwell Wounded

The boys all seated themselves, behind the works, & about eaqually divided on either side of the gun, & had engaged in a general conversation — in a manner becoming insensible to the deadly conflict in progress — when we were startled by the sharp crack of a shell, which was supposed to be from a twelve pound Napoleon gun — which entered one corner of the embrasure exploding at the same time — killing Lieutenant McBride instantly, shattering my Brothers left arm near the shoulder & wounding my friend "Bob" Welch in the foot. As soon as the smoke cleared away so that I could see the dire effects of the explosion, immediately sprang to my Brothers side — with the query — Oh! Caldwell are you hurt? He not being conscious of the dreadful calamity which had befallen him — replied, No! not much! but his arm hanging limp by his side — the large hole torn in his jacket sleeve by a fragment of the shell — the blood spurting from his arm — his palid countenance — told the tale of horror.

Georgia Campaign

One of the men by the name of "Pat" Quinn, took a small silk tie from his own neck — & assisted me in tying it tightly above the wound, to check the blood, & with the assistance of the boys placed him upon a litter, & carried him a short distance down the mountain to the company Surgeons quarters. Oh!! who can imagine the horror & grief that stifled me to silence — as I helped to bear from the field — my best friend — my only relative in the company. Why could it not have been some one else? Or if die why not die together! All this & more flitted through my mind with more rapidity than it can be told. Amputation was pronounced the only remedy — & the captain ordered me to go with him — twas well he did — for I do not think I could have seen him go, without accompanying him. An ambulance was soon procured, & placing him in it, ordered the driver to go to Marietta, where the Surgery was performed — although only two & a half miles — it seemed ten times the distance, & an age consumed in traveling it. The yankee shells were falling around us a good portion of the way — the road cut up by travel was very rough — & every jolt caused the bones in my Brother's arm to grate together — almost throwing him into spasms; although I did my best to hold it in such a manner as to prevent it.

Georgia Campaign

When we arrived after some delay, he was placed upon the amputating table — Dr. Wm Gough adminestering the chloroform & Dr Fluellen assistant Medical director of the army of Tennessee, amputated his arm within an inch of the Shoulder joint. I will always kindly remember my old friend Dr Gough for his services on this occasion & the deep interest he took in my Brothers welfare. After the work was completed — & in answer to my question; Will he get well? The Dr said — if he ever revives from the chloroform — there is some show — but he is so weak from loss of blood — chances are against him. He was removed to the back part of the building — where I made him as comfortable as possible — upon the hard floor with a bed made of our blankets — where I watched in breathless silence for some time before I could see signs of returning life — & when I did words cannot express the great joy that came over me — & who but one who has been so situated can imagine my feelings — when his blue eyes caught mine — & in trembling tones — asked, Is that you Sam? The house was filled with men wounded in all conceivable ways — whose groans & pleadings for help were very pitiful indeed. This place was considered too near the line of battle & was too much danger of our wounded falling to the enemies hands — & by Johnstons orders were sent to Atlanta as fast as conveyance could be procured.

A Confederate army was organized as follows: Three infantry corps were each commanded by a lieutenant general. A corps was made up of three infantry divisions, each commanded by a major or a brigadier general and an artillery battalion was commanded by a brigadier general. An artillery battalion was made up of four to six regiments, each of which was composed of ten companies called batteries. Each battery could consist of over 100 men armed with six cannon, but generally had less men and four cannon (Heiser).

The range of the cannon to which Caldwell and Sam were assigned was like that of all other cannon used in the Civil War. For effectiveness, the cannoneer's target had to be within a range of 1,500 yards or less and the cannoneer needed to see his target, even though most could reach a much longer distance. The armies depended upon their infantries for numbers, as artillery damage, such as that done to Caldwell, McBride, and Welch, only amounted to six to eight percent of the war casualties, although the wounds were often mutilating (Kelly 8).

Caldwell's position on Little Kennesaw Mountain overlooked thirty-five-year-old Gen. James Birdseye McPherson's Army of the Tennessee amassed below. The ridge tops of Big Kennesaw, Little Kennesaw and a spur named Pigeon Hill, the southern most extension of the Appalachian Mountain Range gave their position a panoramic view of General McPherson's troops and northwest Georgia beyond.

Caldwell was wounded during pre-battle skirmishing that occupied both Union and Confederate armies before the main battle for Kennesaw Mountain on June 27, 1864. At that time, Maj. George S. Storrs commanded Capt. John J. Wards Alabama Battery, Capt. James A. Hoskin's Brookhaven (Mississippi) Artillery, and Capt. Henry Guibor's Missouri Battery (Johnson).

Twenty-five years after, an article written by one of the survivors in Captain Hoskin's Battery appeared in the May 15, 1889, issue of *The Kennesaw Gazette*. The writer described at length the series of events experienced by Caldwell and Sam. One month following, Maj. George S. Storrs answered with a letter to the editor of *The Kennesaw Gazette*. Headlined "The Artillery on Kennesaw, A Confederate Commanders Authoritative Statement about the Operations of North Georgia in 1864," Major Storrs supported a portion of the first article and corrected the errors which he deemed "to have elegantly and glibly flowed from the pen of a 'Fairy Tale' writer." Both articles discussed the event that occurred in Lieutenant McBride's section. Major Storrs reported, "I gave him [McBride] the order, when in a hearty and cheerful tone he says: 'Major, we have just loaded this gun; hadn't we better empty her?' I said 'Yes,' and just as he delivered his last shot, a shell from the enemy exploded right over his gun."

General Storrs ran to him and offered him water from a canteen, but McBride had been struck on the head and was unable to drink or speak. General Storrs wrote, "The Catholic priest with the battery, a noble man, administered the dying unction under the brow of the mountain while the enemy's shells by the hundred were shrieking and bursting in the air overhead" (Storrs).

The Mississippi survivor recalled ". . .twelve heavy Parrot guns planted to bear on our little battery of four guns" which ". . .resulted to us in the death of Lieut. E.D. McBride, the best lieutenant in the battery. Caldwell Dunlap, brave fellow, lost his left arm; Bob Welch was wounded badly, and Sergt. Billy Robinson had his leg broken. The enemy commenced on us with twelve guns and ceased with three; we supposed the rest were disabled" ("Guibor's").

Although Union reports were made on a monthly basis during the Atlanta Campaign, many Confederate documents were lost in the fires during the evacuation of Atlanta; estimates placed Union casualties at Kennesaw Mountain at 3,000 and Confederate at 1,000 (Kelly 59).

Georgia Campaign

About 1.O.C. AM on the 24th I placed Caldwell in a box car & the train pulled out for that place — where we arrived at daylight — I had considerable delay & trouble, before finding out, how & where to go — but finally succeeded in getting Caldwell to the Institute hospital. I also got Wm H. Robinson, a young man of our company, who lost a leg in the same engagement — & tried to find Welch — & after a long search found him at another hospital, but the managers, would not allow him to be removed. I visited him several times during the few days I was allowed to remain. His wound although not thought to be dangerous at first, proved fatal. His health was not very good at the time of the accident, & when suffering from any cause — was always discouraged & melancholy.

Institute Hospital Atlanta

The Hospital where Caldwell was — took its name from being near the Medical Institute — the building was already full, & Caldwell with many others were assigned a place, in tents upon nice clean cots — which made a very pleasant berth, compared with what he had experienced since wounded. Anything outside of what was furnished by the hospital Corps — that would benefit or add to the comfort of My Brother, that could be had — I cheerfully furnished. The Ladies of the City frequently visited the hospital, bringing many necessaries & delicacies to the wounded — rousing up their drooping spirits, by pressing their hands upon their fevered brows, at the same time smiling only, as a pure Heroine could — speaking in cheerful tones & expressing a desire for their early recovery. The ladies were also kind enough to furnish the wounded with old, soft clean rags — very essential articles for a tender hurt. Although not a desirable task — yet it was a great pleasure to me — to keep cold water & fresh cloths upon my Brothers wound, & watch with eager delight — the returning gleam of the eye & flush upon his cheek. The most critical stage had been passed, & with good nursing would have soon been up & around. But it was a sad thing to think of a seperation at that time — notwithstanding on the 4th of July, Gen. Johnston issued orders, for every man, who was able to bear arms, to be sent to the front, & I was notified to get ready. About 10.O.C. AM grasped the only hand of my Brother, as I murmered good bye.

July

This was the most heartrending trial I ever experienced. The Idea of leaving him, all that was near & dear to me in the south, in this mangled condition — to be nursed & cared for by a crippled stranger — who was hardly able to dress himself — was well calculated to fill the heart with agony, cause a tear to drop, & make the lips quiver when the time of such seperations came. Only those who have had similar experiences can imagine my feelings. Many will say — I would have remained with him — No! You wouldn't! & been branded, a shirk & a coward. or put under guard for disobeying orders.

Georgia Campaign

At 4- O.C. P.M. boarded the cars & after a short run arrived at Vine station. Found a wagon there loaded with medical stores for our battallion, ready to leave, & thinking it the quickest & most certain way to reach the company started with it — but had not gone far before ordered to countermarch, & I received orders to remain with the wagon. We went back one & a half miles south of the Chatahoochee river & the entire army fell back to near the north side. There had been quite a change in affairs since I left Kennessaw — the army had fallen back several miles — but "Old Joe" familiarly called — was bitterly contesting every foot of ground — he did not give Sherman an inch unless dearly purchased by northern blood. On the morning of the 5th being anxious to see my company again — started on foot early in search for it, & after considerable travel & inquiry — came upon them, just as they were hitching up to take position in line of battle one mile north of the Chatahoochee river. My mess mates & most intimate associates, seemed completely dumbfounded at my early return — & after several hurried & anxious inquiries, regarding Caldwell & the other boys — advised me to return as soon as possible — volunteering to do my portion of camp duty, as well as fighting. This was very magnanimous indeed, & to show such marked respect for my Brother, was truly gratifying to me, & one which will always be appreciated. But I could not return without a pass — which had to be signed by Captain Guibor Maj. Storrs & Gen. Johnston. I concluded to make a trial — & the preliminary steps were immediately taken. There had been considerable change in the Officers of the company since my departure. Corporal Sam. Kinnard was elected to fill the vacancy caused by the death of Lieut. McBride — also Sergeant Murphy was elected as Lieut to fill out the deficiency in officers.

I spent the am with the drivers & caisons having been ordered to do so until the return of my pass. The guns were at the position taken the previous day, but did not fire a shot. Some cannonading & sharpshooting at other points around the line. The 7th was passed with a restless impatience, so far as I was concerned. & the same monotonous proceedings in regard to military affairs. In the afternoon of the 8th I was greatly rejoiced, when my pass was handed me, containing the proper signatures of approval — & was soon on my return to Atlanta, where I arrived a short time before night — & immediately proceeded to the Hospital where I had left My Brother — only a few days since — but was completely dumbfounded, when I didnot find him & was told that he had been removed.

Feeling greatly disappointed, I turned my weary foot steps toward the depot — & made diligent inquiry at every place & from every one, whom I thought could give me information as to his whereabouts — only to find out that he had left on the cars — but where could not be ascertained. I spent the night as best I could, renewing my search with increased diligence on the following morning — but was met with disappointment & negative answers on every hand.

Completely worn out — & thinking it useless to prolong the search — in despair & bewilderment, was almost ready to climb on the cars & return to the company, when I was accosted by a friend of mine by the name of Henry Newman, belonging to the first Mo. infantry Brigade — with the query, have you Seen Welch? No! Where is he? was the answer & question in return.

"Bob" Welch's Death & Burial

He said he's at the Medical College hospital here — & very bad. After explaining to him the nature of my errand & sad disappointment — told him if I could not find my Brother — would spend the short time alloted me with "Bob," & parting from my friend, but a few moments intervened before I was at his bedside — & as soon as I arrived could see, the sad message of my friend was only too true — his emaciated form, feverish brow, wild staring eyes — & random conversation, while tossing his head from side to side upon his hard pillow — told that his time on earth was short, a few more days at best & all would be over. He was rational only at short intervals — & when those did come — recognizing in me a friend — his joy was unbounded & feelings uncontrollable — yet realized that he was bound to die. His wound was badly gangreened — which had eaten the flesh from his foot & ankle, so ~~as~~ the bones & leaders were almost all bare. The fracture in the main bone of the foot could be plainly seen which was made by a fragment of shell at Kennessaw Mt,. I cheered him up & administered to his wants as best I could — many times wiping the cold clamy sweat from his palid brow — but he had to yield to the grim monster death. Away from home, family & but one lone friend, to drop a tear at his grave. 'Twas sad, very sad indeed.

He died on July 13th 3-30-O.C. PM. In his death the south lost a brave & true soldier — & his companions a jovial & lasting friend. I examined his pockets & knapsack for some little memento, to take back to his aged parents in North Mo. — & finding a silver half dollar & razor — putting them away for safe keeping until the close of the war — when I delvered them in person to the old folks. On the morning of the 14th I assisted in attending to the last sad rites of my dear young friend. His remains were placed in a coffin made of rough pine boards — & buried in the Soldiers burying ground near the hospital. I took the spade & dug the grave deeper after the men detailed for that purpose pronounced it deep enough — & put his name upon the head board. This done the last evidence of respect — that could be shown by me at that time was completed — and as the time for which my leave of absence was granted, would expire with the close of the day — turned my face toward the post of duty. In order to facilitate maters — in case of men returning to their commands, a camp of direction had been established whose business it was to keep posted as to the whereabouts of the different Corps' Brigades & Regiments — there by assisting the enquirer to a hasty return. The day was about gone when I arrived at the camp, & I remained until morning. Early in the morning of the 15th having received directions, started on foot for my command, which I found about ~~2~~ 1- O.C. PM. doing picket duty at the bridge across the Chatahoochee river eight miles north of Atlanta. All the army except a strong picket force along the south side of the river — were two & a half miles to the rear on peach tree creek fortifying. The Feds & our men kept up a constant cannonading across the Chatahoochee river.

Georgia Campaign

Received a letter from my Brother, the first word from him, since the parting of the 4th, was greatly rejoiced, to find out he was doing well & in good spirits. He was at Covington Ga. about forty miles south of Atlanta, having been taken there from the Institute hospital at the time of my fruitless search.

On picket at the Chatahoochee

On the 16th the yankees amused themselves firing at our parapets with twenty pounder parrott guns — while we remained silent, not caring to waste our ammunition & having works that could not be easily battered. Our position was a good one, & where we could not be troubled to any great extent by sharpshooters; finding time occasionally, to retire a short distance to the rear & shade ourselves under some trees, from the burning rays of a July sun. 17th cannonading was kept up all day. About noon two Confederate batteries to the right of our position, replied to the Federals, silencing them the greater portion of the afternoon, but our opponents continued to throw their long shot & shell at us without effect. The distance was too great for our guns to do much execution, & our orders were to save our ammunition until they moved up in range. Late in the evening the Feds succeeded in crossing the river about three miles above & to the right of our position, & commenced skirmishing heavily. This created some excitement all along the line, but soon died out as the evening shades appeared. Soon after dark we were relieved by Hoskins battery — & retired to the rear four miles — where we had the pleasure of the greater portion of a nights rest, & on the morning of the 18th the baggage wagon came up — & we once more cooked our own rations, & ate them around the mess fires —

For some time past our rations had been prepared & sent to us, by men detailed for that purpose — but this privilege of doing our own cooking was not to be extended long & our rest was much disturbed, by receiving orders at 9 AM, to harness the horses & hold ourselves in readiness, as the enemy ~~was~~ were reported advancing in force.

Georgia Campaign

At 3- O.C. P.M. hitched up, moved out & took position in line of battle two & a half miles south of the Chatahoochee river — ~~which~~ where it was currently reported & generally believed, that the enemy would be met on open field.

Peach Tree Creek
Johnston Superseded By Hood

In the afternoon Johnston was Superseded by Hood — an action which caused great surprise & dissatisfaction. Johnston was acting a little too much on the defensive to suit President Davis & some others who were agging on the removal. But subsequent events will show that Johnston was doing, & had been conducting affairs, in the best manner calculated to produce the best final results to the south. And by his ceaseless efforts in trying to protect the lives of his men — had become so endeared to them, that the most implicit confidence was placed in any order he gave or move he made. Hood was nervous & excitable — while Johnston was calm.

Hood's tactics were to the reverse of Johnston's. He believed in the aggressive — & by this mode of warfare — in opposition to a far superior foe, soon diminished his force, so that he could not remain in front of Sherman's Army — or atleast the torch of Sherman was applied to Atlanta several days sooner than it would have been — had Hood not weakened his already inferior force, by charging a superior one in his strongholds. It was a generally conceded fact, that Hood was one of the best corps commanders in the Confederacy — that he was one of the best to execute an order after it had been planed by some one else, was never successfully disputed.

Georgia Campaign

He never yielded a position unless driven from it at the point of the bayonet by great odds — & if ordered to storm the enemy in his strongholds, seldom ever failed to come out victorious. This change put an entirely new face on affairs, & happening at the time it did — upon the eve of an anticipated open field battle, the rank & file soon found it out & commented freely upon the cause & effect — notwithstanding it met with almost universal disapprobation, we could only fight on & hope for the better. Just as day was breaking on the morning of the 19th the work of fortifying was commenced, which surprised us greatly — as there had been an open field engagement in contemplation; But digging in the earth had become so prevalent with the troops on this campaign, 'twas said if a man happened to ly down upon the ground, face foremost, would naturally "scratch" a place to hide — especially if he heard a minnie whistle.

Near Peach tree Creek

However this by the way — we never commenced digging until ordered. Late in the evening the Feds made an attempt to cross peach tree creek, one mile in our front — but made a failure loosing forty five "Blue coats", prisoners, besides several killed & wounded. There was also a heavy engagement on the right, our side coming out victorious. We worked hard all day & half the night, & did not complete our redoubt, not having but four cannoneers on our gun some were on the sick list. In the fore noon of the 20th we had lively skirmishing in our front.

At noon heavy fighting on the right wing — & for fear the Federals would over power the Confederates at that point — the infantry of our corps was ordered to their assistance. Our battery not receiving any orders, remained in place. Our men also charged the enemy on the extreme right — capturing two lines of breastworks & several prisoners. The engagement was general — the roar of artillery & rattle of musketry was continued for three or four hours, & would have been kept up longer had not night intervened to close the bloody drama.

Georgia Campaign

Our men slept or rested that night in the Federal ditches. About one hour by sun our battery was ordered to follow up — "double quick" — leaving only a skirmish line on the left to guard the works. But a short time elapsed after receiving the orders until we were in range of the yankee bullets — & halted about one hour, where we had to listen & shrug our shoulders from their iron & leaden missils, without getting a position or firing a shot — & during it useless to hold us without benefit, ordered us to return to our former position, after the first hours of the night had passed.

Near Peach tree Creek

The corps also returned & took up their old places of abode. During the day our forces captured four or five hundred prisoners, & a large amount of their dead & wounded were left in our possession. This was a tolerably good days work — but our men being the attacking party — paid for it with the lives of several of our men. When I awoke on the 21st at sunrise — the Feds were thundering away in our front — & a few stray shots from cannon & enfield rifles passing over our parapet.

Georgia Campaign

They had advanced considerable in our absence the previous evening. Heavy cannonading again on the fight. Several troops were sent to their aid — & in order to cover, or hold the distance of breastworks desired, our division were deployed as skirmishes — six feet apart. This was a risky business; but luckily for us, was not found out by the Feds. Late in the afternoon orders were received to fall back to near Atlanta — & soon after dark a move in that direction was commenced. When we arrived near town, a short halt was made to feed the horses — this was done without unhitching or unharnessing. About midnight moved one mile to the left & stopped the remainder of the night — waiting orders. On the 22nd at 9-O.C. AM, our gun took position on the left of our brigade, & the other guns one mile to the right. French's Division was the extreme left except cavalry. At 3.O.C. P.M. heavy fighting again on the right — our drivers were ordered to harness & infantry to be ready for any emergency. Times began to look squally, & the balance, tipping in favor of the enemy. Our forces had to stretch out over too much territory, to guard all points — or when one wing was called upon to reinforce the other — the position from which they went, was weakened to such an extent — that the whole army was in danger of route or capture. And it looked like folly — yes, madness in the extreme, for our forces to charge a superior one — in almost impenetrable fortifications — yet they did — on the right there was one continual roar of artillery & muskitry.

Near Atlanta

The loud mouthed cannon roaring in thundering tones, above the volleys of rifles — raining sheets of balls & fragments of shells, over heads & in the ranks of both adversaries.

Our men had charged — the Feds could not stand — fleeing in confusion four miles, leaving in our possession twenty five pieces of artillery — two thousand eight hundred prisoners, & nine hundred wagons. This was a grand victory — the account of which was received with loud shouts — as it was dispatched by couriers our company was ordered to move out of the ditches, & our place taken by Stephen's Georgia battery — But in the afternoon of the 23rd we were ordered back to our former position, which had been greatly improved, the parapet having been finished in our absence. Our brigade moved still farther to the left & made new works — leaving a small force to guard the old ones. All was quiet on the right except occasional sharpshooting.

Georgia Campaign

The weather was cool & pleasant — a great blessing upon the wounded of the previous days engagement. Reports continued coming in all day, confirming the victory of the day before on the right & in front of the city. There was cannonading & sharpshooting at intervals on the 24th all around the line, during the day & night.

The yanks, also shelled the city day & night, with twenty pounder parrotts, & frequently the heavens were lighted up by the flames ascending from a dwelling, fired by the bursting of a shell or hot shot. Affairs had began to put on the appearance of a besieged city — the citizens having become thoroughly alarmed — began digging caves in the ground — as the people did at Vicksburg.

Atlanta

The contemplation of a siege was awful, especially to those who had been previously engaged in one. The thought that many innocent women & children, had already been rendered homeless, & others would be compelled to flee for safety — while their pathway would be lighted up by the flames of their residences — was calculated to still the heart of any one except one of Sherman's gang. Strong fortifications, were speedily erected by order of Hood — so that a small force could hold them against great odds. The 25th passed with but little change in affairs — our men in their old positions, strengthening them & the yanks booming away at the City. Our brigade drove sharp pickets in front of their works & conceiled them with brush, making an almost insurmountable obstacle.

After dark there was great excitement in our lines — caused by the Federals throwing up rockets, upon the right & left of their lines —and to add more fuel to the flames; a wild rumor was circulated, that the Feds were doing this as a signal for a general retreat.

Georgia Campaign

We closed our eyes that night, with dreams of uncertainty settling upon our brows — but was dispelled early on the morning of the 26th when we heard the booming of cannon at the old places — & we saw the good work of fortifying still going on, also to make assurance doubly sure & the reports of the previous night were only a fake — two seven inch Siege guns were being mounted on a high elevation, to the left & a few rods in rear of our brigade.

Atlanta

A portion of Gen. Walthall's Miss division, moved to the left, & their places in the works taken by Georgia state malitia.

Gen. Edward Cary Walthall was first commissioned 1st lieutenant in the Yalobusha Rifles in 1861, and later he received his commission as brigadier general in December 1862. General Walthall had just recently been promoted to major general before Sam made the above reference to him. Following the war, Walthall served (1885-1898) as a United States Senator for the State of Mississippi (Boatner III 888; "Walthall").

All cannoniers on each gun over No — 6 — & all the drivers except the wheel drivers, drew enfield rifles, to act as Sharp shooters in the redoubts. This put many more muskets in the ditches — which would have rendered great assistance, in repelling an assault, or added great strength in an advance movement.

The 27th day of the month came & brought but little change in affairs in our front, or upon either flank — except the yanks commenced throwing up works one & a half miles in our front — they also took great delight — or seemed to, in shelling the City. Oh! What a great annoyance, this must have been to the citizens — but we could not help them. Brigadier Gen. Ector & Captain Ward of Ward's battery, were wounded by a shell from the enemies artillery while engaged in conversation. Ward's wound was not dangerous — but Ector lost a leg.

In the evening the infantry received orders to draw sixty rounds of ammunition to the man — & be ready to move at a moments warning. We received orders to harness up. The orders for issuing ammunition was soon countermanded. Gen Ectors brigade moved to the left & their places taken by Malitia, who flocked in by hundreds — & seemed anxious for a fight.

Georgia Campaign

However, I would have sooner trusted old veterans for a support — as only a very small number of ~~them~~ malitia had ever heard a bullet whistle, or smelled burned powder except while hunting game. On the 28th quiet prevailed in the morning — About noon orders were received by the infantry to be prepared to move at any time — & our battery ordered to harness up & hitch in. At 1. O. C. PM there was heavy fighting on our left — Our men met the advance of the yanks on the open field, charged, & drove them back upon their main line of works, which was constructed of fence rails —

Atlanta

After which three successive & desperate attempts were made by our men to dislodge them — but, seeing their efforts were vain, & forces fast diminishing, had to fall back under a murderous fire of the enemies artillery & small arms, leaving our dead & wounded on the field. Two hours by sun, a courier came from the left in post haste, after our battery — we immediately limbered up & started in the direction designated — which was four miles from our former position — & farther to the left. We were not long in making the distance, & took position in open field, & prepared to protect ourselves as best we could, by constructing temporary works of fence rails. The field was hedged in on the north by a thick under growth, making a good hiding place for the enemy, while our position was upon a bald hill. We had a great deal of worry & fret — but didnot fire a shot — yet received some effective ones from the enemy, having one man killed & two wounded in our company.

Georgia Campaign

You will no doubt say — Why didn't you fire? I might answer — for several reasons. We were not ordered to do so — 'twas often the case, while we were taking a position, some unexpected change would happen, that our situation was unavailable — or frequently our own troops were in range. We always fired when ordered.

A short time after dark, we fell back about two miles & parked the guns for the night. At least with the expectation of remaining until morning if permitted to do so. We had not remained long before the yankee pickets in our immediate front made two or three assaults upon ours — & were as often driven back. The minnies whistled thick & fast around us, & thinking a general attack imminent, prepared for action, & loaded our guns with four second shell — which were withdrawn after a short time — the infantry having driven them back with considerable loss — this seemed to satisfy the yanks for the night — or at least in our front.

Atlanta

About 9.O.C. P.M. all the left wing of our army withdrew one & a half miles, & commenced throwing up breastworks. This gave us a much better position. On the 29th about 10.O.C. A.M. Our battery received orders to hitch up & move to the left. We soon took the position in line of battle assigned us, & commenced the old business of fortifying. We labored hard with pick & shovel all day — the earth was very hard & weather extremely warm. Our battery was temporarily thrown out of Storrs battallion & attached to Lorings old Division. Two batteries from every battallion in this corps; by order of Gen. Hood, were left in the trenches around Atlanta — all others subject to orders for duty on open field or flank. This gave us plenty of work & exercise — not very agreeable, unless our stomachs could have been more bountifully stored with substancial food.

In early 1864, Gen. William Wing Loring was serving under Lieut. Gen. Leonidas Polk. Following their failed efforts to stop General Sherman's Meridian campaign, General Loring moved into north Georgia in May 1864 to support Gen. Joseph

Johnston's efforts to stop Sherman's move toward Atlanta. After General Polk's death, General Loring took command of the Army of Mississippi. Following the battles of Franklin and Nashville, he rejoined Gen. Joseph Johnston in an effort to stop General Sherman's march through the Carolinas. After the war, General Loring was commissioned brigadier general in the Egyptian army and fought ten years before retiring in 1879 (Heidler and Heidler 1220-1).

Georgia Campaign

The 30th was very warm & sultry — but having our works completed in the forenoon, could ward off the heat much better. In order to protect our flanks & rear — it was necessary to recruit our cavalry force — accordingly orders were received by our Captain, to dismount all the Sergeants & corporals of the company & turn the horses over to the cavalry. Late in the evening there also came an order, to send a detail of four men from the company to assist in manning Siege guns. I was one of the detail & ordered to report to Captain Scoggins in Atlanta for duty. We arrived at our newly assigned post soon after dark — & after being informed by the Captain that our posts would be given us the next morning — were soon asleep near the guns.

Detailed on Siege gun at Atlanta

On the morning of the 31st I was assigned to duty as No. one on a thirty two pounder — seven inch — rifled gun, & with the assistance of others commenced firing. After firing five or six shots at thirty minutes interval, received orders from Gen Hood, to cease as it was Sunday & the Feds were not replying.

This was one of the guns, which I referred to being placed in position a few days since. It was mounted upon a carriage in a round excavation in the earth about fifteen or twenty feet in diameter, & of sufficient depth, to allow the muzzle to be elevated over the surface or about five feet deep.

August

On the 1st day of August military affairs were somewhat quiet in the forenoon — but we kept up firing at intervals from our gun. At noon we fired six shots as fast as possible, to silence a Federal battery which was playing upon a working party of our men — the desired effect was accomplished, & we sat down to rest. Helping to man one of these guns was very hard work — & when it was discharged, the jar would almost "lift" a person off their feet. When I had time, & could think of it — often stood on tip-toe, stopping my ears, & opening my mouth to avoid concussion.

Georgia Campaign

At 3- O.C. PM. the Feds opened up on our fort with twenty guns, ranging in caliber from twenty pounder parrots down to ten pounder Shrapnells, raining the solid shot, balls, Scraps of iron & shell around us with terrible velocity, covering us with dirt & pieces of turf. We immediately opened upon them, with our thirty two pounders, & Captain Hoskins with three guns from the fort. A very spirited duel was kept up until sundown — & the Feds not showing a disposition to continue hostilities — silence was again restored in our quarters, & the smoke soon settled away in the distant valleys. When we ceased firing I was almost as black as a "nigger" having to handle both spung staff & rammer.

Atlanta On detail

Our gun fired twenty four rounds — & we must have torn up a great deal of ground & cut down several trees — if we did not kill any Feds. In the forenoon of the 2nd we fixed three shots & as our ammunition was getting scarce, orders were to withhold our fire until the Enemy opened. They commenced constructing works for more artillery in our front. At 10- O.C. AM on the third, the yanks charged our pickets on the left in front of our field battery, & were successfully repulsed by our men the second time — they then advanced in two lines of battle, driving our boys from their rifle pits. Our picket line was immediately reinforced, & their adversaries ~~were~~ driven back, & not permitted to halt until they had taken refuge behind their main line of works. While the pickets were contending for supremacy, the Feds ran up a battery in open field, & commenced firing upon our battery — the boys replied with great speed & accuracy, causing them to return behind their works, & with seeming content remained the balance of the day.

Georgia Campaign

At 3.O.C. PM. the Feds charged our works on the right, but were repulsed with great slaughter. We had nothing to do at my position, but listen to the deadly conflict — occasionally taking notes as I could catch them from passing couriers. But our "hole in the ground" was made very disagreeable late in the evening, by a heavy rain & wind storm.

Atlanta On Detail.

During the morning of the 4th quietness prevailed around the entire line — except, the sharpshooters, & their noise rarely ever ceased. About 2-O-C. PM the enemies infantry made another charge on the left, in front of our battery, using their artillery at the same time, with great effect.

Murphy's Death

The cannoniers at the works escaped unhurt — but a twenty pounder parrott shell which passed over them, exploded near where our drivers were situated, a short distance to the rear with the horses — killing Louis ("Polk") Murphy, & slightly wounding three others. About one third of the shell struck Murphy in the breast, tearing a ghastly hold through him — Staggering — he fell back into the arms of one of the boys; calling him by name — exclaiming — O'riley! I'm a dead man!! These were the last & only words spoken by him, & another tongue was stilled forever. Another bosom friend & boon companion of mine gone! The last neighbor boy was taken from my side. Who will it be next? Who is the next to be carted off to the lonely ground without a mourning friend? Oh! can it be possible, it will be me? All these thoughts revolved in my mind & thousands more as I sat by the lonely camp fire — or tossed my head upon the hard ground, at night, as I tried in vain to sleep. He was one of my warmest & most affectionate friends in the company. He was a noble, kind, generous & obliging young man — would divide the last crumb, or mouthful of water with a friend. His career in the army, was that of a patriot, brave & constant — was always at his post, when able for duty regardless if danger or hardships,. He hated a coward or a shirk. He lived happy — was rarely out of humor, & died while performing his duty. He was greatly missed in the ranks as a Soldier, & in camp as a Social & true companion. The mess fire circle was always aglow, with mirth & laughter, at his dry sayings & good humored jokes.

Murphy's Burial

His remains were taken to the field hospital, placed in a rough pine board coffin, his own blanket for a shroud, & buried in Mr. McNant's orchard near Atlanta. Two of his comrads attended to the last sad rites — But there was no kind hand to entwine a wreath of flowers, upon the lonely mound

— or no Father, Mother, Brother or Sister to drop a tear, or imprint a farewell kiss upon his lips, cold & silent in death.

I was yet doing duty on the siege gun, but happened to be at the company baggage wagon, on a short permit — when they passed with his remains in an ambulance — & saw the ghastly hold through his body, from which his life blood had already flown, & I being the only one in the company from his neighborhood, or acquainted with his folks — a horn handled pocket knife of his was given me, as a memento for his family, which I brought back at the close of the war & gave it to his aged Parents living in Buchanan Co. Mo. A short time before sun set the enemy charged our pickets in front of our position, but were driven back leaving a few prisoners in our hands. While the engagement was going on, we fired a few shots from our long guns — & received a severe shelling from our opponents in return — but fortunately no damage was done.

Georgia Campaign

On the 5th we had sharpshooting & cannonading all day — but would not have been troubled at our position, had it not been for a mortar, throwing shells at intervals — several of which fell too close to our position to be agreeable — several times they fell near enough to throw fragments of shell & dirt in our pit. Captain Guibor, who had been absent on a short leave of absence, returned & took command of his old company.

Atlanta on detail

In the forenoon of the 6th Gen. French advanced in force to Strengthen the picket line upon the right of his division. The enemy made a strong opposition — but the object sought was accomplished with but little loss. We gave the yanks a few shots, to assist the General in his work — but our shells being damaged, so they did not all explode — did little or no execution. About 4.O.C. PM the Feds opened a furious cannonade around the entire line — not forgetting to give us a severe shelling — but did us no harm, as those that didnot fall short, passed over us taking effect in the embankment in our immediate rear. Their deadly work & thundering tones, were kept up until after dark regardless of the heavy rain falling. Our ammunition being scarce was ordered to remain silent — & all that we could do was to hold ourselves in readiness, at the same time drawing our bodies up into as small a knot as possible in the front side of the pit. The 7th was Sunday, & there being no signs of immediate danger in our front in the forenoon received permission to attend Divine Servises, being held near our post, by the Army Chaplain.

Georgia Campaign

The meeting was very interesting — resulting in the confession & baptism of thirteen Soldiers. Eight of whom were Missourians. This was a good work in a righteous cause — & at the time, I had some serious thoughts upon the subject of Christianity; & thinking, if all wickedness could be dispelled from our army — victory would crown our efforts in the end, earnestly hoped the good work would go on until a complete reformation was accomplished. The enemy remained quiet in our front all day — but made some heavy charges upon our left — resulting in defeat & loss to them, while our lines were not charged. 8th was quiet. On the 9th the yanks shelled us very heavy — but we escaped unhurt, & remained silent.

Atlanta On detail

News reached us in the afternoon of the surrender of Fort Gains Ala, to the yankee fleet. Col Anderson the man who had command of the Fort, was branded as a traitor, & it was boldly asserted that He justly deserved the ignominious epithet. This gave the enemy another strong foothold upon our southern coast — but some men will do anything for money — or promise of high position, regardless of principle.

Early in the morning of the 10th we opened on the Federal pickets, who approached sufficiently near to reach our parapet with minnies, & as soon as we fired the first shot, the enemy let loose at us with their parrott guns at a lively rate, but we directed our fire at the sharpshooters until they moved back — then turned our attention toward the artillery & a few well directed shots Silenced them the remainder of the day. We fired all day & until 11.O.C PM. alternately at their artillery, working parties, Generals headquarters, Quarter master & commissary departments Etc. The last shot fired, we elevated the gun to the utmost extent, & let her go, as we said, to "wake up" some far off sleeper. The extent to which a shot could be fired was said to be two & a half miles.

Georgia Campaign

I met a man by the name of George. Peel of Michigan, after the close of the war, who said he was a member of a Generals escort, & was about two miles in the rear of their lines, lying under a wagon when one of these shells plowed a large hole in the ground under the tongue. He said their quarters were moved without waiting a second shot or any further orders. 11th We had some lively sharpshooting & cannonading all day & at intervals through the entire night. The yanks did not forget to make war upon the noncombattants of the City, making their lives miserable, by the continual bursting of shells over & in their houses. From our position the burning fuse in their shells as they described a half circle, could be seen resembling in appearance falling meteors.

Atlanta On detail

In the early morning of the 12th the yanks opened upon us with several guns, one thousand yards in our front, which was quite a surprise to us — they having planted them during the night — but surprises had become very familiar to us on this campaign, & however great we soon became ready for any emergency, & reconciled to our fate — we entered into a duel with them, replying as long as we had any ammunition.

That was the great trouble — having to remain silent so much of the time — & often chances to do great execution, passed without a demonstration to grasp it on our part. Had we been furnished with ammunition could have demolished the Federal parapets in our front, as fast as constructed.

On the 13th & 14th there was more sharpshooting than usual & less cannonading. Captain Hoskins strengthened & casemated the works for his ten pounder rifled guns.

The American Heritage Dictionary **defines a casemate as "an armored compartment for artillery on a rampart" ("Casemate").**

Georgia Campaign

The Feds were also busy constructing works for more artillery in our front. We fellows at the "hole in the ground" having no ammunition, had nothing to do but eat, sleep & listen to the booming of artillery, & rattle of small arms. If this manner of doing would have brought a speedy success to our arms, would have been very acceptable indeed — as the weather was extremely warm for active exercise; but this kind of warfare, with us, was only spasmodic. 15th the same hum drum, of anxiously watching & waiting, characterized the sate of affairs near our position. There being but little skirmishing & cannonading — except shelling the City.

Atlanta On detail

A heavy force of the enemy, consisting of infantry, cavalry & artillery — reported as starting on a raid, in the direction of West point — a place of considerable importance southwest of our position. A force was immediately dispatched by Hood to counteract their movements — Having failed to drive us from the front of Atlanta by direct attack — the same old flank movement was commenced. The opperations in our front, were only a repetition of the last several days, as to quietness — in fact there was but little display of hostilities any where around the lines. The gloom that had been hovering around me for the last month past, in regard to the where abouts of My Brother, was lifted by receiving a letter from him, & my heart was made to rejoice & feel glad, when I read it, & found that he was at Augusta Ga. doing well. This removed "mountains" of trouble from my mind — made soldiers duty much lighter to me — having heard once since our seperation, that he was dead, & at another time, his life was dispaired of — as gangreen had set in. From the manner in which he wrote, was eaqually as anxious in regard to my fate — as I had been exposed to the enemies shot & shell, almost the entire time since our parting, & not hearing any reliable report. On the 17th sharpshooting was very slow in the forenoon.

Georgia Campaign

In the afternoon Captain Hoskins — opened from the fort, upon the Feds in our front — but not without receiving several twenty pounder parrott shells, in return, as a compliment to show ~~with~~ how much "veneration" they had for us "Rebs". We were anxious to help the Captain, out of his dilemma — but had no ammunition

Atlanta On detail

18th Our usual silence was observed — but the yanks gave our hill a severe shelling — with the same verdict — no body hurt. We had heavy cannonading on the 19th, & the yanks gave our "posish" the usual rations. In the afternoon the enemy charged upon the left in front of our field battery, with their infantry — shelling at the same time, but they found our infantry & battery boys wide awake, who directed their shots with the same precission & determination as on former ocasions — resulting in a complete reverse of their assailants — but unfortunately our battery had three of their men wounded, & one feared mortally. Communiation was again cut off, from the points south — by the Feds tearing up some of the Macon & Western railroad. This placed us in rather an awkward situation — a powerful army in our front, & a heavy force reported in rear. When I arose from my humble couch of clay on Sunday morning the 21st, the sun had already risen above the tree-tops, & shedding his bright warm rays upon the once happy homes & emblems of peace — as well as the implements of war & death. The chiming of church bells in the City, was the only demonstration, by which us soldiers could tell that another ~~sabbath~~ Lords day had come. But Oh! how hard those yankee's hearts must have been — to hurl shell in the midst of those dear women & children, while on their way to different places of worship.

Georgia Campaign

Could anything be imagined more heartrending, than tearing the mother away from child or child from its Mother on an occasion like this? Yet Sherman hardened his heart, (if he had any) & caused this inhuman treatment to go on — also the sharpshooters were instructed to keep up their deadly work. I earnestly hoped the interval short, between this manner of passing ~~the Sabbath~~ Sunday, & the settlement of hostilities — that all could enjoy the day in a Christian like manner.

Atlanta On detail

On the 22nd nothing occurred around the lines worthy of note — but the restorations of communications, between Atlanta & Macon Ga. was of great importance, & one for which our cavalry deserved great credit. On the 24th having received twenty five rounds of Ammunition for our gun, on the previous day — concluded to fire a few shots — having been silent so long, feared, our "friends" over the way — might think we had left — or their heavy shellings had disabled our gun. They returned the five without hesitation, & a small fragment of one of their shells, cut a slight gash in the cheek of one of our cannoneers, by the name of Blakely — but didnot disable him from duty.

Georgia Campaign

Early in the morning of the 25th we received orders to fire three ~~of~~ or four shots at the casemated parapets in our front, thinking everything so still over in that direction, perhaps our enemy had fled between "two suns" — but it was just like probing a hornets nest — one of our shots brought an answer from five guns. This made a very uneaqual combat, & after the information sought was gained, & the orders given us obeyed — we dropped behind the works, to listen to the whizz & buzz of their shells passing over us.

Atlanta On detail

A short time after daylight on the 26th the first news received after rubbing my eyes open — was the yanks had evacuated our front, except a small, picket force. Some skirmishing with artillery & musketry could yet be heard on the left. In the forenoon our skirmish line in the center & on the right, was advanced two & a half miles without disturbance.

In the evening the detail on the heavy guns & Hoskins men went over in front to tear down the works for artillery, from which the Feds had been firing at us so long — we found our task a very hard one — the works were strongly built, & well casemated with heavy timbers, covered with two or three feet of dirt. We also found it very disagreeable, as well as dangerous, as our movements were soon discovered by the enemies sharpshooters, who peppered the balls around us at a lively rate. I thought sure they would get me before our task was done. On the morning of the 27th the yanks were reported as having fallen back all along the line — & several thousand of our troops were sent out upon a reconnoitering expedition — which proved the report well founded — as our men didnot overhaul them, until the crossing of the chatahoochee river eight miles north of Atlanta was reached, a bout 1- O.C. PM — when a considerable engagement ensued — resulting in the withdrawal of our men, as the enemy was strongly fortified on the north bank of the river.

Georgia Campaign

On the morning of the 28th the exact position of the Feds seemed very difficult to ascertain — & their future movements eaqually as mysterious. All except a small force of Cavalry, crossed to the north side of the river, burned the railroad bridge & leveled the stone piers to the waters edge.

This act was well calculated to vail their movements in darkness, for the present — as it had been, but a few weeks since they rebuilt it, after being distroyed by us. Us fellows, left in the trenches, were an extremely restless mass of humanity — all eager to grasp at the flying reports — as to the whereabouts of the enemy — also our future movements. Later reports had it, that the Feds cut the railroad near West point, & Gen. Hardee's corps went to meet them. The enemy having disappeared from our front

— or atleast beyond the extreme range of our big guns — & indications pointing to a complete change in their base of opperations — our sevises as a detail were considered unnecessary at that time — were ordered to report to our respective companies for duty.

Returned to our Companies

The company had come back near our position, & also to our old division. I was well pleased when the order to return came, & glad to see my old mess mates again. Several familiar faces had dropped out of the ranks, since I left the company — but one especially familiar, had again broken the chain around our mess fire — Poor Murphy was gone.

Georgia Campaign

29th we parked our guns & remained stationary all day. As previously reported, the Feds were making a flank movement upon our left, & Hardee did go to check them. Late in ~~in~~ the afternoon of the 30th having been ordered — our battery moved over & took position in the breastworks in front of the City. This move caused a great deal of comment, as there was not an enemy in our front nearer than the Chatahoochee river. 31st we remained in position — strengthening all the weak points in our works, but the fortifications were already very formidable — as they should be — for it was intended in case of an emergency, a small force could protect the city — while the main army could be used in repelling flank movements.

In the trenches in front of Atlanta

Heavy fighting was heard upon the left, & it was generally believed a bloody battle near at hand — for the enemy had been battering away in our front, for more than a month — & met with the same fate which had been characteristic — of all their direct attacks since the beginning of the Campaign, & from general appearances, a desperate effort to capture the prize would be made by flank movement. Now kind reader if you have been a soldier, you can readily conceive, the great restlessness, & anxiety that made us almost miserable.

Sept 1st

about noon on the 1st day of September — when we received orders to move the guns out of the works & leave the horses hitched to them, & the infantry to fill their cartridge boxes with Sixty rounds of ammunition to the man — there had already been some heavy firing on the extreme left in the forenoon — & to render our dilema more untenable, the "air" was full of rumors of all kinds. Some prophecies that a pitched battle was in progess while the "knowing ones", said it was Hoods intention to go to the rear of the enemy & cut off his communications — a third one said evacuation was the only alternative — but it was generally conceded, that a few hours at farthest would tell the tale, & sure enough about two hours by sun, unmistakable evidence of an evacuation was shown — when the Siege guns were ordered spiked & carriages burned — we then knew our doom was sealed, & that too in a manner which we were unable to avoid. The Feds were reported advancing. Four days rations of "hard tack" & bacon were issued — something extra for us to draw — also received a "jigger" of whiskey each, I suppose to nerve us for the nights march. Soon after dark the destruction of all kinds of army stores that could not be moved began. The flames shot up from the frequent explosions of powder & ammunition maggazines to light up the Heavens & by their loud reports scatter the news abroad, of the final downfall of Atlanta.

Oh! what a pity it was that we could not have fore-seen, the final result — & burned all this powder in thinning the ranks of an enemy that more than doubled our number.

Evacuation of Atlanta

About 8-O-C. P.M. the evacuation commenced. The columns filed out slowly in the places assigned them. Our battery covered the rear. This was a sad, sad! move indeed. Another Spear had been sunk to the hilt in the heart of the Southern Confederacy — & every man marched & looked, as following to the grave the last remains of some dear, departed friend. 'Twas well that darkness vailed the procession in mourning, hiding from view many of the poor, miserable inhabitants, who were begging in all quarters for mercy. Passed a very tiresome night, as we were on our feet all the time, & when daylight came on the morning of the 2nd we were only six miles from Atlanta, & we kept dragging along in this manner all day & a good portion of the night. About 2 O.C.P.M. our corps formed a junction with S. D. Lees' which had been traveling on another road.

Gen. Stephen Dill Lee was serving as Aide de Camp to Gen. Pierre Gustave Toutant Beauregard when General Beauregard ordered the firing on Fort Sumter at 4:30 a.m. on April 12, 1861. He rose in rank, becoming at age thirty the youngest of the seventeen lieutenant generals of the

Confederacy. General Lee fought at Seven pines, Savage's Station, Malvern Hill, Bull Run, Antietam, Vicksburg, Chickasaw Bayou, Champion's Hill, and the Nashville and Atlanta campaigns, Following the war, Lee operated his plantation, served in the legislature, and was president of Mississippi A. and M. College (now Mississippi State University) from 1880-1899. He was a member of a federal commission that established Vicksburg National Park. In 1904, as the last surviving Confederate general, he became the Commander in Chief of the United Confederate Veterans, a post he retained until his death in 1908. (Boatner III 299, 477; Heidler and Heidler 1164-65).

Georgia Campaign

Late in the afternoon cannonading was heard at right-angles to our position. Hardee, the Sturdy old warrior was opposing the advancing columns of the enemy, over there — We continued our march toward the southeast, in the direction of Augusta. Filed out in an open field by the road side, 11- O.C. PM. & filling up my Stomach a little with "hard tack" & raw bacon, immediately stretched myself upon the ground to sleep away the few precious hours allotted. Silence reigned supreme at a bivuoac like this, so far as the men off duty were concerned — the voice of the Sentinel as he stood watch while his comrads slept, or the hoofs of the galloping panting steed, as he swiftly carried the lonely courier from post to post, would often be heard to add solemnity & anxiety to the occasion.

Falling back From Atlanta

Our slumber turned out to be of short duration as the camp was roused on the morning of the 3rd at 3. OC. ~~PM~~. & only a few moments intervened until we were again marking of the distance, step by step, through the darkness, upon our toilsome & uncertain journey. Our baggage wagon train took the McDonald road — as it led in a direction least exposed to the enemy. At this time, prospects for an engagement seemed near at hand. We proceeded very slow & cautious — but were not long in getting close enough to hear the familiar whistle of "Mr minnie", as ~~the~~ he fell around us or passed over our heads.

Georgia Campaign

Our position in line of battle after considerable delay, was assigned us — about one fourth mile east of the Macon & Western railroad, near Lovejoy station & about five miles South of Jonesboro. Our corps relieved Hardee's, & His & Lee's moved a short distance south on the railroad for a little recuperation. We were again in front & to the south of our enemies, & holding them at bay — in silence as far as possible. They kept up a regular fire from their artillery until dark, & their Sharpshooters annoyed us, "as usual" — all night. This mixed with the rain that was coming down upon us, made our lot a very disagreeable one. On the 4th we remained in ~~our~~ position until dark — then our Division moved to the west & left, a short distance, & our old stand taken by Gen. Cheatham's Division. Very little cannonading during the day. The country was very level — breastworks weak, & line of battle poorly arranged — as the distruction of human lives in the first mo. brigade on the 5th demonstrated. The enemy gained a position for their artillery, from which they enfaladed the ditches occupied by them — killing & wounding Seventeen of their number, without an opportunity of retribution. The yanks gained supremacy over us, in getting by far the best position, & our works were very inferior to theirs — compelling us to remain silent most of the day.

Lovejoy Station

Our battery was left in Hardee's corps, & being told by his chief of artillery, that we would remain with them — atleast until another change of position was made — went to work with pick & shovel to make our works stronger. But just how long a body of men would occupy a certain place on the lines, was hard to determine — as orders in the army were~~re~~ often changed in a very short time. We had gotten our works in pretty good shape — & become reconciled to our new assignment. But soon after dark we were ordered back to our old Division, & as we splashed along the road made mudy by the rain that had fallen & yet continued — we heard that it was through the influence of Major Storrs — our battallion commander, that the change was made ~~&~~ & all manner of abusive epithets — which could be applied to man, were heaped upon him.

Georgia Campaign

Had we not been assured of remaining where we were, this abuse would not have been given — & another reason, the night was extremely dark — could scarcely see your hand before you — the road was very narrow, leading through a heavy body of timber, winding in every direction — would have been a difficult undertaking to drive six horses through in day time without running upon an obstruction. As it was the wheels of the guns were frequently catching on the trunks of trees — before we were aware of being so near, & the only alternative was, to put our shoulders to the wheels, & lift them off. After a very tire some travel consuming several hours — arrived at our destination, unlimbered & rolled the guns into the works, & "coiling up" on the wet ground was soon sound asleep.

Lovejoy Station

Our position was considered a very dangerous one — a Georgia battery having failed to mane their guns the previous day — when ordered to reply to the yankee guns playing upon them. Ah! ha! this was what Maj. Storrs wanted with us —What Cowards!

This was a repetition of the same game, played upon us at the "Old hewed log house." I took great delight in belonging to a champion artillery company — but I thought we were sometimes unnecessarily imposed upon on account of the reputation we bore — for always obeying orders, & standing to our posts regardless of danger or consequences. About Sunrise on the 6th I was aroused from slumber by one of the boys calling me by names — telling me to wake up — the yanks were gone! My first impulse was to "yell" for joy — but concluded to withhold such demonstration until further investigations were made, & subsequent reports only confirmed the first — they had fled.

Georgia Campaign

Our boys were soon scattered over the ground previously occupied by them, working like bees — gathering up small packages of coffee, sugar, & crackers, of which we had a grand feast — especially, coffee — for it was almost as scarce as "hens teeth" with us. At 9.O.C. A.M. the first Mo. brigade, & one section of our battery, from our division, was ordered to follow up the enemy. The section to which I belonged was the one selected.

We pursued them with slight resistance to Jonesboro, a distance of Seven miles — where upon investigation found them strongly entrenched, & in large force — deeming a direct attack unwise as well as unsafe — returned to our former position — leaving Gen. Cheathams Division, & other troops to guard & watch their movements. On our advance we caught several prisoners & some other things of minor importance.

Lovejoy Station

On the 7th we moved back half mile from the works, & went into camp. This was an occurrance, very unexpected — yet 'twas thought from the stand still, both armies had assumed, a short stay was anticipated — any way Major Storrs, ordered us to commence building arbors for the guns & horses. The few words of abuse for the Major — which the boys didnot think of, on the march of a night or so previous — were thrown at him — "on the sly". — for putting us at work, without ordering a short rest. This did seem inhuman in him — yet he was excusable to a certain extent — he did not have the hardships to undergo that a private soldier did — & similar to a great many officers —he was blind on that subject.

The 8th was the first day in camp for about four months — & as a matter of course we were several days in becoming naturalized. However, we were not permitted to stretch ourselves out in the sunshine like "lizzards"— but were kept busy building arbors, policing camp etc etc.

Georgia Campaign

On this occasion, the officers exhibited a considerable inclination to tyrany — & in the absence of any very interesting army news — we "high privates", ventillated our feelings towards them while around the mess-fires. 11th was Sunday & in imitation of bygone days — Battallion inspection upon the field was the order of the day. The officers had already forgotten the hardships & trials undergone by the soldiers of the rank & file, on the dreadful campaign that had seemed to cease — for how long no one knew — & added to inspection, daily drill. We had some good officers — while others hearts seemed seared — ears stopped & eyes blinded to the condition of the poorly clad — half "shod" private — while they gloated with the swell & pomp of an aristocrat, when ruling over them.

Lovejoy Station
Truce Commenced

On the morning of the 12th it was announced, that a truce had commenced between the two armies, & to be extended ten days if necessary, the object being to get all the noncombattants out of Atlanta. Sherman dispatched to Hood that he could not feed them, & a choice would be given to them — to take the Oath of Allegiance to the United States government & sent north, & those refusing must be sent south out of his lines. The principal portion of the wagons & ambulances of our army were sent after them. This was the longest truce declared since the war began in which I was a participant. It was not the feeding of the inhabitants of Atlanta that was troubling Shermans mind most — He figured an excuse to gratify his insatiate ravings for destroying private property.

Atlanta Ga. burned

He was anxious to apply the torch. Oh! how could he "muster" up such a fiendish disposition, long enough to make, a wholesale, uncalled for destruction of property as the burning of this beautiful City would render. If he could not feed them, could he not have sent them out as he did, & let their houses remain until they could return again? Why destroy the last thing the people had & cause them to look upon him, with hate, hate, eternal hate! & think of him as the King of fire Demons.

Georgia Campaign

On the 13th camp life began to resume its old state — all was quiet which seemed very strange to me, after having been accustomed to the reverse so long. Several refugees arrived from Atlanta — who looked very pitiful & seemed greatly bewildered, as to where to go, or the best course to pursue. We would gladly have assisted them, had it been in our power.

Lovejoy Station
My 21st Birthday

The 14th was a day long to be remembered — by myself — the coming of which I looked forward to with great delight especially in my younger days — not because any particularly great event happened upon that day, but every time the fourteenth passed another year was added to my age. This was the fourth birthday passed in the Service for the South — & if any difference there were less signs of a reconciliation than the previous year at that date. This is the age at which one generally styles himself his own man —but I wasn't by a "jugfull."

The 15th was a day appointed, for fasting, thanksgiving & prayer — So far as the fasting part was concerned — could be & was frequently obeyed without a proclamation, & I expect if there had been any prayers offered — would have been for more "grub" & the complete annihilation of Sherman's army.

Fasting & Prayer

16th passed off quiet with the exception of the review of Gen. Stewarts corps — but we were some what puzzed, on the morning of the 17th when orders were given to cook one days ration of cornbread, & draw two of "hard tack"

Gen. Alexander Peter Stewart, known by his men as "Old Straight," taught mathematics at West Point, then Cumberland University and the University of Nashville before the war. He was appointed lieutenant general when General Polk was killed, commanding the Army of Tennessee at the time of the surrender. Following the war, he returned to teaching at Cumberland University and later became chancellor of the University of Mississippi. He was park commissioner of the Chickamauga and Chattanooga National Parks (Boatner 798-9).

Georgia Campaign

On the morning of the 18th the corndodge was cooked according to orders, & all necessary preperations for another move made. Various conjectures were heard, as to the significance of the move, the direction mapped out, & destination contemplated — but it was generally conceded that no one knew except Hood, & some ventured the assertion that, it was doubtful if he did. Everything ready — the infantry moved out 2.O.C. P.M. followed by the artillery — traveling in a northwest direction, on what was known as the Mcdonald & Fayettville road. Our progress was very slow, the roads being mudy & rain falling the greater portion of the day — & it seemed to be our luck, when a move was ordered, rain commenced — However we managed to move about nine miles.

Hood's Mystery

19th we had reveille at 5- 30 O.C A.M. & soon after pulled out on the Slippery roads — in the same direction of the day previous, & regardless of the mud made fair headway as the country was level. Passed through Fayettville in the forenoon; also Palmetto station, a short time after sun set — where we crossed the Atlanta & Westpoint railroad, & after a march of three miles directly north camped for the night. Some excitement was created, by a rumor being circulated that a battle was imminent — yet we would not have been greatly surprised at anything just then — as all had failed so far to solve the mystery. 20th the shrill notes of the bugle roused us 3. O. C. A.M. & the march was again taken up at Six — in the same direction of previous days.

Northern March

The movement was somewhat sluggish — giving us ample time to catch all the conjectures, & wild speculations — as to where we were going

— where the yanks were — the long march contemplated etc. etc etc. However, after a move of only three miles — things put on quite a different & very unexpected appearance, in a very short time & when a change in tactics were least anticipated. A line of battles was formed & the work of fortifying commenced.

Georgia Campaign

This seemed a little singular as the enemy was not reported very near — neither were they reported as advancing. Our work of "digging" was resumed with a somewhat reluctant Spirit on the 21st as there wasn't a "single" "Fed" reported nearer than fifteen miles — well I believe there was a small scouting — or thieving party. We had rain almost every day making our work very disagreeable. About this time our variety of food wasn't much & somewhat scarce at that — & several of us concluded to go out on a "nocturnal scout," to se if anything could be found to make an addition — but there had been too many "scouts" of similar character, anticipated us, to make a very great success — we spent the best portion of the night in a ramble of about fifteen miles capturing only a few "wee" sweetpotatoes.

Hoods Mystery

22nd the work of fortifying was again followed up. A general order was issued to the commisary & forage masters — to gather in all stores of either kind, in front of our lines, to prevent them from falling into the hands of the enemy — This did not consume much time, as the country had already been pretty well sacked.

Building Fortifications

On the morning of the 23rd after eating a hearty breakfast — proceeded to the works with, picks, shovels & spades upon our shoulders — & were soon delving into the hard clay & gravel with a determination of an early completion of our parapets — but were happily disappointed, by being ordered to suspend operations & return to our quarters. We hitched up & moved back one & a half miles & went into camp — which was very muddy & filthy — rain, rain, rain!!

Georgia Campaign

The 24th & 25th were very pleasantly spent in camp — as the clouds disappeared — & sun shone out, giving us hopes of good weather. While here we had a very amusing incident to happen — illustrating how easily the innocent & unsuspecting — could be lead into a trap, to cause their cheeks to burn with Shame while their persecutors "chuckled" in their sleeves at their ignorance & modesty.

"Old Sweat's" Bee tree

There were two & some times more, notoriously bad characters in the shape of women — who followed the army for an "unmentionable" purpose — pitching their tent in a convenient place to the troops — generally in a thick cluster of bushes or deep hollow. Well, we had two men in our company, eaqually as bad — as to morality — & while we were at this camp, they discovered the whereabouts of these notorious strumpets, & concluded to have a "little fun", out of an old man in the company by the name of Sweat, who had some queer ways, & some of the boys were always plaguing him. He had passed his Sixty summers — but was yet very fond of hunting bees. A big story about the bee course they had struck, was painted to the old man in the most flattering colors — so much so that the old man was induced to accompany them & assist in the location of the tree. After going quite a distance, feeding the old man on "taffy" — to keep him from suspicioning any thing wrong — was at the tent & walked in — before his eyes were "opened", Arrangements with the inmates had been previously made, & they knew the character of their victim before he arrived —& the old man was almost crazed with madness when he made his exit. But through the influence of his betrayers — was induced to report back to the other boys — a "sure enough" bee tree — & a rich one at that. When the old man returned to camp, & reported as they directed him — it raised a great deal of excitement, & when night came — the time decided upon to take the honey — it was really amusing to see the boys making preperations — a couple of the best axes were selected — some got buckets, while others filled their pockets with "corndodge". The "procession" was about ready to move out — when the Old Gentleman said he was too tired & would like to be excused from going — & said the other two men would lead them through alright. I had almost decided to go — when the old man plucked me to one side — & told me it was a "sell". His reason for befriending me — was, that I never teased him any, while many others in the company did, & he didn't care if some of them did get fooled. Shortly after 10. P.M. about a dozzen or two of the maddest boys you ever saw returned to camp — & some of us were compeled to do a little good talking to keep them from wrecking vengeance upon the trio. "Old Sweats bee hunt" — as it was styled, was quite a noted event, & one which created a great deal of merriment in the company the remainder of the war.

Review By. Pres. Jeff. Davis

On the 26th Stewarts corps was reviewed by President Davis — but made rather a poor appearance owing to the situation of the ground — However it was a great satisfaction to have the honor of a personal review, by the person who was at the head of affairs of the Southern Confederacy. True — alike all others, he had his faults — but his Veteran appearance, upright figure & frosty locks, which he uncovered, while stopping a short time at every stand of colors, as he rode with his staff down the lines — brought forth loud & prolonged cheers. Fond hopes were entertained that the day of reconciliation was not far distant, that the arms of the south, would finally triumph, & He be continued at the helm of the ship of State.

Georgia Campaign

27th camp policing was commenced, which was thought to be an intimation of a short stay — any way, we began to predict, more tight "reins". While at this camp I was greatly surprised yet very agreeably — by seeing my Brother come walking up. He was looking well & almost entirely recovered from his wound. Not having heard a word from me, since our seperation at Atlanta — was greatly alarmed, as I had been in several engagements, & more or less exposed to the enemies ball & shell, all the time. He expressed a desire to remain with the company — said he would be better satisfied with us than among strangers but, I said, no. Telling him to go to the country & save the limbs he had, if by staying with us, had lost the other arm — or one of his legs — would have been almost helpless — as he was could make his own living — also advised him to go to Alabama. He went — & stopped near Faunsdale Station, on the Demopolis & Selma railroad, with an old planter, by the name of Walker, remaining until the close of the war.

Following the Confederates' surrender at Vicksburg, the officers and men were offered parole. Caldwell wrote in his diary that about one-half of his company refused parole and were sent up river to prison. Caldwell and Sam accepted parole and were sent from Vicksburg to Mobile via New Orleans and then to a parole camp at Demopolis, Alabama. While there they received furloughs and were able to travel about the area, staying with various families. On September

16, 1863, Caldwell and Sam learned from a day-old newspaper that all paroled Missouri troops had been exchanged. From that time until November 2, 1863, the troops remained in camp with opportunities to travel briefly within the area.

On September 29, 1863, Caldwell and Bob (R. D.) Welch rode out on horseback to the Charles Walker plantation and stayed overnight. Caldwell's October 1, 1863, diary entry reported, "We had a pleasant time, for a more chivalrous family I never met with before. Mrs Walker gave me three pairs of socks. She also gave us a sack of potatoes & cooked rations enough to last us a day or two. Welch had stayed there some time before" (Lehr 92).

It was this introduction to the Walker family that Caldwell remembered when, unable to return to Augusta, Georgia, in September 1864, he sought refuge with the Walker family for the remainder of the war. The Mrs. Walker (Jane Ann Jordan Jemison) Caldwell knew was the second wife of Charles Walker. Walker's first wife, Margaret, died fourteen months after her sixth child, a daughter, was born. George and Jane Ann had no children together (Alison).

The Walker plantation was built on the 160 acres originally granted to Dougal and Malcom McAlpin in 1830. In 1852, George and Jane Ann Walker bought the McAlpin land on the old trail between Uniontown, Alabama, and the tiny hamlet of Faunsdale. They added 1,800 acres and built their plantation home around the McAlpin's four-room log cabin. The cabin became the dining room, a bedroom, and an upstairs storage area for their antebellum home known as Cedar Grove. In 1860, just prior to the start of the Civil War, Charles Walker's canebrake plantation and 154 slaves made him a considerably wealthy planter with assets valued at over $257,000. Within ten years, the economic impact of the Civil War reduced his assets to $70,000 (Alison; "Cedar Grove: Palatial"; "Front Porches").

It is not surprising that Caldwell was a welcome guest for the eight months he spent at Cedar Grove. Mr. Walker had three sons who also served in the Confederate army. Caldwell would have arrived for his lengthy visit shortly after the death of Mr. Walker's eldest son Capt. John Marshall "Mack" Walker of the 36th Alabama Regiment. Mack died May 24, 1864, a week after being wounded at the battle at Resaca, Georgia. David Walker served with the Independent Troop of Uniontown, although their company did not engage in active battle. Mims Walker served under Gen. James Longstreet in the I Corps, Confederate Army of Northern Virginia, as a

captain with the 4th Alabama Infantry, also called the Canebrake Rifle Guards (Boatner III 178-9; Harris).

During the war, Mims met the German artist Nicola Marschall and invited him to paint portraits of his family. These portraits have been handed down through the Walker family and today are in the possession of Nancy and George McKee of Faunsdale, Alabama (Alison; McKee).

Nicola Marschall is credited with designing the first official Confederate flag, the Stars and Bars. Although his design was presented by the flag committee to the Congress of the Confederate States on March 4, 1861, there is no record of a recorded vote, but there is a written record in the journal of the Congress. It had seven stars and flew over Fort Sumter in Charleston Harbor, South Carolina, in 1861. Marschall is also credited with designing the Confederate uniform ("Banners of Glory"; Hume; "Stars and Bars flag").

Captain Guibor left the Company

On the 28th quite a damper was thrown over the company, by Captain Guibor having to leave us — & there were sad hearts & moist eyes — when the members of the company one by one, took a farewell shake of the Old Veterans hand, & bid him good bye!. We all knew him to be a noble man, & a kind, conscientious Officer — one who would be missed by all,. But his seperation from field duty was unavoidable — the service being too arduous for his feeble constitution. He was assigned a position at the post of Taladega Ala.

Hoods North Ga Expedition

On the 29th the signal for a general wake up was given about 1- O.C. A.M. — & for some time there was a great bustling around issuing, drawing & cooking rations. I got up & commenced cooking, the order having been given to prepare three days rations — also to move at 9. AM, but owing to some unaccountable delay — the troops didnot move out until 3. O.C. PM. After a travel of five miles the Chatahoochee river was crossed on a pontoon, & our line of march ~~was~~ taken on a road leading to Cave springs Ga. This move was looked upon by all, as very mysterious. Hood's motive in turning his back upon the enemy — & marching right away from them, & in the direction exactly contrary to the course pursued by our army for the last several months — & leaving the interior of our country wide open to the ravages of Sherman's Army — was a problem — which no one attempted to solve except Hood himself. 30th Reveille at daylight — & our march was again resumed at 8- O.C. A.M. on the Powder spring road.

Near Kennesaw Mountains

Passed in sight of the memorable Kennesaw mountains — a description of which I have given Some time since. After traveling twelve miles parked the guns by the road side at 3. O. C PM. This gave us a long time to rest — & we enjoyed it "muchly". This placed us in rear of the enemy — & many thought without discovery. I always thought this a matter of speculation only — Sherman was undoubtedly aware of Hoods movements — as it had been about twelve days since the truce was broken — but he didnot care to look back — from his contemplated march to the Sea.

Oct 1st

On the 1st day of October we remained in camp — & cooked four days rations, according to orders. The latest rumor was to the effect that the Feds had evacuated Marietta, without resistance & fell back in the direction of Atlanta. The weather was again very disagreeable — for our anticipated move.— As rain commenced falling on the 2nd we had an early reveille with orders to move at daylight — but didnot leave camp until 10- AM. & after all the commands had fallen to the places allotted them, everything moved along smoothly — making good progress — until 4. O.C P.M. We bivuoaced about four miles from Lost mountain, where the yanks were said to be in force — & the cannonading heard in that direction at the time was proof of the assertion — or atleast denoted an enemy in that direction.

Hoods North Ga expedition

On the morning of the 3rd we had reveille at daylight. The early part looked very gloomy — the rain of previous day had caused an almost impenitrable gloom to settle in the valleys, & was very slow in clearing away. A short time after sunrise all the infantry of the division, & Kolbs battery moved out toward the front — or in the direction of the mountain, to ascertain the enemies position & strength. Our battery remained stationary awaiting orders. Lee's corps also passed us going in the direction taken by the division. At noon we harnessed up, & moved about one mile, to join the camp of Truharts battallion & Hoskins battery — & act in conjunction with them as reserve artillery of the corps. Occasional cannonading was heard in the direction of Marietta — it seemed there were some of the enemy left there yet — although a contrary report had been circulated. The movement of the Feds seemed very tardy. Contrary to Hoods expectations, they didnot follow in pursuit — they were at a stand still, & slow in moving any way.

Tearing up the railroad

On the 4th the artillery remained in camp. The infantry of the Corps not finding an enemy in force at the Mountain, busied themselves tearing up the railroad, the same which was destroyed by our Army during the spring & summer campaign, as we fell back upon Atlanta but had since been rebuilt by the Federals. The work of destruction was made complete — by first tearing up the rails, then piling the ties in heaps with the rails across them — the ties were fired, & when the rails became well heated — were taken from the fire & bent in all conceivable shapes around telegraph posts & trees.

Hoods North Ga Expedition

5th was spent by us in camp. The work of demolishing the railroad was about completed — or that portion intended to be destroyed at that time, & our Army was nearing Allatoona, where the enemy were reported to be three thousand strong & well fortified, & while the other portion of our Troops were otherwise engaged, French's division stormed the works at that place, & drove the enemy from two lines — but not receiving reinforcements, were compelled to fall back — leaving their dead & wounded in possession of the yanks. Our loss was considerable & no advantage in position gained — the first Mo brigade lost heavy. If Hood had concentrated his whole force upon this place, the enemy could have been easily dislodged — but he made this one attempt & moved on. His motive in this was never satisfactorally explained to me. On the 6th we had reveille at 2. O. C. AM, & left camp at daylight, through a heavy rain & deep mud. The whole army moved north in the direction of the Etawah river.

The Etowah River begins its journey in the mountains north of Dahlonega, Georgia, and flows 60 to 75 river miles southwest to empty into Lake Allatoona. Sam makes no mention of the discovery of gold there in 1828, but the Etoway River became an important site to the gold miners of Dahlonega's "Gold Rush" days. Today, limited gold panning still occurs on part of the river (*Dahlonega Georgia;* "Etowah River").

During our days march, passed by New Hope Church, & through the lines of intrenchments occupied by both armies during the past summer — where occurred a very bloody battle, & defeat of the enemy. The place looked very natural — the trees that were torn in shreds & houses demolished, were unmistakable evidence of how bitterly the ground was contested by both armies — but the destruction of property during the few hours the troops were engaged — will take many years to replace. We also passed several Federal graves — which looked as if they had been made in haste & without ceremony. Crossed a small stream called Pumpkin Vine Creek & camped near by 4. O. C. PM. after a travel of twelve miles. 7th Reveille at daylight & the march was again taken up — at 8. O. C. AM, on the road leading west in the direction of Rome Ga.

Hoods North Ga. Expedition

The country was mountainous & very poor — the principal settlements were along the creek bottoms, where a narrow strip on either side, was cultivated in corn & cotton. Inhabitants generally ignorant — but seemed happy & contented.

They seemed to believe that — "Ignorance was bliss 'twas folly to be wise" — Had been born & reared there — & were very reluctant in believing our stories of the existence of a better country than that. The report was freely circulated & generally believed, that Sherman had evacuated Atlanta & pursuing us with his entire Army. Camped 5. PM near Vanwert — a small village, twenty two miles from Rome. I was really glad to see a "stopping" place — true, we had only marched fifteen miles, but the country over which our march extended was so rocky & rough, I was almost worn out.

On the morning of the 8th we had reveille at 4. O.C. A.M. & moved out at sunrise. The morning was cool, sky clear — making beautiful weather for marching — if the troops had been in a corresponding shape — all would have been well — but many of them were barefooted, & all were very poorly & thinly clad. Our days march extended over the best country that I had seen up to that time in Georgia.

Hoods Traveling Sorghum Mills

This was a great country for raising Sorghum cane — & we called ourselves "Hood's traveling Sorghum Mills" — from the amount of cane carried off by us. When passing a field — every fellow, got a stalk or two & sometimes more — which was cut in pieces eight or ten inches long & put in his haversack — which was again cut in short bits — as we marched along the road — juice sucked from it & the dry "cuds" spit upon the ground, resembling in comparison, a place where hogs had been fed green corn stalks. Large fields were destroyed in this manner.

Hoods North Ga Expedition

Several times on this march some of the boys "straggled", a little — or got off the road a short distance — to get something a little extra from our regular rations. At a certain time one of them approached a house & asked the Lady if she had any Sorghum? She hesitated a moment — & said we havn't any. This answer didnot satisfy the enquirer who said, She certainly had — for he had just passed a "big" pile of stalks from which the juice had been pressed.

Queer Names For things

This made her understand — & she exclaimed, It's molasses you want! W'y yes, we've got plenty! You Soldiers have such queer names for things! Some of them frequently ask my negro woman for "things"— & go off without them — when we may have an abundance about the house! This reminds me of another instance, in which a person was not posted in regard to the proper names of "things"— but it wasn't a "woman" this time.

About the close of the second year of the war, a soldier who prided himself a "good" deal upon his looks, & what he "knew"— went out into the country to spend a short furlough with an Old north Miss. Planter — & while in conversation one day — the Old Gentleman asked him, if he kept a diary of his travels, while in the service? When the young man exclaimed! No! By george — he had it for about six months once — & it "liked" to "a" killed him — before he got "shet" of it — & didn't want it any more! He mistook the old mans meaning of course — & wasn't any better posted than the lady.

Hoods Expedition continued

Well — to return to business — the latest "Grape vine" news — said the yanks had left Rome. When the day was far spent — camp was pitched near Cedartown — which was the county seat of Polk county. About noon on the 8th all the infantry & one battery for each division — started on a raid in a northern direction — their chief aim, was to destroy the railroad — & final destination was said to be Nashville Tenn. However this was only speculation at this time — but enough had already been hinted, to venture an assertion.

Our battery was left behind with the wagon train, not having a sufficient number at that time of men to opperate on open field. Orders issued to stop all bugling & drumming — for the present — as the Federals were liable to take advantage of our unguarded artillery & baggage train. The weather was considered a little cool for that country — as the first frost fell the previous night.

The Infantry & Some Art. Started on a raid
Baggage Train & the rest of Art. Sent South

We were aroused at 4. O. C. A.M on the 10th & at Seven the artillery & baggage train started for Blue Mountain, or that vacinity. Shortly after leaving camp — passed through Cedartown, a small village, near the state line. Stopped at Cavesprings, for water & a short rest — after which we moved out on the Jacksonville & Blue Mountain road — which we traveled about three miles — & took a right hand road leading west — & in the direction of Centerville. Crossed the state line between Ga. & Ala. & camped about 7 P.M. in Cherokee County Ala. I had been in north Ga. so long, & the country had become so near destitute of anything to live upon — as soon as I crossed the line between the two states — made a wish that my foot prints, would not be again seen in North Georgia; only to march across it with a victorious army. But in a very short time subsequent to this I saw my wish would never be granted — unless some very miraculous event happened in our favor. 11th Reveille at 4. O.C. AM. moved at sunrise. The road we traveled was very bad — The country was level, covered with a very luxuriant growth of pine — Soil sandy — but enclined to be marshy — frequently the guns sank to the axle in mud holes — & we cannoneers had to "wade" in & roll them out — but this didn't matter, so far as our clothing was concerned, as it was almost thread bare — & the Georgia clay well rubbed in — our shoes were so full of holes the mud that entered — could soon escape.

Hood's North Ga. Expedition

Our manner of traveling gave us a splendid opportunity, to catch all the "Grape" — as we termed it — in regard to the movements of both armies — & about this time we received a large & fresh supply — Stating that Stewart's corps had been sent to Rome. — Lee's to Resaca — and Hardee's to Tunnelhill — Also that Sherman had left one corps to guard Atlanta, & was pursuing us with the ballance of his Army.

This gave vent to a great deal of restlessness & the wildest comments imaginable. Left the road leading to Centerville, & took the Edwards ferry road. We traveled sixteen miles before camping 4- O.C. P.M. two & a half miles from the Coosa river. The country for some distance from the river, was very swampy — & before we could move on the 12th were compelled to build a corduroy road over some of the worst places. At 2.O.C. P.M. we moved one & a half miles nearer the river & parked the guns, to await our turn crossing. We had a heavy shower of rain at night — almost "swamping" us sure enough.

Several northwestern Georgia mountain tributaries, including the Etowah River previously mentioned, join to form the Coosa River which begins in Rome, Georgia, and flows across Alabama to merge with the Tallapoosa River and form the Alabama River. The Coosa River Basin ranks just behind areas of Hawaii, Washington, and Oregon in receiving the most rain in the United States. The average precipitation is 52 to 64 inches per year ("Coosa River").

Chestnut & Squirrel Hunt

13th Not having moving orders — I with some others, went out over the hills in search of chestnuts — & took with us an old musket to kill some squirrels. We returned to camp after quite an extended ramble, feeling well paid for our trouble. In the forenoon — our cavalry — Gen. Armistead's Division, was surprised twelve miles south of Rome, by a superior force of Federal cavalry & Infantry. He was almost surrounded, before aware of the presence of such a large force — & many of his men were killed & captured in cutting their way out. However, reinforcements were near at hand — & his loss was more than recompensed & enemy driven back.

As an undergraduate, Gen. Lewis Addison Armistead was dismissed from the United States Military Academy in 1836 for breaking a plate over the head of his classmate Jubal Early. However, he was later commissioned in the Regular Army in 1839. He joined the Confederate army in 1861 as a major. On April 1, 1862, he was appointed brigadier general. General Armistead was mortally wounded at Gettysburg, falling dead over Union officer Alonzo Hersford Cushing's cannon (Boatner III 26, 215).

Hood's North Ga Expedition

Shortly after midnight, on the morning of the 14th our slumbers were brought suddenly to a close — & drivers ordered to harness their horses immediately. Federal cavalry ~~were~~ reported between us & our supply train.

This created great excitement — & the whole camp was roused at 2. O. C. AM & ordered to cook "grub". The pontoon bridge which had been stretched across Coosa river, for the purpose of crossing on our northern march, was taken up — a short time before day — & about twilight came back by our camp — when the artillery all filed in behind it, & moved off in a direction, contrary to the one contemplated.

Passed through Centre, a small Village & took the Jacksonville road, leading south. This very sudden change in our course, was quite a surprise — yet changes were frequent — especially when compelled to do so — & deemed best at the time. Our march was very laborious, the roads were muddy. The country was sandy & well watered, a great convenience — also an almost indespensible article for an army. After a travel of sixteen miles, a camp was pitched 4. O.C. PM.

Officers caught Butchering

We found several "mud-larks" running "loose" in the woods — & being very hungry for pork — a whole sale butchery was commenced. Even Majors & Lieutenants were caught taking a hand — something very unusual, but this only had a tendency to "re-license" the private soldier — who was already — going his "full length". 13th Reveille at 4. O.C.A.M. & after a short breakfast — our move was again commenced at sunrise, & continued down a valley between two mountains — spurs of the Blue ridge range.

Some good land — but of limited extent, & almost destitute of anything to eat for man, or forage for horses. The country had been stripped by foraging parties previous to our coming.

Hood's North Ga Expedition

We marched eleven miles — filed out of the road at noon & went into camp four miles from Jacksonville, Ala. Remained in this camp afew days — but nothing happened in military affairs worthy of note. On the 18th Hoskins battery was sent but several miles, upon our contemplated, future course, to guard the pontoon across Coosa river.

Chestnut & Chinkypin Hunt

I, with some of my mess mates took a "tramp" over the hills in search of chestnuts & chinkey-pins. Our time was very pleasantly spent, & labors rewarded — by finding all the nuts we could eat. The day was delightful — resembling, an Indian summer day in North Mo.

> **Sam is probably referring to the Allegheny Chinkapin (*Castanea pumila* Mill.), a shrub-like tree found in the area through which he was traveling. According to the *National Audubon Society Field Guide to Trees* for the eastern region, the earliest information on the nut of this tree was published in 1612. Captain John Smith wrote, "They [the Indians] have a small fruit growing on little trees, husked like a Chestnut, but the fruit most like a very small acorne. This they call *Checkinquamins*, which they esteem a great daintie." (379-80).**

Our party becoming wearied — & the evening more than half spent, all returned to camp — except one fellow — not being satisfied, thought he'd look out a potato patch — ready for a night "raid". After we had been in for some time, & the sun was almost hidden in the west — he came in — & sure enough — reported one — but said, it was considerable distance away. Distance wasn't anything to us — when a mess of "taters" was considered in it. Early in the morning of the 19th Gen. Beauregard, passed by our camp, & we having been apprised of his coming a short time previous — a large number of us had collected along the road side — & cheered him with loud & unlimited huzzas. It made my bosom swell with emotion, when I saw the brave warrior, experienced artillery man & engineer, pressing onward to his much needed & well merited position. When night came — & about the time all "honest people" should go to bed — a dozzen or more of us, with the fellow who said said he found t__ (corner of page missing) potato patch —as our leader — got a sack each ~~a pail~~ & started out to bring in the delicious "roots". We did not dare to enter a patch in daylight — as they were closely watched by the owners, upon the appearance of the army — & many sat up at night to guard them.

Hood's North Ga Expedition

Well! we "tramped" along by pairs, through the tall chestnut trees, scaling the hills, climbing over rocks & logs, until we thought, we had gone about far enough to find the place — when some of the party called to the leader & asked, how much farther? Oh! it's only a short distance now!

A nights Ramble Without Any "Taters"

We went on & on — for some time, merrily chatting with each other — occasionally joking our guide — until finally he began to think the distance too long — a short halt was made — & sure enough he had missed the way & was at a loss to know which course to pursue. A short consultation was held — the direction decided upon, & we again "plunged" into the darkness — & only a short time intervened, until we found ourselves — not at the potato patch though but — where we entered the woods, when we started, not very far from camp. Our leader was completely dumbfounded, & almost plagued to death. We sat down upon a log to rest — & "argue" the question awhile — & it was finally decided to make another effort, rather than return to camp with out anything — & stand the ridicule of the other boys. We again struck out through the woods, & I think we must have traveled all of five miles — the "sack brigade" was again checked — & it was announced that we were nearing our long hoped for destination, & as in all cases where danger was apprehended — a picket was sent out — & as a matter of course, in this case, the discoverer was the one to select. He started & while we were awaiting his return & announcement, were almost afraid to speak above a whisper, for fear of detection. But imagine our feelings, when he returned after half hours absence, & reported Peanuts! by _ g_d, Boys! Peanuts! Well! this "stumped" us completely — we didn't know what to do. Being so badly disappointed & so very tired, could not avoid being out of humor. But (Harrisson) our leader swore that he didnot try to "sell us out". Said he didnot go very close to the patch in daylight — but was sure that he had found potatos. The only alternative, was to hang our heads in sad disappointment — & turn our weary foot steps toward camp — & upon our arrival — found that we had intruded on the morning of the 20th about two hours — "nary tater" in our sacks — & a more tired — hungry — sleepy set of boys, are seldom every found — as we had traveled atleast twenty miles. We were not long in finding our humble & poorly furnished beds, & being "encompassed" in the "arms" of morpheus — but our nap was of short duration — as we were aroused by the sharp notes of the bugle at daylight.

Hood's North Ga Expedition

I rubbed my eyes open as quickly as possible, & fell into line — to say here! When my name was called we had scarcely finished breakfast — before the order came to harness up & move out, but remained in place until 8. O. C. A.M. then our march was taken up on the Jacksonville road leading south — our course was soon turned to northwest in the direction of Gadsden Ala.

The country was very rough & rocky — & a greater portion of the day was consumed in traveling eight miles. On 21st we had reveille at 2. O.C. AM. & before the gray streaks of day appeared in the eastern horizon — we were again on the move, our line of march leading across Mount Pope — which was very precipitous & difficult to ascend — with our jaded horses. Passed through Hokes Bluff — a very small village, of but little importance.

Formed a junction with the army at Gadsden

Crossed Coosa river at Howards ferry, at which place Gadsden, a very nice little town was situated upon the west bank. Here we found the army in camp, & in fine spirits — having just returned from a raid on the railroad, which was inaugerated soon after we entered Ala.

Hood's North Ga Expedition

After a march of twenty miles — bivuouced five miles from town 4-30- O.C. P.M. On the morning of the 22nd we were awakened at 1- O.C. AM — & in order that our train might be shortened, thereby increasing our accellertion —all extra baggage & ordinance, were sent to the rear for safe keeping. We were only allowed what clothing & blankets could be carried upon our backs — & only one wagon allowed to haul messkit for the battallion — (three companies). According to orders, our corps (Stewarts) & Hardee's marched on the same road & Lee's to the left, & parallel. Crossed Sand mountain, which was very difficult to ascend, on account of its sandy & rocky surface — also crossed Big Wills Creek — which is one of the most important tributaries of Black warrior river, & near its banks about 7- O.C. PM found camp, after consuming the whole day marching thirteen miles.

Crossed Sand Mountain

The nights were very cool & we could have slept under more blankets than we had & yet been more comfortable. On the 23rd we were aroused at 2. O.C. AM. & marched at four, & worse than all without beef — not being allowed sufficient time to cook it. These mountains were great for hale, hearty — robust & rosy young ladies. The breeze was very refreshing — giving the rosy tint to their cheeks — & their figures were made Symetrical & firm by scaling the hills in search of black haws & chestnuts — which grew in abundance — and some of the finest looking children — I ever saw — "Arkensaw" couln't hold a "candle".

The *National Audubon Society Field Guide to Trees* for the eastern division describes two species of blackhaw shrubs or small trees, either of which may have been the variety Sam mentioned. Both the blackhaw *Viburnum prunifolium* L. (known as stagbush or sweethaw) and the rusty blackhaw *Viburnum rufidulum* Raf. (known as the bluehaw or rusty nannyberry) grow in the area where Sam was marching. It is more likely the area residents gathered the small, blue fruit of the bluehaw, as this shrub or small tree tends to grow in the uplands rather than in valleys. Whereas, the stagbush, which produces a small blue-black fruit, prefers the moist soil of valleys and slopes (674-6).

Passed through Summit, a very small village which took its name from being the center & highest portion of the mountain. Crossed Black Warrior river about noon. The country was very rough & rocky — nevertheless inhabited, & as invariably the case, by the most ignorant class. It seems almost incredible — but absolutely true — some of them could not tell us the character of the country ten miles from where they lived — the name of the county in which they resided, or county seat. After a travel of seventeen miles we again "hung up" for the night. On the morning of the 22nd reveille was sounded at 4. O.C. & about daylight our march was resumed on the Decatur road.

Hood's North Ga Expedition

The lay of the country & character of its citizens were, about of the same "stripe", as had been seen for a few days previous. The valleys between the hills — which were almost mountains — were the only ground suitable for cultivation — & they were thickly dotted with cabins — the inmates of which didnot denote much thrift — yet seemingly happy. Their appearance, reminded me of the old adage — "Ignorance is bliss, 'Tis folly, to be wise". Our camp was pitched at 4.O.C. PM on Sixmile creek — said to be twenty miles from Decater. I was very much fatigued — as we had marched twenty miles. I enjoyed my nights slumber very much — but it was cut a little short, by an early reveille on the 25th, but didnot move out until noon — having to wait for other troops to pass in our front — when once started, our travel was uninterrupted, & progress good — as the country was level — yet the soil was thin.

March Continued

We camped again a short time before sunset — one mile from Summerville, Morgan. Co. Ala. Soon after camping, reports were circulated that the yanks were ten thousand Infantry & thirteen Gunboats, strong at Decater. On the 26th our tiresome march was again taken up at daylight. Soon after leaving camp — passed through Summerville — & took the most direct road leading to Decater. A cold rain commenced falling in the early morning — & constant travel on the roads made them very muddy, & our march was extremely disagreeable.

Hood's North Ga Expedition

The rain fell so hard the night previous, that sleep or rest was impossible. We were forced to get up & build large fires of logs — to keep warm & dry a side at a time. About the middle of the afternoon we arrived within five miles of the Town to which our march had been directed, & one section of Hoskins battery (rifled guns) was sent in front to act as an artillery guard. When about two miles from Decater, a halt was called — guns parked in regular order — but horses left hitched to await orders. Some cannonading was heard at the fortified little City — although some time had intervened between "showers" the noise sounded very familiar. All the rifled artillery of the army, was ordered forward by Gen. Beauregard — & a brisk fire at once opened upon the strongly fortified enemy — the fire was kept up for some time, with as much rapidity as possible — & when a cessation was ordered, the Gen sent in a flag of truce, asking the immediate surrender of the garrison — but being bluntly refused — the shelling was again resumed, with increased vigor, & kept up until compelled to desist on account of a heavy rain falling & extreme darkness of the night.

Hood's North Ga Expedition

As soon as day peeped on the morning of the 27th the Sharpshooters on both sides were wide awake, & at their work of attempting to destroy human lives. After the immense fogg had cleared away — cannonading was commenced & continued at intervals all day. The enemy had some gunboats — or small transports which had been turned into, "war" vessels by using cotton bales as breastworks — which were cruising up & down, the Tennessee river, ransacking the adjacent country of every thing that could be utilized, & in many cases the work of destruction was entered into, sooner than let them remain in possession of their rightful owners. They became bold enough to fire upon a working party of ours — constructing breastworks upon the river bank. Captain Hoskins section of rifled pieces were ordered down to protect the working party — but thinking their adversaries too "many" deemed it policy to remain silent — & only intefere, sould they attempt to land.

Attempted Capture of Decatur Alabama

During the forepart of the night our infantry forced the enemies pickets around Decatur, back & established a line of works in close proximity to theirs & at 2. O.C. on the morning of the 28th our pickets stimulated by their success in the early night — made a desperate charge — but were greeted with a heavy "shower" of grape & cannister from the enemies cannon, checking their movements — our artillery immediately opened & the "ball" was kept going all day ~~mingled~~ intermingled with heavy sharpshooting. About 3 O.C in the afternoon our battery was ordered to prepare for an engagement with these gunboats a description of which has been given above — boots & saddles was immediately sounded & our company, accompanied by Captain Hoskin's battery was soon on the move.

Hoods North Ga Expedition

Our march was very slow — meeting many obstacles & extending three or four miles — winding & twisting through the thick woods & swamps along the river bottom — scarcely passable for footmen — which I think we could have never passed through — had we not been piloted by an old citizen who was familiar with the country — However success being our motto — crept stealthily along through the thick underbrush, & succeeded in getting eight guns in position upon the bank of the river almost unnoticed by the occupants of two gunboats — which were anchored near the opposite bank & some of their men on shore — but they "scrambled" on board & soon pulled up stakes & started down the river firing one shot from their artillery as they receded.

Engagement with gunboats on the Tenn. R

We immediately & simultaniously opened with eight guns & kept up a brisk fusilade until our adversaries were out of range. The sharpshooters from the boats made the minnies hail around us very lively for a short time — making our position anything but a pleasant one — but "fortune" smiled upon us — & delivered us without a scratch. We fired five founds to the gun two of the shots from the one I helped to man — struck the boats — the only ones which hit the mark. My post of duty on the gun was No four — or the one who pulled the laniard which fired the gun. After the enemy had disappeared, & were were satisfied that a return was not probable — limbered up & returned to camp. This was my first time to see the Tennessee river — & my "introduction" was rather abrupt & visit too short — to gain much information or secure long & mutual acquaintance.

Corn issued for rations

Our rations at this time were running very low — in fact we had no meal & drew corn on the cob in its stead — three ears to the man — one pound of "blue beef" partly dried for a ration, was the only meat issued. Men walking up to draw corn in this manner — made us almost "imagine" we were horses. Some of the boys created a great deal of merriment — by complaining that the commissary should have thrown in a bundle of fodder for "ruffness". The corn, we parched & put in our haversacks — which was eaten while marching. This was dry eating — & I came so near "foundering" upon the "stuff", that it was some time before I regained my former appetite for parched corn — but this was a "Ground Hog" case — that or nothing.

Hood's North Ga Expedition

Our rest was cut short on the morning of the 29th by being aroused at 3. O.C. & at daylight — the wagon train having preceded us a short time — the army moved out to the south of Decatur, in a western direction, leaving the "Old Gridiron" floating above the yanks — in peacable possession of the town. 'Twas said by those who professed to know, that our generals didnot care to capture the garrisson. To make a pretense, & keep their attention attracted while another important move could be accomplished, was the chief object desired.

From Decatur to Tuscumbia

Our line of march led us across the Memphis & Charleston railroad, two miles from Decatur, & parallel with it in the direction previously indicated.

Our progress was good, as the country was level — soil good, dotted here & there with beautiful residences — & "by the way" — some of the portico's were ornamented with beautiful young ladies — & being the first seen for some time — "kinder" took my eye — & caused great broad smiles to appear. We marched about twenty miles & camp was pitched 4. O.C PM in Laurence County Ala. 30th we had reveille at 4 O.C. AM. & moving was again resumed at daylight on the Courtland & Tuscumbia road. Passed through Courtland — a pretty little Village & station on the M & C. RR. There was but one business house open, & that was a drug store — hard times & Federal raids had closed the others out. The country over which our days march extended was very good — but the fences had almost entirely been destroyed & many houses burned — presenting the appearance of a vast plain. The citizens wore a downcast, disheartened look — the ravages of war had "ploughed" great furrows in their cheeks, the torch of a cruel enemy had destroyed their palacial residences, & at the same time stopped them of all means of cultivating the soil. The rail road was also a complete reck — nothing to be wondered at — but the wholesale, wanton destruction of private property, was very unmanly.

Hoods North Ga Expedition

On our march we crossed Clinch river nine miles from Courtland, & after completing a gravel of seventeen miles, camped 4. PM near Leyton a small town on the line between Laurence & Franklin Co's Ala. We had reveille at 4. O.C on the morning of the 31st — & at daylight our tiresome & uncertain march was again taken up. We moved very rapidly the infantry followed the railroad, & artillery the highway. Being thus seperated — a jam, so common in a moving army — was avoided & country being level — the distance traveled almost doubled.

Camp Near Tuscumbia Ala
November

Arrived at Tuscumbia Ala. about noon & camped near by — upon the same ground occupied by Gen. A. S. Johnston's Army just before the memorable battle of Shilo — or Pittsburg landing Miss — was fought. We had been on the march for some time past — & when, the order was given out, on the 1st day of November that the army would remain in camp, those who had a change of clothes took off their dirty ones, in which the mud had been well ground — & as if by magic, the whole army seemed to adopt it as a general wash day. Those who did not have an extra shirt (&

unfortunately there were many) remained in their filth — or took their shirts off, replacing their jackets, to protect their nakedness, while attending to the "Laundry" — & the rap- rap- rap! of the battling sticks the sounds of which were echoed back & forth by the banks of the creek upon which the army was camped, making such a grating sound scarcely anything else could be heard — but this was the beating of the last "Tattoo", by which the life of many "G B's" went out. This manner of washing, reminded me of my young boyhood days — when my Step-Mother had me pounding away with a paddle, to "loosen" up the dirt in the clothes, that she might be able to cleanse them upon the old home-made wooden wash boards — as they would not ~~cleanse them~~ do the work as the patents of later days. The quietness that prevailed at this camp for several days, was very noticeable — as we had been accustomed to an active life for some time past. The time of those whose duty it was to look after the needs of the troops in general, was consumed in supplying them as best they could from the limited stock, in store. 'Twas said as far as practicable, the army would be outfitted with wagons & good mules, sufficient to stand a force march of twenty days.

The men were badly in need of clothing of all kinds, & especially shoes — many of the poor fellows were barefoot — my toes would have been more comfortable, if better protected from the sloppy ground, continually stirred by travel, & kept moist by an almost constant drizzling rain, driven by a north wind. We presented rather a ragged, dilapidated appearance — especially when crossing of the Tennessee river, was contemplated at an early date — it was not an uncommon thing to see a man with two holes in the seat of his pants — & both knees out. On the 5th a small amount of clothing was issued — I was fortunate enough to draw a jacket — & I needed it so badly — was almost tempted to sleep with it on as I did my first pants. On Sunday 6th the blankets & clothing of the company — also horses & harness were inspected, by Lieut Col. William's.

Camp Near Tuscumbia Ala

The wants could have been easily seen without inspection — or in other words what benefit would grow out of inspection — when our supplies were so limited? — yet a winters campaign & in a much colder climate, than the one to which we had been accustomed, was in contemplation. We were even deprived the comforts of tents — many of us built small huts of poles, thatched & chinked with straw & grass to shield us from the wind & rain. Had we been supplied with a sufficient quantity of good wholesome food, to brace up the physical man — could have weathered the storm with less inconvenience — as it was our "eyes fell" upon an empty plate — when our stomachs were only half filled. The stage of water from incessant rain, was partly the cause of short rations.

The streams, which were numerous — & some large, were bank full & ~~some~~ running over the lowlands. Wagons sent out in the country after forage, were often detained by high water, or stuck in the mud. Such a state of affairs, caused the troops to become very restless — not having any of the surroundings, canculated to make permanent camp comfortable — yet only having the lease of a day at a time, & a winters campaign in contemplation — were well calculated to unsteady men & cause them to wish for a hastening of the crisis. Tuesday 8th the voters of the states which had not ceceded from the Union cast their ballots for another Presedend. The candidates were Lincoln, Republican, & McClelland Democrat. The sympathies of the south were with McClelland, & not withstanding we were deprived of a vote — many loud cheers were given & earnest wishes expressed for the success of the Democratic candidate. In the groups knotted around the camp fires — the political situation, of the country was fully discussed — many conjecturing that our destiny hinged upon the election — doubtless quite a turn in affairs would have transpired, had George. B. McClelland been given the supremacy.

Abraham Lincoln received 2,330,552 popular votes; Gen. George B. McClellan received 1,835,985. Lincoln and Andrew Johnson (vice-presidential candidate) received 212 electoral votes; McClellan and George H. Pendleton (vice-presidential candidate) received 21. McClellan and Pendleton only carried Delaware, Kentucky, and New Jersey. McClellan's popularity as a general was not sufficient to overcome the disillusionment within the Democratic party. Shortly after the election, General McClellan resigned from the army and wrote, "For my country's sake I deplore the result...." Lincoln stated the results of the election "will be to the lasting advantage, if not to the very salvation, of the country." (Long 594).

Capture of Johnsonville By Gen. Forest

As it was another gloom was case over the Confederacy — another eye "knocked out" from which she never recovered sight. But while our sympthizers were defeated by ballot at the north — our enemies were yielding in the South. — & we had great reason to rejoice at retreat roll call by hearing the reading of the Official report of Gen's Hood & Forest confirming the capture of Johnsonville by Gen. Forest — a small town situated upon the south bank of the Tennessee River — with four gunboats, eleven steamers, seventeen barges; also quartermaster & commissary stores — to the amount of seventy five or one hundred thousand tons.

Gen. Nathan Bedford Forrest, having enlisted as a private shortly before his 40th birthday, rose in rank to major general in December 1863. While General Sherman believed there could be no peace in Tennessee until Forrest was dead, General Johnston ranked Forrest as the war's greatest soldier. Five of Forrest's brothers and two of his half brothers also served in the Confederate army. Following the war, General Forrest returned to his plantation, took part in railroading, and became involved with the Ku Klux Klan soon after it was organized. It is believed he served as its Grand Wizard (Boatner III 288-9).

The boats were consigned to the flames, as were the stores that could not be taken away. It was a great pity to burn anything when it could have been utilized by our own army — & when so very badly needed — but the place was some distance from our main army & liable to be recaptured by the enemy.

This was a most brilliant achievement — & was the occasion of another plume being added to the already well filled hat of the "Wizzard of the saddle." The election, which had been the all absorbing theme of conversation, was for the time forgotten — & the woods were made to ring with loud shouts of victory.

Camp Near Tuscumbia Ala

The weather continued cold & blustering — intermingled with rain, & many murmerings were heard from the poorly clad soldiers. On the 10th we had a nice sunny day for the first for some time; & as our private commissaries had added pork, dried fruit, & turnips to the bill-of-fare — we stretched out in the rays of "old sol" like stuffed toads — enjoying ourselves hugely. But this private foraging caused the adoption of a strict battallion guard — with orders to allow no man beyond camp limits, without a written pass from the proper Officers & business stated.

This gave us double guard duty — having to furnish our quoto for the battallion — in addition to our regular duty in company. However this extra service was of short duration — as it was revoked the following day. Yet we had a very stringent one — but of entirely different character —

'Twas issued by Maj. Gen. Elza, Chief of Artillery of the Army of Tennessee — regarding the feeding & care of horses — forage for them was becoming very scarce — hence the necessity of economizing.

Gen. Arnold Elzey was born Arnold Elzey Jones, however during his time at West Point, he dropped Jones and began using his middle name, which was his paternal grandmother's name. General Elzey served as Chief of Artillery for the Army of Tennessee from September 8, 1864, to February 19, 1865. Following the war, he returned to his farm in Maryland (Boatner III 264-5).

On the 12th Stewarts corps was reviewed by Gen. Beauregard — & as he passed down the lines upon his beautiful steed — the troops by regiments greeted him with three cheers — an expression of their heartfelt gratitude & great rejoicing, occasioned by his reappearance in the saddle — after a short absence, on the sick list. The 13th was Sunday — & as usual, the order was read at reveille roll call to be ready for inspection 10 O.C AM — That meant for us to shave & every fellow to don his clean linen — "if he had it." Soon after the horses were harnessed, the order to inspect was substituted by one to prepare to move at noon — three or four hours were passed, in watching, waiting & wondering — what next?

Camp Near Tuscumbia Ala

The burden was finally lifted from our minds, for the time, by moving orders being countermanded — & our old quarters resumed & cooking commenced. Perhaps, the reported breaking of the pontoon across the Tennessee river, while loaded with cattle — caused the change in moving orders — & time posponed until sunrise next morning. Reveille at 4 .O.C A.M & everything in readiness to move at time specified on subsequent evening — but were delayed, half hour.

Ruins of Tuscumbia

Soon after leaving camp passed through Tuscumbia — or what was left of it — after the yankee "house burners," partly satiated their unquenchable desire to use the torch. The buildings yet remaining — from which many of the occupants had fled for safety — denoted great taste — & prosperity of the once happy owners. Some places whole blocks were burned — in the ashes of which, the birds & winds of Heaven deposited seeds — the thorn & thistle prospered — giving the once beautiful inland city a ragged — forlorn appearance — nestling disease, to torture the few remaining inhabitants. Would to God! I could pass these thoughts, as buried — never again to be "resurrected" — but when I contemplate the happy, prosperous, contented people, who once lived in that town — & its beautiful surroundings — & then think of what my eyes have seen — the burned stubs of ornamental shade trees — the piles of brick, mortar & ashes — the only thing left to mark the spot where stood many costly business houses — in town, as well as residences in country — I cannot refrain from, again entering my condemnation — against those who used the torch — or the General who sanctioned such a barbarious warfare. The march was continued on the Florence road until within half mile of the pontoon crossing the river & went into camp, to await our turn. The crossing was very slow — to be cautious was considered the best policy — as the bridge was very shackling.

Camp Near Tenn. R

The 15th was some what gloomy — rainy — foggy weather continued. All troops reported across the river, but our corps (Stewarts) who were put to work, throwing up fortifycations — while Gen. Cheathams division were engaged in the same work upon the opposite bank. The purpose being, to leave the defenses, so the pontoon could be safely guarded by a small force — while the campaign could be completed.

Thanksgiving & Prayer

The 16th was set a part by the Gen. commanding, as a day of thanksgiving & prayer. All pioneer work & military duty unless, compulsory, were suspended. If such proceedings could have been put off until the following day — many of us would have had a desire to offer up thanks to "Uncle Jeff" — when he loosened up his purse strings, & paid us four months wages.

The appearance of the Paymaster — notwithstanding the cash value of our money had greatly depreciated — made many happy faces in the company — smiles were seen to reappear upon countenances, where sadness had predominated for sometime past. The sporting class were soon observed gathering in groups — the old rusty — greasy decks, brought out, & the successful ones soon carried off the booty. Many were penniless, before another sun dawned & cursing themselves for gaming. I kept my resolve, also my money. On the morning of the 18th at reveille rollcall of

Capt. Hoskins Miss battery, seven men were reported missing — who disappeared very mysteriously, during the night previous. Supposed to have deserted. Early in the fore-noon Forests cavalry commenced crossing the river — all the forage wagons were also sent across the river to procure forage for the horses.

Bivuoac Near Tenn R

About 10- O.C. AM our battery received orders to cross — as soon as the horses could be harnessed & mess-kit loaded — moved down near the river bank — where we came up with — an almost impenetrable mass — cavalry, wagons etc etc. The rain was yet pouring down, the road being very narrow, & mud mirey — we were ordered to park the guns by the road side & bivuoac the remainder of the day & a portion of the night. Our uncomfortable rest was shortened several hours in the following morning, by being roused 1- O.C. AM — soon after moving out in the road, where we remained stamping around in the mud until almost daylight — waiting for some other batteries in our front to cross. Crossing a body of swift running water, & as wide as the river was at this point, was very slow after night — especially when our means of crossing was considered unsafe.

Crossing Tenn R

If our pontoon had not been partially supported by stone piers from which the Feds had burned the bridge — the high water would have soon swept it down the stream, carrying with it many precious souls. The pontoon was lighted up by large fires made of logs on either bank. Just as the last shades of night, were disappearing, from which appeared a few faint streaks in the heavy clouds — as if the sun would be permitted to shine, our battery moved on the old rickety bridge & moved slowly across, & I tell you I was greatly relieved when I put my feet upon terriferma on the opposite shore.

Only a short distance from the landing was situated Florence, Ala. Lauderdale. Co. which had, but a short time previous, been a considerable trading point & possessed of a great deal of wealth — but as usual, the torch of the yanks had been applied & the blackened brick walls, stood towering above the ruins, as tombstones to mark the fiendish deeds of the despoilers, upon which was inscribed in thought of the citizens, hate! hate!! eternal Hate!!!

Tennessee Campaign

Moved out three miles & camped — without any forage — the poor horses having to stand in the mud & shiver in the cold bleak rain which continued to fall. At this time I wrote in my pocket diary — If the cold rain continued — I pitied the poor Confederate ~~Rebel~~ soldier who saw Tennessee that winter — supplies of all kinds were being reduced & gradually growing shorter — the troops were becoming discouraged — which would soon initiate trouble, & finally end in defeat & complete disorganization of the army — yet I hoped for the better. But subsequent events were not long in fulfilling my prophecy. On the morning of the 20th Lee's corps (formerly Hood's) moved out in a northern direction — our command remaining in camp. They were experienced in traveling — the roads had become so worked up, were almost impassable. Wagons & artillery were continually miring down to the axle — horses & mules rearing & plunging for dear life — in an endeavor to extricate themselves from the mudy prison — riders & drivers applying the lash to the poor creatures — cannoniers rolling at the wheels — while the pioneer corps was busy cordurroying the worst places — in order to push forward on the "mysterious move" & it looked as if the worst had not yet come, as rain continued to fall.

Tennessee Campaign

We drew three days rations of bacon (something new) & two of "hard tack," Also "drew" an order to move on the following morning at 7 O.C. A.M. — & after a hasty breakfast of hardtack — some of which had become wet from rain — & bacon — moved out one hour later than was on the programme — upon the Lawrenceburg, or military road, each battallion of artillery marching with their respective Division of infantry. Our progress was very slow — the road being so mudy. Soon after leaving camp, the rain changed to snow & continued to fall for three or four hours — after which a driving wind set in from the north — howling over the bare fields & whistling through the tall forest trees — causing the teeth of the thinly clad soldier to chatter with cold — as he drew his scanty wrappings closer, bending forward on his northbound — uncertain march. In a general order (No 35) Gen Hood expressed a most earnest desire for all true soldiers, to stay with him, in that hour of victory (In his own imagination).

If his soldiers had not been true to their convictions, & patriots in every sense of the word — Hood never could have held a "handfull" of them together until a recrossing of the Tennessee river was affected. In his "exhortation" — said rations might be scarce — especially bread but insisted that we bear it cheerfully, & the honor gained would more than recompense our hardships. We could have stood the march a great deal better had it not been for rain & mud. Our stock were in poor condition, & forage for them very scarce, & as a consequence becoming weak & chilled, stalling on every hill — & we the cannoniers had to wade mud kneedeep & roll at the wheels. About 4 O.C. AM. we pulled out of the road, to camp — almost worn out, cold, wet, mudy & had only traveled eight miles.

On the morning of the 22nd had reveille at 5 O.C. ~~AM~~ & continued our march at 8- & I tell you, it looked as if winter had commenced in earnest — the ground being frozen hard & Snowing. Facing those cold "northerners" was very pinching to us — having been accustomed to spending our winters in a much warmer climate.

Tennessee Campaign

A short time previous to camping — crossed the Tennessee state line — and after a weary travel of fifteen miles, stopped for the night in a narrow valley, down which ran a small stream, called Bakers Creek. This was Wayne. County.

Deer in Camp

The major portion of the country, was rough, some rock & covered with heavy timber, sparsely inhabited — partaking of a wild nature, as one would naturally infer, by what happened on the following morning about 10 OC. — as we were preparing to leave camp — were startled by a hideous yelling, shooting, throwing of stones, axes & the appearance of five deer, running at a break neck speed through the midst of camp. One of my mess threw a skillet at them as they jumped the log by which our mess fire was built — but we didn't get "a smell" of venison. Three escaped unhurt — two were killed near the outskirts of the camp. Our march extended up the creek valley for several miles — then we had to "take to" the hills — which looked like mountains, & were in reality spurs of the Blueridge range. This country was filled with armed men, who we termed bushwhackers, but were in reality — outlaws, whose business was to prey upon either army — honor was a thing of the past, with them — booty was their chief aim — but they seemed to be more antagonistic toward the Southern cause.

All the citizens with whom we conversed did not hesitate to denounce us as traitors — the women were especially bitter. One principal characteristic in my Diary, is eulogizing the ladies — but in this case please pardon me — if I did, would not speak my convictions; Most all the able bodied men were in the woods heavily armed. Depradations were daily committed upon our men. In some instances when one was found alone, a short distance from the main army — his gun was taken, robbed & sometimes sent back to quarters in an almost nude condition.

Tennessee Campaign

A regiment of Infantry was marched single file upon both sides, a short distance from the supply train to protect it from the depradations of these men. Our march was very slow — the horses so weak & hills so steep, the assistance of the cannoniers was required in many places. We worked hard all day & until 10 O.C. in the night, before we found camp & only traveled twelve miles. On the morning of the 24th it was about 7. O.C. before camp was evacuated — & then did not move with much rapidity, the horses were cold & hungry — & didn't like to "get into" the collar, worth a cent.

Bush Whackers Lynched

We were attended by the same quoto of bushwhackers — Gen. Stewart was fired upon three times from ambush while riding along the road. Several robberies committed, some of our men ~~were~~ stripped of their clothing — bodies disfigured & sent back to camp. "Twas said some of the miscreants "looked up a limb" with a rope around their necks — for their misdeeds. "Judge lynch" should always pronounce & execute sentence in all such cases. During the days march we passed a house which had been used as a rendezvoux for these fellows — & judging from what had been left in their hurried flight — it was easy to judge the character of the former occupants — yes — there were some women left — who gave us a severe tongue-lashing. Our march extended up the valley of what was called Factory creek — which was extremely crooked for I think we must have crossed the stream about fifty times during a march of ten miles.

After a short disagreeable nights rest & a scanty breakfast, we were again moving at sunrise the 25th in a northeast direction. During the forenoon we intersected the main Nashville & Columbia road, which had been graded for a pike — but not macademized that far down. The country was generally poor & thinly populated by a people whose resourses were not very extended. Camp was again pitched, about 4. O.C. PM. Lawrence Co.

Tennessee Campaign

Our advance was very slow — but could not well have been otherwise — considering the crosses & "stumbling blocks" in the way. At this time Hood was in full command of the Army of Tennessee. Gen. Beauregard — who had been in charge of the Artillery up to the time of our departure from Tuscumbia — was transfered to another department. Hood was not the man to be at the head of affairs at that time — the men had never regained confidence since the uncalled for slaughter of them, in his "bull dog" fighting — when attacking the enemy in his stronghold at Atlanta — this should not have been — when men are thinly clad & poorly fed they should think their commander a second Moses, who could smite "the rock" for ~~good~~ water.

On the morning of the 26th we were roused from our cold beds, by the sharp notes of the bugle at 5 O.C & continued our north bound march, at day light, which was very laborious, the mud was almost knee deep & the rain fell all day. Fortunately, though after traveling ten miles — struck the pike where the Macadam began. As we passed through Mountpleasant, a small village, situated on Sugar creek were forcably reminded, that we were again in a country inhabited by civilized people & friendly to our cause, as the ladies were out in all directions with flying handkerchiefs & smiles — instead of frowns & abuse as their mountain sisters gave us. When a halt for the night was made about dark — we had passed twenty mile posts during the day — was ten miles south of Columbia, Murry Co. Bread rations scarce again.

Tennessee Campaign

On the 27th at daylight — Same "old seven & six — pull up stakes & move on — somebody knew. But I don't think any one in our army did — it was very tiresome, we were aware ~~at~~ of that — but our thoughts were for the time lifted from our sore distress, by the beautiful scenery that presented itself to our view — compared with that of a few days previous — was well calculated to enliven us; 'twas said we were marching through one of the fairest portions of the state. Soil rich & adorned with magnificent residences — yards tastefully decorated with beautiful flowers & evergreens. The citizens were greatly surprised, yet highly pleased at our coming & welcomed us with open arms.

Pillows Residence

Passed by Gen. Pillow's (of C.S.A) residence — an elegant structure, denoting great pride of its former occupant. In the Gen's absence the yanks cultivated his farm, in corn & cotton, the Season previous to our arrival. Surely none of Sherman's men had been around — as there were no signs of fire.

Gen. Gideon Johnson Pillow, formerly a criminal lawyer and partner of James K. Polk, wielded significant power in the Democratic party. As a Douglas Democrat, he had hoped compromise would prevent the southern states from seceding, but when the war began, he first led the Tennessee state troops, then transferred to the Confederate army. His last major command was at Fort Donelson in 1862. Gen. John Buchanan Floyd, first in command at Fort Donelson, saw little chance against General Grant's force of 15,000 men and gave his command to General Pillow, who was second-in-command. General Pillow, in turn, relinquished command to Gen. Simeon Bolivar Buckner and escaped with General Floyd, leaving General Buckner to face General Grant, and ultimately an unconditional surrender. As a result, both General Floyd and General Pillow were relieved of their commands by President Jefferson Davis. General Floyd died in August 1863, and General Pillow never received another significant appointment. Following the war, he returned to the practice of law (Boatner III 95-6, 286, 394-7, 653-4).

Left the pike marching in a northeast direction on the Columbia & Pulaski road — camping about two miles distant from Columbia — where the Federals were reported several thousand strong & well fortified. Some skirmishing could be heard — which sounded very natural, although our ears had been unused to such for a short interval. Forest had been fighting them along the pike for several miles south. About 8 O.C. PM the enemy burned most of their valuables on the south side of the Duck river — where Columbia was Situated — falling back to the opposite side — burning the bridge behind them — also Strengthened their fortifications.

Columbia Tennessee

Early in the morning of the 28th the reported evacuation of Columbia by the Feds — had been confirmed — & our camp was almost wild — considering it a great victory — without the shedding of much blood — to follow up & capture the fleeing enemy — would be delightful & Nashville would soon be ours. Gen. Hood & Staff rode into town — were met by a large crowd of excited citizens, who were very anxious to show him welcome. The ladies were especially frank in their devotion. In the afternoon, having received orders — one section of our battery, went down to the river near town, to shell the yankee batteries & sharpshooters upon the opposite side — who seemed to take great pleasure in annoying the people & soldiers, on the side from which they had just departed.

Tennessee Campaign

The section fired forty rounds, which seemed to satisfy our adversary for the time & returned to camp. Columbia at that time, was a nice town beautifully situated upon quite a promonance overlooking the south side of Duck River.

Pat. Quinn Wounded

One of our company "Pat." Quinn, received a wound here by his own, reckless daring & foolhardiness — which cost him his life. The engagement with the section didnot satisfy his thirst for "yankee" blood — & with a companion — "Tom" Burgess — procured an enfield rifle each — returned to the seat of conflict — & engaged in a sharpshooting duel with the Feds across the river. Sometime after night Burgess returned to camp & reported Quinn dangerously wounded in the knee, & sent to the hospital. Quinn was one of my mess-mates, & I received word from him to take care of his valise & blankets until his return.

Quinn's Death

A few days afterward, news came to camp that poor "Pat" was dead. He was a good natured, jovial Irish man, a true friend — or an inveterate foe. He did a great deal of barbering for the company — frequently shaving a half dozzen or more of the boys on Sunday morning. After his death was confirmed, I made dilligent inquiry to find some of his relatives — but failing contributed his valise & contents to my own use. I brought his razor strap — valise etc etc. home with me, & have a small fragment of them yet remaining.

Tennessee Campaign

Just as day was peeping on the 29th at reveille rollcall, our company received orders to report to the aadjutant Gen. of Stewarts corps — & was requested to select the best horses of the company. At 7 O.C AM we left camp, to join the infantry — who had preceded us about two hours. Four miles from camp & east of Columbia crossed Duck river at Davis ferry — on a pontoon — after which were ordered to report to Brigadier Gen. Brantly to bring up the rear.

> **According to Mark M. Boatner III, Marcus Wright's *General Officers of the Confederate Army* lists Gen. William F. Brantly as a brigadier general, but Robert C. Wood's *Confederate Hand-Book* and Clement A. Evans' *Confederate Military History* do not list him as a general officer. General Brantly was assassinated on November 2, 1870.**
> **(Boatner III 82, 970, 974).**

Our movements were executed with as little noise as possible — so as to keep the enemy in ignorance of our circuitous march — & intercept them between Columbia & Franklin Tenn. The route was very rough & attended with many dangers — notwithstanding our observed silence, the keen eye of the enemies Sharpshooters detected our movements & repeatedly fired upon us. The Feds were reported several thousand strong, opposite Columbia. When night came, it was one of the dark ones, & found us traveling over a country which in ordinary times — one would think himself lucky, to pass, in a two wheeled cart without capsizing. The hills in some places were very precipitous — & covered with ledges of rock from six inches to a foot "Jump off".

While passing over one of these bad places — & being prevented by the darkness — from detecting the worst — & check the horses to prevent an accident — one of the wheels of the gun to which I belonged, jumped from a huge boulder — & the heavy weight of the cannon — smashed every spoke in it.

A Broken Artilley Wheel

We had an extra wheel, with the ordnance wagons — which was tried — but contrary to expectations would not fit. This was quite a dilemma — a broken wheel — a night almost pitch dark — & within gun shot, of an inveterate enemy — whose pickets took great delight in annoying us with their whizzing minnies.

Tennessee Campaign

Again the old proverb was verified & "necessity proved to be the mother of invention" in this case — under the circumstances 'twas indespensibly necessary that we think fast & act accordingly — Some one suggested a wagon wheel might do — & immediately a couple of men, were started in the direction of a dim light, which was seen flickering through the darkness & heavy timber & proved to be emanating from a residence the occupant of which was the owner of an old fashioned Tennesse wagon, with a "schooner" bed.

The Old Wagon Wheel

The, "Old Cit" remonstrated with the boys, when the object of their errand was made known — but something must be done, & that quickly. One of the rear wheels was removed, & but few moments intervened before the boys reappeared — & our gun was soon on the move again. I remarked to the boys — the first big rock that wheel encountered — would smash into kindling wood — but it stood up just like a "little man". While we were feeling our way through the darkness, heavy cannonading was heard at Columbia in our left rear & occasionally at Spinghill in front. The firing in rear, was our men trying to attract the attention of the enemy — until our detachment could surround them. After making a circuitous march of twenty miles or more from our starting point in the morning — stopped for a short rest at midnight. The horses had become greatly fatigued, by the steady march over a country, seldom, if ever traveled by a wagon — & without feed or water. A rest & food were greatly needy by them — & a much longer one than was in store, would have been especially appreciated by the men. Owing the condition of the road, & the misfortune of breaking a wheel — the infantry had left us in their rear some distance, & after a rest of two hours, we again pulled out, having orders to push forward as rapidly as possible & over take them.

Tennessee Campaign

Just as day was dawning on the morning of the 30th — came up with the corps a short distance from the Nashville pike, & to find the yankee's had fled only a short time previous, in the direction of Franklin with Forest in hot pursuit. 'Twas hard for us to become reconciled to our unexpected disappointment — that our "game" had flown after being so near bagged — & had we been successful — how easy the capture of Nashville would have been. But no one could be blamed — we had done remarkably well — taking into consideration the condition of men horses & the country over which we were compelled to pass, in order to gain the enemies rear. We came to the pike at the town of Spring Hill — & followed in the direction the enemy had fled. From appearances the Feds had been stopping there for some time, & the manner in which army stores of all kinds, & dead horses were scattered, was indicative of a hurried departure. They had attempted to burn the wagons & stores, which they could not take with them — but were not as successful — as when using the match upon private property — some failing to ignite.

They halted & formed a line of battle about two miles south of Franklin — but were soon dislodged by a flank movement — which forced them to fall back in their entrenchments around the little City — & would to God, the flank movement had been continued for a few miles farther, & until the enemy had been forced to evacuate Franklin — & thus saved the needless butchery of so many precious souls —; lost confidence — & disorganization of the army. There were three lines of entrenchments, on the south side of Franklin — the direction we were advancing — upon an eminence — sloping south — in an open plain overlooking & commanding the country for miles around. When within gunshot range of their outer line of works — about 4 O.C. PM. our troops were quickly formed in three lines of battle — & as some of our artillery had not yet arrived from Columbia — our battery was divided in sections with the corps — one going to the right & the one of which I was a member remaining in the center.

Tennessee Campaign

Our section was ordered to go out in front of the advance line & commence firing. We were soon in position — guns loaded, & at the command fire! sent two shells screaming through the air in the direction of the fortified little city.

Battle of Franklin Tennessee

This was a signal for our men to prepare for a charge all around the lines — & a deafening roar of artillery — attended with the bursting of shells & whizzing of minnies — from the enemies guns, was heard in return. Our pieces fired as rapidly as possible & until our first line of battle passed — then limbered up — fell in their rear to join in the charge. This was the first & only instance during the war in which we were ordered to charge as artillery — but Hood's intention on this occasion was to take everything by storm — & had he been successful — when a good position for artillery had been reached — we would have been ready to plant our guns. Our advance extended down an open field, over a small ravine & railroad — up an inclined plain in full view of the enemy. Our horses had become almost wild with excitement — rearing & pitching to free themselves from their drivers — & escape the "hailstorm" of shot & shell, that was tearing up the ground around them.

Canteen Spoiled

In crossing the railroad, one of the wheel tugs on my gun broke which necessitated a short halt. While I was assisting the wheel driver to mend it — a minnie ball from the enemies gun, hit my canteen, mashing one side into the other — I was excited! & didnot feel the jar. My companion hearing the sharp crack — asked — Sam didn't that strike you? I said no. & was not aware of what a protector it had been until sometime afterward. My canteen, when the ball struck it, was full of water, a short time had expired — becoming thirsty, thought to take a drink of water — then it was I realized what had happened, the water was all gone & stopper lost. The escape of the stopper & water admitted air, & perhaps saved me of a dangerous wound in the hip. It did seem to me if a hat had been held up one second, when were mending that tug, would have been pierced with twenty bullets. This may sound a little "fishy" — but It did seem as though the Heavens had opened & raining shot & shell.

Battle of Franklin Continued

We had moved but a few paces from where the breakage occurred — when this same wheel driver (Stubbs) was hit on top of the head with a fragment of shell — & fell forward between his horses — lodging upon the bridle reins & end of pole. He was born from the field & place filled by one of the cannoniers. We succeeded in driving the enemy from their first & second line of works but our first line of battle becoming so decimated by the continuous hail of shell, grape, canister & minnies into their ranks — had to be filled up by the second & third. Not being able to obtain a position, from which we could do execution, without endangering the lives of our own men — the battery was halted at the first line of works — but our infantry kept steadily on — on! until their enemy was driven behind the last line of entrenchments. We were told to remain in place, subject to orders — & I assure you the continual rain of shot, shell & the sight of our comrads falling around us — made our position anything but a pleasant one. To be a silent & helpless spectator, when death in all its horridness, is hovering over you — listen to the cries of the wounded & dying as they are being "carted" off the field — requires greater nerve — than to face the cannons mouth in heat of battle.

Tennessee Campaign

Our infantry after reaching the last line of entrenchments — met with such stubborn & overwhelming resistance, & failing to rout their adversaries, dropped down in the outer ditch, where they kept up firing at each other across the works — by elevating the breech of their rifles, with one hand — at the same time crouching as low to the earth as possible, to avoid exposing their bodies. Some of our infantry told me after the battle — the Feds threw shovels & picks over the works at them, & were hurled back from whence they came, with as much force as possible.

Battle of Franklin

The outer ditch was filled with our men sweltering in their own blood while the inner one in like manner was filled with the enemies dead & wounded. Some time after dark our company moved back a short distance, & at 9 O.C. PM firing ceased all around the lines, excdept occasional sharpshooting. The casualties in our company ~~were~~ were two men. Stubbs died & a man by the name of Axton, in the other section received a painful wound in the leg. Once more I thanked God, for protecting me, in the dark hours of danger. This was a bloody & hotly contested field — although we were given possession, the price paid in blood, overballanced the gain.

Hood's "Bull dog" fighting again lost us many brave souls, that could have been saved by a little strategy. When we entered the conflict, I thought the part we had to play in the bloody drama, would be of short duration — on account of the old wagon wheel — as I believed it certain to crumble — at the first discharge of the gun, & I being the one to pull the lanyard, was liable to be caught in the reck, stood as far from the wheel as possible — but to my great surprise, it stood the "racket" like an "Old Veteran". The only difference or inconvenience experienced — in firing the gun — the narrow tire cut down into the soft earth — while the broad one on ~~of~~ the origial wheel, remained upon the surface — describing a half circle, necessitating a brisk movement on the part of the cannoniers to dodge the gun trail as it swept around.

December 1st

We had scarcely got our places warm upon the damp ground in an attempt to rest & sleep — when we received a sharp shake of the shoulder & a summons to rouse up at 3- O.C. AM, Dec 1st & we were just about as sleepy, dirty, ragged, red-eyed — wornout set of human beings as you ever looked upon.

All the artillery of the army was ordered up & to be in position by 7-O.C. A.M. to shell the enemy. At 4 O.C. we moved up to within eight-hundred yards of the position occupied by the Feds on the previous evening — & halted to await orders. The appearance of daybreak — brought us the news — the enemy had fled. They left some time in the after part of the night. Quite a commotion was heard over in their quarters at that time — but the night ~~was~~ being very dark — was difficult to distinguish by sound alone — whether they were evacuating — or reinforcing — to receive another attack. During the afternoon of the 30th about two thousand prisoners were captured, with four pieces of artillery — which were immediately turned upon them & their shells used to destroy the ones who moulded them.

Evacuation of Franklin by the Feds

They fled in the direction of Nashville, leaving their dead & wounded in our possession. A short time after daylight, a companion & myself — walked over a portion of the battle field, & I beheld a sight which stifles description, & causes a cold shudder to run over me, when in contemplation of that field of blood — although many years have elapsed. We walked along the last line of entrenchments, over which the last death struggle for victory occurred — of which my previous description, only gives the reader a faint idea of the desperate & memorable hand to hand conflict.

Tennessee Campaign

One can scarcely imagine the horrible sight that presented itself. On the south side laid our men, in pools of blood, many of whom were cold in death — while others were gasping as if almost ready to "pass over the river". Upon the north a similar scene was beheld — the distorted corpses, of the enemy with upturned faces, & almost nude bodies, from which the outer clothing had been stripped by our men, & some of the poor fellows were feebly crying for help.

"Pat." Cleburns death

Far over to the left of our lines, lying across the works was the body of the dead gray charger, which was ridden the previous day by the gallant Brig. Gen. "Pat." Cleburn, who fell a lifeless corpse at the same volley, while leading his men in the dreadful charge on the previous evening.

Gen. Patrick Ronayne Cleburne failed French, Latin, and Greek in the apothecaries' test in his native Ireland, then came to America where he was a druggist and lawyer when the Civil War began. Responsible for organizing the Yell Rifles, a militia that seized the Little Rock Arsenal, he received his first commission when Arkansas seceded. He rose from the rank of captain to major general by 1862. Known as "Stonewall Jackson of the West," General Cleburn fought at Stones River, Chickamauga, Chattanooga, and in the Atlanta campaign before the Battle of Franklin where he was killed on November 30, 1864 (Boatner III 158-9).

He had been unjustly accused of cowardice, & said he would rather die than bear the name. Near the last & awful pit, stood a dwelling, where resided the parents of a young volunteer in the confederate army who in the fatal charge on that memorable afternoon — in a vain endeavor to reach his once happy home — fell forward while grasping his bayonetted rifle, a corpse, only a few paces from the door-sill around which he had passed his happy childhood days. No doubt, but when that young man entered the charge, all thoughts of danger, were enveloped by the great desire, to assist in driving the enemy from his Fathers door & the happy meeting of loved ones there.

If the historian, who gives the details of the Battle of Franklin Tenn — fails to record it as one of the bloodiest & most hotly contested battles of the civil war will fail to do justice to both Federal & Confederate & ignore the truth.

Tennessee Campaign

Franklin is situated on the south side of Stone river, which was up to the time of the departure of the enemy — spared by a bridge — which was burned by them to delay our pursuit. About 3. O.C. in the afternoon according to orders — we hitched up & moved to the right of town with the intention of crossing the river, at a place which was fordable in dry weather, but the stream had become so enlarged by continued rain & that it was considered dangerous for artillery to cross — in consequence of which, we went into camp to wait until a pontoon was constructed at the old crossing, near town. Reveille 4 O.C. A.M. on the 2nd.

Exchange Wheels

About sunrise received orders to countermarch; went back to Franklin, where we found in the principal street, the rear ammunition chests & wheels of a federal caisson — upon which was also fastened a fifth wheel — as our gun wheels did not "match up" very well, a short halt was made & when tried, found the yanks in their hurried nocturnal evacuation, had left — though not intentional — just what we needed. The Old Citizens wheel was left in the street — & I have never heard whether he recovered his property or not. But I have often thought — special word should have been left, that he might recover his wheel — memory was very short in wartimes, necessity often caused us to act speedily & without decorum — when we received a favor, forgot to acknowledge our thankfullness — or return one as an offset. Crossed the river & continued our march on the pike leading to Nashville. Near the crossing — near some timbers — (part of the old bridge) — several of the enemies dead, laid bleeching in the rain — & from their position, we supposed had been mortally wounded & crawled there for protection. Everything indicated that we had them almost whipped, & their departure was made in haste — But they had us so terribly crippled — were too weak to push matters.

Tennessee Campaign

The thin mud was about six inches deep on the pike — which had been worked up by continued rain & travel — but we managed to get over about twenty miles of it — & camped within four miles of Nashville. Williamson. Co. Country good soil & had the appearance of being cultivatged by industrious husbandmen. Lee's corps, having arrived several hours in our advance — had already formed a line of battle in front of the City.

Near Nashville

In the forenoon of the 3rd there was some skirmishing. About 12 Oclock our Infantry formed in solid column — advancing some distance to establish a permanent line of battle. The enemies skirmishes were easily driven before them. At 4 O.C. PM the first shot from artillery was fired by the Feds & we were annoyed the remainder of the evening by their shells. Nashville was strongly fortified upon three sides by earthworks — the fourth by the Cumberland river — defended by a large & well equipped army under Gen. Thomas US.

As a result of his success at Chickamauga, Gen. George Henry Thomas, a Virginian, but loyal to the Union, earned the nickname "The Rock of Chickamauga" and was

appointed brigadier general. His achievements at Franklin and Nashville (where Sam encounters him) brought him an appointment as major general and the Thanks of Congress for both Franklin and Nashville. He was one of only fifteen army officers to receive this honor during the Civil War. In 1869, General Thomas died of apoplexy in San Francisco while in command of the Division of the Pacific (Boatner III 836; "George Henry Thomas").

Reported capture of two U.S. steamers by Gen. Forest, on the Cumberland river. Early in the morning of the 4th our battery received orders to move to the front & build breastworks — were soon at the position pointed out to us, & began cutting the timber, to get a better view of the enemy. The clearing was about completed, when an order to suspend, opperations was received. Our rations of meal was running low, & the public crib was almost drained — & as a matter of compulsion had to again depend upon our private commissary.

Going to Mill

A few willing hands soon shelled a sack of corn, & I started on horseback to mill, about five miles distant, as a detail from my mess. This reminded me of my first experience in milling — when a small boy — a stride of "Old Marth" the blazed faced family mare. After some inquiry & a tiresome ride — succeeded in landing the bag of corn in the mill. The noon hour had almost arrived — & the good miller in informing me, I would have to wait my "turn" — & there were several ahead concluded to go out a short distance in the country & if possible get a "square meal". Fortune smiled upon me, & I was not long in finding a place to shove my knees under a Table — although it was not "groaning" beneath turkey, & delicacies of all kinds — I found sufficient substantials to gratify my gnawing appetite — returning to camp with a full "bag" & belly. The nearest mill at that time was in Nashville, but being under yankee jurisdiction — was fearful it would all be taken for "toll" — as they had announced their intention to suspend grinding for "Cornfeds". On the morning of the 6th Hoskins battery was ordered to report to Gen. Chalmer's cavalry division. We yet kept knocking away at the door of Nashville — but were stubbornly refused admittance by the "bosses".

In front of Nashville

About 4 O.C. PM we received orders to report to Brig. Gen. Sears Miss.

Infantry brigade. Various conjectures, as to the meaning, were made by the members of the company — & as it generally fell to our lot to do the "tramping" for the army, some of them correctly guessed a raid.

It was a great satisfaction to be honored with the name of being the best moved battery of field artillery belonging to the Army of Tennessee; but I sometimes wished that we could enjoy the praise without having to be exposed to as much danger & hardships.

We soon became aware — our contemplated destination, was Murfreesboro, about twenty five miles south east of Nashville, & at dark left camp with our new commander. One battery & brigade were sent from each division of the Army. The route we had to make, was similar in point of obstacles — as the Columbia's expedition. The road being seldom traveled, was narrow, rough & rocky.

Tennessee Campaign

The moon which had been dimly lighting our uncertain pathway — had "retired" for the night — & sky becoming clouded — compelled us to pull to one side of the road at midnight to await the coming day. Here Lieut. Cockery — formerly of Guibors old battery — but had been an officer in the company since the consolidation at Demopolis Ala — took command of our section. On the 6th we had reveille at daylight — notwithstanding we marched hard half the previous night — were yet in hearing of the rifles at Nashville.

Murfreesboro Raid

After several miles of hard pulling through mud & over rocks, arrived at the Nashville & Murfreesboro pike, where the small Village of Lavern was situated — formerly guarded by two hundred Federal cavalry — who Forest surprised & captured the previous day. We again bivuoaced seven miles from Murfressboro. This expedition was entirely under the supervision of Gen. Forest.

After a poor nights rest, we arose from our wet steaming beds upon the cold ground — on the morning of the 7th & moved out in the direction of Murfreesboro, which was quite an auxillary to Nashville — & a place of considerable importance to the enemy — there being a large amount of army supplies packed away. To capture it would be quite a bonanza to us — just what we needed — & would also be a heavy blow to the enemy. Left the pike about five miles from the Fort, going to the right wing of our army which was situated southeast of town. Upon our arrival, found some of the troops, in line of battle & others forming — & from the signs of the times — couriers galloping to & fro etc etc an engagement seemed imminent. The Federals were strongly fortified & well equipped. Some places our men had constructed very temporary works of fence rails & logs. Forest's tactics on this occasion were to draw them out of their stronghold, by advancing a small force then fall back to our main line & whip them on open field.

Tennessee Campaign

About 2 O.C. PM. the Feds. were reported advancing upon our left — to which point our battery was ordered to report in double quick — upon our arrival, we were ordered to go out in advance of our skirmish line, to open the "fracus". Everything seemed ready & waiting for a starter. We fired several shots at a moving column of "blue coats" some distance off — but were greatly surprised — at the expiration of only a few moments, to see their skirmishers, only one hundred & fifty yards in our front, advancing rapidly through the timber & firing as they came.

Second Battle of Murfreesboro

We immediately turned our guns upon them — but soon had to abandon our position, & fall back as hasty as possible to the main line — where our limbers were again dropped in double quick time — ready for action, & pouring two second shells & grape into them — who by this time were almost close enough to count their buttons on their coats — but I didnot take the pains to count them. — Their columns were solid. I am sure the wheel of the gun, saved my life at this position — a ball no doubt, was aimed at me — just as I was in the act of inserting a friction primer — struck the tire, & went whizzing over my head — I felt the air, & dodged, after the danger was all passed — I stepped to one side, pulled the lanyard — & let "her go" with as much vehemence as possible, & this was the last shot fired from that position. Our Infantry became badly confused — some of whom didnot stop to fire a shot — but ran like turkeys. Had it not been for a detachment of Forests' cavalry coming to our rescued — capture would have been inevitable — as it was, by a very quick movement escaped.

Tennessee Campaign

Just as we were emerging from a small growth of under brush, which fringed an open field — & only a short distance from where we had been driven; met two guns of the Louisiana battery — member of which was kind enough to give me whisky at Grenada. Miss. where I got the "ducking" in the Yalabusha river — they had heard of our close quarters & said were coming to our assistance. We told them to turn back with us — but no — they dashed on in a gallop — a few paces — unlimbered, fired one shot — the enemies advance was upon them & in an instant their guns were gone — with most of their men & horses. Poor fellows! I felt so sad over their misfortune. A braver, truer set of men, never unfurled a flag in battle, than those La. Boys.

Second Battle of Murfreesboro

We fell back about one thousand yards, in an open field & prepared for action again — the sweeping columns of the enemy came upon us with a crash — despite our charges of grape — & they demanding us to halt & surrender the guns — but to give up our guns, was the last remedy with us — in an instant the guns were limbered up & horses in a sweeping gallop — a short distance to the rear, our third & last position was taken.

Gen. Forest by this time had become very much excited — realizing the day had been lost by the cowardice of some of the Infantry. At our last position was directly in rear of the guns on horseback — raising high up in his stirrups waving a flag which belonged to an infantry regiment — yelling at the top of his voice that he could be heard above the din of battle — & using every endeavor to rally them. The infantry were straggling to the rear, in squads of four to a dozzen. Forest said — Men for God's sake, rally! don't run off the field & leave the artillery to do all the fighting! If you cannot fight, raise one yell, any how! Finding his pleadings, didnot accomplish anything — threw the flag to one of them — saying take the d-m-d dirty rag & go to the rear! that's where you belong!

We fired several shots from this position — our infantry as I described before, were running pell mell — to the rear, in groups — & when the command was given by the gunner to fire! I said, hold on! we'll kill some of our own mess! The order was repeated, with greater animation, Pull the lanyard! they are no account any way. The concussion of the shell as it passed over their heads — knocked them sprawling for an instant — but soon rose with increased velocity & in a half bent position continued in the direction started.

Tennessee Campaign

'Twas hard to realize, they battle had been lost — when one hours stubborn resistance would have given us the victory — & the capture of army stores would have been immense.

The attack upon the place, was carefully planed by Gen. Forest. Gen. Armstrong's Cavalry brigade, was placed in the rear, or north, sufficiently far as not to attract attention. Forests' plan was for us upon the south side, to draw the enemy out sufficiently far to meet them on open field — & we having time to place our line of battle — thought a victory certain.

Second battle of Murfreesboro

When they left their fortifications in our pursuit, Gen. Armstrong, as had been previously arranged — came sweeping over the entrenchments, capturing the small detachments the enemy had left to guard the fort in their absence, using their artillery upon our belligerents. It was well for us, they did — had Armstrong failed to act his part well — our battery would have certainly been captured, & most of our army. One more complete victory for the yanks — & a disgraceful defeat for the Rebs. As soon as Armstrong opened upon the enemy — they realized to pursue us farther, meant the loss of their fort & stores — an about-face was immedately executed; Armstrong driven from his new possessions; — Soon after, & about nightfall firing ceased, & thus ended another fatal disaster, in the downfall of the South. When one is so confident of victory — the reverse is very humiliating. Never in all my Soldier life, did I feel the pangs of defeat, so keenly, as on this occasion. The enemies force was estimated at five to eight thousand, under command of Gen. Ranssam ours about six thousand.

Gen. Thomas Edward Greenfield Ransom, a civil engineer and realtor prior to the war, was wounded four times during his service on the battlefields at Charleston (Missouri), Fort Donelson, Shiloh, and the Red River campaign. His illness during the pursuit of Hood (September - October 1864) forced him to lead his command from the ambulance in which he rode. He was taken from the field at Gaylesville, Alabama, and died October 29, 1864. When Sam encountered General Ransom's troops in December 1864, he was apparently unaware of General Ransom's death just slightly more than a month before (Boatner III 679-80).

Tennessee Campaign

A portion of the ground where this running engagement occurred — was the same over which Gen. Bragg Confederate, & Gen. Rosecrans

Federal fought in 1862. At our first position the timber had been cut down by cannon balls — several trunks of trees yet standing, indicative of the fierce struggle between the antagonists.

We fell back about ten miles & camped near the pike leading to Nashville. Forest dispatched to Hood for another division of infantry intending to renew his attack upon Murfreesboro, as soon as his men rested & reorganized.

Camp Ten Miles From Murfreesboro

On the 8th we remained in camp, & Federals fell back in their works at Murfreesboro. Reported that reinforcements were coming from Nashville to assist in another attempt to capture Murfreesboro. 9th was passed in, inactivity as its predecessor, so far as we were concerned, looking for every "minit" to be the next, "as "Zack." Lear of our company rendered, such a predicament. Snow fell to the depth of two inches, accompanied by a cold wind, making it very uncomfortable for man & beast situated as we were. Affairs in reagard to the movements of the armies at Nashville remained at a standstill. In the forenoon of the 10th moved camp two miles down the pike toward Nashville. Rutherford County — & as ordered reported to Olmstead's infantry brigade — where we remained several days, & some ventured the prediction that we would remain inactive until the weather moderated — while others extended the time as far as spring. The weather was extremely cold, ground covered with snow & frozen hard. We were without tents & had been for several months past. Our portion of the army was very scarce of food & all kinds of clothing — especially shoes. I was almost barefoot — my toes were "grinning at the snow".

Tennessee Campaign

The consequence was, the men became very much dispirited. The disorganization & destitution, concerning which I prophesied, when camped near Florence ~~Tenn.~~ Alabama had come — with a prospect of a more ponderous calamity awaiting us — & it was impossible to shake off the almost impenetrable gloom that overshadowed our pathway. One glorious thing, & almost a "Savior" in this case, our camp was situated in a heavy body of timber — which acted as a wind break, & the huge logs, were piled "high" upon the fires, to keep us from freezing. Logs were also piled up before the fires, leaves gathered upon which our well worn blankets were spread, where we slept in a half frozen condition.

Between Nashville & Murfreesboro

This state of affairs, was well calculated to cause us to look upon the dark side; every "page" was a blank. The Feds seemed very quiet, & at times one would be impressed with the thought — they had sure enough concluded to suspend hostile operations until spring. But Hood being of an aggressive disposition, continued to "thunder" away at their fortified cities. The 15th was marked by a great change in the base of opperations taking place, the weather having "softened" up.

Heavy cannonading in the direction of Nashville, which had the "ring" of an artillery duel. 'Twas also currently reported, that the enemy charged our works with three lines of battle & were repulsed with heavy loss. About 10 O.C. PM I "nestled" myself away in the bed of leaves, & was using every exertion in my power to wrap myself in the arms of "Morpheus", but notwithstanding, the counting of fingers — repeating the multiplication table — covering up my ears, & thinking of home & a good warm feather bed, with covers "tucked in" etc etc was all in vain, sleep or rest was impossible.

Tennessee Campaign

The heavy tread of infantry — rolling of wheels, & clatter of horses feet upon the turnpike nearby, indicated an important & necessary move. I understood afterward it was some of the troops which had been under Forest, on the late expedition returning to Nashville. Half hour later, the company bugler sounded boots & saddles — every man was roused & only a few moments intervened, before we were wending our way through the mud in the direction of Murfreesboro — but left the pike a short distance from town, going to the right. A halt was ordered at 2 O.C. AM on the 16th, & we had scarcely parked the guns before an order was given, to cook three days rations immediately.

Second Advance on Murfreesboro

This was the means of "shutting " off our nap again & rest was ostracised. At 8 O.C. AM orders to advance on Murfreesboro — we had scarcely commenced moving when the order was countermanded & our former camp reoccupied.

Company Seperated

After an hour was passed in suspense, the section to which I belonged was ordered to report to Gen. Forest for duty, near town. We were very much displeased at the seperation of our company — but the game of "displease", with out asking your pleasure — was often "played" in the army. It was not until we made a considerable circuit, & a hard march of several miles, that we found ourselves within five miles of town & with Forest's troops. After a short stop & another move was inaugerated, & kept up until 8 O.C PM. we bivuoaced on the south of town, to rest the stock which was almost over come with fatigue — the artillery horses reeled as they walked — the men also cooked rations.

Tennessee Campaign

While this seemingly, meaningless maneuvering was going on near Murfreesboro — great change in affairs had taken place at Nashville, & as a result there was great excitement.

Retreat Commenced

About 12 Oclock on the night of the 16th camp was aroused & we began falling back toward the Nashville pike. This retrograde movement was caused by our forces giving away at Nashville. The Federals after several futile & repeated efforts — finally concentrated an overwhelming force upon the weakest point in our lines, & succeeded in breaking them. Our troops had met with so many reverses & disappointments, on this campaign, to break their lines, was eaqual to a defeat. Some of the men scattered in all directions, & for a while the retreat, took the form of a regular stampede; but enough were finally prevailed upon to rally & check the enemy, who had become almost crazed by their victory. In our detachment near Murfreesboro, were two brigades of infantry & Forest's cavalry — & being cut off from the main avenue of exit, were compeled to make a circuitous march, in which we passed over Some of the roughest road, it is possible to imagine, & to make matters more unpleasant, rain began to fall soon after the retreat commenced. But often in the darkest hour we were made to rejoice; this time the "swelling" of the heart came when we arrived at the Nolansville turnpike, which let us out of mud knee deep. About three miles from where we struck the pike — passed through Tryune a small village, & the name of the place was rendered indelible upon our minds by the liberality of our commander.

Forests Present

Forest's cavalry had quite a drove of hogs — which had been collected —

& were being driven along to feed the troops — also to keep them out of the enemies hands. One fine "porker" gave out, & Gen. Forest riding up about that time — told us we could have it — a moments halt was made, hog knocked in the head & thrown upon one of the caissons.

Tennessee Campaign

About three miles farther on we crossed Harpeth creek, & its current was considerably aggravated by rain — in the middle of which stood "stock still" a team of mules, hitched to an old Tennessee wagon, & an old gray haired negro vigorously applying the lash to make them pull out & avoid the "soljers". He had been to mill, exchanged his wheat for flour, & on his return, misled by high water, got off the road, & "stuck" fast.

The Negro & flour

Some of the boys scented the flour — as they were always "up to snuff", & when the battery was passing the wagon, three sacks were placed upon the caissons, regardless of the old darkeys pleadings & threatening to tell his "Massa". This was too rich a thing for a hungry soldier to pass.

The liberality of our "private" commissary, revived our drooping spirits very much — we could stand almost anything with a full stomach. Stopped 10 O.C. PM near Chapelhill, after a march of more than thirty miles, without rest. Oh! So tired. but never so tired that we could not prepare something to eat — if we had it — & while some of the boys were engaged in skinning the hog, others stuck their arms in the flour, up to their elbows making buiscuit, & after "wrapping" ourselves around a good supply of pork & "wheat bread", slept the remainder of the night as soundly as a babe that had been freshly starched by its mother. Reveille on the morning of the 18th at daylight, & soon after moved out leaving the pike, & marching directly to Duck river, which was three miles from Chapelhill — with the intention of fording it — but finding it too deep — turned our course toward Columbia.

Tennessee Campaign

The river made a considerable bend south from Columbia to this point — so that in turning back had to march northwest, in the direction of Nashville, from whence came the roaring of cannon & rattle of small arms. Our condition was a very precarious one, & had the enemy succeeded in their attempt to cut through our lines on the main pike — would have been irretrivably lost. Soon after leaving camp, I was compelled to abandon my old pieces of Shoes, which had become more of a hindrance, than protection, & scale the rocks, wade mud almost knee deep, besides roll on the wheels of the gun on every hill.

Retreat Continued

I had often heard of the old proverb — "put your shoulder to the wheel" — but not until this campaign was it practically demonstrated. For two or three days previous, the innumerable small gravel, which being worked up with the mud — intruded upon my feet, through the "air holes" in my old shoes — was the occasion of my dropping behind frequently for a few moments, to make an "emptying".

Abandoned My shoes

I was not the only one in this fix, & I assure you our lot was a hard one — But we had to "splash" on or be captured, & that was the very last extreme with our company. Frequently we were compeled to hitch twelve horses to one gun, in order to pull through the mud. After the seperation of our battery, near Murfreesboro — the other section went on with the baggage train, & at this time was out of immediate danger — having crossed Duck river. Our main force had fallen back to within four miles of Columbia, & were holding the enemy in check at Battle Creek. We received orders to hurry on as fast as possible — but with all our whipping, yelling & pushing our progress was very slow.

Tennessee Campaign

The constant roaring of cannon, mingled with the rattle of small arms — told how hard the enemy were struggling, to cut us off. Soon after dark, we were compelled to halt, await the rising of the moon, that its rays might enable us to avoid some of the worst mud holes & rocks, many of which were two feet high. A portion of this ground was the same passed over by us in our attempt to cut off the enemy, just before the battle of Franklin — & in my previous description — I believe — that I termed it the roughest road I ever saw, to be traveled by an army — the truth of which I yet verify.

Retreat Continued

At 1- O.C. AM on the 19th, the moon having risen, but being cloudy

& raining, did not give us much light, though an effort was made to move with the usual number of horses — but they were so near wornout, had to double team before a wheel could be turned.

The rain continued to fall as it had been on most of our trip & hills as steep as ever, our movements were very slow & arduous. The wind shifted to the north, turning the rain to sleet, & afterwards a light snow fell. By this time we had arrived near the crossing. Soon after noon, I in company with another member of our battery (Taylor from north Ark) got a permit from our Lieutenant (Sam. Kennard of St Louis Mo) to go in advance of the section & cross the pontoon, & overtake the other section before it turned too cold. We got across alright — & as Taylor & I ascended the hill — I remarked, I'm going to do my best for a pair of shoes before leaving that town, & when passing through Columbia, concluded to stop in at a place, which had been run as a livery stable, in antebellum days — but at that time, was filled with soldiers, trying to dry & warm themselves, around some ~~smoking~~ smouldering fires. Immediately upon entering — I yelled out — Is there any one in here, that has a pair of shoes to sell or give away? A boy of about fifteen years, an attendant of the stable — was standing in the office door. Said yes! walk in! I stepped in closing the door behind me.

Bought "Some" Shoes

He produced a pair of halfworn cloth shoes, two numbers too large for me — & thinking they'd beat none — asked the price. Fifteen dollars, sir. (Confederate money having greatly depreciated in value) — I, said, alright! I'll take them, at the same time handing him a twenty dollar bill. Not having change, said he'd have to go out & get some. In his absence a soldiers inquisitiveness, induced me to make a reconnoisance, & I spied an old blue Federal overcoat under his bunk, ~~which~~ and upon investigation, found it covered a pair of half worn leather shoes. They were soon changed from their hiding place under the bed — to under a coat of the same color worn by myself — & when the boy returned, I was looking as innocent as a "lamb". Failing to find the proper change — said I could have the cloth shoes for ten dollars. Alright! Good bye! & stepping out, gave Taylor — (my six foot partner) a "nudge", leaving the stable with a quicker step, than we entered. After we had gone sufficiently far, as not to fear the discovery of the loss by the boy, I handed the cloth shoes to my comrad — & both had a complete fit. By this time our barefoot tracks could be seen in the snow, which were tinged with blood & Notwithstanding, we "pulled" through — & came up with our advanced section, in camp about one mile from town near the Pulaski pike. I hunted up my valise, in which I found a pair of good warm socks, & after my feet healed up — was in good shape for foot wear.

In later years, Sam wrote about the shoe incident in three different articles he submitted to the *Confederate Veteran*, a monthly magazine. The first article, "Hard Times on Hood's Retreat," was published in June 1899. The second, "Missouri Battery in Tennessee Campaign," was published in August 1904. The third, "Experiences on the Hood Campaign," was published April 1908. In all three articles, Sam describes the brutal conditions for the Confederates in this campaign and always includes a retelling of the shoe tale. In his second article, Sam mentions he hopes he will hear from the boy soldier, if he is still living, and in the third, he reminds his readers he was just a boy when he made the appropriation, and he still hopes to hear from that "other fellow," as he hasn't yet paid for those shoes (266, 389, 187-8).

Retreat Continued

A short time after dark my section arrived, & there was great rejoicing at the reunion — company together again & all accounted for. Capt Fenner La. lost his guns, by the pontoon breaking while crossing. The rear guard of our army were compelled to cross in haste — 'twas said the last mile on the north side of the river was made in twenty minutes, with a ravenous enemy upon their heels. There seemed to be no desire on the part of Hood, to offer battle, except to check them until the recrossing of the Tennessee river could be accomplished. There were a great many modes of covering the feet resorted to on the campaign; some cut out pieces of green hides which were skinned from the beeves, which fed the army — sewed them over the feet with a "whang" of the same material, & their tracks in the snow resembled an elephants more than a human.

Tennessee Campaign

In the morning of the 20th moved out on the Pulak's pike — but our speed was very slow, some of the guns having but four horses — several having given out on the escapade. After a travel of about seven miles — pulled off the road, fed the horses & remained until dark — then moved on. This was queer proceedings — but was not the first, by a "long shot" since Hoods "wild goose" chase began.

Retreat Continued

The weather had moderated some, & a cold steady rain came down upon us all night. I straggled for the first & only time during the war, but I had a companion or two from the company with me. In passing a vacant house near the turnpike — to which was attached an old fashioned chimney — a bright blazing fire within, & seeing other soldiers around it — concluded to step in & take a warm.

Straggled

The heat of the fire made us stuped, & the time passed more rapidly than we were aware of. About Midnight one of the guns upset in a ditch — & the whole company had to stop until daylight — & lucky for us "stragglers", we arrived in time to assist in "resurrecting" the gun, also to receive a little scolding from the officers. The pike had become cut up, in holes & ditches from six to eighteen inches deep, which were filled with a thin mud, & many poor unfortunates, while feeling their way through the darkness — stepped into one of them, & went sprauling in the mud.

Hood & The Infantryman

Rather an amusing conversation took place on this retreat, between an Infantryman & Gen. Hood. The Gen. rode up to one, seated upon a log in the woods, who had his gun across his lap — elbows upon his knees — holding his head in his hands, as if in deep meditation & unaware of any ones presence — Saying, what, are you doing here? Well Gen — I'm worn out, sleepy, hungry, half naked & barefooted, but I'll be d_m_d if you can call me scattered.

Tennessee Campaign

About noon of the 20th left camp, continuing our exit. The wind again shifted to the north, & rain turned to snow in the evening. Forest had charge of eight picked brigades of Infantry & his cavalry, with which he had been holding the enemy in check at Columbia since the rear guard of our army crossed. The mark of destruction was seen on every side — especially in horses & mules — many were dead — while others were yet alive stuck in the mud, but too weak to get out. Passed through & camped two miles south of Linnville.

Retreat Continued

22nd was also spent on the "pad", near the close of which, we passed through Pulaski, a place of considerable business — also county seat of Giles County. Our camp was pitched near the suburbs. During the night some of our "private commissaries", found some flour, & appropriated it to their own use (or messes) without the owners consent. We needed it — "in our business" — as the "Harpeth creek flour", was running low. Had we depended entirely upon our general commissary — our buiscuits would have been "few & far between", especially on this trip. Before leaving camp on the 23rd our company, according to orders — destroyed all the ammunition, except thirty two shells to the gun, our horses being reduced in number, & those yet remaining, so badly "jamed" up — & country over which our line of march lead us, so hilly was useless to attempt hauling it farther. Our Orderly Sergeant — John. Dickenson was reduced to ranks, for disobeying orders. We were not at all pleased with having to leave the pike at this place. The road led us down a narrow valley, hemed in on two sides by almost perpendicular hills — which looked as if it would almost be impossible for a person to assend — yet corn had been grown on the sides. Some of the boys suggested, it had been planted with a shot gun — while the "planter" was standing at the bottom — but they trusted it to a "higher" power to tell how the cribbing was done — as the ground was too steep to pass over with a wagon.

Tennessee Campaign

The log cabins many of which had mud & stick chimneys, were built near the edge of the valleys & the bluffs being so much higher, we could almost look down the chimneys & see the children & cats playing around the fire. Don't you believe it? If not go & see for yourself.

Retreat Continued

For several days about this time we marched on rather an independent scale, & depended a great deal upon our own exertions for support, & "you bet" we lived fat, & were anxious to have some more "of it." Our stopping place was abandoned about 8. O.C. AM on the 24th & continued the retreat on the Banebridge or Florence road, which was very bad. Passed over some very poor country & after a tiresome march of twelve miles, camped 4 OC PM three miles from the southern line of Tennessee.

Christmas Day

On the 25th we again pulled up stakes, & moved out to pass another day — mud, rain & a repetition of all the vicissitudes, which had been our almost constant companions during the retreat. Of course we were aware of the fact — that another anniversary of the birth of our Savior had come around — & also, that it was impossible to pass it as in by gone days — but to "grin & bear it," was all we could do. Contentment, generally was one of the leading characteristics of our company — Some of the "Sons of Erin" — members of it — said they'd a "loiked" a "wee droph" of the "Crather".

We camped about 3.O.C. PM in the edge of Lexington. Lauderdale Co. Ala. My mess did their cooking, eating & sleeping in an old log stable — & this frail structure was a great protection, & while we could not have a table filled with choice viands — we could sit in the horse trough & eat buiscuit & pork. On the 26th at the usual hour, bid adieu to our humble habitation, & while the slow rain was falling through a dense fog, which seemed to be hesitating as if awaiting a breeze to waft it away — whipping the poor horses through the stiff mud — frequently rolling on the wheels, getting our clothing so badly besmeared that they would almost "stand alone.

Retreat Continued

Our stock being so near worn out — pulled out of the road about sunset & stopped for the night. On the morning of the 27th our march was continued regardless of the rain, & although the roads were as rough & mudy as ever — having heard of our near approach to the river, were stimulated by the thought, that fortune might again smile upon us in another delivery — & six miles from camp, we did cross the Tennessee river — not between "divided waters" as in the case of the ~~Egyptians~~ Isrealites, but upon a pontoon at Banebridge ferry & camped one mile from the crossing.

Recrossing of the Tenn. R

Our army all succeeded in crossing during the night. The river was pontooned above the shoals to prevent any hindrance from the enemy — but it did not prevent them from trying. Their gunboats from below, approached as near as possible — but their shells only made a splash in the water, a safe distance below. Having the river between us & the enemy, felt very much relieved — & we "high privates" could have enjoyed an extended rest — but our officers thought best to move on while we had such good "backing," & the principal portion of the 28th was consumed in marching.

Passed through Tuscumbia — a discription of which I gave when advancing — traveling on the Cherokee road three miles to Bear creek, before camping. For several subsequent days, we marched in a northwest direction near a branch of the Mobile & Ohio Railroad. Every stream of any importance had to be pontooned on account of high water. All the bridges having been previously burned by one army or the other, as this had been a point subject to raiding parties of both almost since the beginning of the war.

Tennessee Campaign

On the 29th passed through Barton station — a place of but little importance, except railroad business. On the 30th Feds having crossed the river — were reported near our rear — but not in sufficient force to do any damage. Our movements were very slow — because of rough, mudy roads & bad condition of stock. 31st Passed through & camped near Iuka Miss. The town & surrounding country looked very natural — but no chance to replenish our commissary — as in the fall of 1862 when we drove the Feds before us.

1865

Jany
Iuka Miss

On Sunday Jany 1st 1865 I wrote in my pocket memoranda as follows. "The fourth new year ushered in since my enlistment to battle for the south — & yet this cruel war is waged with increased bitterness, on the part of the enemy. The dark & gloomy clouds are gathering thick & fast, over the noblest cause that "ere" on earth was lost.

Tennessee Campaign

Dark & stormy as the clouds may seem — yet "me thinks" at times I can see a flickering light — to nerve & cause us to renew our pledges, & make one more grand effort to rid our beloved south of her tyranical oppressors." It was natural for us to have these gloomy forebodings, after having endured so many hardships — fought so many battles, & gained so little. But 'tis said, "while there is life, there is hope", & as I previously remarked, we could only hope on! fight on! & endure all — trusting the ballance to the one who rules all things. On the 2nd left Iuka, at sunrise, marching in the direction chosen at Tuscumbia — arriving at Burnsville 10- OC AM. twelve miles distant — where an order was given, to dismount & ship all the guns & ammunition chests, belonging to the corps — except one battery, & those thus relieved of their guns, to go down in the country where forage was plenty, & recruit themselves & horses.

Retreat Continued

As usual we were "elected" to remain, & were greatly displeased at our ill luck. However about 9 O.C. PM. our spirits were greatly lifted up, by receiving orders to do as the others had done. Accordingly we had a very early reveille on the morning of the 3rd — 3 oclock & were not long getting our guns to the depot. The guns & chests were soon dismounted & loaded on the cars — ready for shipment to Columbus Miss. We returned to camp as light as a "feather" — moving on with the rest of the column, in a Southern direction on the Russellville road, which lead us through a very swampy country — but having nothing but the running geer, pulled through with but little trouble. On the 4th we were greatly surprised, at hearing of the capture & burning of a large wagon train of ours, by a small force of yankee cavalry — twenty miles in our front.

This caused a great deal of uneasiness for the time — as we were unarmed & no Infantry with us. But the alarm proved to be a farce — as did another dispatch received over the "Grape vine" wire — announcing the death of Jeff. Davis.

This line of march, extended down the eastern tier of counties near the state border. The country at that time was thinly settled — some places very marshy — almost impassable — while other portions were poor & sandy, covered with pine timber. Forage for the horses was very scarce — sometimes entirely without. On the 7th passed through Smithville, Monroe. Co. Also passed through Athens on the 8th, a very small, unimportant place — where we took the road leading to Columbus.

Tennessee Campaign

On the 9th we had a very early reveille, & soon after moving out, rain commenced, making the roads very sloppy. Crossed the Buttahatchee river, which was very deep fording, & only a short time afterward became impassable by incessant rain.

The Buttahatchee River is a tributary of the Tombigbee River, previously mentioned by Sam. The river has had at least twenty-two different spellings. The river's official name and spelling was selected by The Board on Geographic Names in 1947 and is the same as Sam's spelling more than eighty years prior ("Buttahatchee").

Retreat Continued

The country was very flat & marshy some distance from the river — which had to be corduroyed with fence rails before we could get through. We did a great deal of kicking about having to turn into a pioneer corps — but it was that, or worse. Instead of going where we could "rusticate & recuperate", as we expected when leaving Burnsville, found the opposite — little to eat, & no rest. On the 10th although the weather was disagreeable, our burdens were greatly lightened up, by merging into a good country, which yet bore the marks of prosperity. We stopped late in the afternoon one mile from Columbus. On the 11th we had an early reveille, but didnot move out until 10. O.C. AM. & before starting, the Officers issued very stringent orders against straggling while passing through Town.

Retreat Ended

We managed to "get through" all together & crossed the Tombigbee river on a pontoon, camping one mile distant, in thick under brush — low marshy ground — swamp water to drink — & pine the principal wood, for cooking purposes. A great many thought, this a singular move, as the side from which we came was by far the best camping ground. Our Colonel — Williams — in charge of the artillery — was a little despotic — & the boys thought he only wanted to river between us & town — than "draw the reins", as tight as he pleased. At this time our company was considerably disorganized — or in other words, had the "blues".

Camp Near Columbus Miss

We had become accustomed to constant moving & seeing something new or different every day — which caused the monotony of a settled camp & become tiresome — especially, when "swamped". The day was spent in rambling around through the woods, near camp — or at night one could see us, seated around the mess fires, debating upon the "war question". It was rumored, the Infantry would soon be ordered to Meridian Miss — & from what we could gather from reading & observation — it seemed, the whole base of Military operations were upon the eve of a great change — & it was not surprising, under the circumstances — that we became restless — & began to wonder, what next?

Johnston Reinstated

On the 12th our camp was almost wild with joy — when news came that

Gen. Joseph E. Johnston had been reinstated, as commander in chief of the Army of Tennessee — Although considered rather "late in the day", to accomplish any great good — by the change — yet it was thought — "better late than never —" & all agreed that it would shed new light upon the Southern cause, — we also knew full well, by the broad smile that played upon the careworn countenances of the soldiers — that they were well pleased. We also realized, whatever he did, was the very best that could be done under the circumstances, & when an order was given by him, it emanated from a soul full of love for his fellow man & patriotism for the country of his adoption. On the 15th having received information on the previous evening, that our guns which were left at Burnsville, had arrived at the depot, on the opposite side of the river. The horses were soon harnessed, guns remounted & parked in camp. This was ~~the Sabbath day~~ Sunday & the most striking Sign by which we could determine its arrival — was the "Gutta perchas" promonading the streets, in their white cotton costumes, "donned" every Sunday morning.

Sam previously had noted seeing the white Sunday outfits of the slaves as the troops marched through the towns and past the plantations. According to the *Cassell Dictionary of Slang*, a "gutta-percha" is an aboriginal inhabitant of Victoria, Australia, so named for the prevalence of the gutta-percha tree (*Isonaudra Gutta*) in that region. Perhaps, Sam's classical education led him to apply the appellation for the Australian aborigines to Southern slaves (Green; "History of Victoria"; "Indigenous"; "Victoria").

The chief population of the City, seemed to be aristocratic, which put rather a "rough edge" on the troops. Most of them would sooner look through their windows, at the ragged, hungry soldier passing, than meet him on the street, & offer him a crumb.

Camp Near Columbus

For everything we obtained here, outside army supplies, we paid exhorbitant prices. The town seemed to be a general rendevous for "dead beats," mixed up with a superfluity of "Brassmounted" men — hunting a position in the ordinance, quartermaster, or commissary department. We soon settled down in a regular routine camp life, & passed several days in restive inactivity — occasionally visiting town — buying a paper, filled with wild rumors, such as the recognition of the south, by foreign powers — although not believed, kept up an excitement. Our company drew some clothing on the 18th — which was very much needed.

Furloughs Issued

It had become an established custom in the army, when not engaged in active sevice — to issue furloughs — & on the 21st our company drew, at the rate of one for every seven men for duty. I, as on all other similar occasions — drew a b_l-a-n-k. The news that reached us on the 24th made us believe that our rest was nearing an end. Sherman had commenced a return trip — as if to invade the two Carolina's. Two corps of Infantry Lee's & Cheatham's were sent from our army to meet him.

Moving Camp

On the 26th we moved camp to the opposite or east side of the Tombigbee river — also across the Luxulila, or Sleeping Terrapin. Luxulila was said to be the Indian name, While the name Sleeping Terrapin was American, & given because of its slow & crooked current. It was narrow & very deep. This camp was about four miles from Columbus & much better situated in regard to wood & water.

> **Columbus, Mississippi, known before its incorporation in 1821 as Possum Town, was a hospital town during the war. It was a destination for many of the wounded from the Battle of Shiloh, and thousands were buried there in Friendship Cemetery. On May 29, 1866, ladies from Columbus decorated both Union and Confederate graves, part of the founding of Memorial Day. Poet Francis Miles French commemorated the event with his poem *The Blue and the Grey*. The Tombigbee River borders the eastern edge of Columbus; the Luxapalila Creek bisects the town, separating East Columbus from Columbus ("Columbus").**

Camp Near Columbus

27th A companion & I — with permission, took a trip, out in the country, with a wagon on a private foraging expedition for the company. Found some very obliging openhearted citizens — while others were very penurious — but we were fortunate enough to find a good supply of sweetpotatoes — eggs & homespun socks — with which we returned to camp on the following day — These were great luxuries, as well as substantials to us.

On the 31st I was detailed as wheel driver to serve in place of one who received a furlough. I was very much displeased at the change — but was promised to be relieved at the close of one month. Our time was passed lounging around, & speculating about the future of the south.

February

My mess thinking the chances to remain for sometime, good — hauled up some hickory wood in the forenoon of 4th Feb. & was seated around a bright blazing fire, of the same — merrily chatting — when we were startled by the reception of an order at company head quarters, to move the battery down to the Tombigbee rive immedately, & load it on the Steamer Admiral. Then it was, I had to harness my first wheel team, since my enlistment in the Artillery. "You bet" — I did not like it — but my "likes & dislikes" were not consulted — To do as ordered, was my duty — if not my pleasure.

Several steamers have had the name Admiral. Sam may have been referring to the Admiral Farragut, a sternwheeler built in Beardstown, Illinois, in 1864. The machinery for this packet came from Key West No. 2. In 1871, it was dismantled and the engines were transferred to the Mary E. Poe (Way, Jr. 6).

Leaving Columbus

By sunset our outfit was loaded. All the artillery had orders to leave Columbus. Our battallion was all shipped on the Admiral. We were somewhat mystified, in regard to the move — & puzzled as to our future destination — but some how — we heard it whispered — that we were going to Northcarolina, where Gen. Johnston was massing his forces, to check Sherman, & save the helpless people, from another "torch light" procession. About 10 O.C. AM on the 5th we started upon our unknown voyage — or atleast not known to a private soldier —

We bid adieu to Columbus & were soon wending our way down the crooked current of the Tombigbee — but I cannot say our trip was a pleasant one. Before drawing in the anchor, Gen. Elza & Staff came on board — & you know it required a "heap" more room for an officer than a private — & the consequence was, we were crowded up in so small a space as to render our position very uncomfortable —especially when traveling all night when it was raining & boat leaking.

Leaving Columbus

However by drawing ourselves up in as small a "knot" as possible, in a half reclining position, "nodded" away the night as best we could — arriving at Demopolis Ala 10- O.C. AM on the 6th & having previously ascertained, the course traveled by the troops would take them up the Alabama river by way of Selma, I was granted a three days leave of absence to visit my Brother Caldwell, who was stopping in the country near the Demopolis & Selma railroad, which connected these two points. I debarked with a light step, & in a few moments was at the depot — but was greatly "set back," when informed that there was a reck on my contemplated route, which would occasion a delay until the next evening. Having remained here on parole, after the surrender of Vicksburg, was well acquainted with the Town, & found pleasure in noting the change which had taken place in our absence, until late in the afternoon of the 7th when the conductor signaled the engineer to pull out; & when we had traveled twenty five or thirty miles I dismounted at Faunsdale station & after a tiresome walk of one & half miles through the mud & darkness, was ushered into the large & handsome residence of Charles. Walker — a wealthy old planter — where I found my Brother, who I had not seen for several months, comfortably ensconsed, with all the luxuries of a southern home before the war.

Visiting Caldwell

It is needless to say, that the two subsequent days were passed as pleasantly as heart could wish. The unlimited supply of "grub" — & colored waiters to "stick it under your nose"; a nice bed to to sleep in, & a carriage ride, was sufficient to make me wish that I had an unlimited pass — without taking into consideration the shock, my modesty, received, when the parlor door was thrown open, & I invited with my old dingy soldier clothes, to take a seat upon the sofa, & listen to the sweet vocal & instrumental music made by two charming young ladies, daughters of the noble Host & Hostess.

Charles Walkers

"Twas delightful to watch their nimble fingers, passing from key to key over the piano, & calculated to cause one to rejoice that they had enlisted to defend such noble creatures.

Selma Ala

It was a happy meeting — a welcome sojourn — but an unpleasant seperation — on the morning of the 10th when I grasped the one hand of my brother, in an affectionate farewell — extended the hand of friendship to my newly — but lasting acquaintences, thanking them for their kindness & hospitality — receiving their blessings in return — left for Uniontown to take the cars for Selma. Arrived 2 O.C. PM. The boat upon which I left the battallion, had passed up the river — but came up with several of the company boys, who had also received passes at Demopolis to visit friends who cared for them while on parole. At 5 PM we took passage on the steamer Henry King, for Montgomery Ala.

The Henry J. King was a wooden-hulled sternwheeler built in New Albany, Indiana, in 1856. It was sent to Mobile, Alabama, and was registered to the Confederacy in 1861 (Way, Jr. 212).

From Selma to Montgomery

After a good nights rest, awoke at daylight on the morning of the 11th to find that I was yet moving gently up the smooth current of the Alabama river, several miles from our starting point — arriving at Montgomery 1- OC. PM. Remained over night at the Way side Home, where we were bedded & fed gratis. The rations were cornbread & poor beef in small "doses". Montgomery, as it appeared then, was a nice City & pleasantly situated. On the following day Sunday took the cars for Columbus Ga. the command having gone in that direction. The long train was crowded with citizens & soldiers — So I with others, were compelled to ride on top. It was a great sight to behold the immense crowds of citizens collected at the crossroads & stations, to witness our passing, greeting us with songs, cheers, flying handkerchiefs, smiles & kind words — which were echoed back from the passengers. And I tell you the appearance of so many good looking young ladies —made me feel like I could jump off & stay awhile.

From Montgomery Ala. to Columbus Ga

Arrived at Columbus, situated on the Chatahoochee river & ninety eight miles from Montgomery 5 O.C. PM, but not in time to overtake the company, they having left a few hours in advance. Here I met a Mr Johnson formerly a resident of St Louis Mo — who after finding out my native state — kindly invited me to accompany him to his home, & spend the night. The bed was so good, I slept like a "log" — & didnot wake in time to meet the train due at 6 O.C. AM. Although disappointed, I spent the day very pleasantly looking over the town — besides having an opportunity of sharing the Hosts hospitality another night.

From Columbus to Macon Ga

On the 14th I was at the depot on time & took the cars for Macon Ga. arriving at 2. O.C. PM to find the company, yet a day in advance. I had come up with some of the company boys — & we were all perplexed — but could not leave until the arrival of another train — & to pass off the time & have some amusement — attended the theater at night — which wore off all the "blues" for a week. On the following morning our train was on time & we boarded it for Miledgeville, at that time capital of the state.

In 1803, Governor John Milledge was honored with the establishment of a town named for him. The following year, Milledgeville became the fourth capitol of Georgia. The young town prospered, becoming the political and social center of antebellum Georgia. On January 19, 1861, a great celebration occurred on Milledgeville's statehouse square in response to the news that Georgia had joined the Confederate States of America; three years later the town lay in ruins. Sherman's army had ransacked the statehouse, destroyed the state arsenal, burned the penitentiary, depot, and Oconee bridge, and destroyed the cotton plantations. During reconstruction, the state capitol was relocated to Atlanta ("Milledgeville").

We arrived at the station bearing the same name — two miles from the City 11- O.C. AM. When we dismounted, found some of the boys belonging to the company with a wagon who informed us the command had left the previous day by highway, in the direction of Mayfield, then the terminus of a railroad leading to Augusta Ga.

Miledgeville to Mayfield

We started on foot to shorten the space between us as fast as possible — after we had traveled sixteen miles — night came upon us, & being so very dark & roads mudy — we begged the privilege of an old gentleman to sleep on the floor, in front of the fire place. This revived us very much & before day light on the 16th, were again on the "pad", & stimulated by hearing of the company camping — on the night previous — only four miles in our advance — increased the length & rapidity of our steps — & at

10 O.C. AM, overtook the boys, moving along very slow, the roads being in bad condition. I was almost as well pleased at the meeting, as the seperation of a few days past. Camped at sundown four miles from Mayfield station. We had an early reveille on the 17th breaking camp at daylight, & moving in the direction of Mayfield station — By 10- O.C. AM we had everything loaded on the cars & started for Augusta, distant sixty three miles.

Augusta

We steamed into the depot about sunset — but owing to some unaccountable delay, it was 9 oclock in the night before orders were given us to unload — in consequence of which we were compelled to remain at the depot — passing a rough night. On the 18th after "going down", in our haversacks, for a very small allowance of corndodge & blue beef for breakfast — harnessed up & moved out at 7 AM — passing through the City — crossing the Savannah river upon a stationary bridge — traveling out into South Carolina Seven miles — camping near Cherokee Pond on the Columbia plank road — where we were ordered to remain, until the baggage wagons arrived which had been sent by highway, from Columbus Ga — transportation being scarce when the battery was shipped from that point. The surrounding country was very poor — & but few citizens remaining — many having left, because the had no money — no food & no means of raising it. In some localities rice was cultivated on a limited scale.

Cherokee Pond SC

This was a very lonely appearing camp — only a few residences of the most ordinary construction in view, & a barren sandy plane, made us think that starvation "station", was not very far in advance of that place — & being badly in need of clothing, caused us to act a little stubborn — when late in the afternoon of the 21st we received orders to draw five days traveling rations — & prepare for moving on the following morning.

A great many of the troops had been furnished clothing — & by some means our company had been overlooked. Feeling the keen insult — which we imagined, had been intentionally offered — & knowing it to be without a cause — Our Captain resolved not to turn a wheel until our wants were supplied. Suffice to say — the clothing was soon forthcoming — & about dark on the evening of the 22nd we pulled out on the Chapelbridge road — to overtake the command — which had preceded us several hours.

Beginning of the March through South Carolina

The sky was covered over with a heavy cloud — making the night so dark, we were forced to camp at 11. O.C PM. And in our effort to overtake the army — had an early reveille on the 23rd traveling as briskly as possible. The men & stock becoming very much wearied, after marching twenty three miles — stopped again without gaining sight of the main army. The guns were parked where the mud was almost knee deep — which displeased the boys very much, & in order to express their indignation called it camp "Toby" — which was the nickname of our Captain — On the following morning early, we pulled out in the rain, which had commenced the previous evening. We caught the army at Saluda river — which we crossed at Higgin's ferry — in a very shackling flat boat 11- OC. PM. camping one mile distant, as wet & mudy as "drowned rats" — having marched in the rain all day. After making an "impression" of short duration — upon the ground, in an endeavor to sleep a little — our march was continued on the Newberry road.

March Through S.C

Passed through Newberry, situated in the district bearing the same name. The town had several hundred population — but was constructed on a very antique style — & presented the appearance of retrograding. South Carolina was divided into districts, instead of counties. Our course extended northeast. Found camp about 3. O.C. PM in an old field — also found Sand as deep as the mud was a few nights previous. On the morning of the 26th our hearts were made glad, by the appearance of the sun, soon after leaving camp. "His" sparkling rays as they came beaming through the heavy dew drops hanging from the trees — caused gleams of joy to flash across the hardy countenance of the trooper — as he plodded along through the mud — hoping for better roads. On the 27th our march was continued in a northeast direction. We were greatly buoyed up by the cool breeze, & although our route lead us through a hilly country — yet the marks of prosperity could be seen on every hand — whle the patriotism of the people was shown in the hospitality, toward those who volunteered to defend their state, against the encroachments of an inveterate enemy. In many places they presented us with — bacon, potatoes, bread, molasses, butter & milk. I assure you the interval between such "treats" had been so long — their liberality was highly appreciated, by the soldiers, & caused us to place South Carolina upon an equality with all others on free donations. About 2 O.C. PM we pulled to one side of the road to camp, & had scarcely unharnessed, when an order was received, to cross the Ennerree river, a short distance in our front — & it was said the battery which arrived first, would cross first — which caused a race between the different artillery companies, & our battery came out ahead — but the boat was pronounced unsafe by Gen. Cheatham — for the crossing of artillery.

The Enoree River, a shallow, narrow river flowing through Sumter National Forest in South Carolina, was named by the Cherokee Indians. Their word, "river of muscadines," referred to the wild, green grape vine that grew profusely among the ash, sycamore, and hickory trees, providing ideal habitat for red-shouldered hawks, blue herons, barred owls, mink, muskrat, and otter. The river teems with catfish, bream, and redeye bass ("Enoree River Canoe"; "Enoree River Canoe Trail").

We parked the guns on the river bank, to await the construction of another. But I didnot admire the guard duty which followed that night, especially when raining all the time. About 10. O.C. PM. while the Infantry were crossing — the old rickety flat sank in the middle of the river — but luckily the occupants all escaped with their lives, except one. The river at this place was very swift & greatly swollen by rain. All the beef cattle & loose horses with the army — were driven in & made swim across — & assisting in making them take water, proved to be great sport & pass time for us.

Water levels on the Enoree River depend on the time of year and the amount of rainfall. Heavy rains in early spring create brisk currents and, although today the river is significantly important for recreational use, at flood stage, it is considered unsafe and boating is not recommended ("Enoree River Canoe").

March 1st

The construction of a rude flat was pronounced complete, & about 1- O.C. PM on March 1st was launched, & we were ordered to make ready for crossing — but didnot get all the battery over until midnight. Our passage was very difficult as well as dangerous. It was raining & very dark — rendering our crossing impossible — had not our way been lighted by large log fires on both banks.

Our camp one miles from the river, was reached with great difficulty — the guns sticking in the mud axle deep on several occasions. After "steaming" ourselves in a very short nap upon the cold wet ground, roused up at daylight on the 2nd to repeat the mud "measuring" business & again try our strength rolling on the wheels. Our days march had been very hard — but our drooping spirits were greatly revived, when arriving in camp, by drawing four days rations of bacon & flour. This happened so seldom, it was worthy of note.

On the 3rd we passed through the Town of Union, arriving at Swerves ferry on Broad river about noon. The crossing was very slow & dangerous, the boat being very old & held to its place by means of a guy rope, extending from one bank to the other. The boats at these crossings had been used as neighborhood facilities, during high water — most of the streams were fordable in ~~dry weather~~ ordinary Seasons.

March Through S. C.

I had not fully recovered from my shock at Grenada Miss — & being no swimmer, endeavored to select the lightest load to cross with, & the consequence was, I waited until after dark, & the last trip was being made for the company — then had to cross with a full load & the boat within an inch of dipping water all the way — I imagined the distance four times as great as it was — I carried my heart in my mouth — while my hair stood on end — But if the boat had capsized I made up my mind to cling to one of the horses & let him pull me out. I tell you, I felt more than thankful, when my feet again struck "terrifirma." On the 4th our camp was pitched within five miles of Chesterville South Carolina. On the 5th we moved camp to within one mile of town — which was then the terminal point of the Richmond & Danville railroad — It being the intention to take shipping here as soon as transportation could be procured.

Chesterville S. C.

We had been subjected to a great deal of exposure on this march — scarcely a day passing — without some rain, & it was not uncommon to continue all day & night, making the roads very disagreeable, & so many rivers to cross — the rude contrivances prepared for our passage — the time for our company to be ferried over, was generally after night — it was marvelous that we escaped without loss.

North Carolina Expedition

And it is not surprising, when it was announced that we would remain in camp on the 6th, & the early morning hours were lighted up, with the sparkling rays of the sun, & not a cloud appearing between Heaven & earth, to cast a shadow during the day — that I would give vent to my feelings in the following manner. "It makes my soul rejoice, to behold the Sun in his Heavenly home — shedding his refulgent beams from a cloudless sky — after being hidden so long, to dispell the gloom, which has been overshadowing the earth & dry up the rain, which has fallen in his secrecy. The little birds are singing songs of praise — the chickens have perched themselves upon the fence, spreading their wings as if to dry — the old farm dog has stretched himself upon the grass, breathing lazily — the negroes move around over the plantation with a lighter tread — whistling & singing melodies — on which they have remained silent for some time, & there were none other beings in all nature, who could be more happy than the soldiers — while basking in the beautiful light — stretching their wearied limbs upon a blanket, in quiet rest — or while they softly slumber — living in dreams of long ago — enjoying the blessed sunshine in the most comprehensive form of the expression. Oh! how beautiful & cheering is coming spring, in the dearly loved Sunny South.

Charlotte N C.

Our camp was situated a short distance in front of an Old Planters residence — the surroundings of which, suggested a great portion of the subjects from which I wrote. On the 8th having orders to move, loaded the guns on the cars; while raining — but cars being scarce, had to leave the horses & baggage wagons behind. A short time after dark, arrived at Charlotte N.C. fifty five miles distant.

The railroad was in bad condition, necessitating slow time. About 10 O.C. AM on the 9th pulled out — the train moving very slow, giving us ample time to survey the poor piney woods, through which we passed — which at that time was anything but attractive.

Salsburg N.C

Arrived at Salsburg N.C. 5. O.C. PM — unloading the guns to wait the coming of the horses. Our army was considerably recruited here by the return of exchanged prisoners. Among them were some of our old company (Landis battery) who refused paroles at Vicksburg. That was a sad mistake of theirs — which they were frank to confess upon the return. True they had not been exposed in battle — yet the tortures through which they had passed in the miserable dens — to face death upon the battle field, would have been far more preferable & honorable.

N C Expedition

On the 11th our horses having arrived, hooked on to the guns & moved out to camp two miles — to remain until cars could be furnished, to transport us farther on toward the seat of war. While in camp & at the depot we had some nice weather — but the sign which had been indicative — on former occasion — was again a true forteller on the morning of the 15th when we received orders to load the guns on the cars while raining.

Greensboro N C

About 2. O.C PM the signal was given to pull out & the men were compelled to ride on a flat car in the rain — 10. PM halted at Greensboro N.C. for the night. The following morning our uncomfortable trip was resumed — as on the previous day, attended with the usual amount of "dampness.' Soon after starting we procured a tent, which we managed by the "skin of our teeth" to pitch while the train was in motion. About twenty of us piled into it & amused ourselves telling yarns — singing etc etc, until far into the night — when we melted down into a huge heap & slept until day light.

Raleigh N C

Arrived at Raleigh in the early forenoon of the 17th —but didnot remain but a short time, receiving orders to pass on to Smithfield Station, twenty five miles distant — at which place we pulled up — 3 O.C. PM — unloading the guns & rolling them by hand out into the piney woods, a short distance from the depot — to await the arrival of the horses, which had been traveling by highway from Salisburg.

Smithfield Station

The occasional booming of cannon was heard about eleven miles distant — where our line of battle was established, on the road leading to Wilmington N.C. All reports received from the front were favorable to our side — & prospects of an engagement at an early date seemed probable — but the position in which our company was placed appeared rather awkward as well — as dangerous — when our means of moving were considered.

N C Expedition

We were again near our beloved Gen. Joseph. E. Johnston — who had gathered up the fragments of the Army of Tennessee — to make one desperate, though feeble effort, to check the invasion of Sherman's overwhelming force. Like chickens flying to their mothers wings to avoid the keen eye of the hawk — we always felt perfectly composed when under the Guardianship of our noble Johnston.

We knew his vigil never ceased, & his commands were dictated, by a pure heart — & a soul full of love for his fellow man. About noon on the 18th we received an order from Gen. Beauregard to return to Raleigh — not having horses — were too much exposed to raiding parties of the enemy.

Return to Raleigh

A short time after dark our guns were loaded, & I almost imagined the cars took wings & flew back to Raleigh — they rocked from side to side & the guns rolled back & forth — still the engineer went on in his mad career — but all we could do, was to crawl under the carriages between the wheels, in as small space as possible & hold on for dear life. The miles were counted by the minutes — & when we checked up at our destination I heaved a long sigh of relief — & thanked my maker for the miraculous deliverance. This was all caused by one of the engineer's mad freaks — he became angry at having to make an extra trip — after his usual days work was done. On the following day our guns were unloaded & parked near the depot.

Some fighting reported near Smithfield. The city of Raleigh was beautifully situated & handsomely constructed — but the citizens generally bore rather a selfish bigoted appearance. They turned their backs, instead of receiving us with open arms. But when we think how often they had been called upon to extend their generosity — & how many of their noble sons had offered themselves as martyrs upon the altar of their beloved country — we cannot wonder that they didnot meet us with a smiles & extended hand. This being ~~the Sabbath~~ Sunday day attended church at night. We remained at this place for several days — during which time there was but little change in affairs — military.

N C Expedition

The enemy made several attacks upon our front — but were repulsed every time. All that Johnston could do, with his diminutive forces — was to resent an attack, when offered — & prevent a wholesale invasion, & maybe burning, by Shermans troops. Our horses had not yet arrived on the 21st & Gen. Beauregard ordered us to return to Hillsborough N. C. by way of the same railroad we traveled going up. On the forenoon of the 23rd the guns were loaded preparatory to moving — but owing to some unaccountable delay didnot leave until 2. O.C. PM. This sudden retrograde movement was rather unexpected, & caused us to wonder what it all meant.

Hillsborough N C.

Arrived at Hillsborough soon after dark — unload the guns & parked them near the depot. In the evening of the following day our horses arrived from Salisbury, but too late to move out. Early in the morning of the 25th hitched up & pulled out to camp one mile north of town; where we found a pleasant situation, & an abundance of good wood & water near at hand.

We were camped there as reserve artillery. Hillsborough at that time, was a nice little City & county seat of Orange County.

> **Hillsborough, North Carolina, was established by William Churton in 1754. Although originally called Orange, the town was renamed Hillsborough in 1766 to honor William Hill, the Earl of Hillsborough. Built on four hundred acres, at the site where the Great Indian Trading Path crossed the Eno River, Hillsborough soon became the colonial capitol of North Carolina. The North Carolina Constitutional Convention was held here in the late 1700s; at this event the Bill of Rights became an official part of the United States Constitution. Prior, the Trading Path connected Indian tribes in the area, and later served commercial enterprise between the James River colonial settlements and the Catawba and Cherokee tribes in the Carolinas, Tennessee, and Georgia ("North Carolina"; "Trading Path"; "Welcome to Hillsborough").**

26th was Sunday again, & after taking a bath & shave — donning a clean cotton shirt, & brushing the mud off my uniform — attended servises at the Episcopal Church. The singing by the choir was excellent — but the manner of conducting the servises, was so different from anything I had previously seen, proved very interesting as well as instructive, & I returned to quarters feeling well recompensed for attending.

Saterwhites Death

The 29th was a very sad day in our company. One of our comrads lay cold in death — true his death was not altogether unexpected — no matter, the announcement of a death, creates a sensation peculiar in its effects. As the old adage, runs — "Eat, drink & be merry, for tomorrow you may die."

N C Expedition

To day we may be enjoying good health — but tomorrow placed beneath the cold, cold, sod. Early in the morning, my attention was attracted to one of the company, William Saterwhite, groaning with severe pain, from which he had been a sufferer more or less — for several years — but the last pain had struck him, though he struggled & reached out his feeble hands, as if grasping for a few more moments — yet despite his efforts — was soon wrapped in the strong arms of death — the last sad moan soon died away — he fell asleep, to awake no more to the troubles of this world. He died without a relative to drop a tear beside his humble couch — but not without friends. He was a believer of the Episcopal doctrine, & the congregation at that place honored him with a burial in their cemetery.

Chapelhill N C

On the 28th I went out in the country with one of the company teamsters after forage — & there wasn't anything that could have pleased me better. Our route lead through Chapelhill — only a few miles from camp — a town of eighthundred inhabitants, pleasantly ~~situated~~ situated upon high rolling ground, & near by it was the University of of North Carolina, which was a model structure, & far famed for its educational facilities.

> **The University of North Carolina at Chapel Hill was chartered by the General Assembly in 1789, the same year George Washington became president of the United States of America. During the Civil War, many colleges and universities closed, but this university remained open ("Carolina — A Brief History").**

One mile from town we enjoyed the hospitality of Mr Purefoy for the night. In the forenoon of the next day we found some corn at Dr. Smith's — & had a very lengthy parlez, with him & his sister — who by the way was an old maid — She entered a plea of scarcty, starvation etc etc — at times was very abusive — but we had foraged in scarce countries before — the wagon was filled & we returned to camp. The majority of the country was poor & but little surplus raised. In fact the soil was not adapted to corn & oats.

N. C. Expedition

Our camp was situated under the outspread branches of some ancient forest oaks — ~~of~~ which we appropriated a portion of for fuel —

that while young, sheltered from the burning rays of a summers Sun — the ranks of the British army, in the year 1781. I saw the remnants of a small log cabin in the suburbs of Hillsborough — in which the old citizens said Cornwallis had his headquarters, at that time.

This is quite an ancient town — although not noted for the area it covers, or the number of inhabitants — yet the events which transpired in the town & vacinity — made it renowned.

Camp Near Hillsborough

On the 31st had inspection by Col. — once Lieut Gen Pemberton. He had been greatly reduced in rank since the surrender of Vicksburg — but not as much as he deserved. He should have been reduced to "High-private" in the rear rank. Pemberton — "had been" — but he wasn't "in it," then — "small potatoes & few in a hill". He had withered like a leaf — but not before he should.

April 1st

The 1st day of April was very beautiful — the sun shone forth from a cloudless sky, & all nature seemed to be dressed in her brightest robe — it was hard that one could not enjoy freedom, as the birds of the air. The 2nd was Sunday & feeling it my duty to honor it in some manner went to church — which was largely attended by ladies & Soldiers. We spent some time at this camp as reserve artillery — and if there ever was such a thing as happiness in camp life — we certainly had some of it here — plenty of good rations — wood — water, & no duty to perform except guard duty for the company. We could occasionally get out in the country for a "square" meal — butter & milk. Sunday again came on the 9th & in the forenoon I attended church. The text from which the minister preached was — "Remember now thy Creator in the days of thy youth." His sermon was very impressive — & I realized that I was one who had failed to comply with that command. I spent the afternoon in promonading the streets, & had the pleasure of seeing some goodlooking young ladies.

N C Expedition

The peace & quietude of our camp was suddenly disturbed, about 3. O.C. pM. by receiving orders to move immediately — Our camp had been so pleasant — was almost like home — & an order to leave on such short notice, was a great surprise. Started 4 PM on the Greensboro road — our wagons being out after forage — were compelled to leave without rations or cooking utensils. It seems that our Officers were in a kind of quandary — or some misunderstanding in regard to moving — as we were only five miles from Hillsborough, when we bivuoaced, 11. O.C. PM. Soon after camping we were agreeably surprised by receiving orders to return to the place we left. The news was received with shouts of joy, & on the following evening were comfortably ensconsed in our old quarters — after having been without rations for twenty four hours. To say we were pleased by having to return, is enough. The boys who had gathered in groups, passing off the time in pleasant conversation — was an expression of their acquiesence in the turn of our private affairs. But as I have previously remarked — for every step forward there were always two backward, & every pleasure a sad disapointment — especially so with a Confederate Soldier.

Hillsborough
Gen Lee Surrendered Apr 9

Instead of peace & tranquility continuing to reign supreme — the camp was soon all agog — & the wildest excitement prevailed, hearing of the defeat of Gen. Lee's army, & surrender of Gen. Gordons force five thousand strong.

> **Gen. John Brown Gordon, a lawyer and coal mine superintendent prior to the war, entered the C.S.A. as colonel of the 6th Alabama. Although he has been mistakenly considered a lieutenant general as of 1865, he finished the war as a major general. He served at Antietam, Chancellorsville, Gettysburg, the Wilderness, and Spotsylvania. General Gordon's wife, Fanny Haralson Gordon, left their children with his mother so that she might be General Gordon's companion throughout all of his campaigns. Gen. Jubal Early "was once heard to wish to God that the Federals would capture her" (Boatner III 348-9).**

In fact Lee's whole command had surrendered to Grant on the 9th Inst. but the news was kept from us. As we imagined at that time — the dark clouds of Anarchy, despotism, dictatorship & tyrany, seemed to be hanging over the south — her advocates, by a slender thread & to make an open confession, I was feeling very despondent — when contemplating the critical position in which we were placed — we were trembling upon the very brink of destruction — our beloved nation was invaded to its very center — & stood gasping ~~ready~~ as if to receive the awful deluge, which seemed ready to complete its destruction. But despite the gloomy forebodings, we yet lingered upon the verge hoping for a "Moses". On the 13th we had reveille at daylight, & as usual moved in the rain.

N C Expedition

While passing through Hillsborough — the question was frequently asked us by the ladies, who had knotted in groups upon the balconies & portico's. If we were going to leave them to the mercy of the yankees? We hung our heads in sadness — answering in an almost inaudable tone — We can't help it. God bless the noble ladies! They were always first to cheer us on to victory — & last to dispair. On the following day our march was continued — crossing Haw river & passing over some good country. The citizens were all very much frightened, as well as surprised at our retrograde movement — who seemed to entertain the most inveterate hate — for the yankees — as they termed them — & hearing of their depredations in other quarters, thought they would soon be subjected to a similar fate.

On the March to Deep River

On Sunday our march also extended through a good farming comminity — & well improved — & by way of a change got my dinner at a farm house. Passed through New Salem, Guilford County N.C. — Camping 4. O.C. PM near Union Factory on Deep river. Early on the morning of the 17th after crossing Deep river — & we had gone about five miles, when ordered to return to the river & go into camp.

The Federal cavalry were reported as having the crossings of Yadkin river twenty miles in our front heavily guarded, & Sherman only ten miles in rear & advancing slowly. This was a very precarious situation, & calculated to cause us to think, the time of surrender, was not far distant. We remained in the bluffs which fringed Deep river several days — the time seemed to drag Slowly by — it was an hour of great expectancy — all kinds of rumors flooded the camp — there was but little discipline among the troops — deserting from some portions of the Army was of nightly occurrence. Occasionally the boys would almost go wild, over the rumor, that England & France had declared war against the Federal government.

1865 Lincoln Assassinated Apr 19 – 1865

On the 19th News reached us of the attempted assassination of Lincoln & Seward at the Ford Theater in Washington city — by Booth, & the wildest enthusiasm followed — hats were thrown, time & again in the air — the deafening shouts — which made the woods ring, reverberating from bluff to bluff — & ~~val~~ valley to valley — dying away on the still waters of Deep river — made one almost believe the south had gained her independence. Booth was a Virginian — & as many others — aggravated by the manner in which his relatives & friends had been treated by the Lincoln government — selected these two as victims. When he committed the deed — leaping from the stage — cried out! Virginia! Revenged!! Sic Semper Tyrannus!!

In *Manhunt*, James L. Swanson wrote that Booth "thrust his bloody dagger triumphantly into the air" and shouted, "Sic semper tyrannis" (the state motto of Virginia). "Thus always to tyrants. The South is avenged" (48).

This occurrence — although late in the "day" had a tendency to buoy us up. We knew it would create a great confusion all over the north — & we hoped while this state of affairs existed, the people would become divided — & give us another chance for victory. On the 20th we became aware, there was something of great importance, ~~being~~ under advisement — as our Officers & the Federals were in consultation under a flag of truce. About 10- O.C. AM Our company was assembled to listen to the reading of an order from Gen Hardee — temporary in command of the Army — in which he stated that terms of surrender had already been agreed upon — & both armies were to remain in their present positions until further orders. This only confirmed in my mind — that upon which I had long since become convinced — I felt confident, unless, something appeared in the form of a miracle — the Confederacy was doomed to wear the conquerors yoke.

'Tis said while there is life there is hope & upon this declaration I based the following — and to show with what zeal I as others clung to the cause we loved so dearly, I repeat my writings upon the occasion. In the darkest hour, there is yet some hope — however thick the gloom ~~may be~~ appears — there may be a light, that will save our way worn ship — that has been tossed upon the rugged waves of the sea of war — a light that will enable her to reach the harbor of Independence safely — & feast upon sweet liberty — for which some of the best & bravest sons of the South have poured out their warm hearts blood.

To wait as patiently as possible, was all we could do & in order to "kill" the time as fast & agreeable as could be — I frequently went fishing on Deep river.

Epilogue

Sam's last days as a private in the Confederate States Army were spent on the banks of Deep River in North Carolina. On April 14, 1865, Abraham Lincoln was assassinated. By April 16, the news had reached Sam's unit, and by April 20, Sam was aware the commanding generals were meeting under a flag of truce. The Confederate generals still in the field would soon follow Lee's action, and the war would officially end. On one level, it is clear Sam knew there was no hope. Yet, on another level, all of the passion Sam had brought to the cause still burned within his heart.

Caldwell wrote in his diary that when Sam was released from the army, sometime in mid-May, he and two friends came to the Walker plantation to get Caldwell, and the four made preparations for the long journey home. Caldwell confessed he was glad the war was ended, but sorry for the humiliation of the South. Leaving about the middle of May, the young men planned to ride the train to Memphis, but because in places the tracks had been destroyed, they had to walk part of the way. Near Memphis, they were stopped by federal pickets and forced to show their papers before being allowed to pass.

When they reached Memphis, the young men were invited to a large unfurnished church, where they were fed well, but they were required to get a permit from the provost marshall to wear their Confederate uniforms on the streets. Before they left Memphis three days later, the ladies of the church had given them each a set of summer clothing. Although there is no information as to who furnished their transportation on a steamboat from Memphis to St. Louis, Caldwell does mention their onboard discussions about the unsettled conditions in Missouri, and all of them decided to toss their Confederate uniforms into the Mississippi River.

At St. Louis, the four went to find Sam Kennard, who had been a lieutenant in their battery. They found the Kennard Carpet Company, but Sam was away from the city. His father invited the young men to his home for dinner and helped them make arrangements for traveling the rest of the way.

An army friend in St. Louis gave Sam ten dollars, and one of

Caldwell's friends arranged credit for their trip on the steamboat to Atchison, Kansas, where their parents now lived. During the war years, many residents of northwest Missouri had been forced to leave their homes and seek haven in places more favorable to their beliefs. Many Union supporters had moved their homes and businesses to Elwood, Kansas, and many of the pro-southern families had taken residence in Atchison, Kansas. Atchison was one of about twenty pro-slavery towns that had emerged along the Missouri River following the Kansas-Nebraska Act of 1854. This small river town had been named for a pro-slavery U.S. Senator from Missouri, David Rice Atchison, in the hope his name would command political influence. There is no information as to how long J. C. Dunlap III and his family remained there, but at some point they all returned to the DeKalb area.

On January 22, 1866, Sam's brother, James Wallace, who had been named for the famed Scottish warrior William Wallace, succumbed to the heart ailment that had troubled him through the early months of the war. He was buried in the tiny cemetery on the Dunlap farm, where his great-grandfather, mother, and step-mother Polly had been laid to rest some years earlier. His brother Alvan had died in 1845, just two and one-half weeks after his mother. He was six-years-old. A fragile marble spire stands yet today, marked with inscriptions for J. C. III's wives Patsy, Polly, Sallie, and M.G. (Mahala) and sons Alvan M. and James W. They are still legible, despite the passage of well more than a century since the last one was buried there.

The December following Wallace's death, Sam's brother Caldwell married Geneva "Jennie" Hurst, and a year later, Sam married Nancy I. Brown, a daughter of Dave and Margaret Hill Brown who lived on the farm adjoining J. C.'s. Both Sam and his brother returned to farming when they came home from the war. By 1876, Sam was farming and raising stock in Township 55 North, Range 35 West, Section 6 of southern Buchanan County. Caldwell and Sam's dad were farming near each other in Township 55, Range 36.

Within a year of their marriages, both brothers began raising families. Caldwell had five sons and five daughters between 1868 and 1889. Sam had four sons and two daughters between 1869 and 1879. The DeKalb Christian Church membership records indicate the brothers were members. Caldwell's admission record is incomplete, but he and his wife maintained memberships until death removed them from the rolls. Sam and his wife both came into the church by letter from Old Union Church on September 9, 1910, and they also remained members until their deaths.

According to Charles Spencer, who retains the abstract (the land record) for the fifty acres Sam farmed, the land can be traced back to William Harrington who obtained the land on June 12, 1843. Harrington sold to George W. Jenkins in 1853 for $4,000. Jenkins sold to James A. Matney in 1871 for $24.21. The Civil War had great economic impact on many parts of the United States, including northwest Missouri. Matney sold the land back to George W. Jenkins in 1871 for $75.00. Jenkins sold to James Thomas and John F. Tyler in 1875 for $175.00. Thomas and Tyler sold to B. J. Woodson in 1876 for $525.00. Woodson sold to James Sampson March 25, 1876 for $1,250.00 and James and Mary Sampson sold to Samuel B. Dunlap January 25, 1881, for $1,600.00. Four and one-half weeks after Sam's death, the land was transferred on February 8, 1932, to his wife Nannie and some of their children. (It is unclear as to why the 1876 plat for Township 55, Range 35, Section 6 names Sam B. Dunlap, rather than James and Mary Sampson.)

On July 29, 1886, Sam's father, James III, handwrote his last will and testament, leaving all of his "real estate to wit North End, (containing (70) seventy acres) of West half of South West Quarter of Section (16) sixteen, Township fifty five (55) range thirty six (36) and the South East Quarter of Section seventeen (17), Township fifty five (55) in Range thirty six (36) in Bloomington Township Buchanan County Missouri" to his two sons, Samuel B. and Robert C. Dunlap. He also left all of his "personal property, Stock, Money, Notes, and household and kitchen furniture" to his sons, except for twenty dollars, which he bequeathed to his daughter, Sarah Isabell Jones and her husband A. D. Jones. James III died July 13, 1894, and was buried in the family cemetery where four wives and two sons preceded him. It is not known when his fifth wife died and where she was buried. Sam's inheritance increased his land holdings to one hundred twenty acres in Section 6 (Archives).

The similarities of brothers less than two years apart in age, growing up and attending school together in rural northwest Missouri, serving much of their time in the same unit in the Missouri State Guard and later the Confederate army, returning from war together, marrying, farming, and raising families in close proximity contrast with two known differences:

Caldwell was blonde with piercing blue eyes; Sam had brown hair and dark eyes.

One was succinct and terse; the other was considerably more verbal.

A comparison of Caldwell's writing style with Sam's reveals a few similarities, but several noteworthy differences. Both men wrote in pen, and few words in either diary are illegible, even with fading over time. However, Caldwell's small, thin diary measured approximately four inches wide by six inches high. His capital letters were two mm. high, and the lower case letters were one mm. high; he would have been able to easily carry his diary in a shirt pocket, if he had one, through three years of the war. Sam's memoir is a large book measuring six by ten inches, with average sized script on four hundred eighty-one pages. He indicated he kept more than one diary through the war and recopied them into the one book in 1890.

The two brothers were together for much of their service in the Missouri State Guard, as well as the Confederate army. Their observations were never contradictory, but in many cases they focused on different incidents. When they did tell the same tale, it was not unusual for Sam to give considerably more detail. For ease of comparison, Sam's entry regarding "the coon hunt" appears below, followed by Caldwell's entry for the same event.

> Sam: *We had not been in camp a sufficient length of time to commence drill — yet several days rest afforded us considerable recuperation, from our long arduous march, & we had began to grow restless — many things sugjested themselves to ward off the monotony of camp life, & for a little recreation on the morning of the 12th one of our company boys, Charles Marent, proposed that he, Caldwell & myself take a hunt. To which we willingly consented; & after Marent had procured an old condemned army musket, the old "piece" used as a company safeguard to keep at bay, "fighting hogs", Caldwell & I with an ax — started off through the swamps at a lively pace — at the same time annoyed by the taunts & jeers of our messmates — with such expressions as "Fishermans luck" etc etc. After we had left the camp some miles in our rear, & becoming some what foot weary from tramping around through the swamps & marshy lands of the Yalabusha river, sat down on an old moss covered log to rest, for a few moments but our rest was of short duration — One of our party espied a young coon playing around in some grape vines hanging from a tall cypress tree, a short distance from where we were seated.*
>
> *A Coon Hunt*
>
> *We were soon at the tree, when Marent put the "Old trusty" musket to his shoulder, & as the deafening roar of the immense charge of*

powder reverberated through the swamps, Marent attained his equlibrium & the smoke cleared away sufficiently to see — discovered one coon tumble to the ground. The firing was kept up until three of the "ring tailed" monsters of the hen roost, were on the ground & the fourth lodged in the vines. Not knowing to what extent the tree was inhabited by these midnight ramblers — concluded to fall it ~~the tree~~, as it was too large to climb; Shed our jackets, & by turns plied the ax, after more than an hours hard chopping — the top commenced wavering, & in the absence of dogs two of us stood picket with uplifted clubs & glaring eyes, while the third used the ax with all his might — but to our great surprise when the tree fell, the war was over, our game was all dead, the old ones were gone. After resting a short time Caldwell & I suggested a return to camp. Marent being more disposed to ramble — was not yet satisfied — said he would take the gun & hunt for a short time, while we if preferable could take the four coons & ax, & return to camp. The last half of the evening was pretty well consumed, thick clouds o'erspread the sky, from which a fine mist was descending through the tall boughs of the cypress, from which was dangling the moss in long silky shreds, to meet the immense fogg rising from the surrounding swamps & ponds of stagnate water, where the toad wallowed in filth & slime uttering his shrill screams, to mingle with the sweet melodies of the lonely whippoorwill as he perched himself on the branch of a weeping willow near by. Well, we seperated & according to the previously arranged programme, divided our burdens as eaqually as possible, and started as we supposed in the direction of camp. Our travel was uninterrupted for some time; the distance between us & the coon tree seemed to be increasing very fast, we feeling so much elated on our success in so short a time, hastened on to tell the good news to our comrads — not taking the time or precaution to survey the surroundings until sometime had elapsed — in fact "Old Sol" had just about consumed all the time allotted him, to complete the days journey; we began to think we had traveled far enough to be near camp, finally we stopped & held a hurried consultation, the sound of axes as the men were preparing wood for the evening meal could be heard in the distant camps — the sharp notes of the bugle sounding stable call, the neigh of the horses & bray of the mules mingling in one confused mass, rang in our ears; finally we heard a noise! one we seemed to recognize as a familiar one, & said, That's our company!! let's go that way; so on & on our wearied limbs carried us, & the echoes as they proved to be, came no nearer. At last, after several miles travel, we very reluctantly came to the conclusion, that we were lost, & as such cases generally terminates, under such circumstances, after an other vain attempt to find our way, came up to the Identical tree for which we had fallen to get the coons. Well, kind reader were you ever in a cypress swamp? if ~~you~~ you never have been — when ever you see one, you will not be so much amazed, at two North Missouri Boys loosing their way who had never seen one previous to that — I tell you every tree looks alike, the huge roots of one is an exact duplicate of its neighbor which stands in close proximity, the thick undergrowth interwoven with muscadine vines & briars of all kinds, have a great tendency to misguide the already confused traveler.

Not Yet found

We were seated side by side on the trunk of the old coon tree, conversing in earnest under tones, in regard to our bewildered situation. But having become habituated to disappointments, by our experience in "rough & tumble" life — had about concluded to spend the night, listening to the hoo! hoo! Owl, or the lonesome song of the whipporwill. We did not need a Mothers lullaby then to put us to sleep, or a feather bed on which to dream — no! Hush! What's that? I hear someone's foot steps coming through the brush! They are coming toward us! — in an instant later, the familiar voice of Marent, was heard in greatly surprised tones, as he exclaimed W'y Boys! I thought you had gone to camp? We thought so too! but didnot quite make the trip was the subdued reply. At first we denied the real cause of our predicament, saying we just thought, we'd rest until he finished his hunt. But our countenances betrayed us, & his looks showed that our story was disbelieved — & believing in the old adage — "an open confession good for the soul" acknowledged that we were lost. However we were cautious enough to obligate him not to tell the boys in camp. After a short rest Marent remarked, let's be going boys; night is almost upon us. We staggered again to our wearied feet to follow our deliverer, with feelings intermingled with joy & doubt. Joy, because our friend had come ~~to~~ in the moments of despair, & proposed to lead us, out of this troubled situation as Moses did the Isrealites when under Egyptian bondage. Doubt, as to his ability to do so, as we had experienced eaqual confidence within ourselves, but a few hours previous, when we started out for camp. But we were soon aware that he knew just what he was doing, & where he was going — having been reared in the south was more familiar with the swamps than us. A short time after night fall, we wearily trudged into camp, & piled the fruits (four coons) of our days hunt before the mess fire; & you ought to have seen the surprised look & glaring eyes of our mess mates, remembering their prophecies & fun at our expense when we left camp on the memorable coon hunt — true — we were "wet" but had plenty of game "all the same". The boys were all willing enough to assist us, & the coons were soon skinned & dressed ready for the "pot". But those best posted in regard to the character of such meat, thought best to let them hang out all night in order to get off — the "coon smell". So the cooking was posponed until the morrow. For our noonday meal on the 13th the coons were cooked in the most magnificent style our limited means afforded, with sweetpotatoes & brown gravy. I had often heard ~~of~~ the old darkies at home, talking about what a delicious dish — "de possum & sweet-taters" were (I always took their word for it) but we had coon & "taters" & "you bet" we helped ourselves until the skillet was sopped dry; as we had almost uncontrollable appetites for "something fresh". This was my first mess of coon, & I guess will be the last unless I am caught in "Rome" again.

Caldwell: *Dec 12th Went coon hunting & got lost in the woods on the way back after killing four. Have coon soup tomorrow aha!.*

A discussion with descendants of both Caldwell and Sam bears out the observation that such proclivities may be genetic. Sam and his descendants share the characteristic of being quite verbal; Caldwell and his descendants are much more reserved and concise.

Sam died on January 7, 1932, at his home at Willis and Main Streets in DeKalb, Missouri, where he had lived for the last twenty years of his life. Sam's wife "Nannie" lived another eleven years; both are buried at Westlawn Cemetery in DeKalb.

Sam had been born to a intensely pro-southern family and had given four years of his life in service to the Confederate cause. When he died, a Confederate flag draped his coffin. A family member recalls that even after eighty-eight years, Sam's beliefs had not changed. Despite the refusal of some pro-Union family members to attend his funeral, Sam went to his grave with the flag dearest to his heart, prominently displayed in honor of his committed service (Sampson).

A Researcher's "Rest of the Story"

When I finished my research for Pvt. Robert Caldwell Dunlap's *As the Mockingbird Sang*, published in December 2005, I was still puzzled as to how the diary became separated from Caldwell, following his wounding on Kennesaw Mountain and how it had come to be returned to him. After researching Sam's memoir, I have drawn some conclusions.

Fifty-four years after his wounding, Caldwell wrote a summary in the back of his diary to explain what happened from the time he was injured until he returned home at the end of the war. He explained that immediately after "a shell from the enemy's gun burst just inside the embrasure sending its fragments in every direction killing Liut McBride," [and] "wounding Bob Welch in the foot," a piece of shrapnel tore through his arm, causing it to fall limp at his side. A tourniquet was put in place, and Caldwell was immediately removed to a field hospital, then taken by ambulance to Marietta, Georgia, where his left arm was amputated.

Soon after the amputation, Caldwell was transferred to Atlanta, where he received treatment for about thirty days. Sam was able to stay with him for nine of those days, but was then ordered to report back to his company. About July 24, Caldwell had gained sufficient strength to walk alone and was helped to the depot where he boarded a train for Covington, Georgia. The Covington Court House had been converted to a hospital, and Caldwell was allowed to recuperate there for a time before being moved to a college building, where he stayed an additional month.

Sometime in late August, Caldwell was sent to Augusta, Georgia. He does not record where he lived, but he mentions daily visits from a Mrs. Ward and her niece, and at some point, the two women took Caldwell with them by train to southwest Georgia, where he stayed with her father, Mr. Stripling.

After Caldwell heard that a battle had been fought at Franklin, he returned with Mrs. Ward to Augusta. Soon after, he arranged for a pass on the railroad to find his brother Sam. He traveled "to where Hood's army was encamped quite a distance north and west of Augusta."

Sam recorded that after General Hood (Sam was now in his command) retreated from Atlanta, the troops began moving west on the Atlanta-Montgomery railroad, arriving at Palmetto before the end of the month. When Caldwell left Augusta, he had intended to find Sam and remain with him and his unit. I believe Caldwell intentionally left his diary at Mrs. Ward's home, as he intended to return there after visiting Sam or, more likely, after the war ended. Being left-handed and having lost his left arm, it would be some time before Caldwell would learn to write with his right hand. Since he could no longer journal, he had no reason to take the diary with him. Caldwell did stay a few days with Sam, but Sam insisted he not put himself at risk for another injury. Caldwell then tried to get a pass on the railroad to return to Augusta, but the pass was denied. Although neither Caldwell, nor Sam explain why, it would not have been safe to travel, as by now Sherman's troops were strongly amassed in the area and beginning their march across Georgia. The railroad to Augusta would likely have been closed to Confederates. Because Caldwell never had the opportunity to return to Augusta, his diary would have remained behind.

Caldwell wrote that when the pass to Augusta was denied, he got a pass on the railroad to Uniontown, Alabama. From there he walked a mile and a half to the Charles Walker plantation, where he stayed for the remainder of the war. He does not mention the Ward family again. On April 26, 1865, Sam received an honorable discharge by parole from service to the Confederate army. He made his way to the Walker plantation, and together, the young men began their long journey home. They rode the train and walked part of the way to Memphis, then traveled by steamboat to St. Louis, and then by another to Atchison, Kansas, where their parents now lived.

Twenty-five years later, Sam copied his diaries into one book. My personal experience with transcribing his memoir on computer has convinced me that pursuing this task in long hand would have taken weeks, if not months to complete. Because the two men lived near one another in the same small town, I suspect Caldwell and Sam may have discussed Sam's work on his diaries, and this may have occasioned Caldwell to wonder what became of his own.

Sam dated his memoir 1890, but it is not possible to know when he finished the transcription. We do know that on December 17, 1891, Caldwell wrote a letter to someone in Augusta inquiring about his diary. The response from Mr. P. H. Ward has survived, and thus, we know Ward offered his apology that the diary had been detained so long and wrote that he was returning it by Express, as he believed this the "safest and surest mode of delivery."

During Caldwell's stay in Augusta, he mentioned frequent visits from a Mrs. Ward and her niece. We have no knowledge as to whether P. H. Ward was perhaps Mrs. Ward's husband or son, but I believe the diary was preserved by the Ward family, and P. H. was familiar with it when Caldwell's letter arrived.

The brief summary written in 1918 gives no clues about the above, nor did Sam's memoir. However, because both the diary and the memoir were preserved by Caldwell and Sam's descendants, I was able to extract information from both to piece together, what I believe, is a plausible explanation of events.

All of the tasks associated with publishing both the diary and the memoir have been most interesting, but fitting together the puzzle pieces to solve such mysteries has been truly intriguing.

Photographs

Key Sites in Samuel Baldwin Dunlap's Memoir

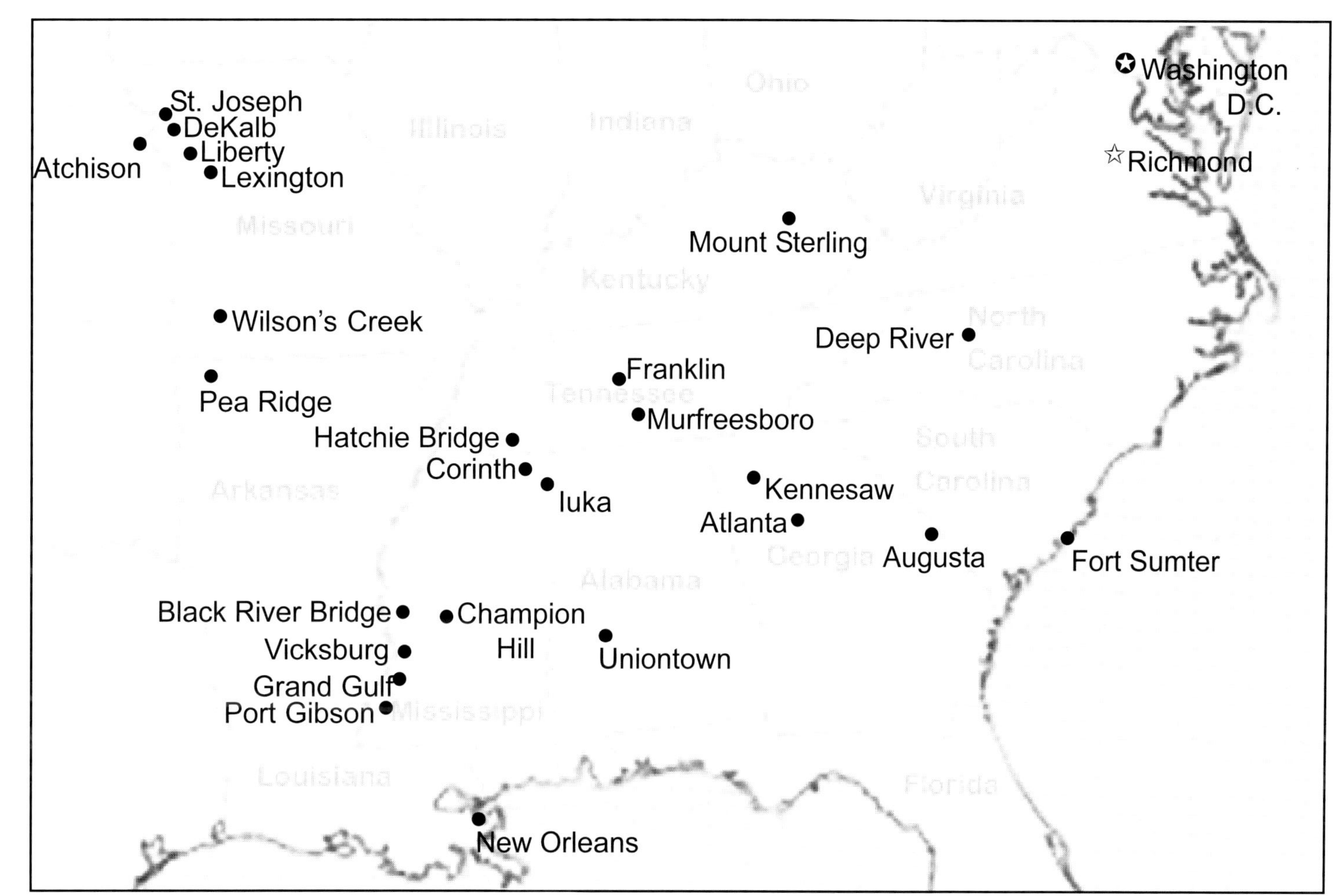

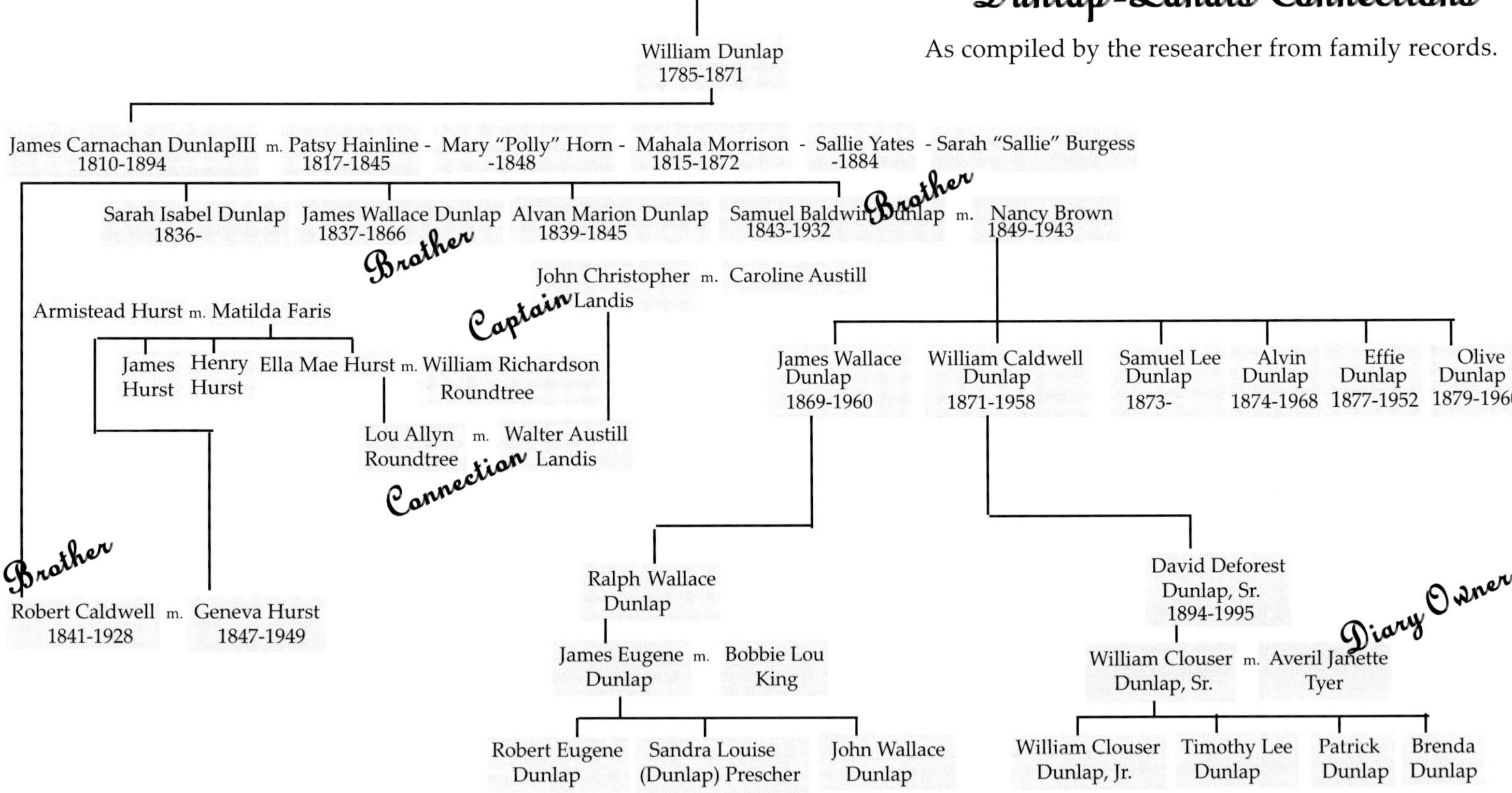
Dunlap-Landis Connections
As compiled by the researcher from family records.
James Carnachan Dunlap I m. Jane Wills
1740-1844
William Dunlap
1785-1871
James Carnachan DunlapIII m. Patsy Hainline - Mary "Polly" Horn - Mahala Morrison - Sallie Yates - Sarah "Sallie" Burgess
1810-1894 1817-1845 -1848 1815-1872 -1884
Sarah Isabel Dunlap
1836-
James Wallace Dunlap
1837-1866
Brother
Alvan Marion Dunlap
1839-1845
Samuel Baldwin Dunlap m. Nancy Brown
1843-1932 1849-1943
Brother
John Christopher Landis m. Caroline Austill
Captain
Armistead Hurst m. Matilda Faris
James Hurst
Henry Hurst
Ella Mae Hurst m. William Richardson Roundtree
Lou Allyn Roundtree m. Walter Austill Landis
Connection
Brother
Robert Caldwell m. Geneva Hurst
1841-1928 1847-1949
James Wallace Dunlap
1869-1960
William Caldwell Dunlap
1871-1958
Samuel Lee Dunlap
1873-
Alvin Dunlap
1874-1968
Effie Dunlap
1877-1952
Olive Dunlap
1879-1960
Ralph Wallace Dunlap
James Eugene Dunlap m. Bobbie Lou King
Robert Eugene Dunlap
Sandra Louise (Dunlap) Prescher
John Wallace Dunlap
David Deforest Dunlap, Sr.
1894-1995
William Clouser Dunlap, Sr. m. Averil Janette Tyer
Diary Owner
William Clouser Dunlap, Jr.
Timothy Lee Dunlap
Patrick Dunlap
Brenda Dunlap

Above: Sam Dunlap's memoir. Front cover is on left. Back cover is on right.
Courtesy of Janette Dunlap, Saint Joseph, Missouri.

Below: Janette Dunlap, Suzanne Lehr, and Bill Dunlap with Sam Dunlap's memoir.
April 30, 2006. *Courtesy of Jim Lehr, Saint Joseph, Missouri.*

Left: James Wallace Dunlap
Right: Samuel Baldwin Dunlap and Robert Caldwell Dunlap
Courtesy of Janette Dunlap, Saint Joseph, Missouri.

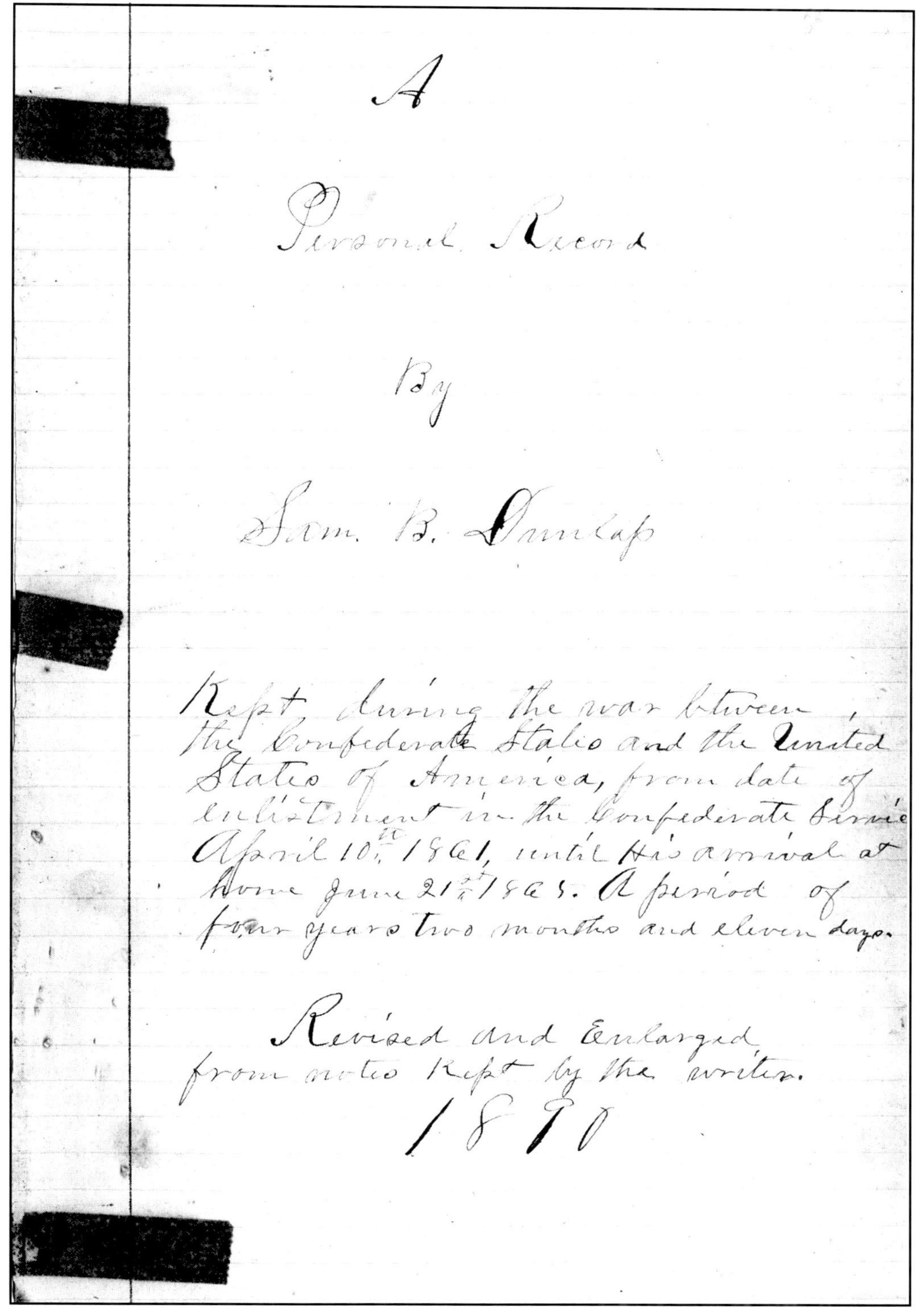
A

Personal Record

By

Sam. B. Dunlap

Kept during the war between the Confederate States and the United States of America, from date of enlistment in the Confederate Service April 10th 1861, until His arrival at Home June 21st 1865. A period of four years two months and eleven days.

Revised and Enlarged from notes Kept by the writer.

1870

First page of the memoir of Pvt. Samuel Baldwin Dunlap, C.S.A.
Courtesy of Janette Dunlap, Saint Joseph, Missouri.

1865 Lincoln Assassinated Apr 19 – 1865
April

an hour of great expectancy– All Kinds of rumors flooded the camp– there was but little discipline among the troops– deserting from some portions of the Army was a nightly occurrence. Occasionally the boys would almost go wild, over the rumor– that England & France had declared war against the Federal government.

On the 19th News reached us of the attempted assassination of Lincoln & Seward at the Ford Theater in Washington city by Booth, & the wildest enthusiasm followed– hats were thrown, time & again in the air. the deafening shouts– which made the woods ring, reverberating from bluff to bluff– & valley to valley– dying away on the still waters of Deep river– made one almost believe the South had gained her independence. Booth was a Virginian– & as many others– aggravated by the manner in which his relatives & friends had been treated by the Lincoln government– selected these two as victims; When he committed the deed– leaping from the stage– Cried out; Virginia; Revenged!! Sic Semper Tyrannus!! This occurrence– although late in the "day" had a tendency to buoy us up, We Knew it would create a great confusion all over the north– & we hoped while this state of Affairs existed, the people would become divided– & give us another chance for victory. On the 20th we became aware, there was something of great importance, under advisement– as our Officers & the Federals were in consultation under a flag of truce. About 10 O'C, Am Our company was assembled to listen to the reading of an order from Gen Hardee– temporary in command of the Army– in which he stated that terms of surrender had already been agreed upon– & both armies were to remain in their present positions until further orders. This only confirmed in my mind– that upon which I had long since become convinced– I felt confident, unless, something appeared in the form of a miracle– the Confederacy was doomed to wear the conquerors yoke. 'Tis said while there is life, there is hope– & upon this declaration I based the following– and to show with what zeal I as others clung to the cause we loved so dearly– I repeat my writings upon the occasion. In the darkest hour, there is yet some hope– however thick the gloom appears– there may be a light, that will save our way worn ship– that has been tossed upon the rugged waves of the sea of war– a light that will enable her to reach the harbor of Independence safely– & feast upon sweet liberty– for which some of the best & bravest sons of the South have poured out their warm hearts blood.

To wait as patiently as possible, was all we could do & in order to "Kill" the time as fast & agreeable as could be– I frequently went fishing on Deep river.

Last page of the memoir of Pvt. Samuel Baldwin Dunlap, C.S.A.
Courtesy of Janette Dunlap, Saint Joseph, Missouri.

Landis Artillery Battery re-enactors with limber and ammunition chest.
Courtesy of Jim Lehr, Saint Joseph, Missouri.

Charles Walker's plantation (Cedar Grove) as it appears today.
Courtesy of Thomas and Catherine Alison, Faunsdale, Alabama.

Left: Charles Walker
Courtesy of Nancy and George McKee, Faunsdale, Alabama.

Charles Walker's plantation, 1880.

Charles Walker, right.
Son Mims Walker, left.

Courtesy of Thomas and Catherine Alison, Faunsdale, Alabama.

OATH OF ALLEGIANCE.

I, Samuel R. Dunlap of ... County State of Missouri do hereby solemnly swear that I will bear true allegiance to the United States, and support and sustain the Constitution and laws thereof; that I will maintain the National Sovereignty paramount to that of all State County or Confederate powers; that I will discourage, discountenance, and forever oppose secession, rebellion and the disintegration of the Federal Union; that I disclaim and denounce all faith and fellowship with the so called Confederate Armies, and pledge my honor my property, and my life, to the sacred performance of this my solemn Oath of Allegiance to the Government of the United States of America.

Samuel R. Dunlap

Subscribed and sworn to before me this 15 day of June 1865.
at

Geo H Richardson

WITNESSES:

C. C. Williams

DESCRIPTION:

Age

Height

Color of Eyes

Color of Hair

Office of the Provost Marshal,
DISTRICT WEST TENNESSEE,
Memphis Tenn June 12th 1865

The bearer has permission to wear his Confederate uniform for the space of days from this date

By Order of Brevet Maj. Gen. JOHN E. SMITH.

Capt. and Asst. Provost Marshal.

MISSOURI ELECTION.

1st District—THOMAS L. SNEAD.
2d District —THOMAS A. HARRIS. N. L. NORTON.
3d District,—CASPAR W. BELL. R. S. BEVIER. T. H. PRICE.
4th District—A. H. CONROW.
5th District—G. G. VEST.
6th District—T. W. FREEMAN. PETER WILKES.
7th District—R. A. HATCHER.

Excerpt from framed collage: Oath of Allegiance signed by Sam Dunlap, June 15, 1865. Permission form from Memphis Provost Marshall for Sam to wear his Confederate uniform, June 12, 1865. Missouri Election Ticket for the Confederate Congress. Sam cast his first vote in this election on May 2, 1864.

Courtesy of James "Gene" and Bobbie Dunlap, Faucett, Missouri.

Sam and Nancy "Nannie" Dunlap with their six children.
Courtesy of James "Gene" and Bobbie Dunlap, Faucett, Missouri.

Front row: William Caldwell Dunlap, Nancy "Nannie" Dunlap, Olive Patsy Dunlap, Samuel Baldwin Dunlap, James Wallace Dunlap.
Second row: Samuel Lee Dunlap, Effie A. Dunlap, Alvin Brown Carnachan Dunlap
Courtesy of James "Gene" and Bobbie Dunlap, Faucett, Missouri.

Samuel Baldwin and Nancy "Nannie" (Brown) Dunlap.
Courtesy of James "Gene" and Bobbie Dunlap, Faucett, Missouri.

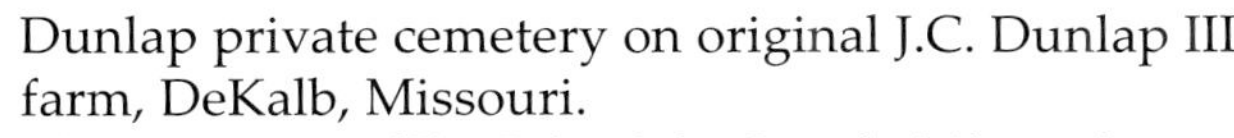

Dunlap private cemetery on original J.C. Dunlap III farm, DeKalb, Missouri.
Photo courtesy of Jim Lehr, Saint Joseph, Missouri.

Above: Monument to each of James C. Dunlap III's wives and son Wallace.
Photo courtesy of Jim Lehr, Saint Joseph, Missouri.

Right: Sam Dunlap's father's tombstone.
Below: Marker for Sam Dunlap's great-grandfather, James Carnachan Dunlap I.
Photos courtesy of Bill Dunlap, Saint Joseph, Missouri.

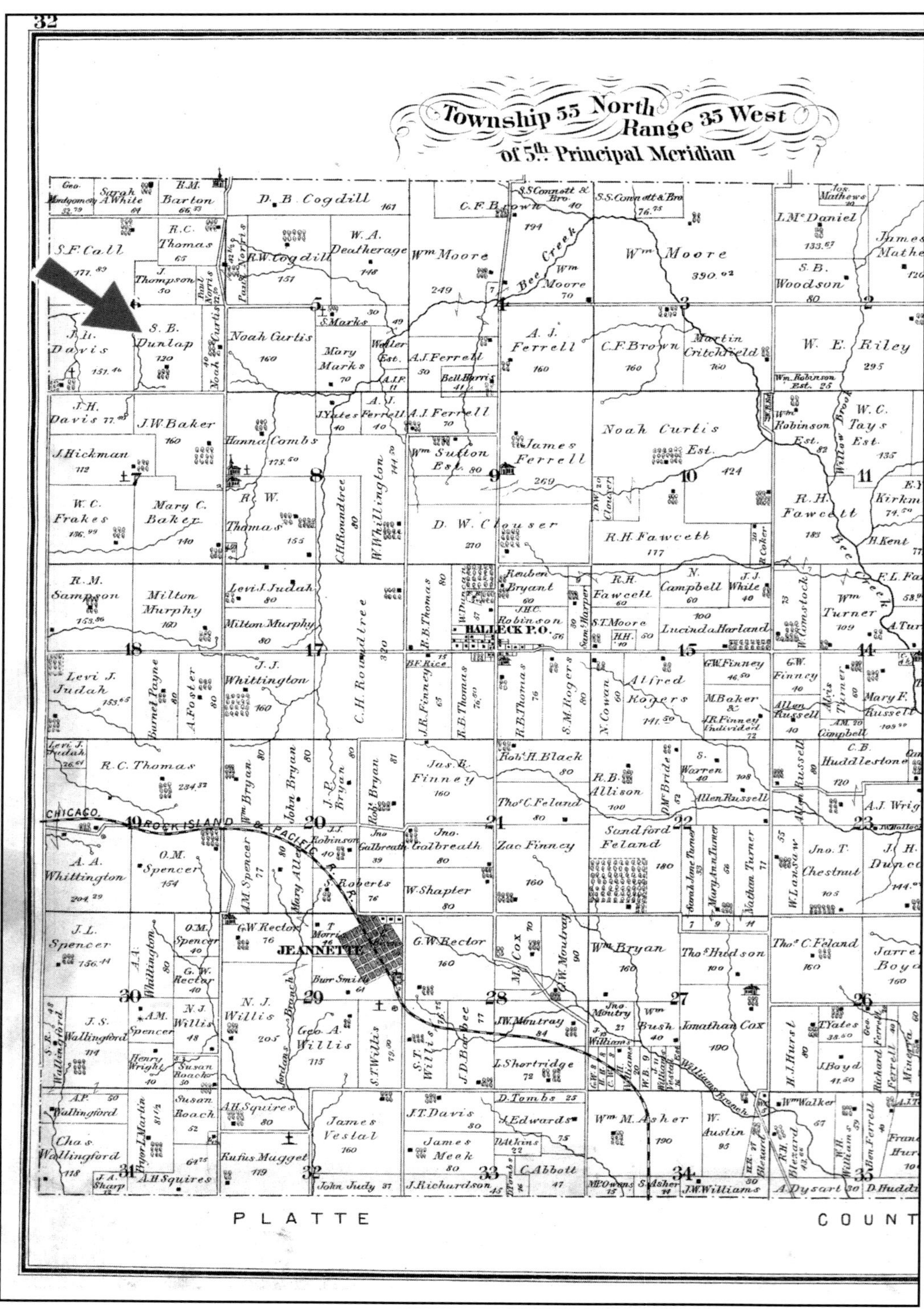

1876 plat from *An Illustrated Historical Atlas for Buchanan County* indicating location of Sam Dunlap's farm.
Courtesy of The St. Joseph Museums Inc.

St Joseph Mo June 3 1901

To the United Daughters of the Confederacy:

The undersigned, residing at DeKalb Buchanan Co Mo *who is an Ex-Confederate Soldier and a member of Camp No.* 807 *U. C. Vs., hereby, at your request, presents this Certificate of Eligibility for a Confederate Cross of Honor. He entered the service of the Confederate States on the .... day of* March *1862, as a* Private *in Company* Artillery *of the* Landis Battery Missouri *Volunteers, ... C. S. A., and was at that time a resident of* Buchanan County Mo

He was honorably discharged from said service by Parole at Greensboro N.C. *on the* 26th *day of* April *1865, at which time he held the rank of* Private Landis Mo Battery

Respectfully,

Sam. B. Dunlap

We endorse the above certificate.

P E Chesnut

L H Read

Members Camp No. 807 *United Confederate Veterans.*

Approved by order of

James W Boyd

Commander Camp No. 807 *United Confederate Veterans*

Jno C Landis

Adjutant.

Sam Dunlap's application for the Confederate Cross of Honor from the United Daughters of the Confederacy, Sterling Price Chapter No. 401, collection.
Courtesy of The St. Joseph Museums Inc., Saint Joseph, Missouri.

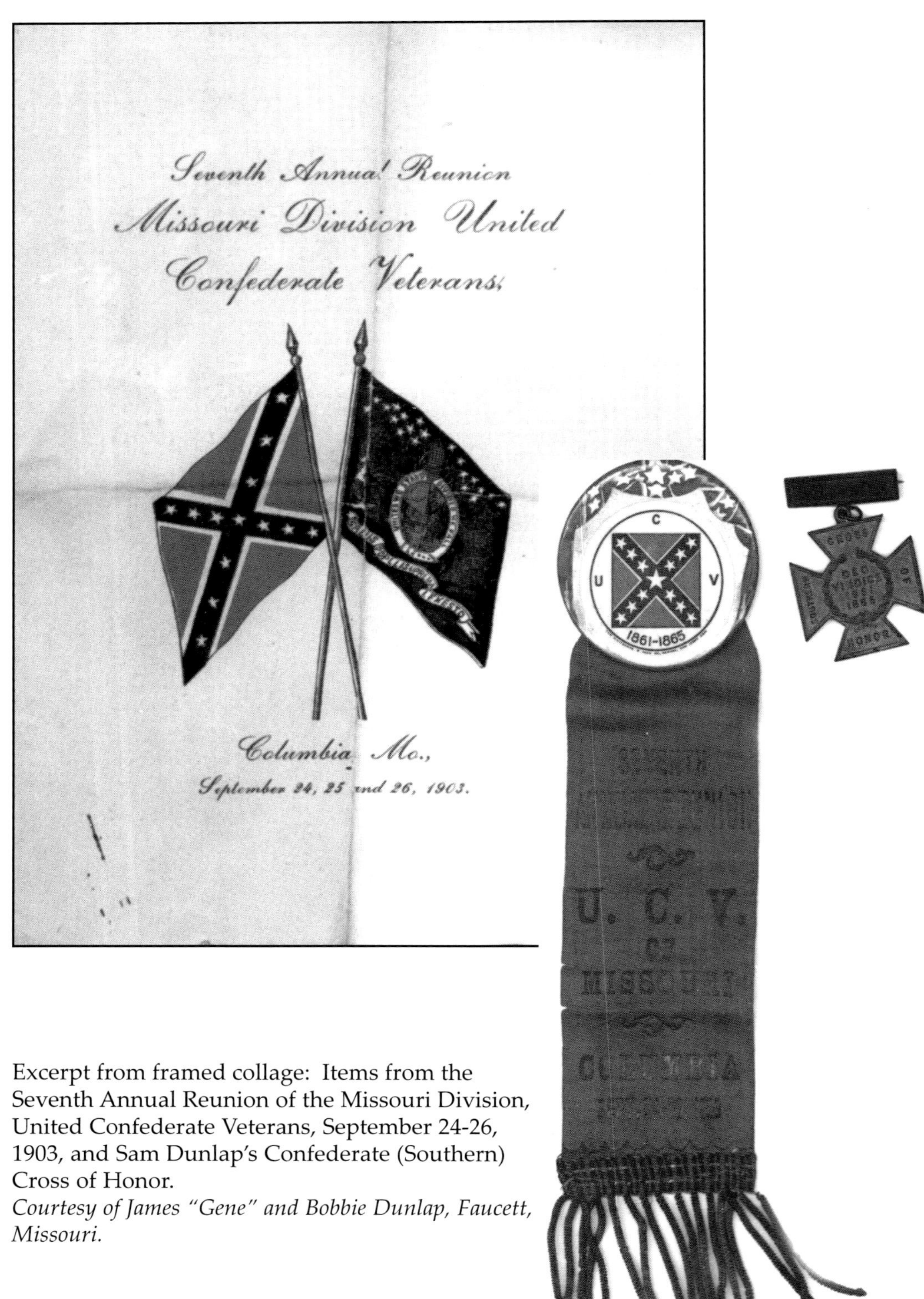

Excerpt from framed collage: Items from the Seventh Annual Reunion of the Missouri Division, United Confederate Veterans, September 24-26, 1903, and Sam Dunlap's Confederate (Southern) Cross of Honor.
Courtesy of James "Gene" and Bobbie Dunlap, Faucett, Missouri.

Cannon at Fort McBride position on Little Kennesaw Mountain.
Courtesy of Jim Lehr, Saint Joseph, Missouri.

Above: Foundation remnants of the Bloomington Academy (later the Sleepy Hollow School) at DeKalb, Missouri.

Courtesy of Jim Lehr, Saint Joseph, Missouri.

Below: Sam and "Nannie" I. Dunlap's tombstone, Westlawn Cemetery, DeKalb, Missouri.

Courtesy of Jim Lehr, Saint Joseph, Missouri.

Works Cited

Ainsworth, Brig. Gen. Fred C. and Joseph W. Kirkley. *The War of the Rebellion: A Compilation of the Official Records of the Union and Confederate Armies.* Series III, Vol. II. Washington: Government Printing Office, 1899.

Ainsworth, Brig. Gen. Fred C. and Joseph W. Kirkley. *The War of the Rebellion: A Compilation of the Official Records of the Union and Confederate Armies.* Series III, Vol. V. Washington: Government Printing Office, 1900.

Alison, George H. Unpublished Walker family information. 11 May 2006.

"America Singing: Nineteenth-Century Song Sheets." *American Memory.* 22 Oct. 1999. The Library of Congress. 9 Feb. 2006 <http://memory.loc.gov/ammem/amsshtml/amsshome.html>.

"Archeologists uncover historic fort." 21 Dec. 2004. *Talk History.* 10 Feb. 2006 <http://www.talk-history.com/forum/showthread.php?t=1300>.

Archives. Files of Northwest Missouri Genealogy Society Library, St. Joseph, Missouri. "Last Will and Testament of James C. Dunlap III." Filed June 27, 1894.

"Arkansas Traveler." *Popular Songs in American History.* 20 Jan. 1999. Contemplator.com. 7 Feb. 2006 <http://www.contemplator.com/america/arkansas.html>.

Bailey, Kristi. "Missouri Brigade leader honored." *St. Joseph News-Press* 14 July 2002: B1, B3.

"Banners of Glory Key." *Vicksburg.* 9 Mar. 2005. ParkNet National Park Service. 4 May 2006 <http://www.nps.gov/vick/eduguide/chp_6/bnrglryk.htm>.

Bennett, Andy. "Fort Morgan." *Coastal Fortification on the Gulf of Mexico.* 28 Aug. 2002. 25 Mar. 2006 <http://andy_bennett.home.mindspring.com/morgan.html>.

"Black fly." *The American Heritage Dictionary of the English Language.* 4th ed. 2000.

"Black Warrior River." *Wikipedia, the free encyclopedia.* 5 Dec. 2005. 5 Apr. 2006 <http://en.wikipedia.org/wiki/Black_Warrior_River>.

Boatner III, Mark M. *The Civil War Dictionary.* Rev. ed. 1991.

Boni, Margaret Bradford. *Fireside Book of Folk Songs.* New York: Simon & Schuster, 1947.

"Bots Latin Name: Gasterophilus species." *HorseData.co.uk.* 2005. 17 Oct. 2005 <http://www.horsedata.co.uk/bots.htm>.

"Bug juice." *Dictionary of Civil War Slang.* Tripod. 11 Sept. 2005 <http://atleb.tripod.com/ordbok/dictionary_of_civil_war_slang.htm>.

"Buttahatchee River." *Wikipedia, the free encyclopedia.* 9 Apr 2006. 18 Apr. 2006 <http://en.wikipedia.org/wiki/Buttahatchee_River>.

"Caltrop." *Wikipedia, the free encyclopedia.* 17 Oct. 2005. 20 Oct. 2005 <http://en.wikipedia.org/wiki/Jack_rock>.

"Capt. Landis, War Veteran, is Dead." *St. Joseph News-Press* 2 Apr. 1913: 1-2.

"Carolina - A Brief History." *University of North Carolina at Chapel Hill.* 2003. 21 Apr. 2006 <http://www.unc.edu/about/history.html>.

"Casemate." *The American Heritage Dictionary of the English Language.* 4th ed. 2000.

"Cedar Grove: Palatial Canebrake Plantation." *Cooperative Farming News.* Dec. 2005. Alabama Farmers Cooperative, Inc. 26 Apr. 2006 <http://www.alafarmnews.com/1204archive/1204lure.htm>.

"Cedar Grove Plantation." *Sankofa's Slavery Data Collection.* 28 Oct. 2004. RootsWeb.com. 22 Apr. 2006 <http://www.rootsweb.com/~afamerpl/plantations_usa/AL/cedargrove.html>.

Centre College. *The Thirty-Seventh Annual Catalogue of the Officers and Students in Centre College, Danville, Ky., For The Year 1861.* Frankfort, Ky: A. G. Hodges & Co., 1861.

"Chicot County, Arkansas Historical and Geneaological Page." *Arkansas GenWeb Project.* Seark.net. 6 Feb. 2006 <http://www.seark.net/~sabra/chicotco.html>.

"Cholera morbus." *The American Heritage Dictionary of the English Language.* 4th ed. 2000.

"Chunky River." *Wikipedia, the free encyclopedia.* 22 Mar. 2006. 5 Apr. 2006 <http://en.wikipedia.org/wiki/Chunky_River>.

"Cincinnati." *Naval Historical Center.* 18 Jan. 2006. Department of the Navy. 22 Mar. 2006 <http://www.history.navy.mil/danfs/c9/cincinnati-i.htm>.

Civil War Action Around Latimer's Farm. Historical Marker on Latimer Farm site at Marietta Country Club, Marietta, Georgia. 8 May 2006.

"Civil War Medicine: An Overview of Medicine." *eHistory.* 2006. Ohio State University. 6 Feb. 2006 <http://ehistory.osu.edu/uscw/features/medicine/cwsurgeon/introduction.cfm>.

"Clara Dolsen." *Dictionary of American Naval Fighting Ships.* 18 Jan. 2006. Naval Historical Center. 10 Feb. 2006 <http://www.history.navy.mil/danfs/cfa2/clara_dolsen.htm>.

Clark, James G., LL.D. *History of William Jewell College, Liberty, Clay County, Missouri.* St. Louis: Central Baptist Print., 1893.

"Col. Gates, St. Joseph's 'Grand Old Man,' War Hero, Dead." *St. Joseph Gazette* 5 Mar. 1915: 1,3.

"Columbus, Mississippi." *Wikipedia, the free encyclopedia.* 3 Apr. 2006. 18 Apr. 2006 <http://en.wikipedia.org/wiki/Columbus,_Mississippi>.

Cook, John, comp. *The Book of Positive Quotations.* Minneapolis: Fairview Press, 1997.

"Coosa River." *Wikipedia, the free encyclopedia.* 9 Apr. 2006. 14 Apr. 2006 <http://en.wikipedia.org/wiki/Coosa_River>.

"Cotton gin." *Wikipedia, the free encyclopedia.* 20 Apr. 2006. 23 Apr. 2006 <http://en.wikipedia.org/wiki/Cotton_gin>.

"Crathur." *A til azed.* BBC Homepage Northern Ireland. 4 Feb. 2006 <http://www.bbc.co.uk/northernireland/voices/atilazed/c.shtml>.

Crossno, Henriella Prather. "History of DeKalb." *Buchanan County Farmer* 27 May 1982.

Dahlonega, Georgia. 2006. Dahlonega-Lumpkin County Chamber of Commerce. 13 Apr. 2006 <http://www.dahlonega.org/aboutus.asp?id06=90&par06=23>.

Daily News' History of Buchanan County and St. Joseph, Mo. St. Joseph: St. Joseph Publishing Company, 1898.

"David Glasgow Farragut." *Vicksburg.* 27 Feb. 2005. ParkNet National Park Service. 25 Mar. 2006 <http://www.nps.gov/vick/visctr/sitebltn/farragut.htm>.

Davis, Varina Jefferson. *Jefferson Davis Ex-President of the Confederate States of America. A Memoir by His Wife.* Vol. 1. New York: Belford Company, Publishers, 1890.

"Dear Evelina, Sweet Evelina." *Lester S. Levy Collection of Sheet Music.* Lester Levy. 15 Oct. 2005 <http://www.contemplator.com/america/evelina.html>.

"Death of Gen. M. Jeff. Thompson." *Daily Morning Herald* 6 Sept. 1876: 2.

"Dick Keys." *Naval Historical Center.* 18 Jan. 2006. Department of the Navy. 22 Mar. 2006 <http://www.history.navy.mil/danfs/cfa3/dick_keys.htm>.

"Dodger." *The Oxford English Dictionary.* 2nd ed. 1989.

"Dog fennel." *The American Heritage Dictionary of the English Language.* 4th ed. 2000.

Drake, Rebecca Blackwell. "Old Port Gibson Road: Civil War Route to Raymond." *The Battle of Champion Hill.* 14 Jan. 2006. James and Rebecca Drake. 21 Mar. 2006 <http://battleofchampionhill.org/history/road.htm>.

Dunlap, Sam. "Experiences on the Hood Campaign." *Confederate Veteran.* Vol. XVI, No. 4. April 1908: 187-8.

Dunlap, Sam. "Hard Times on Hood's Retreat." *Confederate Veteran.* Vol. VII, No. 6. June 1899: 266.

Dunlap, Sam. "Missouri Battery in Tennessee Campaign." *Confederate Veteran.* Vol XII, No. 8. August 1904: 389.

"Enoree River Canoe." *South Carolina State Trails Program.* 30 Nov. 2005. South Carolina Department of Parks, Recreation and Tourism. 19 Apr. 2006 <http://www.sctrails.net/Trails/ALLTRAILS/WaterTrails/EnoreeRvr.html>.

"Enoree River Canoe Trail." *Sumter National Forest South Carolina.* 27 Mar. 2003. USDA Forest Service. 19 Apr. 2006 <http://216.109.125.130/search/cache?p=Enoree+River+Canoe+Trail&fr=FP_tab_web_t&toggle=1&cop=&ei=UTF_8&u=www.fs.fed.us/r8/fms/rec/Enoree%2520River%2520Canoe.pdf&w=enoree+river+canoe+trail&d=As_YREaqMljn&icp=1&.intl=us>.

"Etowah River." *The Atlanta Chapter of The Hoverclub of America.* 13 Apr. 2006 <http://www.mindspring.com/~lpb3/Etowah.html>.

"Fionn McCool Cocktail." *The Art of Drink.* 21 Dec. 2005. 4 Feb. 2006 <http://www.theartofdrink.com/blog/2005/12/fionn_mccool_cocktail.php>.

Flagel, Thomas R. *The History Buff's Guide to the Civil War.* Nashville: Cumberland House, 2003.

Flayderman, E. Norman. *Flayderman's Guide to Antique American Firearms . . . and their values.* Iola, Wisconsin: Krause Publications, 2001.

"Foolscap." *The American Heritage Dictionary of the English Language.* 4th ed. 2000.

"Front Porches." *Alabama's Front Porches.* 2004. Tourism for Rural Southwest Alabama. 22 Apr. 2006 <http://www.alabamasfrontporches.org/marengo/marengo.html>.

Garrison, Webb and Cheryl Garrison. *The Encyclopedia of Civil War Usage an Illustrated Compendium of the Everyday Language of Soldiers and Civilians.* Nashville: Cumberland House, 2001.

"George Henry Thomas." *Wikipedia, the free encyclopedia.* 29 Mar. 2006. 17 Apr. 2006 <http://en.wikipedia.org/wiki/George_Henry_Thomas>.

Gillespie, Michael L. *The Civil War Battle of Lexington, Missouri.* Lone Jack, MO: Private Printing, 1998.

Goodrich, Thomas and Debra Goodrich. *The Day Dixie Died.* Mechanicsburg, Penn.: Stackpole Books, 2001.

"Grease-heel." *Common Problems Horse Owners Encounter and How to Cope.* 2006. About, Inc. 6 Feb. 2006 <http://horses.about.com/od/mmonproblems/index_r.htm>.

Green, Jonathon. *The Cassell Dictionary of Slang.* London: Wellington House, 1998.

"Greenfield." *Welcome to Key to the City's page for Dade County, Missouri.* 2006. Key to the City. 15 Oct. 2005 <http://www.usacitiesonline.com/mocountygreenfield.htm>.

Grimm, William Carey. *The Book of Shrubs.* New York: Bonanza Books, 1957.

"Guibor's Missouri Battery in Georgia." *The Kennesaw Gazette.* Atlanta: Western and Atlantic Railroad. 15 May, 1889: 2-3.

Harper, Douglas. "Pine-top." Nov. 2001. *Online Etymology Dictionary.* 11 Feb. 2006 <http://www.etymonline.com/index.php?1=p&p=17>.

"Harris, Thomas Alexander (1826-1895)." *The Political Graveyard.* 10 Mar. 2005. Lawrence Kestenbaum. 6 Apr. 2006 <http://politicalgraveyard.com/bio/harris8.html>.

Harris, W. Stuart. "A Letter of Sympathy." *Alabama Department of Archives and History.* 17 May 2006 <http://www.archives.state.al.us/marschall/SLetter.html>.

"Hartford." *Naval Historical Center.* 18 Jan. 2006. Department of the Navy. 22 Mar. 2006 <http://www.history.navy.mil/danfs/h3/hartford.htm>.

Heidler, David S. and Jeanne T. Heidler, eds. *Encyclopedia of the American Civil War*. New York: W. W. Norton and Company, Inc., 2000.

Heiser, John. "Army Organization during the Civil War." *Gettysburg National Military Park Virtual Tour.* Sept. 2000. National Park Service. 15 May 2006 <http://www.nps.gov/gett/getttour/armorg.htm>.

Hillix, Mary. Unpublished Hillix family information. 20 Mar. 2006.

History of Clay and Platte Counties, Missouri. St. Louis: National Historical Company, 1885.

"History of Victoria." *Wikipedia, the free encyclopedia.* 12 Apr. 2006. 23 Apr. 2006 <http://en.wikipedia.org/wiki/History_of_Victoria>.

Hodges, Nadine and Mrs. Howard W. Woodruff, compilers. *Buchanan County, Missouri, Abstracts of Wills and Administrations From Books "A" and "B" 1839-1857.* Kansas City: Self-Published, 1969. Archives of Northwest Missouri Genealogy Society, St. Joseph, Missouri.

Horn, Stanley F. *The Army of Tennessee.* Norman: The University of Oklahoma, 1993.

Hume, Edgar Erskine. "Nicola Marschall." *Alabama Department of Archives & History.* 4 May 2006 <http://www.archives.state.al.us/marschall/german.html>.

"Iatan, Missouri." *Wikipedia, the free encyclopedia.* 24 Dec. 2004. 5 Feb. 2006 <http://en.wikipedia.org/wiki/Iatan,_Missouri>.

"Indigenous Australians." *Wikipedia, the free encyclopedia.* 22 Apr. 2006. 23 Apr. 2006 <http://en.wikipedia.org/wiki/Indigenous_Australians>.

"Jabez Lamar Monroe Curry." *Shotgun's Home of the American Civil War.* 3 Mar. 2006. 5 Apr. 2006 <http://www.civilwarhome.com/currybio.htm>.

"Jabez L. M. Curry Elementary School." 5 Apr. 2006 <http://www.bhm.k12.al.us/schools/curry/home/home.htm>.

Jacoby, Oswald and Albert Morehead. *The Fireside Book of Cards.* New York: Simon and Schuster, 1957.

"Jimsonweed." *The American Heritage Dictionary of the English Language.* 4th ed. 2000.

"Johnny-cake." *The Oxford English Dictionary.* 2nd ed. 1989.

Johnson, Willie R., Park Ranger/Historian, Kennesaw Mountain National Historic Park, Kennesaw, Georgia. Personal interview. 8 May 2006.

Kelly, Dennis. *Kennesaw Mountain and the Atlanta Campaign.* Atlanta: Kennesaw Mountain Historical Association, 1990.

King, Bart. "Last Marks of Civil War Are Being Erased from Jewell Hill." *Kansas City Times* 14 Dec. 1956.

Lehr, James. Personal interview. 28 April 2006.

Lehr, Suzanne. *As the Mockingbird Sang.* St. Joseph: Platte Purchase Publishers, 2005.

Libel, Shane. Personal interview. 28 April 2006.

Little, Elbert L. *National Audubon Society Field Guide to North American Trees - Eastern Region.* New York: Alfred A. Knopf, 1980.

Logan, Sheridan A. *Old Saint Jo Gateway to the West, 1799-1932.* Lunenburg, VT: The Stinehour Press, 1979.

Long, E. B. *The Civil War Day by Day: An Almanac 1861-1865.* New York: Da Capo Press, Inc., 1971.

Lovinger, Robert. "Friday the 13th." *SouthCoastToday*. 13 Feb. 1998. The Standard-Times. 5 Apr. 2006 <http://www.s-t.com/daily/02-98/02-13-98/b01li042.htm>.

"Malvern Hill." *CWSAC Battle Summaries.* National Park Service. 8 Feb. 2006 <http://www.cr.nps.gov/hps/abpp/battles/va021.htm>.

Marengo County Heritage Book Committee. *The Heritage of Marengo County, Alabama.* Clanton, Alabama: Heritage Publishing Consultants, Inc., 2000.

Marszalek, John F. and Clay Williams. "Mississippi Soldiers in the Civil War." *Mississippi History Now.* 2004. Mississippi Historical Society. 6 Feb. 2006 <http://mshistory.k12.ms.us/features/feature16/ms_cw_soldiers.html>.

McCartney, Harry. "The Bonnie Blue Flag." *The Civil War Music Site.* 12 Sept. 2005 <http://www.civilwarmusic.net/display_song.php?song =bonnieblue>.

McKee, Nancy and George. Telephone interview. 6 May 2006.

Mershon, Robert. Telephone interview. 15 Mar. 2006.

M'Lean, John. *Notes of a Twenty-five Years' Service in the Hudson's Bay Territory.* Vol. 1. London: Richard Bentley, 1849. 4 Feb. 2006 <http://www.ibiblio.org/pub/docs/books/gutenberg/1/5/3/4/15342/15342.txt>.

"Milledgeville." *New Georgia Encyclopedia.* 30 Sept. 2003. Georgia Humanities Council. 19 Apr. 2006 <http://www.georgiaencyclopedia.org/nge/Article.jsp?path=/CitiesCounties/Cities&id=h-769>.

Miller, Mack. "Big Howdy From the Man From Guntown." 18 Apr. 2001. 10 Feb. 2006 <http://users.ev1.net/~mackm/welcomemain.html>.

"Missouri: June-October 1861: Liberty (Blue Mills Landing), Missouri (MO003), Clay County, September 17, 1861." Houghton Mifflin. 15 Oct. 2005 <http://college.hmco.com/history/readerscomp/civwar/html/cw_000906_libertybluem.htm>.

"Mobile." *2006 Word Origin Calendar* (March 4-5). Denver: Accord Publishing LTD/WO, 2006.

"Monarch." *Naval Historical Center.* 18 Jan. 2006. Department of the Navy. 22 Mar. 2006 <http://www.history.navy.mil/danfs/m13/monarch.htm>.

Moran, Daniel. "Malvern Hill - The Last of the Seven Days." *Military History Online.com.* 2001. 8 Feb. 2006 <http://www.militaryhistoryonline.com/civilwar/misc/malvernhill.aspx>.

"Music of the Southwest Web Site." *The University of Arizona.* 16 June 2003. 28 Feb. 2006 <http://parentseyes.arizona.edu/msw/westernfiddle/tmy_fiddlers_1987.html>.

"North Carolina Communities: Hillsborough." *Younce & Vtipil.* 2006. 22 Apr. 2006 <http://www.attorneysnc.com/hillsborough_north_carolina.html>.

"Old Time Disease Names." *The US Gen Web Project.* 27 Mar. 2005. Rootsweb Homepage. 10 Feb. 2006 <http://www.rootsweb.com/~njmorris/disease.htm>.

"Ordinance of Secession." *Wikipedia, the free encyclopedia.* 17 Sept. 2005. 15 Oct. 2005 <http://en.wikipedia.org/wiki/Ordinance_of_Secession>.

"Osceola, Missouri." *Wikipedia, the free encyclopedia.* 15 Nov. 2005. 7 Feb. 2006 <http://en.wikipedia.org/wiki/Osceola,_Missouri>.

"Palmetto." *The American Heritage Dictionary of the English Language.* 4th ed. 2000.

"Pioneer Cooking: Johnny Cakes." *Easy Fun School.* 2005. 15 Oct. 2005 <http://www.easyfunschool.com/article1497.html>.

Proctor, Victoria. "Life of Francis Marion." *SCGenWeb's The Swamp Fox: Francis Marion.* 17 Jan 2004. 5 Feb. 2006 <http://www.geocities.com/BourbonStreet/1786/swampfox.html?20065>.

"Provost Marshall." *The American Heritage Dictionary of the English Language.* 4th ed. 2000.

"ProZ.com - Directory of Professional Translation Services by Freelance Language Translators & Translation Agencies." *ProZ.com.* 20 Nov. 2004. 11 Sept. 2005 <http://www.proz.com/kudoz/870471?&print=1>.

"Quire." *The American Heritage Dictionary of the English Language.* 4th ed. 2000.

Radford, E. and M.A. Radford. *Encyclopaedia of Superstitions.* New York: The Philosophical Library, 1949.

Rutkow, Ira M. *Bleeding Blue and Gray.* New York: Random House, 2005.

Sampson, Glenn. Personal interview. 16 Aug. 2005.

Sansing, David G. "Charles Clark Twenty-fourth Governor of Mississippi: 1863-1865." *Mississippi History Now.* Dec. 2003. Mississippi Historical Society. 5 Apr. 2006 <http://mshistory.k12.ms.us/features/feature47/governors/19_charles_clark.htm>.

"Sashay." *The American Heritage Dictionary of the English Language.* 4th ed. 2000.

"Skedaddled." *Dictionary of Civil War Slang.* Tripod. 11 Sept. 2005 <http://atleb.tripod.com/ordbok/dictionary_of_civil_war_slang.htm>.

Southern Heritage. *The Southern Heritage Breads Cookbook.* Birmingham: Oxmoor House, 1983.

"Southern Roots." *Special Collections Library.* Aug. 1998. The University of Michigan. 3 Feb. 2006 <http://www.lib.umich.edu/spec-coll/faulknersite/faulknersite/sroots/roots.html>.

"Spice-wood." *The Oxford English Dictionary.* 2nd ed. 1989.

"Sponge." *The Encyclopedia of Civil War Usage.* Nashville: Cumberland House Publishing, 2001.

"Stars and Bars flag (U.S.)." *allstates-flag.com.* 13 Mar. 2006. AllStates Flag & Banner Company. 4 May 2006 <http://www.allstate-flag.com/fotw/flags/us-csal.html>.

"Sterling Price." *Wikipedia, the free encyclopedia.* 4 Feb. 2006. 7 Feb. 2006 <http://en.wikipedia.org/wiki/Sterling_Price>.

Stiffler, Angela. "Re: James Wallace Dunlap." E-mail to the researcher. 18 Oct. 2005.

Storrs, Maj. George S. "The Artillery on Kennesaw." *The Kennesaw Gazette.* Atlanta: Western and Atlantic Railroad. 15 June 1889: 6-7.

"Sutler." *The American Heritage Dictionary of the English Language.* 4th ed. 2000.

Swanson, James L. *Manhunt.* New York: HarperCollins Publishers, 2006.

"Swinny." *The Oxford English Dictionary.* 2nd ed. 1989.

"Synonyms for Sashay." *infoplease.* 2006. Pearson Education. 5 Apr. 2006 <http://www.infoplease.com/thesaurus/sashay>.

"The Arkansas State Historical Song." *Arkansas.* 19 Nov. 2004. Netstate. 6 Feb. 2006 <http://www.netstate.com/states/symb/song/ar_arkansastraveler.htm>.

"The Battle of Lexington." *Battle of Lexington State Historic Site.* 24 Feb. 2004. Missouri State Parks and Historic Sites. 25 Nov. 2004 <http://www.mostateparks.com/lexington/battle.htm>.

"The Bonnie Blue Flag." *The Civil War Music Site.* 2000. Antonio Lupher. 12 Sept. 2005 <http://www.civilwarmusic.net/display_song.php?song=bonnieblue>.

"The Gal I Left Behind Me." *Digital Tradition Mirror.* 2003. The Mudcat Café. 12 Sept. 2005 <http://sniff.numachi.com/~rickheit/dtrad/pages/tiGIRLLFT5;ttBRGHTON.html>.

"The goose hung high." *ProZ The Translators Workplace.* 2005. 9 Feb. 2006 <http://www.proz.com/kudoz/870471?&print+1>.

"The Yocona River Bridge in the Early 1900s." *The Internet Guide to Mississippi Writers.* 18 Mar. 2005. Mississippi Writers Page. 3 Feb. 2006 <http://www.olemiss.edu/mwp/dir/faulkner_william/yocona.html>.

Thomas, Dr. Jack Ward. "Just What is a Trophy." 30 Nov. 2005. *Boone and Crockett Club.* 5 Feb 2006 <http://www.boone-crockett.org/doc/jwt_fairchase_whatisatrophy.doc>.

"Thomas Hill Watts." *Alabama Department of Archives & History.* 14 Mar. 2006. 11 Apr. 2006 <http://www.archives.state.al.us/govs_list/_wattst.html>.

"Trading Path Story." *Trading Path Association.* 14 Nov. 2005. 22 Apr. 2006 <http://www.tradingpath.org/content/view/17/2/>.

Tucker, Phillip Thomas. *The South's Finest.* Shippensburg, Penn.: White Mane Publishing Co., Inc., 1993.

Union Historical Company. *The History of Buchanan County, Missouri.* Birdsall, Williams and Company, 1881.

"Upper ten." *Webster's New International Dictionary of the English Language.* 2nd ed. 1937.

"Vest, George Graham, (1830-1904)." *Biographical Directory of the United States Congress.* United States Senate. 20 Mar. 2006 <http://bioguide.congress.gov/scripts/biodisplay.pl?index=V000091>.

"Victoria." *The Columbia Gazatteer of the World.* New York: Columbia University Press, 1998.

"Walthall, Edward Cary." *Biographical Directory of the United States Congress.* United States Senate. 12 Apr. 2006 <http://bioguide.congress.gov/biosearch/biosearch1.asp>.

Way, Frederick, Jr. *Way's Packet Directory, 1848-1994.* Athens: Ohio University Press, 1994.

"Welcome to Hillsborough and Orange County." *Hillsborough/Orange County Chamber of Commerce.* 2003. 22 Apr. 2006 <http://www.hillsboroughchamber.com/>.

"Welcome to the Boone and Crockett Club web site!" *Boone and Crockett Club.* 2005. 30 Nov. 2005 <http://www.boone_crockett.org/>.

"What does the Boone and Crockett Club do?" 2006. 5 Feb. 2006 <http://www.boone-crockett.org/more.asp>.

William Jewell College. *Catalogue of the Officers and Students in William Jewell College, for the Year Ending June 23, 1859, With a Statement of the Course of Study Pursued in the Various Departments.* St. Louis: R. P. Studley, 1859.

Willis, Becky. Telephone interview. 6 May 2006.

"Yalobusha County, Mississippi." *Wikipedia, the free encyclopedia.* 24 Jan. 2006. 3 Feb. 2006 <http://en.wikipedia.org/wiki/Yalobusha_County,_Mississippi>.

Index

D

E

F

G

H

I

J

K

L

Q

R

S

T

About the Author

Suzanne Staker Lehr, first Research Associate of The St. Joseph Museums Inc., has been actively involved with research at Mount Mora Cemetery since 2001. The results of her research have already placed her in the 2004 *Tent of Many Voices* sponsored by the Missouri Arts Council during the 200th anniversary celebration of Lewis and Clark's Corps of Discovery Expedition and in "Stories Under the Stone," a 2005 PBS documentary featuring historic cemeteries. Her article, "A Cemetery: A Great Resource for Stories," appeared in the November-December 2005 issue of *Storytelling Magazine*. Her first book, *As the Mockingbird Sang, Civil War Diary of Pvt. Robert Caldwell Dunlap, C.S.A.*, was published in 2005 by Platte Purchase Publishers.

Lehr was in the field of education from 1963 to 2000 at the elementary, middle school, high school, and graduate levels, retiring as a school counselor in 2000. She was named Northwest Missouri School Counselor of the Year, 1991; Outstanding Middle School Counselor, Missouri School Counselor Association, 1992; one of "Twenty Who Count," *St. Joseph News-Press*, 1993; and most recently profiled in *Who's Who of American Women* 2006-2007 and *Who's Who in American Education* 2006-2007. She resides in St. Joseph, Missouri, with her husband, Jim, and their cat, Chloe.